Ancient Examples:

Writings of the Early Christians for Today

St. Justin Martyr

and

St. Perpetua

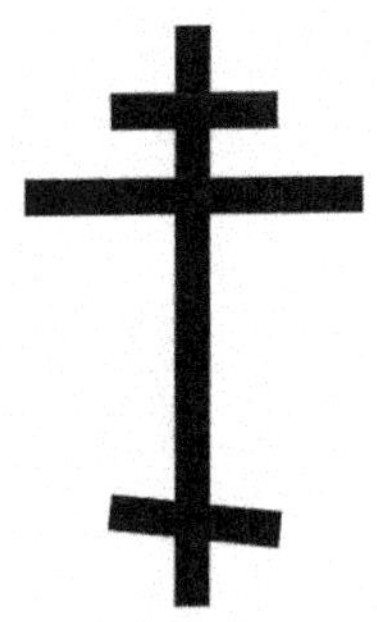

Ancient Examples:

Writings of the Early Christians for Today

St. Justin Martyr

and

St. Perpetua

Compiled and edited
with a preface and additional commentary by

Donna Perpetua

Saints Justin and Perpetua Orthodox Christian Books
an imprint of
DMS Onge Publishing, LLC
Hartland, Michigan
2019

For information about bulk quantities, please email your request to:
info@DMSOngePublishing.com
or, send a letter to:
DMS Onge Publishing, LLC,
ATTN: Saints Justin and Perpetua Orthodox Christian Books
9552 East Highland Road, #30, Howell MI 48843

Ancient Examples: Writings of the Early Christians for Today:
St. Justin Martyr and Saint Perpetua
First Trade Edition: June 2019
ISBN: 978-1-944976-05-7 Expanded Edition (trade paperback)
ISBN: 978-1-944976-04-0 Limited Edition (genuine leather with slipcase)

Printed in the United States of America

Dedicated to

Our Triune God,
the Father, Son, and Holy Spirit,

to those seeking the faith and to those who have found it

and especially to

Perpetua and Justin
and
Liora Dorothea,
their daughter in heaven

and to
the newly illumined everywhere

And we therefore pray you
to publish this little book,
appending what you think right,
that our opinions may be known to others,
and that these persons may have a fair chance of being freed
from erroneous notions
and ignorance of good . . .

Saint Justin Martyr
The Second Apology of Justin

. . . these modern examples
will one day become ancient and available for posterity . . . .

O truly called and chosen
unto the glory of our Lord Jesus Christ!
whom whoever magnifies, and honors, and adores
assuredly ought to read these examples
for the edification of the Church,
not less than the ancient ones,
so that new virtues also may testify
that one and the same Holy Spirit
is always operating
even until now. . .

The Passion of Saints Perpetua and Felicity

Contents

Preface to this Edition

The eyewitness[1] to Saint Perpetua's martyrdom and Saint Justin Martyr's prayers are answered, yet again, with the works collected in this edition. Saint Justin's prayer that his work be published has been repeatedly answered across the centuries, and continues today with this volume so that people once again have a fair chance of being free from error and from ignorance of what is good. And, what was modern in Saint Perpetua's time is now ancient and available for posterity, even after more than 1,800 years, just as her eyewitness predicted and hoped.[2] This edition collects in one volume the collected writings of Saint Justin the Martyr and the Philosopher, *The Martyrdom of Saint Justin and Others*, and fragments supposed to be written by Saint Justin Martyr, with *The Passion of Saints Perpetua and Felicity.*[3]

Although this volume was created in commemoration of the chrismations of one newly illumined Justin and one newly illumined Perpetua on the occasion of their marriage of thirty-two years being

---

[1] We have Tertullian's preservation of Saint Perpetua's martyrdom account, but it is unclear that he wrote the eyewitness portions of it. Thomas J. Heffernan is of the view that textual differences between Tertullian's use of Latin in his other works and the eyewitness portions of the *Passion* counsel against a conclusion that Tertullian is the author of the account. Heffernan cites other authorities who differ, and conclude that Tertullian is either the author or the editor. This editor will refer to the author of those portions as "the eyewitness" (Heffernan chooses to refer to this person simply as "R" for redactor). See *The Passion of Perpetua and Felicity*, Thomas J. Heffernan, (Oxford University Press, 2012), pp. 8-17, 437-439, 441.

[2] See Heffernan's App.I.C. pp. 431-42 for a thorough list of the numerous printed editions and major translations of her *Passion* at the time of his work's printing in 2012.

[3] The term "Passion" is usually used in connection with the trial, crucifixion and death of our Lord Jesus Christ. Accounts of similarly brutal deaths of saints are customarily referred to as a "martyrdom" or "witness." This is true of the account reprinted herein for Saint Justin Martyr, titled *The Martyrdom of the Holy Martyrs Justin, Chariton, Charitas, Paeon, and Liberianus, Who Suffered at Rome.* Such is not the case with Saint Perpetua. With most accounts of her martyrdom being in Latin, the title usually has been translated as *The Passion of Saints Perpetua and Felicity*. This is true of the version reprinted herein. Moreover, the recent scholarly work about her martyrdom has also used the term "passion" in its title, Heffernan's *The Passion of Perpetua and Felicity*. This editor has chosen to respect the long publishing history of Saint Perpetua's martyrdom and retained references to it as her *Passion*.

blessed, it is fitting that the written works of these two Saints be joined. For, you see, Saint Perpetua is oft considered the earliest known female Christian writer. And Saint Justin Martyr is generally considered the earliest pagan (i.e., non-Jewish) Christian writer and apologist. Together they represent some of the oldest surviving Christian texts, and are among the most notable.

Interestingly, both Perpetua and Justin of our time, both newly illumined as Orthodox Christians, which, next to the Roman Catholic Church is the most ancient of the Christian faiths, and to whom this volume is dedicated, also both write in a variety of genres. So, this volume is a fitting way to honor the recent blessing of their union as one flesh for over thirty years.

* * *

Saint Perpetua and Saint Justin Martyr both lived during times of great persecution of Christians: in the Roman city of Carthage in Africa for Saint Perpetua, and in Greece for Saint Justin Martyr, both of which were heathen states at the time. Both Saints were martyrs for our Lord and Savior Jesus Christ, both being put to death by their respective governments *solely* because they professed to be Christians. The records of their trials both show this:

> *Rusticus said, "Are you not, then, a Christian?"*
> *Justin said, "Yes, I am a Christian."*
>
> The Martyrdom of Saint Justin

> *Hilarianus said, 'Are you a Christian?'*
> *And I replied, 'I am a Christian.'*
>
> The Passion of Saints Perpetua and Felicitas

Saint Perpetua, just twenty-two years of age at the time, is generally considered to have been martyred in 202 or 203 A.D., while Saint Justin Martyr preceded her in 165 A.D. Their Christian endings, especially in light of the more recent persecutions we Christians face around the world today, should inspire us all to be steadfast in our faith, even unto death for the greater glory of our Lord Jesus Christ, who so sacrificed Himself for us on the Cross after enduring betrayal by one of His chosen disciples, a farce of a trial, denial by His chosen people, the Jews, scourging, and various humiliations.[4]

Today, Christians face persecution in a variety of countries, sometimes from government, whether from atheist-oriented communist or socialist governments, Muslim-majority or other non-Christian countries, or from governments of largely Christian nations where the faith is under attack by the imposition of a number of different kinds of anti-Christian regulatory regimes. But oftener, persecution comes at the hands of private and non-state actors, those we now generally label as terrorists, especially radical Muslim terrorists.

Radical Muslim terrorism has been increasing over the past few decades. Especially starting here in the United States with the first terrorist attack on the World Trade Center in New York City on February 26, 1993, which was largely unsuccessful[5] but which was fulfilled on September 11, 2001,[6] in the attacks by Al Qaeda,[7] when the towers of the World Trade Center and other nearby skyscrapers fell, along with the other nearly simultaneous attacks that targeted the Pentagon and, presumably Congress or the White House, the latter of which was thwarted by the passengers of Flight 93 over the countryside of Pennsylvania, who now rest near Shanksville.

---

[4] Lest one think the tortures and cruelty of the ancient Greek and Roman world are over, and that such barbarity as being fed to wild beasts, scourgings, torchings, beheadings, and other barbaric practices no longer occur, one should recall especially the recent treatment in our own present century of Christians and others at the hands of ISIS. This terrorist organization prides itself on barbarity, engaging in televised beheadings, stonings, slow roasting over pits and setting afire caged victims, drowning caged victims, pushing victims off the roofs of tall buildings, and other horrific brutalities.

[5] The first attack was unsuccessful in that the Muslim terrorists had planned for the building to topple and, in toppling, to crash into the other main tower, toppling it as well. Neither tower fell, although severe damage was done to the north tower. Six people were killed and 1,042 people were injured.

[6] On September 11, 2001, at least 2,753 people were killed in New York City, including civilians, in and around the buildings, and fire and police personnel who had arrived at the scene of the bombing before or shortly after the Twin Towers fell. In total, 2,996 people were killed and over 6,000 were injured at the various sites attacked or who were on the airplanes that the nineteen Muslim terrorists used to bomb the buildings.

[7] Sometimes spelled Al Qaida. This was the terrorist organization headed by the now deceased terrorist Osama bin Laden, who was killed by our U.S. military forces. It's leader is now Ayman al-Zawahiri.

Indeed, this volume was compiled and initially edited during a time when terrorist attacks were occurring around the globe seemingly daily just before and during the Ramadan of the Muslims in 2017, especially in Europe. Repeatedly in Great Britain children and young people have been specifically targeted, and even in Islamic countries attacks have increased, such as in Iran which had largely escaped ISIS[8] terrorist attacks up until now. And while ISIS ever increasingly seeks to establish its proclaimed Muslim Caliphate to rule the entire globe under Sharia[9] law, governments in both the West and the East, (whether of largely Christian, Jewish, or Islamic faith), seem powerless to either

---

[8] ISIS refers to the Islamic State of Iraq and Syria, sometimes referred to as ISIL (Islamic State of Iraq and the Levant), or as Daesh, an Arabic acronym sometimes spelled as Daish. It is headed by Abu Bakr al-Baghdadi, who claims to be the Caliph. ISIS proclaimed itself the worldwide Caliphate in 2014, thereby claiming to be the global authority over all Muslims for religious, political and military purposes. It has conquered territory in Syria and Iraq, where it enforces Sharia law, and has been thought by some to have operations in as many as 18 countries, although such an estimate does not include the formation of small cells or lone individuals that clearly exist throughout the West, especially in Europe, and arguably here in the United States as well. For example, the May 2015 Garland, Texas, shooting attack outside a Mohammed art exhibit, injuring one; the July 2015 shootings at a military recruitment center in Chattanooga, Tennessee, killing five and wounding two; the December 2015 San Bernardino, California, shooting attack at a county health department's holiday party killing 14 and injuring 23; the June 2016 Orlando, Florida, nightclub shooting that killed 49 people and wounded 53; the September 2016 pressure cooker and pipe bomb bombings in New York and New Jersey that injured 32; the November 2016 car ramming and knife attack on the Ohio State University campus that injured 11; the January 2017 shooting in Denver by a recent convert to Islam killing one; the April 2017 shooting in Fresno, California, that killed four. These are just incidents since 2015 in the U.S. The full list of terrorist attacks around the world and the loss of life is sobering. (Search Wikipedia with the phrase "list of terrorist incidents in" and add the year. You will see how horrific the carnage is around the world, although these lists include "terrorist" incidents other than those carried out or inspired by radical Muslim terrorists because a broad definition of the term is used.)

[9] Shariah law is the theocratic law of Islam. It governs all aspects of a Muslim's life as well as the lives of non-Muslims within its territory. It is essentially a theocratic governance system, not simply a set of religious beliefs and practices. In other words, there is no separate church and separate state. Muslims who do not adhere to the Sunni Muslim ideology of ISIS are considered apostates and subject to a sentence of death. Non-Muslims are expected to convert to Islam, pay an often onerous tax called the *jizya,* or suffer death. ISIS has issued formal statements to Christians offering these alternatives in areas such as Mosul, a major city in Iraq and the birthplace of Assyrian Christianity, and in Raqqa, Syria, the purported headquarters of ISIS. The call for the *jizya* in Raqqa was reportedly demanded to be paid with an ounce of gold.

understand these threats or to act effectively to mitigate them, much less stop them. We can only pray unceasingly that the leaders of nations around the world come to understand the true nature of this evil and act to thwart it, for truly it is of the devil's work.

* * *

After all these many centuries, the ancient words of Saints Justin Martyr and Perpetua still have relevance today to all those seeking the true faith or to defend their faith. Saint Perpetua's *Passion* is a witness to the mysteries of faith as well as a witness to her martyrdom, and is deeply grounded in Scripture. Saint Justin Martyr's works and his *Martyrdom*, on the other hand, are a clear and logical defense of the faith using Scripture and pagan texts. It is not for nothing that he is called Saint Justin the Martyr *and* the Philosopher. The following are brief descriptions of these works.

About the Works of Saint Justin Martyr

Saint Justin Martyr was born circa 114 A.D. and was martyred in 165 A.D., when he was in his early fifties. The works of Saint Justin include his *First Apology*, his *Second Apology*, his *Dialogue with Trypho, The Discourse to the Greeks*, the *Hortatory Address to the Greeks, On the Sole Government of God*, extant fragments of his lost work *On the Resurrection*, and other fragments from his lost writings which were preserved by quotations in various texts written mostly by others. Also included in this collection is a record of *The Martyrdom of Justin and Others*.

The following is a brief synopsis, with some limited commentary on each of Saint Justin Martyr's works.

About *The First Apology*

In Saint Justin Martyr's *First Apology*, he presents a petition to the Emperor, the Roman senate, and the people of Rome on behalf of those in all the nations being persecuted as Christians. This is a work of some length, sixty-eight chapters in all, with three appended epistles containing testimonies on behalf of Christians.

The intent of the work is to demand justice for himself and all those Christians who were being "unjustly hated and wantonly abused." This *Apology* is filled with Scripture, both from the New Testament, principally passages from the Gospels of Saint Luke and Saint Matthew, but also from the Old Testament books such as Genesis, Exodus, Psalms, and a few others, and the prophets Isaiah, to a substantial degree, as well as more briefly Jeremiah, Ezekiel, Daniel, Micah, and Zechariah. It should be kept in mind while reading that Saint Justin's quotes from Scripture are not always exact, sometimes being paraphrases, other times combining Scripture from different authors, such as quoting from the Gospels of Luke and Matthew in a single paragraph, or from a single Gospel but in an order of his own preference as they support his argument.

Saint Justin Martyr presents a variety of arguments in his *First Apology*. He refutes that Christians are atheists because the gods to whom they are being asked to pray are not actually gods at all, but objects created by men inspired by demons that are meant to deceive man and to keep him from the true God. He discusses the folly of idol worship and how idols are mere creations of men, often men who are then entrusted to guard the very creatures they fashion, as if men could ever be guardians of God. Saint Justin discusses at length what Christ taught, including obedience to civil authorities, but not to the worship of false gods or idols. He also discusses proofs of immortality and the Resurrection.

In the main, he presents three arguments: (1) that the prophets who foretold Christ are older than other writers who have existed, (2) that Christ is the only begotten Son of God, Who became man according to God's will for the restoration of mankind, and (3) that demons have, through poets and others, fabricated scandalous reports of Christians, among other things.

Throughout his *First Apology*, Saint Justin provides the many prophesies of Christ in the Hebrew holy books, including his birth, miracles, rejection by the Jews, humiliation, and crucifixion. He also makes an argument that Scripture is actually the origin of heathen mythology and that devils have misled men into perverting God's history—and that they still do so after Christ's crucifixion, and work to persecute Christians, as well as raise up heretics in the true faith. He particularly notes imitations of Christian baptism, among other practices. That ancient Scripture is the source of the pagan works revered by the authorities of his day is a subject to which he repeatedly returns in his other works.

The epistles include testimonies by others on behalf of Christians. They include one by Adrian, one by Antoninus, and one by Marcus Aurelius to the Roman senate. Adrian's Epistle expresses concerns over unjust persecutions that are either not based on what "men *do*" or are based on accusations of accusers who are villainous themselves. He suggests the latter who make false complaints receive more severe punishments proportionate to their wickedness. Antoninus's Epistle cautions that Christians, when persecuted, actually serve to conquer the authorities to the extent that they are "lavish with their lives" rather than yielding to authority. He also chastises the authorities for seemingly ignoring the gods and their temples and right worship, and instead are jealously persecuting those who do worship God. He cautions against acting on accusations of mere Christianity, without more, urging acquittal of Christians and bringing their accusers to justice instead.

The Epistle of Marcy Aurelius is different, in that it is a witness of his own experience of the Christian God. He retells how he was surrounded by a vast army of the enemy in Germany and took to pray to the gods, fruitlessly. But when he called on Christians in his midst, they prepared for battle not by arming themselves, but by prostrating themselves and praying for him and his army as well as for relief from famine and thirst, there having been no rain for days. He reports that as the Christians prayed, it began to rain on them, but to hail on his enemies in a withering way. He then expresses fear that Christians could pray for such hail to be used against the Roman army, so no one should be brought up on charges of being a Christian only, and, that their accusers be burned alive. He also does not want the Christians to be compelled to retract their faith. He ends by requesting the senate to issue such a decree and commands that his edict be published, and that "no one who wishes to make use of or to possess it be hindered from obtaining a copy from the document I now publish."

About *The Second Apology*

In his *Second Apology*, a short work of fifteen chapters, none of which contain Scripture, Saint Justin Martyr addresses his arguments to Romans under Urbicus to explain how Urbicus was persecuting Christians. Like parts of his *First Apology*, this *Second Apology* centers on descriptions of malicious conduct of accusers and persecution solely for professing Christianity, as opposed to real crimes of murder, robbery, adultery, and the like, and Saint Justin's prediction that he, too, would become accused merely as a Christian and persecuted solely for professing his faith.

In this *Second Apology*, he elaborates on the fall of angels, their influence over men, and how men came to worship them as gods of various names. He briefly explains God's plans for Christians and their role in the salvation of man, as well as how Socrates was essentially condemned in like manner as Christians, arguing that Socrates at some basic level understood about God and Christ. He also explains the Christian view of death and the fearlessness of it because they believe in a salvation by God and a resurrection into a better life than exists on earth. He also condemns hypocrites for accusing Christians of horrific and immoral conduct they themselves engage in but which Christians abhor. He concludes with a teaching that the Word is and has always been within man and prays that his appeal be published.

About the *Dialogue with Trypho*

In his *Dialogue with Trypho*, Saint Justin Martyr essentially refutes the Jewish view of Christianity and shows how Judaism is meant to lead to Christianity. This is the lengthiest work, consisting of 142 chapters. It is also filled with Scripture, both from the New Testament, principally passages from the Gospels, but also from such Old Testament books as Genesis, Exodus, Deuteronomy, Psalms, and a few others, and virtually all of the prophets.

In the *Dialogue*, Saint Justin shares his testimony of how he strived for knowledge of truth and then retells a conversation he had with Trypho, a Jew, and his friends. Saint Justin describes how he had searched for truth in all the major philosophies of his day, including those of Plato, the Stoics, as well as in Peripatetics, Theoretics, and the

Pythagoreans. He then describes his conversion to Christianity after meeting a certain man with whom he had a conversation about God and ancient Hebrew writers.

The vast majority of the *Dialogue*, however, is taken up with explaining Christianity to Trypho, who as a Jew does not accept Christ, showing him the Hebrew texts that foretell Christ, and the precepts in Christian Scripture, as well as how the Jewish people fail to uphold the Jewish Law and fail to understand their own prophets. As such, they are actually an affront to God, while Christians are the righteous ones in God's eyes, because one may only become righteous through faith in Christ, the only begotten Son of God. And, that one may only be saved through Christ, not merely by following Jewish Law.

The range of discussion is vast and the explication comprehensive. Saint Justin Martyr parries Trypho's objections at every turn. The discussion is especially helpful for its focus on all the types of Christ that are set forth in the Old Testament, types which pertain to Christ Himself, but also to the Eucharist, the Apostles, the Cross, the Church, and other Christian matters. There is also great attention given to the role of the Virgin Mary, our Theotokos, the divinity of Christ, and His two Advents, the conversion of the Gentiles, and the differences between the physical circumcision of Jews and the circumcision of the hearts of Christians. Saint Justin also notes various alterations made by Jews to their Hebrew books, changes made principally to deny the Word of God, and that these and other distortions are the result of the works of demons.

In the end, Saint Justin prays for Trypho and his friends to come to faith in Christ and exhorts them to conversion. Yet, while Trypho and his friends are pleased with their conversation with Saint Justin and his commentary on Scripture, they cannot renounce their Jewish faith. This is an unfortunate conclusion to his *Dialogue*, although it is probably a realistic one in that many Jews cannot be convinced.

About the *Discourse to the Greeks*

Saint Justin Martyr does much the same in his *Discourse to the Greeks*, a short work of just five chapters, as he does in his *Dialogue with Trypho*. However, here he justifies why he departed from Greek customs, which was largely for the reason that he found nothing in them that was holy or that could be acceptable to God. He also comments on the follies of Greek mythology, in that they honor the vices of humans. He then condemns certain practices of the Greeks, in particular their gluttony, lust, fornication and prideful displays, principally at banquets. Saint Justin ends with an appeal for their conversion to the true wisdom of the Divine Word.

About the *Hortatory Address to the Greeks*

Saint Justin Martyr also does much the same in his *Hortatory Address to the Greeks*, which consists of thirty-eight chapters. If one has read any of the classics, this material is quite interesting in that he refutes the ideas of the major thinkers of his day and addresses the sources of their thoughts. Key to his arguments is his witness that the books of Moses predate those of Greek writers and that those writers have passages that acknowledge the truths of Jewish prophets, the very prophets who foretold of Christ.

Some of these early pagan works most readers will recognize, such as Homer's *Iliad* and the *Odyssey*, as well as works of Plato, Aristotle, and Sophocles. Other historians, philosophers, poets and oracles are more obscure or at least less well known to us today, such as Diodorus, Pythagorus, Epicurus, Polemon, Appion, Ptolemaeus, Solon, Philo, Josephus, as well as Orpheus and the Sibyl.

The most attention is given to Homer and Plato. Saint Justin Martyr maintains that both, especially Plato, owe much to the writings of Moses and other Scripture, which he believes both learned while in Egypt. He asserts that Plato contradicts himself on key points because he feared persecution from those who practiced polytheism. In the end, he argues that true knowledge can never be found in the philosophers, as even Socrates acknowledged, and urges instead that knowledge of the true God may be found only in the Jewish prophets of old.

About *On the Sole Government of God*

In Saint Justin Martyr's work *On the Sole Government of God*, which consists of seven chapters, he again resorts to well-known Greek poetic authorities to convince others to worship the true God. He shows by excerpts that these poets have actually acknowledged the unity of God and that He is the Creator of all, as well as their acknowledgement of the future judgment over the conduct of men. He provides excerpts from poets who also acknowledge that God does not want sacrifices made to Him, but righteous living for Him. And, he sets forth numerous excerpts from Greek works demonstrating the folly of belief in false gods. Saint Justin, as usual, ends with an appeal for his readers, here Greeks, to worship the one true God Who is attested to not just by him, but by their own beloved poets.

About the Fragments of *On the Resurrection*

The extant fragments of Saint Justin's work *On the Resurrection* consist of ten chapters in which he addresses various objections to the Resurrection doctrine, often invoking Scripture, especially Christ's life and work on earth. This is a comforting work, in that it discusses how valuable our bodies are in God's sight and that our bodies are resurrected perfect and whole without deformity or sickness. In the end, it is also a work encouraging righteous living. Unlike the other works, the extant fragments do not include a specific concluding appeal to come to faith in Christ and the one true God, but perhaps this is to be expected with a work known only by fragments.

About the Other Fragments

Finally, there are nineteen additional fragments of Saint Justin Martyr's writings, some of which were preserved only by early writers, most being quite brief. The other authors include Tatian, Irenaeus, John of Antioch, Methodius, Leontius, Anastasius, Antonius Melissa, and John of Damascus, many of whom are recognized as Saints by the Orthodox Church. These cover a variety of topics.

About *The Martyrdom of Justin and Others*

Finally, *The Martyrdom of Justin and Others* includes the Roman prefect's examination of Saint Justin Martyr, his examination of Chariton, Charito, Eulpistus, Hierax, Paeon, and Liberius, the threat of death by Rusticus, the sentences imposed, and the executions. In this brief account of the trial, Saint Justin professes his Christianity, as do all of the others. The prefect threatens all with being scourged and beheaded, and Saint Justin continues to profess his faith. The prefect then gives them another chance to offer sacrifice to the gods, but they all refuse to sacrifice to idols. The prefect then sentences them to scourging, followed by decapitation. The account ends with the notation that fellow Christians "secretly removed their bodies" and "laid them in a suitable place."[10]

* * *

About the *Passion of Saints Perpetua and Felicitas*

Saint Perpetua was born circa 182 and died as a martyr circa March 7, 203[11] A.D. Saint Perpetua's *Passion* account is actually a collection of a number of short writings. One is written by her, comprising the first three chapters; another is written by her companion martyr Saint Saturus, found in Chapter IV; and the two final chapters are a third account written by an unnamed eyewitness to their and their other companions' martyrdoms.[12] Whether Tertullian supplies the introduction and certain prefatory sentences, or whether he is merely a copyist or the editor, is unclear and experts continue to be in dispute about these matters.[13] However, he lived during the time of Saint Perpetua's martyrdom in the Roman city of Carthage, in Africa, where she was martyred.[14]

---

[10] A number of churches reportedly have relics of Saint Justin Martyr, including Santa Maria della Concezione in Rome, Italy; San Giovanni Battista e Biagio in Sacrofano, Italy; the Church of the Jesuits in Valletta, Malta; St. Justin Martyr Parish in Anaheim, California. The University of Notre Dame, Notre Dame, Indiana, also claims his relics are in their reliquary chapel in the Basilica.

[11] Some sources say 202 A.D. Roman emperor Septimius Severus outlawed Christianity sometime after 201 A.D.

[12] The translation by Wallis reprinted herein is broken up into these nine chapters. Heffernan's new Latin text is in twenty-one chapters and his new English translation is likewise in twenty-one chapters. See Heffernan, pp. 104-124 and 125-135, respectively.

[13] See n. 1, above.

[14] Tertullian was born circa 155 A.D. and died sometime after 220 A.D., the date of his last known writing, although some put his death as late as circa 240 A.D. He was raised in Carthage, (modern day Tunisia), where Saint Perpetua lived. It seems probable that he knew her. Tertullian was son of a Roman centurion and converted to Christianity circa

Several sources note that her *Passion* was read aloud in the churches of Carthage for centuries after her death.[15] Saint Augustine, another Early Church Father, commented on Saint Perpetua in his sermons some 200 years after her martyrdom.[16]

What is left of the amphitheater where Saint Perpetua and her companions were martyred is located a few miles from the modern-day city of Tunis, in Tunisia.[17] A room was discovered in the amphitheater in 1881, and it is thought to be the cell where the victims waited to be brought into the arena.[18]

The following is a brief synopsis with some commentary of each narrative contained in Saint Perpetua's *Passion*.

About Saint Perpetua's Account of Her Martyrdom

Saint Perpetua begins her account of her martyrdom with basic historical facts about her present situation, her companions, and family, in particular recounting her father's desire that she recant her Christian

---

197 or 198 A.D., just a few years before the persecution of Saint Perpetua and her companions, and at some point married a Christian woman. He was never recognized as a saint in the West or the East despite being considered the father of the Latin Christian Church and the founder of Western Christian theology. Later in life he became a Montanist, but broke with them to form his own Christian sect.

[15] These sources generally cite Saint Augustine's *Sermons* 180. Heffernan notes that Saint Augustine had concerns that Saint Perpetua's *Passion* could rival the Gospels in the churches of Africa given the popularity of her and her companions' martyrdom. See Heffernan, p. 82.

[16] See Saint Augustine's *Sermons* 280-283, and 294. Interestingly, Saint Augustine's sister was named Perpetua, and he spent some time in Carthage, especially in his youth where he studied and later taught. His sister later became abbess of a women's religious community Saint Augustine founded.

[17] The location of her martyrdom is in some dispute. Heffernan favors Carthage. See Heffernan, p. 138.

[18] Relics of Saint Perpetua are reportedly at the Basilica Maiorum in Carthage, Tunisia (along with Saint Felicity's relics); the Paroisse Notre Dame in Vierzon, France (but only publicly presented once a year). The chapel in the right apse of the church in Vierzon is dedicated to Saint Perpetua. The University of Notre Dame, Notre Dame, Indiana, also claims relics for both Saint Perpetua and Saint Felicity are in their reliquary chapel in the Basilica. The Church of the Guardian Angel in Allendale, NJ, may also have relics of Saint Perpetua.

faith, an ongoing conflict throughout most of her story.[19] Evidently he is the only person in the family that is not Christian, as Saint Perpetua comments that "he alone of all my family would not rejoice over my passion."[20] She also discusses at length her infant son, still suckling at her breast. (An incident later, that could be considered a miracle, involves him.) Shortly after her father leaves her, Saint Perpetua and her companions are baptized. This is followed by being thrown into the dungeon where she initially languishes in her anxiety.

Her *Passion* includes revelation via a number of visions. After the first, Saint Perpetua realizes that she will suffer martyrdom. In her first vision, she trods on the head of a large serpent, ascends a narrow ladder without further harm by the sharp weapons around it, and is welcomed in an exquisite garden where she is given a small cake of cheese. The latter being akin to a Eucharistic experience. The serpent is a representation of the devil, and depicts that she is battling dark spiritual forces but will prevail against them. While she understands this vision to foretell her martyrdom, she seems less conscious that her adversary is in reality the serpent, i.e., the devil himself.

After this first prophetic vision, Saint Perpetua learns her sentence, which was to be thrown to the wild beasts in the arena. It is at this point that her father refuses to bring her son to her, that she learns her infant son no longer desires her breast, and realizes that her breasts

---

[19] Saint Perpetua's father attempts a number of times to persuade her to renounce her Christian faith. The third time, he invokes her son and his infancy. She still refuses to renounce her faith. This time, the authorities beat her father. Her father's fourth visit is summarized in a mere sentence, and her response is a terse comment about her grief for him. She is then well on her way to her martyrdom and thus less concerned with the things of this world.

[20] See *The Passion of Saints Perpetua and Felicity*, Ch. II.1. She does not explain why all of her other family members were not also rounded up by the authorities, since by this statement she is testifying that her family is Christian or studying as catachumens to enter the Church, with the exception of her father. And although she is married, she does not refer to her husband at all. It is not clear if "all my family" is meant to include her husband. If so, he too is a Christian or striving to become one. Heffernan notes that Saint Perpetua's marital status is unknown. See Heffernan, p.25. He speculates that the husband may have been deceased, that they divorced, or that it was an ideological necessity to deemphasize her sexual relations, he was edited out of the text, he abandoned his wife, or may have been a Christian in hiding. See id., pp. 147-48, 165, 175-76, 185, and 328.

experienced no pain when no longer being suckled.[21] All these she views as gifts from God.

In the second vision, Saint Perpetua sees her young brother, who died at the age of seven as a pagan from a disfiguring cancer. He is in a dismal and gloomy place unable to reach the water for which he thirsts. This is an indication of his thirst for the true and living water of Christ, as well perhaps as a type of herself, then being in prison but shortly to be in the arena where she will reach her martyrdom. On waking, she prays for her little brother daily with much weeping.

In a third vision, Saint Perpetua again sees her little brother. However, this time the setting is bright, his body is clean and well dressed; instead of a wound, there is a scar; and he can now reach the pool of water and drinks from it before going off to play with joy, as children are wont to do. From this vision, she understands that he is no longer in a place of punishment and that her prayers on his behalf were rewarded. The water and the cleanliness of his body seem indicative of baptism, but may also represent her hope for her resurrected body after her trials in the arena and martyrdom, which would likely mar her physical body.

Her fourth vision occurs the day before she and her companions are to fight in the arena. This last vision consists of seeing her deacon coming for her to guide her into the arena. Once there, Saint Perpetua sees her opponent, an immense Egyptian. While he prepared for the battle by rolling in the dust, she is anointed with oil. A man taller than the amphitheater then announces that if the Egyptian prevails he will slay her, but that if she prevails then she will be awarded a branch with gold apples. The fight commences and she trods on the Egyptian's head, as she did to the serpent in her first vision. The tall man then awards her the branch. Saint Perpetua now consciously understands that her fight is with the devil, not the wild beasts, but that she would prevail in the arena.

At this point, her narrative ends, commenting that "what passed at the exhibition itself let who will write."[22] The *Passion* then continues with a narrative by Saint Saturus.

---

[21] She was allowed to suckle the child for a time while imprisoned.

[22] See *Passion*, below, Ch. III.2.

About Saint Saturus' Account

Chapter IV is a record written by Saint Saturus of his vision prior to his tribulations in the arena. He describes a slow ascendance with Saint Perpetua toward a light while they were being accompanied by four angels, until they arrive in a flower and tree filled garden. There, four more angels who are even brighter welcome them excitedly. The original angels let them down and they walk along a path where they meet three other martyrs, two who were set afire and a third who died inside the prison, asking them where all the other martyrs were. But the angels tell them to meet with their Lord first.

Saint Saturus then describes a light-filled building behind a gate manned by four more angels who provided white robes to them. Upon entering, they hear the ceaseless singing of "Holy, Holy, Holy" and see a man sitting on a throne surrounded by elders and a multitude behind them. As they wondered at the sight, angels lifted them to the throne and they kissed their Lord, after which the elders tell them to leave, urging them to enjoy. Once in the garden again, they meet their bishop and presbyter, who ask the newly martyred to restore them to peace. But angels draw Saints Perpetua and Saturus away, instructing the men to forgive each other and counseling them to rebuke their people for their contentiousness. The two new Saints then begin to recognize other martyrs. The account of the vision ends with a description of a nourishing scent that satisfied them all.

About the Account of the Eyewitness to Their Martyrdom

The final two chapters narrate what happens to Saint Perpetua's companions, especially Saint Felicitas, her young servant, and the trials of each in the arena.

Chapter V begins by noting Saint Secundulus perished in the prison and then describes at length how Saint Felicitas was pregnant at the time of her arrest but had since given birth to a daughter. The birth followed prayers by her and her companions for delivery of the child so that she could join them in the arena, it being unlawful to punish publicly a pregnant woman. And so her prayers were answered. The eyewitness then narrates how the jailor mocks Saint Felicitas, commenting on the suffering from the pain of childbirth and how it will be worse in the arena with the beasts. But she bravely counters by telling her jailor that One within her will suffer with her while she suffers for Him.

The eyewitness then, being inspired by the Holy Spirit, gives an account of Saint Perpetua, including how she argued for better treatment after the tribune began to treat her and her companions severely, and how the tribune acquiesces to her demand. The eyewitness then recounts a speech by Saint Saturus to a crowd who had gathered to mock them at their last meal. He asks them to remember their faces for their own judgment at the last day for their mocking and for taking pleasure in their own hatred. This speech causes some in the crowd to believe.

The final chapter is devoted to the events in the arena, their dress and demeanor. Saint Perpetua is singing Psalms, and the male companions are threatening Hilarianus with God's judgment. This chapter also describes the fate of each Saint. The eyewitness explains the wishes of the companions prior to the event and how each had wanted a certain end and that God granted their desires. Saint Saturninus wished to contend with all the beasts, and he did. Saint Revocatus faced the leopard and the bear; and Saint Saturus, after he was recalled from facing a wild boar and a bear, ultimately suffered one bite of a leopard, which was his desire and which he foretold to a soldier. Saint Saturus later gave the soldier a small ring which he had dipped in his own blood, saying to him, "be mindful of my faith, and let not these things disturb, but confirm you," thus urging the soldier to believe in the saving Christ.

As for Saints Perpetua and Felicitas, the eyewitness describes how they faced a cow who tossed them. The eyewitness describes Saint Perpetua's modesty as to her clothing and hair, and her comforting fellowship with Saint Felicitas in helping her in the arena before being recalled to the gate. The eyewitness also records how Saint Perpetua was so divinely protected as to have been unaware of her injuries until informed of them. Then all were lead back into the arena for slaughter, each receiving a sword thrust, with Saint Saturus being the first to be martyred. The account ends by noting that Saint Perpetua was stabbed by a young gladiator who did not kill her at the first thrust and so she guided the sword to her own throat, whence she gave up her spirit.

About The Elucidation

This *Passion* account ends with a brief elucidation regarding the visions involving Saint Perpetua's young brother. It is written centuries later and republished in 1838, and is appended to the 1885 translation reprinted herein,[23] although it is not found in every edition consulted. It primarily notes that the visions involving the younger brother Dinocrates are subversive of the doctrine of purgatory maintained by the Latin Church, i.e., the Roman Catholic Church in the West, as is Maccabees. It also notes that the Early Church's Prayers for the Dead do not mention purgatory and refute the dogma by limiting "such prayers to the blessed dead" and that bliss is received "at the Last day, and not before." The author relies on Scripture, where 2 Timothy lends support to this view.

* * *

As for the texts themselves, in the rest of this volume brief introductions are provided by this editor, along with any introductory text offered in the prior editions. The translated texts reproduced here are all translations from the late 1800s, and although sometimes difficult to read, they are generally untainted by the highly politicized culture we find ourselves in today. Indeed, this was the main reason that older translations were selected. Too often today translators of religious and other materials translate to reinforce their own religious, and often even political, views and it was difficult to ascertain the extent to which that was true with certain modern day translations. Of course, earlier eras are not immune from this kind of translation practice either, but this editor thought it best to err on the side of history.

Although ladies should go first, this editor has chosen a chronological order. So Saint Perpetua's *Passion* follows Saint Justin Martyr's works and his *Martyrdom*.

[23] Heffernan evidently read a later printing of this version published in 1925, which had few notes. See Heffernan, p. 437.

Saint Justin

The Martyr and the Philosopher

And I, praying for them, said,
"I can wish no better thing for you, sirs, than this, that,
recognizing in this way that
Intelligence is given to every man,
you may be of the same opinion as ourselves,
and believe that Jesus is the Christ of God."

Saint Justin
Dialogue with Trypho

SAINT JUSTIN MARTYR'S WRITINGS

A Brief Introduction to this Reprint

This version of Saint Justin Martyr's writings is taken largely from *Justin Martyr and Athenagoras*, Volume II, of *The Ante-Nicene Christian Library: Translations of the Writings of the Fathers down to A.D. 325*, edited by the Rev. Alexander Roberts, D.D., and James Donaldson, L.L.D., (T. & T. Clark, Edinburgh, 1909). The two *Apologies* were translated by the Rev. Dr. Marcus Dods, D.D. The *Dialogue with Trypho* and the treatise *On the Sole Government of God* were translated by the Rev. Dr. George Reith, D.D. The fragment of Saint Justin Martyr, *On the Resurrection*, was translated by the Rev. Dr. Dods. Other Saint Justin Martyr fragments were translated by the Rev. Dr. Roberts.

The original editors characterized the works included in the volume as comprising "the whole of the certainly and probably genuine works of Justin Martyr."

A number of digital versions of this work were consulted in the creation of this edition, including a copy by archive.org which was digitized by the Internet Archive in 2008 with funding from Microsoft Corporation; the Kindle edition of Church Fathers (2014-06-12), an eBook version of *The Complete Ante-Nicene & Nicene and Post-Nicene Church Fathers Collection*, originally published by Catholic Way Publishing; and other versions.

In the present volume, slight modifications have been made to Americanize most British spellings (i.e., *honor* rather than *honour*, for example), and to fix obvious typographical errors. New chapter headings also have been created for some chapters. Capitalization has been rendered consistent throughout when context is clear. Such minor changes are not noted. And dialogue has been set forth in a dialogue format rather than the running text of Wallis.

Original footnotes have been retained, but have been renumbered. Biblical quotations are in ***italicized bold*** font, in block quotation form if lengthy (more than fifty words), and their citations are given in a more modern citation form. Quotations of pagan authorities are treated similarly.

Material that has been added or replaced by the editor of this present volume is noted by use of curly brackets "{" and "}" instead of straight brackets, "[" and "]" which, when used, are of the original editors' use. Any commentary in footnotes added by this editor is also placed within curly brackets.

The original editors did not refer to Saint Justin Martyr as a Saint. Although the Orthodox Church recognizes his Sainthood, this editor chose not to add this designation to minimize use of brackets within the text to reflect such alterations. His Sainthood is properly honored, as necessary, within any additional commentary in footnotes.

Every attempt has been made to ensure accurate rendering of Greek text, usually found in the footnotes. However, this editor acknowledges that some diacritical marks may be rendered incorrectly because some marks were difficult to see in the editions reviewed.

The original Introductory Notice, next, has been retained, but has been re-titled "The Life and Works of Saint Justin Martyr" to minimize confusion with this introductory material. It begins in the next section.

Any remaining errors are this editor's alone, for which she prays for your indulgence.

The Life and Works of Saint Justin Martyr

Saint Justin Martyr was born in Flavia Neapolis, a city of Samaria, the modern Nablous. The date of his birth is uncertain, but may be fixed about A.D. 114. His father and grandfather were probably of Roman origin. Before his conversion to Christianity he studied in the schools of the philosophers, searching after some knowledge which would satisfy the cravings of his soul. At last he became acquainted with Christianity, being at once impressed with the extraordinary fearlessness which the Christians displayed in the presence of death, and with the grandeur, stability, and truth of the teachings of the *Old Testament*. From this time he acted as an evangelist, taking every opportunity to proclaim the Gospel as the only safe and certain philosophy, the only way to salvation. It is probable that he travelled much. We know that he was some time in Ephesus, and he must have lived for a considerable period in Rome. Probably he settled in Rome as a Christian teacher. While he was there, the philosophers, especially the Cynics, plotted against him, and he sealed his testimony to the truth by martyrdom.

The principal facts of Saint Justin's life are gathered from his own writings. There is little clue to dates. It is agreed on all hands that he lived in the reign of Antoninus Pius, and the testimony of Eusebius and most credible historians renders it nearly certain that he suffered martyrdom in the reign of Marcus Aurelius. The *Chronican Paschale* {of Byzantine Histories} gives as the date 165 A.D.

The writings of Saint Justin Martyr are among the most important that have come down to us from the second century. He was not the first that wrote an Apology in behalf of the Christians, but his *Apologies* are the earliest extant. They are characterized by intense Christian fervor, and they give an insight into the relations existing between heathens and Christians in those days. His other principal writing, the *Dialogue with Trypho*, is the first elaborate exposition of the reasons for regarding Christ as the Messiah of the *Old Testament*, and the first systematic attempt to exhibit the false position of the Jews in regard to Christianity.

Many of Saint Justin's writings have perished. Those works which have come to us bearing his name have been divided into three classes.

The first class embraces those which are unquestionably genuine, viz. the two *Apologies*, and the *Dialogue with Trypho*. Some critics have urged objections against Saint Justin's authorship of the *Dialogue*; but the objections are regarded now as possessing no weight.

The second class consists of those works which are regarded by some critics as Saint Justin's, and by others as not his. They are: 1. *An Address to the Greeks*; 2. *A Hortatory Address to the Greeks*; 3. *On the Sole Government of God*; 4. *An Epistle to Diognetus*; 5. Fragments from a work on the Resurrection; 6. and other Fragments. Whatever difficulty there may be in settling the authorship of these treatises, there is but one opinion of their earliness. The latest of them, in all probability, was not written later than the third century.

The third class consists of those that are unquestionably not the works of Saint Justin. These are: 1. *An Exposition of the True Faith*; 2. *Replies to the Orthodox*; 3. *Christian Questions to Gentiles*; 4. *Gentile Questions to Christians*; 5. *Epistle to Zenas and Serenus*; and 6. *A Refutation of certain Doctrines of Aristotle*. There is no clue to the date of the two last. There can be no doubt that the others were written after the Council of Nicaea, though, immediately after the Reformation, Calvin and others appealed to the first as a genuine writing of Saint Justin's.

There is a curious question connected with the *Apologies* of Saint Justin which have come down to us. Eusebius mentions two *Apologies*—one written in the reign of Antoninus Pius, and the other written in the reign of Marcus Aurelius. Critics have disputed much whether we have these two *Apologies* in those now extant. Some have maintained, that what is now called the *Second Apology* was the preface of the first, and that the second is lost. Others have tried to show, that the so-called *Second Apology* is the continuation of the first, and that the second is lost. Others have supposed the two *Apologies* which we have are Saint Justin's two *Apologies*, but that Eusebius was wrong in affirming that the second was addressed to Marcus Aurelius; and others maintain, that we have in our two *Apologies* the two *Apologies* mentioned by Eusebius, and that our first is his first, and our second is his second.

The First Apology of Justin

Chapter I: *Address and Petition.*

To the Emperor Titus Aelius Adrianus Antoninus Pius Augustus Caesar, and to his son Verissimus the philosopher, and to Lucius the philosopher, the natural son of Caesar, and the adopted son of Pius, a lover of learning, and to the sacred senate, with the whole people of the Romans, I, Justin, the son of Priscus and grandson of Bacchius, natives of Flavia Neapolis in Palestine, present this address and petition in behalf of those of all nations who are unjustly hated and wantonly abused, myself being one of them.

Chapter II: *Demand for Justice.*

Reason directs those who are truly pious and philosophical to honor and love only what is true, declining to follow traditional opinions,[24] if these be worthless. For not only does sound reason direct us to refuse the guidance of those who did or taught anything wrong, but it is incumbent on the lover of truth, by all means, and if death be threatened, even before his own life, to choose to do and say what is right. Do you, then, since ye are called pious and philosophers, guardians of justice and lovers of learning, give good heed, and hearken to my address; and if ye are indeed such, it will be manifested. For we have come, not to flatter you by this writing, nor please you by our address, but to beg that you pass judgment, after an accurate and searching investigation, not flattered by prejudice or by a desire of pleasing superstitious men, nor induced by irrational impulse or evil rumors which have long been prevalent, to give a decision which will prove to be against yourselves. For as for us, we reckon that no evil can be done us, unless we be convicted as evil-doers, or be proved to be wicked men; and you, you can kill, but not hurt us.

---

[24] Literally, "the opinions of the ancients."

Chapter III: *Claim of judicial investigation.*

But lest anyone think that this is an unreasonable and reckless utterance, we demand that the charges against the Christians be investigated, and that, if these be substantiated, they be punished as they deserve; [or rather, indeed, we ourselves will punish them.][25] But if no one can convict us of anything, true reason forbids you, for the sake of a wicked rumor, to wrong blameless men, and indeed rather yourselves, who think fit to direct affairs, not by judgment, but by passion.

And every sober-minded person will declare this to be the only fair and equitable adjustment, namely, that the subjects render an unexceptional account of their own life and doctrine; and that, on the other hand, the rulers should give their decision in obedience, not to violence and tyranny, but to piety and philosophy. For thus would both rulers and ruled reap benefit. For even one of the ancients somewhere said, "Unless both rulers and ruled philosophize, it is impossible to make states blessed."[26]

It is our task, therefore, to afford to all an opportunity of inspecting our life and teachings, lest, on account of those who are accustomed to be ignorant of our affairs, we should incur the penalty due to them for mental blindness;[27] and it is your business, when you hear us, to be found, as reason demands, good judges. For if, when ye have learned the truth, you do not what is just, you will be before God without excuse.

Chapter IV: *Christians unjustly condemned for their mere name.*

By the mere application of a name, nothing is decided, either good or evil, apart from the actions implied in the name; and indeed, so far at least as one may judge from the name we are accused of, we are

[25] Thirlby regarded the clause in brackets as an interpolation. There is considerable variety of opinion as to the exact meaning of the words amongst those who regard them as genuine.
[26] Plato, *Republic*, v. 18.
[27] That is to say, if the Christians refused or neglected to make their real opinions and practices known, they would share the guilt of those whom they thus kept in darkness.

most excellent people.[28] But as we do not think it just to beg to be acquitted on account of the name, if we be convicted as evil-doers, so, on the other hand, if we be found to have committed no offence, either in the matter of thus naming ourselves, or of our conduct *as* citizens, it is your part very earnestly to guard against incurring just punishment, by unjustly punishing those who are not convicted.

For from a name neither praise nor punishment could reasonably spring, unless something excellent or base in action be proved. And those among yourselves who are accused you do not punish before they are convicted; but in our case you receive the name *as* proof against *us*, and this although, so far as the name goes, you ought rather to punish our accusers. For we are accused of being Christians, and to hate what is excellent (Chrestian) is unjust. Again, if any of the accused deny the name, and say that he is not a Christian, you acquit him, as having no evidence against him as a wrong-doer; but if any one acknowledge that he is a Christian, you punish him on account of this acknowledgment.

Justice requires that you inquire into the life both of him who confesses and of him who denies, that by his deeds it may be apparent what kind of man each is. For as some who have been taught by the Master, Christ, not to deny Him, give encouragement to others when they are put to the question, so in all probability do those who lead wicked lives give occasion to those who, without consideration, take upon them to accuse all the Christians of impiety and wickedness. And this also is not right. For of philosophy, too, some assume the name and the garb who do nothing worthy of their profession; and you are well aware, that those of the ancients whose opinions and teachings were quite diverse, are yet all called by the one name of philosophers. And of these some taught atheism; and the poets who have flourished among you raise a laugh out of the uncleanness of Jupiter with his own children. And those who now adopt such instruction are not restrained by you; but, on the contrary, you bestow prizes and honors upon those who euphoniously insult the gods.

---

[28] Justin avails himself here of the similarity in sound of the *Χρcατὸς* (Christ) and *χρηατὸς* (good, worthy, excellent). The play upon these words is kept up throughout this paragraph, and cannot be always represented to the English reader.

Chapter V: *Christians charged with atheism.*

Why, then, should this be? In our case, who pledge ourselves to do no wickedness, nor to hold these atheistic opinions, you do not examine the charges made against us; but, yielding to unreasoning passion, and to the instigation of evil demons, you punish us without consideration or judgment. For the truth shall be spoken; since of old these evil demons, effecting apparitions of themselves, both defiled women and corrupted boys, and showed such fearful sights to men, that those who did not use their reason in judging of the actions that were done, were struck with terror; and being carried away by fear, and not knowing that these were demons, they called them gods, and gave to each the name which each of the demons chose for himself.

And when Socrates endeavored, by true reason and examination, to bring these things to light, and deliver men from the demons, then the demons themselves, by means of men who rejoiced in iniquity, compassed his death, as an atheist and a profane person, on the charge that "he was introducing new divinities;" and in our case they display a similar activity. For not only among the Greeks did reason (Logos) prevail to condemn these things through Socrates, but also among the Barbarians were they condemned by Reason (or the Word, the Logos) Himself, who took shape, and became man, and was called Jesus Christ; and in obedience to Him, we not only deny that they who did such things *as* these are gods,[29] but assert that they are wicked and impious demons, whose actions will not bear comparison with those even of men desirous of virtue.

Chapter VI: *Charge of atheism refuted.*

Hence are we called atheists. And we confess that we are atheists, so far as gods of this sort are concerned, but not with respect to the most true God, the Father of righteousness and temperance and the

---

[29] The word *δαίμων* means in Greek a god, but the Christians used the word to signify an evil spirit. Justin uses the same word here for god and demon {at the end of the next phrase}. The connection which Justin and other Christian writers supposed to exist between evil spirits and the gods of the heathens will be apparent from Justin's own statements. The word *διάβολος*, devil, is not applied to these demons. There is but one devil, but many demons.

other virtues, who is free from all impurity. But both Him, and the Son who came forth from Him and taught us these things, and the host of the other good angels who follow and are made like to Him,[30] and the prophetic Spirit,[31] we worship and adore, knowing them in reason and truth, and declaring without grudging to everyone who wishes to learn, as we have been taught.

Chapter VII: *Each Christian must be tried by his own life.*

But someone will say, Some have ere now been arrested and convicted as evil-doers. For you condemn many, many a time, after inquiring into the life of each of the accused severally, but not on account of those of whom we have been speaking.[32] And this we acknowledge, that as among the Greeks those who teach such theories as please themselves are all called by the one name "Philosopher," though their doctrines be diverse, so also among the Barbarians this name on which accusations are accumulated is the common property of those who are and those who seem wise. For all are called Christians.

Wherefore we demand that the deeds of all those who are accused to you be judged, in order that each one who is convicted may be punished as an evil-doer, and not as a Christian; and if it is clear that any one is blameless, that he may be acquitted, since by the mere fact of his being a Christian he does no wrong.[33] For we will not require that you

[30] This is the literal and obvious translation of Justin's words. But from {Chapters} 13, 16, and 61, it is evident that he did not desire to inculcate the worship of angels. We are therefore driven to adopt another translation of this passage, even though it is somewhat harsh. Two such translations have been proposed: the first connecting "us" and "the host of the other good angels" as the common object of the verb "taught;" the second connecting "these things" with "host of," etc., and making these two together the subject taught. In the first case, the translation would stand, "taught these things to us and to the host," etc.; in the second case the translation would be, "taught us about these things, and about the host of the others who follow Him, viz. the good angels."

[31] {Here, Saint Justin acknowledges the Trinity.}

[32] I.e., according to Otto, "not on account of the sincere Christians of whom we have been speaking." According to Trollope, "not on account of (or at the instigation of) the demons before mentioned."

[33] Or, "as a Christian who has done no wrong."

punish our accusers;[34] they being sufficiently punished by their present wickedness and ignorance of what is right.

Chapter VIII: *Christians confess their faith in God.*

And reckon ye that it is for your sakes we have been saying these things; for it is in our power, when we are examined, to deny that we are Christians; but we would not live by telling a lie. For, impelled by the desire of the eternal and pure life, we seek the abode that is with God, the Father and Creator of all, and hasten to confess our faith, persuaded and convinced as we are that they who have proved to God[35] by their works that they followed Him, and loved to abide with Him where there is no sin to cause disturbance, can obtain these things. This, then, to speak shortly, is what we expect and have learned from Christ, and teach. And Plato, in like manner, used to say that Rhadamanthus and Minos would punish the wicked who came before them; and we say that the same thing will be done, but at the hand of Christ, and upon the wicked in the same bodies united again to their spirits which are now to undergo everlasting punishment; and not only, as Plato said, for a period of a thousand years. And if anyone say that this is incredible or impossible, this error of ours is one which concerns ourselves only, and no other person, so long as you cannot convict us of doing any harm.

Chapter IX: *Folly of idol worship.*

And neither do we honor with many sacrifices and garlands of flowers such deities as men have formed and set in shrines and called gods; since we see that these are soulless and dead, and have not the form of God (for we do not consider that God has such a form as some say that they imitate to His honor), but have the names and forms of those wicked demons which have appeared.

For why need we tell you who already know, into what forms the craftsmen, carving and cutting, casting and hammering, fashion the materials? And often out of vessels of dishonor, by merely changing the

---

[34] Compare the Rescript of Adrian appended to this *Apology*. {This writing is included in this reprint of Saint Justin's *The First Apology*, Ch. LXVIII.}

[35] Literally, "persuaded God."

form, and making an image of the requisite shape, they make what they call a god; which we consider not only senseless, but to be even insulting to God, who, having ineffable glory and form, thus gets His name attached to things that are corruptible, and require constant service. And that the artificers of these are both intemperate, and, not to enter into particulars, are practiced in every vice, you very well know; even their own girls who work along with them they corrupt.

What infatuation! that dissolute men should be said to fashion and make gods for your worship, and that you should appoint such men the guardians of the temples where they are enshrined; not recognizing that it is unlawful even to think or say that men are the guardians of gods.

Chapter X: *How God is to be served by man.*

But we have received by tradition that God does not need the material offerings which men can give, seeing, indeed, that He Himself is the provider of all things. And we have been taught, and are convinced, and do believe, that He accepts those only who imitate the excellences which reside in Him, temperance, and justice, and philanthropy, and as many virtues as are peculiar to a God who is called by no proper name. And we have been taught that He in the beginning did of His goodness, for man's sake, create all things out of unformed matter; and if men by their works show themselves worthy of this His design, they are deemed worthy, and so we have received—of reigning in company with Him, being delivered from corruption and suffering. For as in the beginning He created us when we were not, so do we consider that, in like manner, those who choose what is pleasing to Him are, on account of their choice, deemed worthy of incorruption and of fellowship with Him. For the coming into being at first was not in our own power; and in order that we may follow those things which please Him, choosing them by means of the rational faculties He has Himself endowed us with, He both persuades us and leads us to faith.

And we think it for the advantage of all men that they are not restrained from learning these things, but are even urged thereto. For the restraint which human laws could not effect, the Word, inasmuch as He is divine, would have effected, had not the wicked demons, taking as their ally the lust of wickedness which is in every man, and which draws variously to all manner of vice, scattered many false and profane accusations, none of which attach to us.

Chapter XI: *Christians look for a Heavenly not a human Kingdom.*

And when you hear that we look for a kingdom, you suppose, without making any inquiry, that we speak of a human kingdom; whereas we speak of that which is with God, as appears also from the confession of their faith made by those who are charged with being Christians, though they know that death is the punishment awarded to him who so confesses. For if we looked for a human kingdom, we should also deny our Christ, that we might not be slain; and we should strive to escape detection, that we might obtain what we expect. But since our thoughts are not fixed on the present, we are not concerned when men cut us off; since also death is a debt which must at all events be paid.

Chapter XII: *Christians live as always under God's eye.*

And more than all other men are we your helpers and allies in promoting peace, seeing that we hold this view, that it is alike impossible for the wicked, the covetous, the conspirator, and for the virtuous, to escape the notice of God, and that each man goes to everlasting punishment or salvation according to the value of his actions. For if all men knew this, no one would choose wickedness even for a little, knowing that he goes to the everlasting punishment of fire; but would by all means restrain himself, and adorn himself with virtue, that he might obtain the good gifts of God, and escape the punishments.

For those who, on account of the laws and punishments you impose, endeavor to escape detection when they offend (and they offend, too, under the impression that it is quite possible to escape your detection, since you are but men), those persons, if they learned and were convinced that nothing, whether actually done or only intended, can escape the knowledge of God, would by all means live decently on account of the penalties threatened, as even you yourselves will admit.

But you seem to fear lest all men become righteous, and you no longer have any to punish. Such would be the concern of public executioners, but not of good princes. But, as we before said, we are persuaded that these things are prompted by evil spirits, who demand sacrifices and service even from those who live unreasonably; but as for you, we presume that you who aim at [a reputation for] piety and philosophy will do nothing unreasonable. But if you also, like the foolish, prefer custom to truth, do what you have power to do. But just so much power have rulers who esteem opinion more than truth, as robbers have in a desert. And that you will not succeed is declared by the Word, than whom, after God who begat Him, we know there is no ruler more kingly and just. For as all shrink from succeeding to the poverty or sufferings or obscurity of their fathers, so whatever the Word forbids us to choose, the sensible man will not choose.

That all these things should come to pass, I say, our Teacher foretold, He who is both Son and Apostle of God the Father of all and the Ruler, Jesus Christ; from whom also we have the name of Christians. Whence we become more assured of all the things He taught us, since whatever He beforehand foretold should come to pass, is seen in fact coming to pass; and this is the work of God, to tell of a thing before it happens, and as it was foretold so to show it happening.

It were possible to pause here and add no more, reckoning that we demand what is just and true; but because we are well aware that it is not easy suddenly to change a mind possessed by ignorance, we intend to add a few things, for the sake of persuading those who love the truth, knowing that it is not impossible to put ignorance to flight by presenting the truth.

Chapter XIII: *Christians serve God rationally.*

What sober-minded man, then, will not acknowledge that we are not atheists, worshipping as we do the Maker of this universe, and declaring, as we have been taught, that He has no need of streams of blood and libations and incense; whom we praise to the utmost of our power by the exercise of prayer and thanksgiving for all things wherewith we are supplied, as we have been taught that the only honor that is worthy of Him is not to consume by fire what He has brought into being for our sustenance, but to use it for ourselves and those who need, and with gratitude to Him to offer thanks by invocations and hymns[36] for our

---

[36] *πομχὰς χαὶ ὕμνονς*. "Grabe, and it should seem correctly, understands *πομπὰ* to be *solemn prayers*. . . . He also remarks, that the *ὕμνοι* were either psalms of David, or some

creation, and for all the means of health, and for the various qualities of the different kinds of things, and for the changes of the seasons; and to present before Him petitions for our existing again in incorruption through faith in Him.

Our teacher of these things is Jesus Christ, who also was born for this purpose, and was crucified under Pontius Pilate, procurator of Judaea, in the times of Tiberius Caesar; and that we reasonably worship Him, having learned that He is the Son of the true God Himself, and holding Him in the second place, and the prophetic Spirit in the third, we will prove. For they proclaim our madness to consist in this, that we give to a crucified man a place second to the unchangeable and eternal God, the Creator of all; for they do not discern the mystery that is herein, to which, as we make it plain to you, we pray you to give heed.

Chapter XIV: *The demons misrepresent Christian doctrine.*

For we forewarn you to be on your guard, lest those demons whom we have been accusing should deceive you, and quite divert you from reading and understanding what we say. For they strive to hold you their slaves and servants; and sometimes by appearances in dreams, and sometimes by magical impositions, they subdue all who make no strong opposing effort for their own salvation.

And thus do we also, since our persuasion by the Word, stand aloof from them (i.e., the demons), and follow the only unbegotten God through His Son—we who formerly delighted in fornication, but now embrace chastity alone; we who formerly used magical arts, dedicate ourselves to the good and unbegotten God; we who valued above all things the acquisition of wealth and possessions, now bring what we have into a common stock, and communicate to everyone in need; we who hated and destroyed one another, and on account of their different manners would not live[37] with men of a different tribe, now, since the coming of Christ, live familiarly with them, and pray for our enemies, and endeavor to persuade those who hate us unjustly to live conformably to

---

of those psalms and songs made by the primitive Christians, which are mentioned in Eusebius. *H.E.* v. 28."—Trollope.

[37] Literally, "would not use the same hearth or fire."

the good precepts of Christ, to the end that they may become partakers with us of the same joyful hope of a reward from God the ruler of all.

But lest we should seem to be reasoning sophistically, we consider it right, before giving you the promised[38] explanation, to cite a few precepts given by Christ Himself. And be it yours, as powerful rulers, to inquire whether we have been taught and do teach these things truly. Brief and concise utterances fell from Him, for He was no sophist, but His word was the power of God.

Chapter XV: *What Christ Himself taught.*

Concerning chastity, He uttered[39] such sentiments as these:[40] "***Whosoever looketh upon a woman to lust after her, hath committed adultery with her already in his heart before God.***"[41] And, "***If thy right eye offend thee, cut it out; for it is better for thee to enter into the kingdom of heaven with one eye, than, having two eyes, to be cast into everlasting fire.***"[42] And, "***Whosoever shall marry her that is divorced from another husband, committeth adultery***."[43] And,

> ***There are some who have been made eunuchs of men, and some who were born eunuchs, and some who have made themselves eunuchs for the kingdom of heaven's sake; but all cannot receive this saying.***[44]

---

[38] See the end of Chapter XIII.

[39] {Saint Justin largely quotes the words of Jesus Christ as reported in the Gospels to witness to his audience. He relies almost exclusively on Saints Matthew and Luke.}

[40] The reader will notice that Justin quotes from memory, so that there are some slight discrepancies between the word of Jesus as here cited, and the same sayings as recorded in our Gospels. {This happens with some regularity throughout Saint Justin's works. Moreover, Saint Justin's quotes of verses from Scripture are not always exact, sometimes being paraphrases, other times combining Scripture from different authors, such as quoting from the Gospels of Luke and Matthew in a single paragraph, or multiple verses from a single Gospel but in an order of his own preference as they support his argument.}

[41] {Matthew 5:28.}

[42] {Matthew 5:29.}

[43] Matthew 5:28-29, 32. {The original citation refers to all Scripture quotes in the paragraph. This passage is Matthew 5:32.}

[44] Matthew 19:12.

So that all who, by human law, are twice married,[45] are in the eye of our Master sinners, and those who look upon a woman to lust after her. For not only he who in act commits adultery is rejected by Him, but also he who desires to commit adultery: since not only our works, but also our thoughts, are open before God. And many, both men and women, who have been Christ's disciples from childhood, remain pure at the age of sixty or seventy years; and I boast that I could produce such from every race of men.

For what shall I say, too, of the countless multitude of those who have reformed intemperate habits, and learned these things? For Christ called not the just nor the chaste to repentance, but the ungodly, and the licentious, and the unjust; His words being, ***"I came not to call the righteous, but sinners to repentance."***[46] For the heavenly Father desires rather the repentance than the punishment of the sinner. And of our love to all, He taught thus:

> ***If ye love them that love you, what new thing do ye? for even fornicators do this. But I say unto you, Pray for your enemies, and love them that hate you, and bless them that curse you, and pray for them that despitefully use you.***[47]

And that we should communicate to the needy, and do nothing for glory, He said,

> ***Give to him that asketh, and from him that would borrow turn not away; for if ye lend to them of whom ye hope to receive, what new thing do ye? even the publicans do this. Lay not up for yourselves treasure upon earth, where moth and rust doth corrupt, and where robbers break through; but lay up for***

---

[45] *διγαμίας ποιούμενοι*, lit. Contracting a double marriage. Of double marriages there are three kinds: the first, marriage with a second wife while the first is still alive and recognized as a lawful wife, or bigamy; the second, marriage with a second wife after divorce from the first; and third, marriage with a second wife after the death of the first. It is thought that Justin here refers to the second case.

[46] Matthew 9:13.

[47] Matthew 5:46, 44; Luke 6:28. {Luke 6:27; see also the example of Jesus forgiving enemies at Luke 23:34 (reporting Jesus Christ's forgiving words while crucified). This is the first example of Saint Justin combining passages from different books of the Bible and not necessarily in order.}

> ***yourselves treasure in heaven, where neither moth nor rust doth corrupt. For what is a man profited, if he shall gain the whole world, and lose his own soul? or what shall a man give in exchange for it? Lay up treasure, therefore, in heaven, where neither moth nor rust doth corrupt.***[48]

And,

> ***Be ye kind and merciful, as your Father also is kind and merciful, and maketh His sun to rise on sinners, and the righteous, and the wicked. Take no thought what ye shall eat, or what ye shall put on: are ye not better than the birds and the beasts? And God feedeth them. Take no thought, therefore, what ye shall eat, or what ye shall put on; for your heavenly Father knoweth that ye have need of these things. But seek ye the kingdom of heaven, and all these things shall be added unto you. For where his treasure is, there also is the mind of a man.***[49]

And, "***Do not these things to be seen of men; otherwise ye have no reward from your Father which is in heaven.***"[50]

Chapter XVI: *Concerning patience and swearing.*

And concerning our being patient of injuries, and ready to serve all, and free from anger, this is what He said:

> ***To him that smiteth thee on the one cheek, offer also the other; and him that taketh away thy cloak or coat, forbid not. And whosoever shall be angry, is in danger of the fire. And every one that compelleth thee to go with him a mile, follow him two. And let your good works shine before men, that they, seeing them, may glorify your Father which is in heaven.***[51]

---

[48] Luke 6:30, 34; Matthew 6:19, 16:26; 6:20. {See also Matthew 5:42, 19:21. For Saint Paul's similar instruction to Saint Timothy, see 1 Timothy 6:19. Similar instruction is set forth in the Old Testament, see Leviticus 25:35; Deuteronomy 15:8.}

[49] Luke 6:36; Matthew 5:45; 6:21, 25-26, 31, 33. {See also Job 38:41; Psalm 37:5, 55:22; 1 Peter 5:7.}

[50] Matthew 6:1.

[51] Luke 6:29; Matthew 5:22, 5:41, 16.

For we ought not to strive; neither has He desired us to be imitators of wicked men, but He has exhorted us to lead all men, by patience and gentleness, from shame and the love of evil. And this indeed is proved in the case of many who once were of your way of thinking, but have changed their violent and tyrannical disposition, being overcome either by the constancy which they have witnessed in their neighbors' lives,[52] or by the extraordinary forbearance they have observed in their fellow-travelers when defrauded, or by the honesty of those with whom they have transacted business.

And with regard to our not swearing at all, and always speaking the truth, He enjoined as follows: "***Swear not at all; but let your yea be yea, and your nay, nay; for whatsoever is more than these cometh of evil.***"[53] And that we ought to worship God alone, He thus persuaded us: "***The greatest commandment is, Thou shalt worship the Lord thy God, and Him only shalt thou serve, with all thy heart, and with all thy strength, the Lord God that made thee.***"[54] And when a certain man came to Him and said, "Good Master," He answered and said, "***There is none good but God only, who made all things.***"[55] And let those who are not found living as He taught, be understood to be no Christians, even though they profess with the lip the precepts of Christ; for not those who make profession, but those who do the works, shall be saved, according to His word:

> ***Not everyone who saith to Me, Lord, Lord, shall enter into the kingdom of heaven, but he that doeth the will of My Father which is in heaven. For whosoever heareth Me, and doeth My sayings, heareth Him that sent Me. And many will say unto Me, Lord, Lord, have we not eaten and drunk in Thy name, and done wonders? And then will I say unto them, Depart from Me, ye workers of iniquity. Then shall there be wailing and gnashing of teeth, when the righteous shall shine as the sun, and the wicked are sent into everlasting fire. For many shall come in My name, clothed outwardly in sheep's clothing, but inwardly being ravening wolves. By their works ye shall know them. And every tree that***

---

[52] I.e., Christian neighbors.

[53] Matthew 5:34, 37. {See also James 5:12.}

[54] Mark 12:30.

[55] Matthew 19:16, 17. {See also Mark 10:18.}

> ***bringeth not forth good fruit, is hewn down and cast into the fire.***[56]

And as to those who are not living pursuant to these His teachings, and are Christians only in name, we demand that all such be punished by you.

Chapter XVII: *Christ taught obedience to civil authorities.*

And everywhere we, more readily than all men, endeavor to pay to those appointed by you the taxes both ordinary and extraordinary,[57] as we have been taught by Him; for at that time some came to Him and asked Him, if one ought to pay tribute to Caesar; and He answered, "***Tell Me, whose image does the coin bear?***"[58] And they said, "***Caesar's.***"[59] And again He answered them, "***Render therefore to Caesar the things that are Caesar's, and to God the things that are God's.***"[60] Whence to God alone we render worship, but in other things we gladly serve you, acknowledging you as kings and rulers of men, and praying that with your kingly power you be found to possess also sound judgment.

But if you pay no regard to our prayers and frank explanations, we shall suffer no loss, since we believe (or rather, indeed, are persuaded) that every man will suffer punishment in eternal fire according to the merit of his deed, and will render account according to the power he has received from God, as Christ intimated when He said, "***To whom God has given more, of him shall more be required.***"[61]

Chapter XVIII: *Proof of immortality and the Resurrection.*

For reflect upon the end of each of the preceding kings, how they died the death common to all, which, if it issued in insensibility, would be

---

[56] Matthew 7:21, etc., Luke 13:26; Matthew 13:42, 7:15, 16, 19. {See also Luke 6:46, 13:25-27; Matthew 3:10, 7:20; John 15:2; Hosea 8:2.}

[57] *Φόρους χαὶ εἰΦοράς*. The former is the annual tribute; the latter, any occasional assessment. See Otto's Note and Thucydides III 19.

[58] {Matthew 22:20.}

[59] {Matthew 22:21.}

[60] Matthew 22:17, 19-21. {Matthew 22:21 is the correct citation for this passage.}

[61] Luke 12:48.

a godsend[62] to all the wicked. But since sensation remains to all who have ever lived, and eternal punishment is laid up (i.e., for the wicked), see that ye neglect not to be convinced, and to hold as your belief, that these things are true.

For let even necromancy, and the divinations you practice by immaculate children,[63] and the evoking of departed human souls,[64] and those who are called among the magi, Dream-senders and Assistant-spirits (Familiars),[65] and all that is done by those who are skilled in such matters—let these persuade you that even after death souls are in a state of sensation; and those who are seized and cast about by the spirits of the dead, whom all call demoniacs or madmen;[66] and what you repute as oracles, both of Amphilochus, Dodona, Pytho, and as many other such as exist; and the opinions of your authors, Empedocles and Pythagoras, Plato and Socrates, and the pit of Homer,[67] and the descent of Ulysses to inspect these things, and all that has been uttered of a like kind.

Such favor as you grant to these, grant also to us, who not less but more firmly than they believe in God; since we expect to receive again our own bodies, though they be dead and cast into the earth, for we maintain that with God nothing is impossible.

---

[62] *ἕρμαιον*, a piece of unlooked for luck, Hermes being the reputed giver of such gifts: *vid.* Liddell and Scott's *Lex.*; see also the Scholiast, quoted by Stahllbaum in Plato's *Phaed.* P. 107, on a passage singularly analogous to this.

[63] Boys and girls, or even children, prematurely taken from the womb, were slaughtered, and their entrails inspected, in the belief that the souls of the victims (being still conscious, as Justin is arguing) would reveal things hidden and future. Instances are abundantly cited by Otto and Trollope.

[64] This form of spirit-rapping was familiar to the ancients, and Justin again (*Dialogue with Trypho*, c. 105) uses the invocation of Samuel by the witch of Endor as a proof of the immortality of the soul.

[65] Valesius (on Eusebius *H. E.* IV 7) states that the magi had two kinds of familiars: the first, who were sent to inspire men with dreams which might give them intimations of things future; and the second, who were sent to watch over men, and protect them from diseases and misfortunes. The first, he says, they called (as here) *ὀνειροπομποὺς*, and the second *παρέδρους*.

[66] Justin is not the only author in ancient or recent times who has classed demoniacs and maniacs together; neither does he stand alone among the ancients in the opinion that demoniacs were possessed by the spirits of departed men. References will be found in Trollope's note.

[67] See the *Odyssey*, Book XI line 25, where Ulysses is described as digging a pit or trench with his sword, and pouring libations, in order to collect around him the souls of the dead.

Chapter XIX: *The Resurrection possible.*

And to any thoughtful person would anything appear more incredible, than, if we were not in the body, and someone were to say that it was possible that from a small drop of human seed bones and sinews and flesh be formed into a shape such as we see? For let this now be said hypothetically: if you yourselves were not such as you now are, and born of such parents [and causes], and one were to show you human seed and a picture of a man, and were to say with confidence that from such a substance such a being could be produced, would you believe before you saw the actual production? No one will dare to deny [that such a statement would surpass belief].

In the same way, then, you are now incredulous because you have never seen a dead man rise again. But as at first you would not have believed it possible that such persons could be produced from the small drop, and yet now you see them thus produced, so also judge ye that it is not impossible that the bodies of men, after they have been dissolved, and like seeds resolved into earth, should in God's appointed time rise again and put on incorruption.

For what power worthy of God those imagine who say, that each thing returns to that from which it was produced, and that beyond this not even God Himself can do anything, we are unable to conceive; but this we see clearly, that they would not have believed it possible that they could have become such and produced from such materials, as they now see both themselves and the whole world to be. And that it is better to believe even what is impossible to our own nature and to men, than to be unbelieving like the rest of the world, we have learned; for we know that our master Jesus Christ said, that "***what is impossible with men is possible with God,***"[68] and, "***Fear not them that kill you, and after that can do no more; but fear Him who after death is able to cast both soul and body into hell.***"[69] And hell is a place where those are to be punished who have lived wickedly, and who do not believe that those things which God has taught us by Christ will come to pass.

---

[68] Matthew 19:26. {See also Luke 1:37; Genesis 18:14; Jeremiah 32:17.}

[69] Matthew 10:28.

Chapter XX: *Heathen analogies to Christian doctrine.*

And the Sibyl[70] and Hystaspes said that there should be a dissolution by God of things corruptible. And the philosophers called Stoics teach that even God Himself shall be resolved into fire, and they say that the world is to be formed anew by this revolution; but we understand that God, the Creator of all things, is superior to the things that are to be changed. If, therefore, on some points we teach the same things as the poets and philosophers whom you honor, and on other points are fuller and more divine in our teaching, and if we alone afford proof of what we assert, why are we unjustly hated more than all others?

For while we say that all things have been produced and arranged into a world by God, we shall seem to utter the doctrine of Plato; and while we say that there will be a burning up of all, we shall seem to utter the doctrine of the Stoics; and while we affirm that the souls of the wicked, being endowed with sensation even after death, are punished, and that those of the good being delivered from punishment spend a blessed existence, we shall seem to say the same things as the poets and philosophers; and while we maintain that men ought not to worship the works of their hands, we say the very things which have been said by the comic poet Menander, and other similar writers, for they have declared that the workman is greater than the work.

Chapter XXI: *Analogies to the history of Christ.*

And when we say also that the Word, who is the first-birth[71] of God, was produced without sexual union, and that He, Jesus Christ, our Teacher, was crucified and died, and rose again, and ascended into heaven, we propound nothing different from what you believe regarding those whom you esteem sons of Jupiter. For you know how many sons your esteemed writers ascribed to Jupiter: Mercury, the interpreting word and teacher of all; Aesculapius, who, though he was a great

---

[70] The Sibylline Oracles are now generally regarded as heathen fragments largely interpolated by unscrupulous men during the early ages of the Church. For an interesting account of these somewhat perplexing documents, see Burton's *Lectures on the Ecclesiastical History of the First Three Centuries*, Lect. XVIII. The prophecies of Hystaspes were also commonly appealed to as genuine by the early Christians.

[71] I.e., first-born.

physician, was struck by a thunderbolt, and so ascended to heaven; and Bacchus too, after he had been torn limb from limb; and Hercules, when he had committed himself to the flames to escape his toils; and the sons of Leda, and Dioscuri; and Perseus, son of Danae; and Bellerophon, who, though sprung from mortals, rose to heaven on the horse Pegasus. For what shall I say of Ariadne, and those who, like her, have been declared to be set among the stars?

And what of the emperors who die among yourselves, whom you deem worthy of deification, and in whose behalf you produce someone who swears he has seen the burning Caesar rise to heaven from the funeral pyre? And what kind of deeds are recorded of each of these reputed sons of Jupiter, it is needless to tell to those who already know. This only shall be said, that they are written for the advantage and encouragement[72] of youthful scholars; for all reckon it an honorable thing to imitate the gods. But far be such a thought concerning the gods from every well-conditioned soul, as to believe that Jupiter himself, the governor and creator of all things, was both a parricide and the son of a parricide, and that being overcome by the love of base and shameful pleasures, he came in to Ganymede and those many women whom he had violated, and that his sons did like actions.

But, as we said above, wicked devils perpetrated these things. And we have learned that those only are deified who have lived near to God in holiness and virtue; and we believe that those who live wickedly and do not repent are punished in everlasting fire.

Chapter XXII: *Analogies to the Sonship of Christ.*

Moreover, the Son of God called Jesus, even if only a man by ordinary generation, yet, on account of His wisdom, is worthy to be called the Son of God; for all writers call God the Father of men and gods. And if we assert that the Word of God was born of God in a peculiar manner, different from ordinary generation, let this, as said above, be no

[72] *διαΦορὰν χαὶ προτροπὴν*. The irony here is so obvious as to make the proposed reading (*ὀιαΦθορὰν χαὶ ναρατροπὴν*, corruption and depravation) unnecessary. Otto prefers the reading adopted above. Trollope, on the other hand, inclines to the latter reading, mainly on the score of the former expressions being unusual. See his very sensible note *in loc.*

extraordinary thing to you, who say that Mercury is the angelic word of God.

But if any one objects that He was crucified, in this also He is on a par with those reputed sons of Jupiter of yours, who suffered as we have now enumerated. For their sufferings at death are recorded to have been not all alike, but diverse; so that not even by the peculiarity of His sufferings does He seem to be inferior to them; but, on the contrary, as we promised in the preceding part of this discourse, we will now prove Him superior—or rather have already proved Him to be so—for the superior is revealed by His actions.

And if we even affirm that He was born of a virgin, accept this in common with what you accept of Perseus. And in that we say that He made whole the lame, the paralytic, and those born blind, we seem to say what is very similar to the deeds said to have been done by Aesculapius.

Chapter XXIII: *The three arguments to be made.*

And that this may now become evident to you—(firstly[73]) that whatever we assert in conformity with what has been taught us by Christ, and by the prophets who preceded Him, are alone true, and are older than all the writers who have existed; that we claim to be acknowledged, not because we say the same things as these writers said, but because we say true things: and (secondly) that Jesus Christ is the only proper Son who has been begotten by God, being His Word and first-begotten, and power; and, becoming man according to His will, He taught us these things for the conversion and restoration of the human race: and (thirdly) that before He became a man among men, some, influenced by the demons before mentioned, related beforehand, through the instrumentality of the poets, those circumstances as having really

[73] The Benedictine editor, Maranus, Otto, and Trollope, here note that Justin in this chapter promises to make good three distinct positions: 1st, That Christian doctrines alone are true, and are to be received, not on account of their resemblance to the sentiments of poets and philosophers, but on their own account; 2d, that Jesus Christ is the incarnate Son of God, and our teacher; 3d, that before His Incarnation, the demons, having some knowledge of what He would accomplish, enabled the heathen poets and priests in some points to anticipate, though in a distorted form, the facts of the Incarnation. The first he establishes in Chapters XXIV-XXIX; the second in Chapters XXX-LIII; and the third in Chapters LIV *et seq.*

happened, which, having fictitiously devised, they narrated, in the same manner as they have caused to be fabricated the scandalous reports against us of infamous and impious actions,[74] of which there is neither witness nor proof—we shall bring forward the following proof.

Chapter XXIV: *Varieties of heathen worship.*

In the first place [we furnish proof], because, though we say things similar to what the Greeks say, we only are hated on account of the name of Christ, and though we do no wrong, are put to death as sinners; other men in other places worshipping trees and rivers, and mice and cats and crocodiles, and many irrational animals. Nor are the same animals esteemed by all; but in one place one is worshipped, and another in another, so that all are profane in the judgment of one another, on account of their not worshipping the same objects. And this is the sole accusation you bring against us, that we do not reverence the same gods as you do, nor offer to the dead libations and the savor of fat, and crowns for their statues,[75] and sacrifices. For you very well know that the same animals are with some esteemed gods, with others wild beasts, and with others sacrificial victims.

Chapter XXV: *False gods abandoned by Christians.*

And, secondly, because we—who, out of every race of men, used to worship Bacchus the son of Semele, and Apollo the son of Latona (who in their loves with men did such things as it is shameful even to mention), and Proserpine and Venus (who were maddened with love of Adonis, and whose mysteries also you celebrate), or Aesculapius, or someone or other of those who are called gods—have now, through Jesus Christ, learned to despise these, though we be threatened with death for it, and have dedicated ourselves to the unbegotten and impossible God; of whom we are persuaded that never was he goaded by lust of Antiope, or such other women, or of Ganymede, nor was rescued by that hundred-handed giant

---

[74] We have here followed the reading and rendering of Trollope.
[75] *ἐν γραΦαὶς ατεΦάνους.* The only conjecture which seems at all probable is that of the Benedictine editor followed here.

whose aid was obtained through Thetis, nor was anxious on this account[76] that her son Achilles should destroy many of the Greeks because of his concubine Briseis. Those who believe these things we pity, and those who invented them we know to be devils.

Chapter XXVI: *Magicians not trusted by Christians.*

And, thirdly, because after Christ's Ascension into Heaven the devils put forward certain men who said that they themselves were gods; and they were not only not persecuted by you, but even deemed worthy of honors. There was a Samaritan, Simon, a native of the village called Gitto, who in the reign of Claudius Caesar, and in your royal city of Rome, did mighty acts of magic, by virtue of the art of the devils operating in him. He was considered a god, and as a god was honored by you with a statue, which statue was erected on the river Tiber, between the two bridges, and bore this inscription, in the language of Rome:

Simoni Deo Sancto,[77]
To Simon the holy God.

And almost all the Samaritans, and a few even of other nations, worship him, and acknowledge him as the first god; and a woman, Helena, who went about with him at that time, and had formerly been a prostitute, they say is the first idea generated by him. And a man, Menander, also a Samaritan, of the town Capparetaea, a disciple of Simon, and inspired by devils, we know to have deceived many while he was in Antioch by his magical art. He persuaded those who adhered to him that they should

[76] I.e., on account of the assistance gained for him by Thetis, and in return for it.

[77] It is very generally supposed that Justin was mistaken in understanding this to have been a statue erected to Simon Magus. This supposition rests on the fact that in the year 1574 there was dug up in the island of the Tiber a fragment of marble, with the inscription "Semoni Sanco Deo," etc., being probably the base of a statue erected to the Sabine deity Semo Sancus. This inscription Justin is supposed to have mistaken for the one he gives above. This has always seemed to us very slight evidence on which to reject so precise a statement as Justin here makes; a statement which he would scarcely have hazarded in an apology addressed to Rome, where every person had the means of ascertaining its accuracy. If, as is supposed, he made a mistake, it must have been at once exposed, and other writers would not have so frequently repeated the story as they have done. See *Burton's Bampton Lectures*, p. 374.

never die, and even now there are some living who hold this opinion of his. And there is Marcion, a man of Pontus, who is even at this day alive, and teaching his disciples to believe in some other god greater than the Creator. And he, by the aid of the devils, has caused many of every nation to speak blasphemies, and to deny that God is the Maker of this universe, and to assert that some other, being greater than He, has done greater works.

All who take their opinions from these men, are, as we before said,[78] called Christians; just as also those who do not agree with the philosophers in their doctrines, have yet in common with them the name of philosophers given to them. And whether they perpetrate those fabulous and shameful deeds[79]—the upsetting of the lamp, and promiscuous intercourse, and eating human flesh—we know not; but we do know that they are neither persecuted nor put to death by you, at least on account of their opinions. But I have a treatise against all the heresies that have existed already composed, which, if you wish to read it, I will give you.

Chapter XXVII: *Guilt of exposing children.*

But as for us, we have been taught that to expose newly-born children is the part of wicked men; and this we have been taught lest we should do any one an injury, and lest we should sin against God, first, because we see that almost all so exposed (not only the girls, but also the males) are brought up to prostitution. And as the ancients are said to have reared herds of oxen, or goats, or sheep, or grazing horses, so now we see you rear children only for this shameful use; and for this pollution a multitude of females and hermaphrodites, and those who commit unmentionable iniquities, are found in every nation. And you receive the hire of these, and duty and taxes from them, whom you ought to exterminate from your realm. And anyone who uses such persons, besides the godless and infamous and impure intercourse, may possibly be having intercourse with his own child, or relative, or brother. And there are some who prostitute even their own children and wives, and some are openly mutilated for the purpose of sodomy; and they refer

[78] See Chapter VII.

[79] Which were commonly charged against the Christians.

these mysteries to the mother of the gods, and along with each of those whom you esteem gods there is painted a serpent,[80] a great symbol and mystery. Indeed, the things which you do openly and with applause, as if the divine light were overturned and extinguished, these you lay to our charge; which, in truth, does no harm to us who shrink from doing any such things, but only to those who do them and bear false witness against us.

Chapter XXVIII: *God's care for men.*

For among us the prince of the wicked spirits is called the serpent, and Satan, and the devil, as you can learn by looking into our writings. And that he would be sent into the fire with his host, and the men who follow him, and would be punished for an endless duration, Christ foretold. For the reason why God has delayed to do this, is His regard for the human race. For He foreknows that some are to be saved by repentance, some even that are perhaps not yet born.[81] In the beginning He made the human race with the power of thought and of choosing the truth and doing right, so that all men are without excuse before God; for they have been born rational and contemplative. And if any one disbelieves that God cares for these things[82], he will thereby either insinuate that God does not exist, or he will assert that though He exists He delights in vice, or exists like a stone, and that neither virtue nor vice are anything, but only in the opinion of men these things are reckoned good or evil. And this is the greatest profanity and wickedness.

Chapter XXIX: *Continence of Christians.*

And again [we fear to expose children], lest some of them be not picked up, but die, and we become murderers. But whether we marry, it

---

[80] Thirlby remarks that the serpent was the symbol specially of eternity, of power, and of wisdom, and that there was scarcely any divine attribute to which the heathen did not find some likeness in this animal. See also Hardwick's *Christ and other Masters*, Vol. II 146 (2d ed.).

[81] Literally, "For He foreknows some about to be saved by repentance, and some not yet perhaps born."

[82] Those things which concern the salvation of man; so Trollope and other interpreters, except Otto, who reads *τούτων* masculine, and understands it of the men first spoken of.

is only that we may bring up children; or whether we decline marriage, we live continently. And that you may understand that promiscuous intercourse is not one of our mysteries, one of our number a short time ago presented to Felix the governor in Alexandria a petition, craving that permission might be given to a surgeon to make him an eunuch. For the surgeons there said that they were forbidden to do this without the permission of the governor. And when Felix absolutely refused to sign such a permission, the youth remained single, and was satisfied with his own approving conscience, and the approval of those who thought as he did. And it is not out of place, we think, to mention here Antinous, who was alive but lately, and whom all were prompt, through fear, to worship as a god, though they knew both who he was and what was his origin.[83]

Chapter XXX: *Was Christ not a magician?*

But lest anyone should meet us with the question, What should prevent that He whom we call Christ, being a man born of men, performed what we call His mighty works by magical art, and by this appeared to be the Son of God? we will now offer proof, not trusting mere assertions, but being of necessity persuaded by those who prophesied [of Him] before these things came to pass, for with our own eyes we behold things that have happened and are happening just as they were predicted; and this will, we think appear even to you the strongest and truest evidence.

Chapter XXXI: *Of the Hebrew prophets.*

There were, then, among the Jews certain men who were prophets of God, through whom the prophetic Spirit published beforehand things that were to come to pass, ere ever they happened. And their prophecies, as they were spoken and when they were uttered, the kings who happened to be reigning among the Jews at the several

[83] For a sufficient account of the infamous history here alluded to, and the extravagant grief of Hadrian, and the servility of the people, see Smith's *Dictionary of Biography*: "Antinous." {The reference here is to a Greek youth who was a favorite lover of Emperor Hadrian, who deified him when the young man died. Hadrian also founded a cult in honor of Antinous which spread throughout the Roman Empire, as well as many temples and the city Antinopolis. Antinous is associated with homosexuality.}

times carefully preserved in their possession, when they had been arranged in books by the prophets themselves in their own Hebrew language.

And when Ptolemy king of Egypt formed a library, and endeavored to collect the writings of all men, he heard also of these prophets, and sent to Herod, who was at that time king of the Jews,[84] requesting that the books of the prophets be sent to him. And Herod the king did indeed send them, written, as they were, in the foresaid Hebrew language. And when their contents were found to be unintelligible to the Egyptians, he again sent and requested that men be commissioned to translate them into the Greek language. And when this was done, the books remained with the Egyptians, where they are until now. They are also in the possession of all Jews throughout the world; but they, though they read, do not understand what is said, but count us foes and enemies; and, like yourselves, they kill and punish us whenever they have the power, as you can well believe. For in the Jewish war which lately raged, Barchochebas, the leader of the revolt of the Jews, gave orders that Christians alone should be led to cruel punishments, unless they would deny Jesus Christ and utter blasphemy.

In these books, then, of the prophets we found Jesus our Christ foretold as coming, born of a virgin, growing up to man's estate, and healing every disease and every sickness, and raising the dead, and being hated, and unrecognized, and crucified, and dying, and rising again, and ascending into Heaven, and being, and being called, the Son of God. We find it also predicted that certain persons should be sent by Him into every nation to publish these things, and that rather among the Gentiles [than among the Jews] men should believe on Him. And He was predicted before He appeared, first 5000 years before, and again 3000, then 2000, then 1000, and yet again 800; for in the succession of generations prophets after prophets arose.

Chapter XXXII: *Christ predicted by Moses.*

Moses then, who was the first of the prophets, spoke in these very words: "***The scepter shall not depart from Judah, nor a lawgiver***

[84] Some attribute this blunder in chronology to Justin, others to his transcribers: it was Eleazar the high priest to whom Ptolemy applied.

from between his feet, until He come for whom it is reserved; and He shall be the desire of the nations, binding His foal to the vine, washing His robe in the blood of the grape."[85] It is yours to make accurate inquiry, and ascertain up to whose time the Jews had a lawgiver and king of their own. Up to the time of Jesus Christ, who taught us, and interpreted the prophecies which were not yet understood, [they had a lawgiver] as was foretold by the holy and divine Spirit of prophecy through Moses, "***that a ruler would not fail the Jews until He should come for whom the kingdom was reserved***"[86] (for Judah was the forefather of the Jews, from whom also they have their name of Jews); and after He (i.e., Christ) appeared, you began to rule the Jews, and gained possession of all their territory.

And the prophecy, "*He shall be the expectation of the nations*,"[87] signified that there would be some of all nations who should look for Him to come again. And this indeed you can see for yourselves, and be convinced of by fact. For of all races of men there are some who look for Him who was crucified in Judaea, and after whose crucifixion the land was straightway surrendered to you as spoil of war.

And the prophecy, "***binding His foal to the vine, and washing His robe in the blood of the grape***,"[88] was a significant symbol of the things that were to happen to Christ, and of what He was to do. For the foal of an ass stood bound to a vine at the entrance of a village, and He ordered His acquaintances to bring it to Him then; and when it was brought, He mounted and sat upon it, and entered Jerusalem, where was the vast temple of the Jews which was afterwards destroyed by you. And after this He was crucified, that the rest of the prophecy might be fulfilled. For this "***washing His robe in the blood of the grape***"[89] was predictive of the passion He was to endure, cleansing by His blood those who believe on Him. For what is called by the Divine Spirit through the prophet "***His robe***," are those men who believe in Him in whom abideth the seed[90] of

---

[85] Genesis 49:10. {See also Genesis 49:11.}

[86] {Genesis 49:10.}

[87] {The original editors did not identify this passage. Use of multi-bible concordances could not identify this passage either. Thus, it is not in bold.}

[88] {Genesis 49:11.}

[89] {Genesis 49:11.}

[90] Grabe would here read, not *σπέρμα*, but *πνεῦμα*, the spirit; but the Benedictine, Otto, and Trollope all think that no change should be made.

God, the Word. And what is spoken of as "***the blood of the grape***," signifies that He who should appear would have blood, though not of the seed of man, but of the power of God. And the first power after God the Father and Lord of all is the Word, who is also the Son; and of Him we will, in what follows, relate how He took flesh and became man. For as man did not make the blood of the vine, but God, so it was hereby intimated that the blood should not be of human seed, but of divine power, as we have said above.

And Isaiah, another prophet, foretelling the same things in other words, spoke thus: "***A star shall rise out of Jacob, and a flower shall spring from the root of Jesse;*** *and His arm shall the nations trust.*"[91] And a star of light has arisen, and a flower has sprung from the root of Jesse—this Christ. For by the power of God He was conceived by a virgin of the seed of Jacob, who was the father of Judah, who, as we have shown, was the father of the Jews; and Jesse was His forefather according to the oracle, and He was the son of Jacob and Judah according to lineal descent.

Chapter XXXIII: *Manner of Christ's birth predicted by Isaiah.*

And hear again how Isaiah in express words foretold that He should be born of a virgin; for he spoke thus: "***Behold, a virgin shall conceive, and bring forth a son, and they shall say for His name, God with us {Immanuel}.***"[92] For things which were incredible and seemed impossible with men, these God predicted by the Spirit of prophecy as about to come to pass, in order that, when they came to pass, there might be no unbelief, but faith, because of their prediction.

But lest some, not understanding the prophecy now cited, should charge us with the very things we have been laying to the charge of the poets who say that Jupiter went in to women through lust, let us try to explain the words. This, then, "***Behold, a virgin shall conceive,***"[93] signifies that a virgin should conceive without intercourse. For if she had had intercourse with any one whatever, she was no longer a virgin; but the

---

[91] Isaiah 11:1. {See also Isaiah 4:2; Zechariah 3:8, 6:12; Revelation 5:5. The Scriptural source of the latter half of this quote is uncertain; thus, it is not in bold.}

[92] Isaiah 7:14.

[93] {Isaiah 7:14.}

power of God having come upon the Virgin, overshadowed her, and caused her while yet a virgin to conceive. And the angel of God who was sent to the same Virgin at that time brought her good news, saying, "***Behold, thou shalt conceive of the Holy Ghost, and shalt bear a Son, and He shall be called the Son of the Highest, and thou shalt call His name Jesus; for He shall save His people from their sins,***"[94]—as they who have recorded all that concerns our Savior Jesus Christ have taught, whom we believed, since by Isaiah also, whom we have now adduced, the Spirit of prophecy declared that He should be born as we intimated before.

It is wrong, therefore, to understand the Spirit and the power of God as anything else than the Word, who is also the first-born of God, as the foresaid prophet Moses declared; and it was this which, when it came upon the Virgin and overshadowed her, caused her to conceive, not by intercourse, but by power. And the name Jesus in the Hebrew language means *Σωτὴρ* (Savior) in the Greek tongue. Wherefore, too, the angel said to the Virgin, "***Thou shalt call His name Jesus, for He shall save His people from their sins.***"[95] And that the prophets are inspired[96] by no other than the Divine Word, even you, as I fancy, will grant.

Chapter XXXIV: *Place of Christ's birth foretold by Micah.*

And hear what part of earth He was to be born in, as another prophet, Micah, foretold. He spoke thus: "***And thou, Bethlehem, the land of Judah, art not the least among the princes of Judah; for out of thee shall come forth a Governor, who shall feed My people.***"[97] Now there is a village in the land of the Jews, thirty-five stadia from Jerusalem, in which Jesus Christ was born, as you can ascertain also from the registers of the taxing made under Cyrenius, your first procurator in Judaea.

---

[94] Luke 1:32; Matthew 1:21. {See also Luke 1:31, 33; Matthew 1:20.}

[95] {Matthew 1:21.}

[96] *θεοΦοροῦνται*, lit. Are borne by a god—a word used of those who were supposed to be wholly under the influence of a deity.

[97] Micah 5:2. {See also Genesis 49:10.}

Chapter XXXV: *Other fulfilled prophecies of Isaiah, David and Zechariah.*

And how Christ after He was born was to escape the notice of other men until He grew to man's estate, which also came to pass, hear what was foretold regarding this. There are the following predictions:[98] — "***Unto us a child is born, and unto us a young man is given, and the government shall be upon His shoulders***;"[99] which is significant of the power of the Cross, for to it, when He was crucified, He applied His shoulders, as shall be more clearly made out in the ensuing discourse. And again the same prophet Isaiah, being inspired by the prophetic Spirit, said, "***I have spread out my hands to a disobedient and gainsaying people, to those who walk in a way that is not good. They now ask of me judgment, and dare to draw near to God.***"[100]

And again in other words, through another prophet, He says, "***They pierced My hands and My feet, and for My vesture they cast lots.***"[101] And indeed David, the king and prophet, who uttered these things, suffered none of them; but Jesus Christ stretched forth His hands, being crucified by the Jews speaking against Him, and denying that He was the Christ. And as the prophet spoke, they tormented Him, and set Him on the judgment-seat, and said, Judge us. And the expression, "***They pierced my hands and my feet***,"[102] was used in reference to the nails of the Cross which were fixed in His hands and feet. And after He was crucified they cast lots upon His vesture, and they that crucified Him parted it among them.

And that these things did happen, you can ascertain from the *Acts of Pontius Pilate*.[103] And we will cite the prophetic utterances of another

---

[98] These predictions have so little reference to the point Justin intends to make out, that some editors have supposed that a passage has here been lost. Others think the irrelevancy an insufficient ground for such a supposition.

[99] Isaiah 9:6. {See also Matthew 28:18. Cf. Judges 13:8.}

[100] Isaiah 65:2, 58:2.

[101] Psalm 22:16. {Psalm 22:18; see also Matthew 27:35; Luke 23:33-34.}

[102] Psalm 22:16. {See also Matthew 27:35; Luke 23:33.}

[103] *ἄχτωγ*. These *Acts of Pontius Pilate*, or regular accounts of his procedure sent by Pilate to the Emperor Tiberius, are supposed to have been destroyed at an early period, possibly in consequence of the unanswerable appeals which the Christians constantly made to them. There exists a forgery in imitation of those *Acts*. See Trollope.

prophet, Zephaniah {*sic* Zechariah},[104] to the effect that He was foretold expressly as to sit upon the foal of an ass and to enter Jerusalem. The words are these: "***Rejoice greatly, O daughter of Zion; shout, O daughter of Jerusalem: behold, thy King cometh unto thee; lowly, and riding upon an ass, and upon a colt the foal of an ass.***"[105]

Chapter XXXVI: *Different modes of prophecy.*

But when you hear the utterances of the prophets spoken as it were personally, you must not suppose that they are spoken by the inspired themselves, but by the Divine Word who moves them. For sometimes He declares things that are to come to pass, in the manner of one who foretells the future; sometimes He speaks as from the person of God the Lord and Father of all; sometimes as from the person of Christ; sometimes as from the person of the people answering the Lord or His Father, just as you can see even in your own writers, one man being the writer of the whole, but introducing the persons who converse. And this the Jews who possessed the books of the prophets did not understand, and therefore did not recognize Christ even when He came, but even hate us who say that He has come, and who prove that, as was predicted, He was crucified by them.

Chapter XXXVII: *Utterances of the Father through Isaiah.*

And that this too may be clear to you, there were spoken from the person of the Father through Isaiah the prophet, the following words: "***The ox knoweth his owner, and the ass his master's crib; but Israel doth not know, and My people hath not understood. Woe, sinful nation, a people full of sins, a wicked seed, children that are transgressors, ye have forsaken the Lord.***"[106]

And again elsewhere, when the same prophet speaks in like manner from the person of the Father, "***What is the house that ye will***

---

[104] The reader will note that these are not the words of Zephaniah, but of Zechariah (9:9), to whom also Justin himself refers them in the *Dialogue with Trypho*, Chapter 53.

[105] Zechariah 9:9. {See also Matthew 14:1-11; Luke 19:30-41.}

[106] Isaiah 1:3. This quotation varies only in one word from that of the LXX. {See also Isaiah 1:4; 5:12; Job 34:27.}

build for Me? saith the Lord. The heaven is My throne, and the earth is My footstool."[107] And again, in another place,

> **Your new moons and your sabbaths My soul hateth; and the great day of the fast and of ceasing from labor I cannot away with; nor, if ye come to be seen of Me, will I hear you: your hands are full of blood; and if ye bring fine flour, incense, it is abomination unto Me: the fat of lambs and the blood of bulls I do not desire. For who hath required this at your hands? But loose every bond of wickedness, tear asunder the tight knots of violent contracts, cover the houseless and naked, deal thy bread to the hungry.** [108]

What kind of things are taught through the prophets from [the person of] God, you can now perceive.

Chapter XXXVIII: *Utterances of the Son through Isaiah, the Psalms, and Matthew.*

And when the Spirit of prophecy speaks from the person of Christ, the utterances are of this sort: "***I have spread out My hands to a disobedient and gainsaying people, to those who walk in a way that is not good."***[109] And again:

> ***I gave My back to the scourges, and My cheeks to the buffetings; I turned not away My face from the shame of spittings; and the Lord was My helper: therefore was I not confounded: but I set My face as a firm rock; and I knew that I should not be ashamed, for He is near that justifieth Me.***[110]

And again, when He says, "***They cast lots upon My vesture, and pierced My hands and My feet. And I lay down and slept, and rose again, because the Lord sustained Me."***[111] And again, when He says, "***They***

---

[107] Isaiah 66:1.

[108] Isaiah 1:14, 18:6. {See also Isaiah 1:15; 58:6-7; Proverbs 1:28. The citation to Isaiah 18:6 seems to be a typographical error.}

[109] Isaiah 65:2.

[110] Isaiah 50:6 {-8}.

[111] Psalm 22:18, 3:5. {Psalm 22:16; see also Matthew 27:35; Luke 23:33-34.}

spake with their lips, they wagged the head, saying, Let Him deliver Himself."[112]

And that all these things happened to Christ at the hands of the Jews, you can ascertain. For when He was crucified, they did shoot out the lip, and wagged their heads, saying, "***Let Him who raised the dead save Himself.***"[113]

Chapter XXXIX: *Direct predictions by the Spirit through Isaiah.*

And when the Spirit of prophecy speaks as predicting things that are to come to pass, He speaks in this way:

> ***For out of Zion shall go forth the law, and the word of the Lord from Jerusalem. And He shall judge among the nations, and shall rebuke many people; and they shall beat their swords into ploughshares, and their spears into pruning-hooks: nation shall not lift up sword against nation, neither shall they learn war anymore.***[114]

And that it did so come to pass, we can convince you. For from Jerusalem there went out into the world, men, twelve in number, and these illiterate, of no ability in speaking: but by the power of God they proclaimed to every race of men that they were sent by Christ to teach to all the Word of God; and we who formerly used to murder one another do not only now refrain from making war upon our enemies, but also, that we may not lie nor deceive our examiners, willingly die confessing Christ.

For that saying, "The tongue has sworn but the mind is unsworn,"[115] might be imitated by us in this matter. But if the soldiers enrolled by you, and who have taken the military oath, prefer their allegiance to their own life, and parents, and country, and all kindred, though you can offer them nothing incorruptible, it were verily ridiculous if we, who earnestly long for incorruption, should not endure all things, in order to obtain what we desire from Him who is able to grant it.

---

[112] Psalm 22:7. {See also Psalm 22:8; Matthew 27:39; cf. Job 16:4.}

[113] Comp. Matthew 27:39. {See Matthew 27:41-43; Mark 15:29-31; Luke 23:36-37.}

[114] Isaiah 2:3. {Should be Isaiah 2:3-4.}

[115] Eurip. *Hipp.* 608.

Chapter XL: *Christ's advent foretold by David.*

And hear how it was foretold concerning those who published His doctrine and proclaimed His appearance, the above-mentioned prophet and king speaking thus by the Spirit of prophecy:

> **Day unto day uttereth speech, and night unto night showeth knowledge. There is no speech nor language where their voice is not heard. Their voice has gone out into all the earth, and their words to the ends of the world. In the sun hath He set His tabernacle, and he as a bridegroom going out of his chamber shall rejoice as a giant to run his course.**[116]

And we have thought it right and relevant to mention some other prophetic utterances of David besides these; from which you may learn how the Spirit of prophecy exhorts men to live, and how He foretold the conspiracy which was formed against Christ by Herod the king of the Jews, and the Jews themselves, and Pilate, who was your governor among them, with his soldiers; and how He should be believed on by men of every race; and how God calls Him His Son, and has declared that He will subdue all His enemies under Him; and how the devils, as much as they can, strive to escape the power of God the Father and Lord of all, and the power of Christ Himself; and how God calls all to repentance before the day of judgment comes. These things were uttered thus:

> ***Blessed is the man who hath not walked in the counsel of the ungodly, nor stood in the way of sinners, nor sat in the seat of the scornful: but his delight is in the law of the Lord; and in His law will he meditate day and night. And he shall be like a tree planted by the rivers of waters, which shall give his fruit in his season; and his leaf shall not wither, and whatsoever he doeth shall prosper. The ungodly are not so, but are like the chaff which the wind driveth away from the face of the earth. Therefore the ungodly shall not stand in the judgment, nor sinners in the council of the righteous. For the Lord knoweth the way of the righteous; but the way of the ungodly shall perish.***

---

[116] Psalm 19:2, etc. {through verse 5.}

> ***Why do the heathen rage, and the people imagine new things? The kings of the earth set themselves, and the rulers take counsel together, against the Lord, and against His Anointed, saying, Let us break their bands asunder, and cast their yoke from us. He that dwelleth in the heavens shall laugh at them, and the Lord shall have them in derision. Then shall He speak to them in His wrath, and vex them in His sore displeasure. Yet have I been set by Him a King on Zion His holy hill, declaring the decree of the Lord. The Lord said to Me, Thou art My Son; this day have I begotten Thee. Ask of Me, and I shall give Thee the heathen for Thine inheritance, and the uttermost parts of the earth as Thy possession. Thou shall herd them with a rod of iron; as the vessels of a potter shalt Thou dash them in pieces. Be wise now, therefore, O ye kings; be instructed, all ye judges of the earth. Serve the Lord with fear, and rejoice with trembling. Embrace instruction, lest at any time the Lord be angry, and ye perish from the right way, when His wrath has been suddenly kindled. Blessed are all they that put their trust in Him.***[117]

Chapter XLI: *The crucifixion predicted by David.*

And again, in another prophecy, the Spirit of prophecy, through the same David, intimated that Christ, after He had been crucified, should reign, and spoke as follows:

> ***Sing to the Lord, all the earth, and day by day declare His salvation. For great is the Lord, and greatly to be praised, to be feared above all the gods. For all the gods of the nations are idols of devils; but God made the heavens. Glory and praise are before His face, strength and glorying are in the habitation of His holiness. Give Glory to the Lord, the Father everlasting. Receive grace, and enter His presence, and worship in His holy courts. Let all the earth fear before His face; let it be established, and not shaken. Let them rejoice among the nations.*** *The Lord hath reigned from the tree.*[118]

[117] Psalm 1 and 2.

[118] Psalm 96:1, etc. This last clause, which is not extant in our copies either of the LXX or of the Hebrew, Justin charged the Jews with erasing. See *Dialogue with Trypho*, Chapter 78. {Thus, it is not in bold.}

Chapter XLII: *Prophecy using the past tense.*

But when the Spirit of prophecy speaks of things that are about to come to pass as if they had already taken place,—as may be observed even in the passages already cited by me,—that this circumstance may afford no excuse to readers [for misinterpreting them], we will make even this also quite plain.

The things which He absolutely knows will take place, He predicts as if already they had taken place. And that the utterances must be thus received, you will perceive, if you give your attention to them. The words cited above, David uttered 1,500[119] years before Christ became a man and was crucified; and no one of those who lived before Him, nor yet of His contemporaries, afforded joy to the Gentiles by being crucified. But our Jesus Christ, being crucified and dead, rose again, and having ascended to heaven, reigned; and by those things which were published in His name among all nations by the apostles, there is joy afforded to those who expect the immortality promised by Him.

Chapter XLIII: *Individual responsibility asserted and fate denied.*

But lest some suppose, from what has been said by us, that we say that whatever happens, happens by a fatal necessity, because it is foretold as known beforehand, this too we explain. We have learned from the prophets, and we hold it to be true, that punishments, and chastisements, and good rewards, are rendered according to the merit of each man's actions. Since if it be not so, but all things happen by fate, neither is anything at all in our own power. For if it be fated that this man, e.g., be good, and this other evil, neither is the former meritorious nor the latter to be blamed. And again, unless the human race have the power of avoiding evil and choosing good by free choice, they are not accountable for their actions, of whatever kind they be.

But that it is by free choice they both walk uprightly and stumble, we thus demonstrate. We see the same man making a transition to opposite things. Now, if it had been fated that he were to be either good or bad, he could never have been capable of both the opposites, nor of so many transitions. But not even would some be good and others bad,

---

[119] A chronological error, whether of the copyist or of Justin himself cannot be known.

since we thus make fate the cause of evil, and exhibit her as acting in opposition to herself; or that which has been already stated would seem to be true, that neither virtue nor vice is anything, but that things are only reckoned good or evil by opinion; which, as the true Word shows, is the greatest impiety and wickedness. But this we assert is inevitable fate, that they who choose the good have worthy rewards, and they who choose the opposite have their merited awards. For not like other things, as trees and quadrupeds, which cannot act by choice, did God make man: for neither would he be worthy of reward or praise did he not of himself choose the good, but were created for this end;[120] nor, if he were evil, would he be worthy of punishment, not being evil of himself, but being able to be nothing else than what he was made.

Chapter XLIV: *Not nullified by prophecy.*

And the holy Spirit of prophecy taught us this, telling us by Moses that God spoke thus to the man first created: "***Behold, before thy face are good and evil: choose the good.***"[121] And again, by the other prophet Isaiah, that the following utterance was made as if from God the Father and Lord of all:

> ***Wash you, make you clean; put away evils from your souls; learn to do well; judge the orphan, and plead for the widow: and come and let us reason together, saith the Lord: And if your sins be as scarlet, I will make them white as wool; and if they be red like as crimson, I will make them white as snow. And if ye be willing and obey Me, ye shall eat the good of the land; but if ye do not obey Me, the sword shall devour you: for the mouth of the Lord hath spoken it.***[122]

And that expression, "***The sword shall devour you,***"[123] does not mean that the disobedient shall be slain by the sword, but the sword of God is

[120] Or, "but were made so." The words *are ἀλλὰ τοῦτο γενόμενος*, and the meaning of Justin is sufficiently clear.

[121] Deuteronomy 30:15, 19.

[122] Isaiah 1:16, etc. {through verse 20.}

[123] {Saint Justin often repeats phrases and sentences from lengthier passages. When the quote is short and near the initial excerpt, there will be no additional citation provided.

fire, of which they who choose to do wickedly become the fuel. Wherefore He says, "***The sword shall devour you: for the mouth of the Lord hath spoken it.***"[124] And if He had spoken concerning a sword that cuts and at once dispatches, He would not have said, shall *devour*. And so, too, Plato, when he says, "The blame is his who chooses, and God is blameless,"[125] took this from the prophet Moses and uttered it. For Moses is more ancient than all the Greek writers.

And whatever both philosophers and poets have said concerning the immortality of the soul, or punishments after death, or contemplation of things heavenly, or doctrines of the like kind, they have received such suggestions from the prophets as have enabled them to understand and interpret these things. And hence there seem to be seeds of truth among all men; but they are charged with not accurately understanding [the truth] when they assert contradictories. So that what we say about future events being foretold, we do not say it as if they came about by a fatal necessity; but God foreknowing all that shall be done by all men, and it being His decree that the future actions of men shall all be recompensed according to their several value, He foretells by the Spirit of prophecy that He will bestow meet rewards according to the merit of the actions done, always urging the human race to effort and recollection, showing that He cares and provides for men.

But by the agency of the devils death has been decreed against those who read the books of Hystaspes, or of the Sibyl, or of the prophets, that through fear they may prevent men who read them from receiving the knowledge of the good, and may retain them in slavery to themselves; which, however, they could not always effect. For not only do we fearlessly read them, but, as you see, bring them for your inspection, knowing that their contents will be pleasing to all. And if we persuade even a few, our gain will be very great; for, as good husbandmen, we shall receive the reward from the Master.

However, when a longer portion is repeated, or the phrase appears more distant from the excerpt, the Scripture citation will be provided for the convenience of the reader.}

[124] {Isaiah 1:20.}

[125] Plato, *Rep.* x.

Chapter XLV: *Christ's session in Heaven foretold by David.*

And that God the Father of all would bring Christ to heaven after He had raised Him from the dead, and would keep Him there[126] until He has subdued His enemies the devils, and until the number of those who are foreknown by Him as good and virtuous is complete, on whose account He has still delayed the consummation—hear what was said by the prophet David. These are his words:

> ***The Lord said unto My Lord, Sit Thou at My right hand, until I make Thine enemies Thy footstool. The Lord shall send to Thee the rod of power out of Jerusalem; and rule Thou in the midst of Thine enemies.***
>
> ***With Thee is the government in the day of Thy power, in the beauties of Thy saints: from the womb of morning[127] have I begotten Thee.[128]***

That which he {David} says, "***He shall send to Thee the rod of power out of Jerusalem***,"[129] is predictive of the mighty Word, which His apostles, going forth from Jerusalem, preached everywhere; and though death is decreed against those who teach or at all confess the name of Christ, we everywhere both embrace and teach it. And if you also read these words in a hostile spirit, ye can do no more, as I said before, than kill us; which indeed does no harm to us, but to you and all who unjustly hate us, and do not repent, brings eternal punishment by fire.

Chapter XLVI: *The Word in the world before Christ.*

But lest some should, without reason, and for the perversion of what we teach, maintain that we say that Christ was born one hundred and fifty years ago under Cyrenius, and subsequently, in the time of Pontius Pilate, taught what we say He taught; and should cry out against

---

[126] So Thirlby, Otto, and Trollope seem all to understand the word χατέχειν; yet it seems worth considering whether Justin has not borrowed both the sense and the word from 2 Thess. 2:6-7. {The passage here referred to is Saint Paul's instruction to the Thessalonians about the Second Coming of Christ.}

[127] Or, "before the morning star."

[128] Psalm 110:1, etc.

[129] {Psalm 110:2.}

us as though all men who were born before Him were irresponsible—let us anticipate and solve the difficulty.

We have been taught that Christ is the first-born of God, and we have declared above that He is the Word of whom every race of men were partakers; and those who lived reasonably[130] are Christians, even though they have been thought atheists; as, among the Greeks, Socrates and Heraclitus, and men like them; and among the barbarians, Abraham, and Ananias, and Azarias, and Misael, and Elias, and many others whose actions and names we now decline to recount, because we know it would be tedious. So that even they who lived before Christ, and lived without reason, were wicked and hostile to Christ, and slew those who lived reasonably.

But why, through the power of the Word, according to the will of God the Father and Lord of all, He was born of a virgin as a man, and was named Jesus, and was crucified, and died, and rose again, and ascended into heaven, an intelligent man will be able to comprehend from what has been already so largely said. And we, since the proof of this subject is less needful now, will pass for the present to the proof of those things which are urgent.

Chapter XLVII: *Desolation of Judaea foretold by Isaiah.*

That the land of the Jews, then, was to be laid waste, hear what was said by the Spirit of prophecy. And the words were spoken as if from the person of the people wondering at what had happened. They are these:

> ***{Z}ion is a wilderness, Jerusalem a desolation. The house of our sanctuary has become a curse, and the glory which our fathers blessed is burned up with fire, and all its glorious things are laid waste: and Thou refrainest Thyself at these things, and hast held Thy peace, and hast humbled us very sore.***[131]

And ye are convinced that Jerusalem has been laid waste, as was predicted. And concerning its desolation, and that no one should be

---

[130] *υετὰ λόγου*, "with reason," or "the Word."

[131] Isaiah 64:10-12.

permitted to inhabit it, there was the following prophecy by Isaiah: "***Their land is desolate, their enemies consume it before them, and none of them shall dwell therein.***"[132] And that it is guarded by you lest anyone dwell in it, and that death is decreed against a Jew apprehended entering it, you know very well.

Chapter XLVIII: *Christ's work of miracles and death foretold by Isaiah.*

And that it was predicted that our Christ should heal all diseases and raise the dead, hear what was said. There are these words: "***At His coming the lame shall leap as an hart, and the tongue of the stammerer shall be clear speaking: the blind shall see, and the lepers shall be cleansed; and the dead shall rise, and walk about.***"[133] And that He did those things, you can learn from the *Acts of Pontius Pilate*.[134] And how it was predicted by the Spirit of prophecy that He and those who hoped in Him should be slain, hear what was said by Isaiah. These are the words: "***Behold now the righteous perisheth, and no man layeth it to heart; and just men are taken away, and no man considereth. From the presence of wickedness is the righteous man taken, and his burial shall be in peace: he is taken from our midst.***"[135]

Chapter XLIX: *His rejection by the Jews foretold by Isaiah.*

And again, how it was said by the same Isaiah, that the Gentile nations who were not looking for Him should worship Him, but the Jews who always expected Him should not recognize Him when He came. And the words are spoken as from the person of Christ; and they are these:

> ***I was manifest to them that asked not for Me; I was found of them that sought Me not: I said, Behold Me, to a nation that called not on My name. I spread out My hands to a disobedient and gainsaying people, to those who walked in a way that is not good,***

[132] Isaiah 1:7.

[133] Isaiah 35:6 {See also Isaiah 35:5, 9., 29:18, 32:4; see generally the miracles recorded in the Gospels.}

[134] {See discussion above, n. 103.}

[135] Isaiah 57:1. {The last clause is not in some translations of 57:1. Compare KJV to OSB.}

> ***but follow after their own sins; a people that provoketh Me to anger to My face.***[136]

For the Jews having the prophecies, and being always in expectation of the Christ to come, did not recognize Him; and not only so, but even treated Him shamefully. But the Gentiles, who had never heard anything about Christ, until the apostles set out from Jerusalem and preached concerning Him, and gave them the prophecies, were filled with joy and faith, and cast away their idols, and dedicated themselves to the Unbegotten God through Christ. And that it was foreknown that these infamous things should be uttered against those who confessed Christ, and that those who slandered Him, and said that it was well to preserve the ancient customs, should be miserable, hear what was briefly said by Isaiah; it is this: "***Woe unto them that call sweet bitter, and bitter sweet.***"[137]

Chapter L: *His humiliation predicted by Isaiah.*

But that, having become man for our sakes, He endured to suffer and to be dishonored, and that He shall come again with glory, hear the prophecies which relate to this; they are these:

> ***Because they delivered His soul unto death, and He was numbered with the transgressors, He has borne the sin of many, and shall make intercession for the transgressors. For, behold, My Servant shall deal prudently, and shall be exalted, and shall be greatly extolled. As many were astonished at Thee, so marred shall Thy form be before men, and so hidden from them Thy glory; so shall many nations wonder, and the kings shall shut their mouths at Him. For they to whom it was not told concerning Him, and they who have not heard, shall understand.***
>
> ***O Lord, who hath believed our report? and to whom is the arm of the Lord revealed? We have declared before Him as a child, as a root in a dry ground. He had no form, nor glory; and we saw Him, and there was no form nor comeliness: but His form was dishonored and marred more than the sons of men. A man under the stroke, and knowing how to bear infirmity, because His face***

[136] Isaiah 65:1-3. {See also Isaiah 63:19.}
[137] Isaiah 5:20.

> ***was turned away: He was despised, and of no reputation. It is He who bears our sins, and is afflicted for us; yet we did esteem Him smitten, stricken, and afflicted. But He was wounded for our transgressions, He was bruised for our iniquities, the chastisement of peace was upon Him, by His stripes we are healed. All we, like sheep, have gone astray; every man has wandered in his own way. And He delivered Him for our sins; and He opened not His mouth for all His affliction. He was brought as a sheep to the slaughter, and as a lamb before his shearer is dumb, so He openeth not His mouth. In His humiliation, His judgment was taken away.***[138]

Accordingly, after He was crucified, even all His acquaintances forsook Him, having denied Him; and afterwards, when He had risen from the dead and appeared to them, and had taught them to read the prophecies in which all these things were foretold as coming to pass, and when they had seen Him ascending into heaven, and had believed, and had received power sent thence by Him upon them, and went to every race of men, they taught these things, and were called apostles.

Chapter LI: *The majesty of Christ foretold by Isaiah, the Psalms, and Daniel.*

And that the Spirit of prophecy might signify to us that He who suffers these things has an ineffable origin, and rules His enemies, He spake thus:

> ***His generation who shall declare? because His life is cut off from the earth: for their transgressions He comes to death. And I will give the wicked for His burial, and the rich for His death; because He did no violence, neither was any deceit in His mouth. And the Lord is pleased to cleanse Him from the stripe. If He be given for sin, your soul shall see His seed prolonged in days. And the Lord is pleased to deliver His soul from grief, to show Him light, and to form Him with knowledge, to justify the righteous who richly serveth many. And He shall bear our iniquities. Therefore He shall inherit many, and He shall divide the spoil of the strong; because His soul was delivered to death: and He was numbered with the***

---

[138] Isaiah 52:13-15; 53:1-8. {Isaiah 53:12; see also Mark 15:28. Cf. Isaiah 49:7; Ezekiel 36:25; Psalm 22:6; Matthew 8:17; Acts 8:32; 1 Peter 2:24.}

transgressors; and He bare the sins of many, and He was delivered up for their transgressions."[139]

Hear, too, how He was to ascend into heaven according to prophecy. It was thus spoken: ***"Lift up the gates of heaven; be ye opened, that the King of glory may come in. Who is this King of glory? The Lord, strong and mighty."***[140] And how also He should come again out of heaven with glory, hear what was spoken in reference to this by the prophet Jeremiah.[141] His words are: ***"Behold, as the Son of man He cometh in the clouds of heaven, and His angels with Him."***[142]

Chapter LII: *Certain fulfillment of prophecy foretold by Ezekiel, Isaiah and Zechariah.*

Since, then, we prove that all things which have already happened had been predicted by the prophets before they came to pass, we must necessarily believe also that those things which are in like manner predicted, but are yet to come to pass, shall certainly happen. For as the things which have already taken place came to pass when foretold, and even though unknown, so shall the things that remain, even though they be unknown and disbelieved, yet come to pass. For the prophets have proclaimed two advents of His: the one, that which is already past, when He came as a dishonored and suffering Man; but the second, when, according to prophecy, He shall come from heaven with glory, accompanied by His angelic host, when also He shall raise the bodies of all men who have lived, and shall clothe those of the worthy with immortality, and shall send those of the wicked, endued with eternal sensibility, into everlasting fire with the wicked devils. And that these things also have been foretold as yet to be, we will prove. By Ezekiel the prophet it was said: ***"Joint shall be joined to joint, and bone to bone, and flesh shall grow again; and every knee shall bow to the Lord, and every tongue shall confess Him."***[143] And in what kind of sensation and punishment the wicked are to be, hear from what was said in like manner

[139] Isaiah 53:8-12.
[140] Psalm 24:7 {and verse 8}.
[141] This prophecy occurs not in Jeremiah, but in Daniel 7:13.
[142] Daniel 7:13.
[143] Ezekiel 37:7, 8; Isaiah 45:23.

with reference to this; it is as follows: *"**Their worm shall not rest, and their fire shall not be quenched**;"*[144] and then shall they repent, when it profits them not. And what the people of the Jews shall say and do, when they see Him coming in glory, has been thus predicted by Zechariah the prophet:

> ***I will command the four winds to gather the scattered children; I will command the north wind to bring them, and the south wind, that it keep not back. And then in Jerusalem there shall be great lamentation, not the lamentation of mouths or of lips, but the lamentation of the heart; and they shall rend not their garments, but their hearts. Tribe by tribe they shall mourn, and then they shall look on Him whom they have pierced; and they shall say, Why, O Lord, hast Thou made us to err from Thy way? The glory which our fathers blessed, has for us been turned into shame.***[145]

Chapter LIII: *Summary of the prophecies.*

Though we could bring forward many other prophecies, we forbear, judging these sufficient for the persuasion of those who have ears to hear and understand; and considering also that those persons are able to see that we do not make mere assertions without being able to produce proof, like those fables that are told of the so-called sons of Jupiter. For with what reason should we believe of a crucified man that He is the first-born of the Unbegotten God, and Himself will pass judgment on the whole human race, unless we had found testimonies concerning Him published before He came and was born as man, and unless we saw that things had happened accordingly—the devastation of the land of the Jews, and men of every race persuaded by His teaching through the apostles, and rejecting their old habits, in which, being deceived, they had their conversation; yea, seeing ourselves too, and knowing that the Christians from among the Gentiles are both more numerous and more true than those from among the Jews and Samaritans?

For all the other human races are called Gentiles by the Spirit of prophecy; but the Jewish and Samaritan races are called the tribe of

[144] Isaiah 66:24.
[145] Zechariah 12:3-14; Isaiah 63:17, 64:11. {See also Matthew 24:30-31; Mark 13:27.}

Israel, and the house of Jacob. And the prophecy in which it was predicted that there should be more believers from the Gentiles than from the Jews and Samaritans, we will produce: it ran thus: ***"Rejoice, O barren, thou that dost not bear; break forth and shout, thou that dost not travail, because many more are the children of the desolate than of her that hath an husband."***[146] For all the Gentiles were "desolate" of the true God, serving the works of their hands; but the Jews and Samaritans, having the word of God delivered to them by the prophets, and always expecting the Christ, did not recognize Him when He came, except some few, of whom the Spirit of prophecy by Isaiah had predicted that they should be saved. He spoke as from their person: ***"Except the Lord had left us a seed, we should have been as Sodom and Gomorrah."***[147] For Sodom and Gomorrah are related by Moses to have been cities of ungodly men, which God burned with fire and brimstone, and overthrew, no one of their inhabitants being saved except a certain stranger, a Chaldaean by birth, whose name was Lot; with whom also his daughters were rescued. And those who care may yet see their whole country desolate and burned, and remaining barren.

And to show how those from among the Gentiles were foretold as more true and more believing, we will cite what was said by Isaiah[148] the prophet; for he spoke as follows: ***"Israel is uncircumcised in heart, but the Gentiles are uncircumcised in the flesh."***[149]

So many things therefore, as these, when they are seen with the eye, are enough to produce conviction and belief in those who embrace the truth, and are not bigoted in their opinions, nor are governed by their passions.

Chapter LIV: *Scripture is the origin of heathen mythology.*

But those who hand down the myths which the poets have made, adduce no proof to the youths who learn them; and we proceed to demonstrate that they have been uttered by the influence of the wicked demons, to deceive and lead astray the human race. For having heard it

---

[146] Isaiah 54:1. {See also 1 Samuel 2:5; Galatians 4:27.}
[147] Isaiah 1:9. {See also Romans 9:29.}
[148] The following words are found, not in Isaiah, but Jeremiah 9:26.
[149] Jeremiah 9:26.

proclaimed through the prophets that the Christ was to come, and that the ungodly among men were to be punished by fire, they put forward many to be called sons of Jupiter, under the impression that they would be able to produce in men the idea that the things which were said with regard to Christ were mere marvelous tales, like the things which were said by the poets. And these things were said both among the Greeks and among all nations where they [the demons] heard the prophets foretelling that Christ would specially be believed in; but that in hearing what was said by the prophets they did not accurately understand it, but imitated what was said of our Christ, like men who are in error, we will make plain.

The prophet Moses, then, was, as we have already said, older than all writers; and by him, as we have also said before, it was thus predicted: *"**There shall not fail a prince from Judah, nor a lawgiver from between his feet, until He come for whom it is reserved; and He shall be the desire of the Gentiles, binding His foal to the vine, washing His robe in the blood of the grape.**"*[150] The devils, accordingly, when they heard these prophetic words, said that Bacchus was the son of Jupiter, and gave out that he was the discoverer of the vine, and they number wine[151] [or, the ass] among his mysteries; and they taught that, having been torn in pieces, he ascended into heaven.

And because in the prophecy of Moses it had not been expressly intimated whether He who was to come was the Son of God, and whether He would, riding on the foal, remain on earth or ascend into heaven, and because the name of "foal" could mean either the foal of an ass or the foal of a horse, they, not knowing whether He who was foretold would bring the foal of an ass or of a horse as the sign of His coming, nor whether He was the Son of God, as we said above, or of man, gave out that Bellerophon, a man born of man, himself ascended to heaven on his horse Pegasus.

And when they heard it said by the other prophet Isaiah, that He should be born of a virgin, and by His own means ascend into heaven,

---

[150] Genesis 49:10 {and 11}.

[151] In the manuscripts the reading is *οίνον* (wine); but as Justin's argument seems to require *ὄνον* (an ass), Syllburg inserted this latter word in his edition; and this reading is approved by Grabe and Thirlby, and adopted by Otto and Trollope. It may be added that ἀναγράθουαι {not translated} is much more suitable to *ὄνον* {translated "an ass"} than to *οίνον* {translated "wine"}.

they pretended that Perseus was spoken of. And when they knew what was said, as has been cited above, in the prophecies written aforetime, "***Strong as a giant to run his course***,"[152] they said that Hercules was strong, and had journeyed over the whole earth. And when, again, they learned that it had been foretold that He should heal every sickness, and raise the dead, they produced Aesculapius.

Chapter LV: *Symbols of the Cross foretold.*

But in no instance, not even in any of those called sons of Jupiter, did they imitate the being crucified; for it was not understood by them, all the things said of it having been put symbolically. And this, as the prophet foretold, is the greatest symbol of His power and rule; as is also proved by the things which fall under our observation. For consider all the things in the world, whether without this form they could be administered or have any community.

For the sea is not traversed except that trophy which is called a sail abide safe in the ship; and the earth is not ploughed without it: diggers and mechanics do not their work, except with tools which have this shape. And the human form differs from that of the irrational animals in nothing else than in its being erect and having the hands extended, and having on the face extending from the forehead what is called the nose, through which there is respiration for the living creature; and this shows no other form than that of the Cross. And so it was said by the prophet, "***The breath before our face is the Lord Christ.***"[153]

And the power of this form is shown by your own symbols on what are called "vexilla" [banners] and trophies, with which all your state possessions are made, using these as the insignia of your power and government, even though you do so unwittingly. And with this form you consecrate the images of your emperors when they die, and you name them gods by inscriptions.

Since, therefore, we have urged you both by reason and by an evident form, and to the utmost of our ability, we know that now we are blameless even though you disbelieve; for our part is done and finished.

---

[152] Psalm 19:5.

[153] From Lam. 4:20 (Sept.). {See also Genesis 2:7.}

Chapter LVI: *The demons still mislead men after the time of Christ.*

But the evil spirits were not satisfied with saying, before Christ's appearance, that those who were said to be sons of Jupiter were born of him; but after He had appeared, and been born among men, and when they learned how He had been foretold by the prophets, and knew that He should be believed on and looked for by every nation, they again, as was said above, put forward other men, the Samaritans Simon and Menander, who did many mighty works by magic, and deceived many, and still keep them deceived. For even among yourselves, as we said before, Simon was in the royal city Rome in the reign of Claudius Caesar, and so greatly astonished the sacred senate and people of the Romans, that he was considered a god, and honored, like the others whom you honor as gods, with a statue. Wherefore we pray that the sacred senate and your people may, along with yourselves, be arbiters of this our memorial, in order that if anyone be entangled by that man's doctrines, he may learn the truth, and so be able to escape error; and as for the statue, if you please, destroy it.

Chapter LVII: *And devils cause persecution of Christians.*

Nor can the devils persuade men that there will be no conflagration for the punishment of the wicked; as they were unable to effect that Christ should be hidden after He came. But this only can they effect, that they who live irrationally, and were brought up licentiously in wicked customs, and are prejudiced in their own opinions, should kill and hate us; whom we not only do not hate, but, as is proved, pity and endeavor to lead to repentance. For we do not fear death, since it is acknowledged we must surely die; and there is nothing new, but all things continue the same in this administration of things; and if satiety overtakes those who enjoy even one year of these things, they ought to give heed to our doctrines, that they may live eternally free both from suffering and from want. But if they believe that there is nothing after death, but declare that those who die pass into insensibility, then they become our benefactors when they set us free from sufferings and necessities of this life, and prove themselves to be wicked, and inhuman, and bigoted. For they kill us with no intention of delivering us, but cut us off that we may be deprived of life and pleasure.

Chapter LVIII: *And devils raise up heretics.*

And, as we said before, the devils put forward Marcion of Pontus, who is even now teaching men to deny that God is the maker of all things in heaven and on earth, and that the Christ predicted by the prophets is His Son, and preaches another god besides the Creator of all, and likewise another son. And this man many have believed, as if he alone knew the truth, and laugh at us, though they have no proof of what they say, but are carried away irrationally as lambs by a wolf, and become the prey of atheistical doctrines, and of devils. For they who are called devils attempt nothing else than to seduce men from God who made them, and from Christ His first-begotten; and those who are unable to raise themselves above the earth they have riveted, and do now rivet, to things earthly, and to the works of their own hands; but those who devote themselves to the contemplation of things divine, they secretly beat back; and if they have not a wise sober-mindedness, and a pure and passionless life, they drive them into godlessness.

Chapter LIX: *Plato's obligation to Moses.*

And that you may learn that it was from our teachers—we mean the account given through the prophets—that Plato borrowed his statement that God, having altered matter which was shapeless, made the world, hear the very words spoken through Moses, who, as above shown, was the first prophet, and of greater antiquity than the Greek writers; and through whom the Spirit of prophecy, signifying how and from what materials God at first formed the world, spake thus: ***"In the beginning God created the heaven and the earth. And the earth was invisible and unfurnished, and darkness was upon the face of the deep; and the Spirit of God moved over the waters. And God said, Let there be light; and it was so."***[154]

So that both Plato and they who agree with him, and we ourselves, have learned, and you also can be convinced, that by the word of God the whole world was made out of the substance spoken of before

[154] {Genesis 1:1-3; see also Psalm 8:3, 33:6, 9; John 1:1-5.}

by Moses. And that which the poets call Erebus, we know was spoken of formerly by Moses.[155]

Chapter LX: *Plato's doctrine of the cross based on Moses.*

And the physiological discussion[156] concerning the Son of God in the *Timaeus* of Plato, where he says, "He placed him crosswise[157] in the universe," he borrowed in like manner from Moses; for in the writings of Moses it is related how at that time, when the Israelites went out of Egypt and were in the wilderness, they fell in with poisonous beasts, both vipers and asps, and every kind of serpent, which slew the people; and that Moses, by the inspiration and influence of God, took brass, and made it into the figure of a cross, and set it in the holy tabernacle, and said to the people, "***If ye look to this figure, and believe, ye shall be saved thereby.***"[158] And when this was done, it is recorded that the serpents died, and it is handed down that the people thus escaped death.

Which things Plato reading, and not accurately understanding, and not apprehending that it was the figure of the Cross, but taking it to be a placing crosswise, he said that the power next to the first God was placed crosswise in the universe.

And as to his speaking of a third, he did this because he read, as we said above, that which was spoken by Moses, "***that the Spirit of God moved over the waters.***"[159] For he gives the second place to the Logos which is with God, who he said was placed crosswise in the universe; and the third place to the Spirit who was said to be borne upon the water, saying, "And the third around the third."[160]

And hear how the Spirit of prophecy signified through Moses that there should be a conflagration. He spoke thus: "***Everlasting fire shall descend, and shall devour to the pit beneath.***"[161]

---

[155] Comp. Deuteronomy 32:22.
[156] Literally, "that which is treated physiologically."
[157] "He impressed him as a *χίασμα*, i.e., in the form of the letter χ, upon the universe." Plato is speaking of the soul of the universe.
[158] Numbers 21:8.
[159] {Genesis 1:2.}
[160] *Τὰ δὲ τρίτα περὶ τὸγ τρίτον.*
[161] Deuteronomy 32:22.

It is not, then, that we hold the same opinions as others, but that all speak in imitation of ours. Among us these things can be heard and learned from persons who do not even know the forms of the letters, who are uneducated and barbarous in speech, though wise and believing in mind; some, indeed, even maimed and deprived of eyesight; so that you may understand that these things are not the effect of human wisdom, but are uttered by the power of God.

Chapter LXI: *On Christian baptism.*

I will also relate the manner in which we dedicated ourselves to God when we had been made new through Christ; lest, if we omit this, we seem to be unfair in the explanation we are making.

As many as are persuaded and believe that what we teach and say is true, and undertake to be able to live accordingly, are instructed to pray and to entreat God with fasting, for the remission of their sins that are past, we praying and fasting with them. Then they are brought by us where there is water, and are regenerated in the same manner in which we were ourselves regenerated. For, in the name of God, the Father and Lord of the universe, and of our Savior Jesus Christ, and of the Holy Spirit, they then receive the washing with water. For Christ also said, "***Except ye be born again, ye shall not enter into the kingdom of heaven.***"[162] Now, that it is impossible for those who have once been born to enter into their mothers' wombs, is manifest to all. And how those who have sinned and repent shall escape their sins, is declared by Esaias the prophet, as I wrote above;[163] he thus speaks:

> ***Wash you, make you clean; put away the evil of your doings from your souls; learn to do well; judge the fatherless, and plead for the widow: and come and let us reason together, saith the Lord. And though your sins be as scarlet, I will make them white like wool; and though they be as crimson, I will make them white as snow. But if ye refuse and rebel, the sword shall devour you: for the mouth of the Lord hath spoken it.***[164]

---

[162] John 3:5.
[163] Chapter XLIV.
[164] Isaiah 1:16-20.

And for this [rite] we have learned from the apostles this reason. Since at our birth we were born without our own knowledge or choice, by our parents coming together, and were brought up in bad habits and wicked training; in order that we may not remain the children of necessity and of ignorance, but may become the children of choice and knowledge, and may obtain in the water the remission of sins formerly committed, there is pronounced over him who chooses to be born again, and has repented of his sins, the name of God the Father and Lord of the universe; he who leads to the laver the person that is to be washed calling him by this name alone. For no one can utter the name of the ineffable God; and if any one dare to say that there is a name, he raves with a hopeless madness.

And this washing is called illumination, because they who learn these things are illuminated in their understandings. And in the name of Jesus Christ, who was crucified under Pontius Pilate, and in the name of the Holy Ghost, who through the prophets foretold all things about Jesus, he who is illuminated is washed.

Chapter LXII: *Its imitation by demons.*

And the devils, indeed, having heard this washing published by the prophet, instigated those who enter their temples, and are about to approach them with libations and burnt-offerings, also to sprinkle themselves; and they cause them also to wash themselves entirely, as they depart [from the sacrifice], before they enter into the shrines in which their images are set. And the command, too, given by the priests to those who enter and worship in the temples, that they take off their shoes, the devils, learning what happened to the above-mentioned prophet Moses, have given in imitation of these things. For at that juncture, when Moses was ordered to go down into Egypt and lead out the people of the Israelites who were there, and while he was tending the flocks of his maternal uncle[165] in the land of Arabia, our Christ conversed with him under the appearance of fire from a bush, and said, "***Put off thy***

---

[165] Thirlby conjectures that Justin here confused in his mind the histories of Moses and Jacob.

shoes, and draw near and hear."[166] And he, when he had put off his shoes and drawn near, heard that he was to go down into Egypt and lead out the people of the Israelites there; and he received mighty power from Christ, who spoke to him in the appearance of fire, and went down and led out the people, having done great and marvelous things; which, if you desire to know, you will learn them accurately from his writings.

Chapter LXIII: *How God appeared to Moses.*

And all the Jews even now teach that the nameless God spake to Moses; whence the Spirit of prophecy, accusing them by Isaiah the prophet mentioned above, said "***The ox knoweth his owner, and the ass his master's crib; but Israel doth not know Me, and My people do not understand.***"[167] And Jesus the Christ, because the Jews knew not what the Father was, and what the Son, in like manner accused them; and Himself said, "***No one knoweth the Father, but the Son; nor the Son, but the Father, and they to whom the Son revealeth Him.***"[168]

Now the Word of God is His Son, as we have before said. And He is called Angel and Apostle; for He declares whatever we ought to know, and is sent forth to declare whatever is revealed; as our Lord Himself says, "***He that heareth Me, heareth Him that sent Me.***"[169]

From the writings of Moses also this will be manifest; for thus it is written in them, "***And the Angel of God spake to Moses, in a flame of fire out of the bush, and said, I am that I am, the God of Abraham, the God of Isaac, the God of Jacob, the God of thy fathers; go down into Egypt, and bring forth My people.***"[170] And if you wish to learn what follows, you can do so from the same writings; for it is impossible to relate the whole here.

But so much is written for the sake of proving that Jesus the Christ is the Son of God and His Apostle, being of old the Word, and appearing sometimes in the form of fire, and sometimes in the likeness of angels; but now, by the will of God, having become man for the human

---

[166] {Exodus 3:5; the second clause in the sentence, "and draw near and hear" is not in Exodus; thus, it is not in bold.}
[167] Isaiah 1:3.
[168] Matthew 11:27. {See also John 1:18.}
[169] Luke 10:16. {Compare Matthew 10:40; 18:5.}
[170] Exodus 3:6. {See also Exodus 3:10.}

race, He endured all the sufferings which the devils instigated the senseless Jews to inflict upon Him; who, though they have it expressly affirmed in the writings of Moses, "***And the angel of God spake to Moses in a flame of fire in a bush, and said, I am that I am, the God of Abraham, and the God of Isaac, and the God of Jacob***,"[171] yet maintain that He who said this was the Father and Creator of the universe. Whence also the Spirit of prophecy rebukes them, and says, "***Israel doth not know Me, my people have not understood Me.***"[172] And again, Jesus, as we have already shown, while He was with them, said, "***No one knoweth the Father, but the Son; nor the Son but the Father, and those to whom the Son will reveal Him.***"[173]

The Jews, accordingly, being throughout of opinion that it was the Father of the universe who spake to Moses, though He who spake to him was indeed the Son of God, who is called both Angel and Apostle, are justly charged, both by the Spirit of prophecy and by Christ Himself, with knowing neither the Father nor the Son. For they who affirm that the Son is the Father, are proved neither to have become acquainted with the Father, nor to know that the Father of the universe has a Son; who also, being the first-begotten Word of God, is even God.

And of old He appeared in the shape of fire and in the likeness of an angel to Moses and to the other prophets; but now in the times of your reign, having, as we before said, become Man by a virgin, according to the counsel of the Father, for the salvation of those who believe on Him, He endured both to be set at naught and to suffer, that by dying and rising again He might conquer death.

And that which was said out of the bush to Moses, "***I am that I am, the God of Abraham, and the God of Isaac, and the God of Jacob, and the God of your fathers***,"[174] this signified that they, even though dead, are yet in existence, and are men belonging to Christ Himself. For they were the first of all men to busy themselves in the search after God; Abraham being the father of Isaac, and Isaac of Jacob, as Moses wrote.

---

[171] Ibid.

[172] Isaiah 1:3.

[173] Matthew 11:27. {See also John 1:18.}

[174] Exodus 3:6.

Chapter LXIV: *Further misrepresentations of the truth.*

From what has been already said, you can understand how the devils, in imitation of what was said by Moses, asserted that Proserpine was the daughter of Jupiter, and instigated the people to set up an image of her under the name of Kore [Cora, i.e., the maiden or daughter] at the spring-heads. For, as we wrote above,[175] Moses said, "***In the beginning God made the heaven and the earth. And the earth was without form and unfurnished: and the Spirit of God moved upon the face of the waters.***"[176] In imitation, therefore, of what is here said of the Spirit of God moving on the waters, they said that Proserpine [or Cora] was the daughter of Jupiter.[177] And in like manner also they craftily feigned that Minerva was the daughter of Jupiter, not by sexual union, but, knowing that God conceived and made the world by the Word, they say that Minerva is the first conception [*evvoia*]; which we consider to be very absurd, bringing forward the form of the conception in a female shape. And in like manner the actions of those others who are called sons of Jupiter sufficiently condemn them.

Chapter LXV: *Administration of the sacraments.*

But we, after we have thus washed him who has been convinced and has assented to our teaching, bring him to the place where those who are called brethren are assembled, in order that we may offer hearty prayers in common for ourselves and for the baptized [illuminated] person, and for all others in every place, that we may be counted worthy, now that we have learned the truth, by our works also to be found good citizens and keepers of the commandments, so that we may be saved with an everlasting salvation. Having ended the prayers, we salute one another with a kiss.[178] There is then brought to the president of the

---

[175] Chapter LIX.

[176] {Genesis 1:1-2; see also Psalm 8:3, 33:6, 9.}

[177] And therefore caused her to preside over the waters, as above.

[178] The kiss of charity, the kiss of peace, or "the peace" (ἡ εἰρήνη), was enjoined by the Apostle Paul in his epistles to the Corinthians, Thessalonians, and the Romans, and thence was passed into common Christian usage. It was continued in the Western Church, under regulations to prevent its abuse, until the thirteenth century. Stanley remarks (*Corinthians*, i. 414), "It is still continued in the worship of the Coptic Church."

brethren[179] bread and a cup of wine mixed with water; and he taking them, gives praise and glory to the Father of the universe, through the name of the Son and of the Holy Ghost, and offers thanks at considerable length for our being counted worthy to receive these things at His hands. And when he has concluded the prayers and thanksgivings, all the people present express their assent by saying Amen. This word Amen answers in the Hebrew language to *Γένοιτο* [so be it]. And when the president has given thanks, and all the people have expressed their assent, those who are called by us deacons give to each of those present to partake of the bread and wine mixed with water over which the thanksgiving was pronounced, and to those who are absent they carry away a portion.

Chapter LXVI: *Of the Eucharist.*

And this food is called among us Eucharistia[180] [the Eucharist], of which no one is allowed to partake but the man who believes that the things which we teach are true, and who has been washed with the washing that is for the remission of sins, and unto regeneration, and who is so living as Christ has enjoined. For not as common bread and common drink do we receive these; but in like manner as Jesus Christ our Savior, having been made flesh by the Word of God, had both flesh and blood for our salvation, so likewise have we been taught that the food which is blessed by the prayer of His word, and from which our blood and flesh by transmutation are nourished, is the flesh and blood of that Jesus who was made flesh.[181] For the apostles, in the memoirs composed by them, which are called Gospels, have thus delivered unto us what was enjoined upon them; that Jesus took bread, and when He had given thanks, said, "***This do ye in remembrance of Me,***[182] ***this is My body***;"[183] and that, after

---

[179] *τῷ προεστῶτι τῶν ἀδελΦῶν*. This expression may quite legitimately be translated, "to that one of the brethren who was presiding."

[180] Literally, thanksgiving. See Matthew 26:27. {In the 1909 edition, "Eucharistia" is given in Greek.}

[181] This passage is claimed alike by Calvinists, Lutherans, and Romanists; and, indeed, the language is so inexact, that each party may plausibly maintain that their own opinion is advocated by it. The expression "the prayer of His word," or of the word we have from Him seems to signify the prayer pronounced over the elements, in imitation of our Lord's thanksgiving before breaking the bread.

[182] Luke 22:19.

the same manner, having taken the cup and given thanks, He said, "***This is My blood***;"[184] and gave it to them alone. Which the wicked devils have imitated in the mysteries of Mithras, commanding the same thing to be done. For, that bread and a cup of water are placed with certain incantations in the mystic rites of one who is being initiated, you either know or can learn.

Chapter LXVII: *On the weekly worship of the Christians.*

And we afterwards continually remind each other of these things. And the wealthy among us help the needy; and we always keep together; and for all things wherewith we are supplied, we bless the Maker of all through His Son Jesus Christ, and through the Holy Ghost. And on the day called Sunday,[185] all who live in cities or in the country gather together to one place, and the memoirs of the apostles or the writings of the prophets are read, as long as time permits; then, when the reader has ceased, the president verbally instructs, and exhorts to the imitation of these good things. Then we all rise together and pray, and, as we before said, when our prayer is ended, bread and wine and water are brought, and the president in like manner offers prayers and thanksgivings, according to his ability,[186] and the people assent, saying Amen; and there is a distribution to each, and a participation of that over which thanks have been given,[187] and to those who are absent a portion is sent by the deacons.

And they who are well to do, and willing, give what each thinks fit; and what is collected is deposited with the president, who succors the orphans and widows, and those who, through sickness or any other cause, are in want, and those who are in bonds, and the strangers sojourning among us, and in a word takes care of all who are in need.

But Sunday is the day on which we all hold our common assembly, because it is the first day on which God, having wrought a

---

[183] {Ibid. The clauses are reversed and a few words not included in the quote of this verse in Luke. See also Matthew 26:26; Mark 14:22}

[184] {This is a paraphrase of Luke 22:20; see also Matthew 26:27-28; Mark 14:23-24.}

[185] *τῇ τοῦ Ἡλίου λεγομένῃ ἡμέρᾳ.*

[186] *ὅση δύναμις ςὐτῷ,*—a phrase over which there has been much contention, but which seem to admit of no other meaning that that given above.

[187] Or, of the Eucharistic elements.

change in the darkness and matter, made the world; and Jesus Christ our Savior on the same day rose from the dead. For He was crucified on the day before that of Saturn (Saturday); and on the day after that of Saturn, which is the day of the Sun, having appeared to His apostles and disciples, He taught them these things, which we have submitted to you also for your consideration.

Chapter LXVIII: *Conclusion.*

And if these things seem to you to be reasonable and true, honor them; but if they seem nonsensical, despise them as nonsense, and do not decree death against those who have done no wrong, as you would against enemies. For we forewarn you, that you shall not escape the coming judgment of God, if you continue in your injustice; and we ourselves will invite you to do that which is pleasing to God. And though from the letter of the greatest and most illustrious Emperor Adrian, your father, we could demand that you order judgment to be given as we have desired, yet we have made this appeal and explanation, not on the ground of Adrian's decision, but because we know that what we ask is just. And we have subjoined the copy of Adrian's epistle, that you may know that we are speaking truly about this. And the following is the copy:—

Epistle of Adrian[188] in behalf of the Christians.

I have received the letter addressed to me by your predecessor Serenius Granianus, a most illustrious man; and this communication I am unwilling to pass over in silence, lest innocent persons be disturbed, and occasion be given to the informers for practicing villainy.

Accordingly, if the inhabitants of your province will so far sustain this petition of theirs as to accuse the Christians in some court of law, I do not prohibit them from doing so. But I will not suffer them to make use of mere entreaties and outcries. For it is far more just, if any one

[188] Addressed to Minucius Fundanus.

desires to make an accusation, that you give judgment upon it. If, therefore, any one makes the accusation, and furnishes proof that the said men do anything contrary to the laws, you shall adjudge punishments in proportion to the offences.

And this, by Hercules, you shall give special heed to, that if any man shall, through mere calumny, bring an accusation against any of these persons, you shall award to him more severe punishments in proportion to his wickedness.

Epistle of Antoninus to the common assembly of Asia.

The Emperor Caesar Titus Aelius Adrianus Antoninus Augustus Pius, Supreme Pontiff, in the fifteenth year of his tribuneship, consul for the third time, father of the fatherland, to the common assembly of Asia, greeting:

I should have thought that the gods themselves would see to it that such offenders should not escape. For if they had the power, they themselves would much rather punish those who refuse to worship them; but it is you who bring trouble on these persons, and accuse as the opinion of atheists that which they hold, and lay to their charge certain other things which we are unable to prove. But it would be advantageous to them that they should be thought to die for that of which they are accused, and they conquer you by being lavish of their lives rather than yield that obedience which you require of them.

And regarding the earthquakes which have already happened and are now occurring, it is not seemly that you remind us of them, losing heart whenever they occur, and thus set your conduct in contrast with that of these men; for they have much greater confidence towards God than you yourselves have. And you, indeed, seem at such times to ignore the gods, and you neglect the temples, and make no recognition of the worship of God. And hence you are jealous of those who do serve Him, and persecute them to the death.

Concerning such persons, some others also of the governors of provinces wrote to my most divine father; to whom he replied that they should not at all disturb such persons, unless they were found to be attempting anything against the Roman government. And to myself many have sent intimations regarding such persons, to whom I also replied in pursuance of my father's judgment. But if anyone has a matter to bring against any person of this class, merely as such a person,[189] let the accused be acquitted of the charge, even though he should be found to be such an one; but let the accuser be amenable to justice.

Epistle of Marcus Aurelius to the senate, in which he testifies that the Christians were the cause of his victory.

The Emperor Caesar Marcus Aurelius Antoninus, Germanicus, Parthicus, Sarmaticus, to the People of Rome, and to the sacred Senate greeting:

I explained to you my grand design, and what advantages I gained on the confines of Germany, with much labor and suffering, in consequence of the circumstance that I was surrounded by the enemy; I myself being shut up in Carnuntum by seventy-four cohorts, nine miles off. And the enemy being at hand, the scouts pointed out to us, and our general Pompeianus showed us that there was close on us a mass of a mixed multitude of 977,000 men, which indeed we saw; and I was shut up by this vast host, having with me only a battalion composed of the first, tenth, double and marine legions.

Having then examined my own position, and my host, with respect to the vast mass of barbarians and of the enemy, I quickly betook myself to prayer to the gods of my country.

[189] That is, if anyone accuses a Christian merely on the ground of his being a Christian.

But being disregarded by them, I summoned those who among us go by the name of Christians. And having made inquiry, I discovered a great number and vast host of them, and raged against them, which was by no means becoming; for afterwards I learned their power.

Wherefore they began the battle, not by preparing weapons, nor arms, nor bugles; for such preparation is hateful to them, on account of the God they bear about in their conscience. Therefore it is probable that those whom we suppose to be atheists, have God as their ruling power entrenched in their conscience. For having cast themselves on the ground, they prayed not only for me, but also for the whole army as it stood, that they might be delivered from the present thirst and famine. For during five days we had got no water, because there was none; for we were in the heart of Germany, and in the enemy's territory.

And simultaneously with their casting themselves on the ground, and praying to God (a God of whom I am ignorant), water poured from heaven, upon us most refreshingly cool, but upon the enemies of Rome a withering[190] hail. And immediately we recognized the presence of God following on the prayer—a God unconquerable and indestructible.

Founding upon this, then, let us pardon such as are Christians, lest they pray for and obtain such a weapon against ourselves. And I counsel that no such person be accused on the ground of his being a Christian. But if anyone be found laying to the charge of a Christian that he is a Christian, I desire that it be made manifest that he who is accused as a Christian, and acknowledges that he is one, is accused of nothing else than only this, that he is a Christian; but that he who arraigns him be burned alive.

And I further desire, that he who is entrusted with the government of the province shall not compel the Christian, who confesses and certifies such a matter, to

---

[190] Literally, "fiery."

retract; neither shall he commit him. And I desire that these things be confirmed by a decree of the senate.

And I command this my edict to be published in the Forum of Trajan, in order that it may be read. The prefect Vitrasius Pollio will see that it be transmitted to all the provinces round about, and that no one who wishes to make use of or to possess it be hindered from obtaining a copy from the document I now publish.

The Second Apology of Justin

For the Christians

Addressed to the Roman Senate

Chapter I: *Introduction.*

Romans, the things which have recently[191] happened in your city under Urbicus, and the things which are likewise being everywhere unreasonably done by the governors, have compelled me to frame this composition for your sakes, who are men of like passions, and brethren, though ye know it not, and though ye be unwilling to acknowledge it on account of your glorying in what you esteem dignities. For everywhere, whoever is corrected by father, or neighbor, or child, or friend, or brother, or husband, or wife, for a fault, for being hard to move, for loving pleasure and being hard to urge to what is right (except those who have been persuaded that the unjust and intemperate shall be punished in eternal fire, but that the virtuous and those who lived like Christ shall dwell with God in a state that is free from suffering,—we mean, those who have become Christians), and the evil demons, who hate us, and who keep such men as these subject to themselves, and serving them in the capacity of judges, incite them, as rulers actuated by evil spirits, to put us to death. But that the cause of all that has taken place under Urbicus may become quite plain to you, I will relate what has been done.

Chapter II: *Urbicus condemns the Christians to death.*

A certain woman lived with an intemperate[192] husband; she herself, too, having formerly been intemperate. But when she came to the knowledge of the teachings of Christ she became sober-minded, and endeavored to persuade her husband likewise to be temperate, citing the

---

[191] Literally, "both yesterday and the day before."

[192] *ἀχολ αοταίνοντι*, which word includes unchastity, as well as the other forms of intemperance.

teaching of Christ, and assuring him that there shall be punishment in eternal fire inflicted upon those who do not live temperately and conformably to right reason. But he, continuing in the same excesses, alienated his wife from him by his actions. For she, considering it wicked to live any longer as a wife with a husband who sought in every way means of indulging in pleasure contrary to the law of nature, and in violation of what is right, wished to be divorced from him. And when she was over-persuaded by her friends, who advised her still to continue with him, in the idea that some time or other her husband might give hope of amendment, she did violence to her own feeling and remained with him.

But when her husband had gone into Alexandria, and was reported to be conducting himself worse than ever, she—that she might not, by continuing in matrimonial connection with him, and by sharing his table and his bed, become a partaker also in his wickednesses and impieties—gave him what you call a bill of divorce,[193] and was separated from him. But this noble husband of hers,—while he ought to have been rejoicing that those actions which formerly she unhesitatingly committed with the servants and hirelings, when she delighted in drunkenness and every vice, she had now given up, and desired that he too should give up the same,—when she had gone from him without his desire, brought an accusation against her, affirming that she was a Christian.

And she presented a paper to thee, the Emperor, requesting that first she be permitted to arrange her affairs, and afterwards to make her defense against the accusation, when her affairs were set in order. And this you granted.

And her quondam husband, since he was now no longer able to prosecute her, directed his assaults against a man, Ptolemaeus, whom Urbicus punished, and who had been her teacher in the Christian doctrines. And this he did in the following way. He persuaded a centurion—who had cast Ptolemaeus into prison, and who was friendly to himself—to take Ptolemaeus and interrogate him on this sole point: whether he were a Christian? And Ptolemaeus, being a lover of truth, and not of a deceitful or false disposition, when he confessed himself to be a Christian, was bound by the centurion, and for a long time punished in the prison.

---

[193] *ῥεπουδιον*, i.e., "repudium," a bill of repudiation.

And, at last, when the man[194] came to Urbicus, he was asked this one question only: whether he was a Christian? And again, being conscious of his duty, and the nobility of it through the teaching of Christ, he confessed his discipleship in the divine virtue. For he who denies anything either denies it because he condemns the thing itself, or he shrinks from confession because he is conscious of his own unworthiness or alienation from it, neither of which cases is that of the true Christian.

And when Urbicus ordered him to be led away to punishment, one Lucius, who was also himself a Christian, seeing the unreasonable judgment that had thus been given, said to Urbicus: "What is the ground of this judgment? Why have you punished this man, not as an adulterer, nor fornicator, nor murderer, nor thief, nor robber, nor convicted of any crime at all, but who has only confessed that he is called by the name of Christian? This judgment of yours, O Urbicus, does not become the Emperor Pius, nor the philosopher, the son of Caesar, nor the sacred senate."[195]

And he said nothing else in answer to Lucius than this: "You also seem to me to be such an one." And when Lucius answered, "Most certainly I am," he again ordered him also to be led away. And he professed his thanks, knowing that he was delivered from such wicked rulers, and was going to the Father and King of the heavens. And still a third having come forward, was condemned to be punished.

Chapter III: *Justin accuses Crescens of ignorant prejudice against the Christians.*

I too, therefore, expect to be plotted against and fixed to the stake, by some of those I have named, or perhaps by Crescens, that lover of bravado and boasting;[196] for the man is not worthy of the name of philosopher who publicly bears witness against us in matters which he does not understand, saying that the Christians are atheists and impious, and doing so to win favor with the deluded mob, and to please them. For if he assails us without having read the teachings of Christ, he is thoroughly depraved, and far worse than the illiterate, who often refrain

---

[194] I.e., Ptolemaeus.

[195] On this passage, see Donaldson's *Critical History, etc.*, vol. Ii p.79.

[196] Words resembling "philosopher" in sound, viz. *φιλοψίφου χαὶ φιλοχόμπου*.

from discussing or bearing false witness about matters they do not understand. Or, if he has read them and does not understand the majesty that is in them, or, understanding it, acts thus that he may not be suspected of being such [a Christian], he is far more base and thoroughly depraved, being conquered by illiberal and unreasonable opinion and fear.

For I would have you to know that I proposed to him certain questions on this subject, and interrogated him, and found most convincingly that he, in truth, knows nothing. And to prove that I speak the truth, I am ready, if these disputations have not been reported to you, to conduct them again in your presence. And this would be an act worthy of a prince.

But if my questions and his answers have been made known to you, you are already aware that he is acquainted with none of our matters; or, if he is acquainted with them, but, through fear of those who might hear him, does not dare to speak out, like Socrates, he proves himself, as I said before, no philosopher, but an opinionative man;[197] at least he does not regard that Socratic and most admirable saying: "But a man must in no wise be honored before the truth."[198] But it is impossible for a Cynic, who makes indifference his end, to know any good but indifference.

Chapter IV: *Why the Christians do not kill themselves.*

But lest someone say to us, "Go then all of you and kill yourselves, and pass even now to God, and do not trouble us," I will tell you why we do not so, but why, when examined, we fearlessly confess. We have been taught that God did not make the world aimlessly, but for the sake of the human race; and we have before stated that He takes pleasure in those who imitate His properties, and is displeased with those that embrace what is worthless either in word or deed. If, then, we all kill ourselves we shall become the cause, as far as in us lies, why no one should be born, or instructed in the divine doctrines, or even why the human race should not exist; and we shall, if we so act, be ourselves acting in opposition to the will of God. But when we are examined, we

---

[197] *φιλόδοξος*, which may mean a lover of vainglory.

[198] See Plato, *Rep.* p. 595.

make no denial, because we are not conscious of any evil, but count it impious not to speak the truth in all things, which also we know is pleasing to God, and because we are also now very desirous to deliver you from an unjust prejudice.

Chapter V: *How the angels transgressed.*

But if this idea take possession of someone, that if we acknowledge God as our helper, we should not, as we say, be oppressed and persecuted by the wicked; this, too, I will solve. God, when He had made the whole world, and subjected things earthly to man, and arranged the heavenly elements for the increase of fruits and rotation of the seasons, and appointed this divine law—for these things also He evidently made for man—committed the care of men and of all things under heaven to angels whom He appointed over them.

But the angels transgressed this appointment, and were captivated by love of women, and begat children who are those that are called demons; and besides, they afterwards subdued the human race to themselves, partly by magical writings, and partly by fears and the punishments they occasioned, and partly by teaching them to offer sacrifices, and incense, and libations, of which things they stood in need after they were enslaved by lustful passions; and among men they sowed murders, wars, adulteries, intemperate deeds, and all wickedness.

Whence also the poets and mythologists, not knowing that it was the angels and those demons who had been begotten by them that did these things to men, and women, and cities, and nations, which they related, ascribed them to God Himself, and to those who were accounted to be His very offspring, and to the offspring of those who were called His brothers, Neptune and Pluto, and to the children again of these their offspring. For whatever name each of the angels had given to himself and his children, by that name they called them.

Chapter VI: *Names of God and of Christ, their meaning and power.*

But to the Father of all, who is unbegotten there is no name given. For by whatever name He be called, He has as His elder the person who gives Him the name. But these words Father, and God, and Creator, and Lord, and Master, are not names, but appellations derived from His good deeds and functions.

And His Son, who alone is properly called Son, the Word, who also was with Him and was begotten before the works, when at first He created and arranged all things by Him, is called Christ, in reference to His being anointed and God's ordering all things through Him; this name itself also containing an unknown significance; as also the appellation "God" is not a name, but an opinion implanted in the nature of men of a thing that can hardly be explained.

But "Jesus," His name as man and Savior, has also significance. For He was made man also, as we before said, having been conceived according to the will of God the Father, for the sake of believing men, and for the destruction of the demons.

And now you can learn this from what is under your own observation. For numberless demoniacs throughout the whole world, and in your city, many of our Christian men exorcising them in the name of Jesus Christ, who was crucified under Pontius Pilate, have healed and do heal, rendering helpless and driving the possessing devils out of the men, though they could not be cured by all the other exorcists, and those who used incantations and drugs.

Chapter VII: *The world preserved for the sake of Christians, and man's responsibility.*

Wherefore God delays causing the confusion and destruction of the whole world, by which the wicked angels and demons and men shall cease to exist, because of the seed of the Christians, who know that they are the cause of preservation in nature.[199] Since, if it were not so, it would not have been possible for you to do these things, and to be impelled by evil spirits; but the fire of judgment would descend and utterly dissolve all things, even as formerly the flood left no one but him only with his family who is by us called Noah, and by you Deucalion, from whom again such vast numbers have sprung, some of them evil and others good. For so we say that there will be the conflagration, but not as

[199] This is Dr. Donaldson's rendering of a clause on which the editors differ both as to reading and rendering.

the Stoics, according to their doctrine of all things being changed into one another, which seems most degrading.

But neither do we affirm that it is by fate that men do what they do, or suffer what they suffer, but that each man by free choice acts rightly or sins; and that it is by the influence of the wicked demons that earnest men, such as Socrates and the like, suffer persecution and are in bonds, while Sardanapalus, Epicurus, and the like, seem to be blessed in abundance and glory. The Stoics, not observing this, maintained that all things take place according to the necessity of fate. But since God in the beginning made the race of angels and men with free-will, they will justly suffer in eternal fire the punishment of whatever sins they have committed. And this is the nature of all that is made, to be capable of vice and virtue. For neither would any of them be praiseworthy unless there were power to turn to both [virtue and vice]. And this also is shown by those men everywhere who have made laws and philosophized according to right reason, by their prescribing to do some things and refrain from others.

Even the Stoic philosophers, in their doctrine of morals, steadily honor the same things, so that it is evident that they are not very felicitous in what they say about principles and incorporeal things. For if they say that human actions come to pass by fate, they will maintain either that God is nothing else than the things which are ever turning, and altering, and dissolving into the same things, and will appear to have had a comprehension only of things that are destructible, and to have looked on God Himself as emerging both in part and in whole in every wickedness;[200] or that neither vice nor virtue is anything; which is contrary to every sound idea, reason, and sense.

Chapter VIII: *All have been hated in whom the Word has dwelt.*

And those of the Stoic school—since, so far as their moral teaching went, they were admirable, as were also the poets in some particulars, on account of the seed of reason [the Logos] implanted in every race of men—were, we know, hated and put to death,—Heraclitus for instance, and, among those of our own time, Musonius and others.

---

[200] Literally, "becoming (*γινόενον*) both through the parts and through the whole in every wickedness."

For, as we intimated, the devils have always effected, that all those who anyhow live a reasonable and earnest life, and shun vice, be hated.

And it is nothing wonderful if the devils are proved to cause those to be much worse hated who live not according to a part only of the word diffused [among men] but by the knowledge and contemplation of the whole Word, which is Christ. And they, having been shut up in eternal fire, shall suffer their just punishment and penalty. For if they are even now overthrown by men through the name of Jesus Christ, this is an intimation of the punishment in eternal fire which is to be inflicted on themselves and those who serve them. For thus did both all the prophets foretell, and our own teacher Jesus teach.

Chapter IX: *Eternal punishment not a mere threat.*

And that no one may say what is said by those who are deemed philosophers, that our assertions that the wicked are punished in eternal fire are big words and bugbears, and that we wish men to live virtuously through fear, and not because such a life is good and pleasant; I will briefly reply to this, that if this be not so, God does not exist; or, if He exists, He cares not for men, and neither virtue nor vice is anything, and, as we said before, lawgivers unjustly punish those who transgress good commandments. But since these are not unjust, and their Father teaches them by the word to do the same things as Himself, they who agree with them are not unjust.

And if one object that the laws of men are diverse, and say that with some, one thing is considered good, another evil, while with others what seemed bad to the former is esteemed good, and what seemed good is esteemed bad, let him listen to what we say to this. We know that the wicked angels appointed laws conformable to their own wickedness, in which the men who are like them delight; and the right Reason,[201] when He came, proved that not all opinions nor all doctrines are good, but that some are evil, while others are good. Wherefore, I will declare the same and similar things to such men as these, and, if need be, they shall be spoken of more at large. But at present I return to the subject.

---

[201] These words can be taken of the Logos as well as of the right reason diffused among men by Him.

Chapter X: *Christ compared with Socrates.*

Our doctrines, then, appear to be greater than all human teaching; because Christ, who appeared for our sakes, became the whole rational being, both body, and reason, and soul. For whatever either lawgivers or philosophers uttered well, they elaborated by finding and contemplating some part of the Word. But since they did not know the whole of the Word, which is Christ, they often contradicted themselves. And those who by human birth were more ancient than Christ, when they attempted to consider and prove things by reason, were brought before the tribunals as impious persons and busybodies.

And Socrates, who was more zealous in this direction than all of them, was accused of the very same crimes as ourselves. For they said that he was introducing new divinities, and did not consider those to be gods whom the state recognized. But he cast out from the state both Homer[202] and the rest of the poets, and taught men to reject the wicked demons and those who did the things which the poets related; and he exhorted them to become acquainted with the God who was to them unknown, by means of the investigation of reason, saying, "That it is neither easy to find the Father and Maker of all, nor, having found Him, is it safe to declare Him to all."[203]

But these things our Christ did through His own power. For no one trusted in Socrates so as to die for this doctrine, but in Christ, who was partially known even by Socrates (for He was and is the Word who is in every man, and who foretold the things that were to come to pass both through the prophets and in His own person when He was made of like passions, and taught these things), not only philosophers and scholars believed, but also artisans and people entirely uneducated, despising both glory, and fear, and death; since He is a power of the ineffable Father, not the mere instrument of human reason.

Chapter XI: *How Christians view death.*

But neither should we be put to death, nor would wicked men and devils be more powerful than we, were not death a debt due by

---

[202] Plato, *Rep.* x. c. i. p. 595.

[203] Plato, *Timaeus*, p. 28, C. (but "possible," and not "safe," is the word used by Plato).

every man that is born. Wherefore we give thanks when we pay this debt. And we judge it right and opportune to tell here, for the sake of Crescens and those who rave as he does, what is related by Xenophon.

Hercules, says Xenophon, coming to a place where three ways met, found Virtue and Vice, who appeared to him in the form of women: Vice, in a luxurious dress, and with a seductive expression rendered blooming by such ornaments, and her eyes of a quickly melting tenderness,[204] said to Hercules that if he would follow her, she would always enable him to pass his life in pleasure and adorned with the most graceful ornaments, such as were then upon her own person; and Virtue, who was of squalid look and dress, said, But if you obey me, you shall adorn yourself not with ornament nor beauty that passes away and perishes, but with everlasting and precious graces.

And we are persuaded that everyone who flees those things that seem to be good, and follows hard after what are reckoned difficult and strange, enters into blessedness. For Vice, when by imitation of what is incorruptible (for what is really incorruptible she neither has nor can produce) she has thrown around her own actions, as a disguise, the properties of Virtue, and qualities which are really excellent, leads captive earthly-minded men, attaching to Virtue her own evil properties.

But those who understood the excellences which belong to that which is real, are also uncorrupt in virtue. And this every sensible person ought to think both of Christians and of the athletes, and of those who did what the poets relate of the so-called gods, concluding as much from our contempt of death, even when it could be escaped.[205]

Chapter XII: *Christians proved innocent by their contempt of death.*

For I myself, too, when I was delighting in the doctrines of Plato, and heard the Christians slandered, and saw them fearless of death, and of all other things which are counted fearful, perceived that it was impossible that they could be living in wickedness and pleasure. For what sensual or intemperate man, or who that counts it good to feast on

[204] Another reading is *πρὸς τὰς ὄψεις*, referring to the eyes of the beholder; and which may be rendered, "speedily fascinating to the sight."

[205] *Καὶ φευχτοῦ θανάτυ* may also be rendered, "even of death *which men flee from*."

human flesh,[206] could welcome death that he might be deprived of his enjoyments, and would not rather continue always the present life, and attempt to escape the observation of the rulers; and much less would he denounce himself when the consequence would be death?

This also the wicked demons have now caused to be done by evil men. For having put some to death on account of the accusations falsely brought against us, they also dragged to the torture our domestics, either children or weak women, and by dreadful torments forced them to admit those fabulous actions which they themselves openly perpetrate; about which we are the less concerned, because none of these actions are really ours, and we have the unbegotten and ineffable God as witness both of our thoughts and deeds. For why did we not even publicly profess that these were the things which we esteemed good, and prove that these are the divine philosophy, saying that the mysteries of Saturn are performed when we slay a man, and that when we drink our fill of blood, as it is said we do, we are doing what you do before that idol you honor, and on which you sprinkle the blood not only of irrational animals, but also of men, making a libation of the blood of the slain by the hand of the most illustrious and noble man among you? And imitating Jupiter and the other gods in sodomy and shameless intercourse with woman, might we not bring as our apology the writings of Epicurus and the poets? But because we persuade men to avoid such instruction, and all who practice them and imitate such examples, as now in this discourse we have striven to persuade you, we are assailed in every kind of way.

But we are not concerned, since we know that God is a just observer of all. But would that even now someone would mount a lofty rostrum, and shout with a loud voice,[207] "Be ashamed, be ashamed, ye who charge the guiltless with those deeds which yourselves openly commit, and ascribe things which apply to yourselves and to your gods to those who have not even the slightest sympathy with them. Be ye converted; become wise."

---

[206] Alluding to the common accusation against the Christians. {I.e., that which extends from participation in the Eucharist.}

[207] Literally, "with a tragic voice,"—the loud voice in which the Greek tragedies were recited through the mask.

Chapter XIII: *How the Word has been in all men.*

For I myself, when I discovered the wicked disguise which the evil spirits had thrown around the divine doctrines of the Christians, to turn aside others from joining them, laughed both at those who framed these falsehoods, and at the disguise itself, and at popular opinion; and I confess that I both boast and with all my strength strive to be found a Christian; not because the teachings of Plato are different from those of Christ, but because they are not in all respects similar, as neither are those of the others, Stoics, and poets, and historians. For each man spoke well in proportion to the share he had of the spermatic word,[208] seeing what was related to it. But they who contradict themselves on the more important points appear not to have possessed the heavenly[209] wisdom, and the knowledge which cannot be spoken against. Whatever things were rightly said among all men, are the property of us Christians. For next to God, we worship and love the Word who is from the Unbegotten and Ineffable God, since also He became man for our sakes, that becoming a partaker of our sufferings, He might also bring us healing. For all the writers were able to see realities darkly through the sowing of the implanted Word that was in them. For the seed and imitation impacted according to capacity is one thing, and quite another is the thing itself, of which there is the participation and imitation according to the grace which is from Him.

Chapter XIV: *Justin prays that this appeal be published.*

And we therefore pray you to publish this little book, appending what you think right, that our opinions may be known to others, and that these persons may have a fair chance of being freed from erroneous notions and ignorance of good, who by their own fault are become subject to punishment; that so these things may be published to men, because it is in the nature of man to know good and evil; and by their condemning us, whom they do not understand, for actions which they say are wicked, and by delighting in the gods who did such things, and even now require similar actions from men, and by inflicting on us death or

[208] The word disseminated among men.
[209] Literally, dimly seen at a distance.

bonds or some other such punishment, as if we were guilty of these things, they condemn themselves, so that there is no need of other judges.

Chapter XV: *Conclusion.*

And I despised the wicked and deceitful doctrine of Simon of my own nation. And if you give this book your authority, we will expose him before all, that, if possible, they may be converted. For this end alone did we compose this treatise. And our doctrines are not shameful, according to a sober judgment, but are indeed more lofty than all human philosophy; and if not so, they are at least unlike the doctrines of the Sotadists, and Philaenidians, and Dancers, and Epicureans, and such other teachings of the poets, which all are allowed to acquaint themselves with, both as acted and as written. And henceforth we shall be silent, having done as much as we could, and having added the prayer that all men everywhere may be counted worthy of the truth. And would that you also, in a manner becoming piety and philosophy, would for your own sakes judge justly!

Dialogue of Justin, Philosopher and Martyr, with Trypho, a Jew

Chapter I: *Introduction.*

While I was going about one morning in the walks of the Xystus,[210] a certain man, with others in his company, having met me, and said, "Hail, O philosopher!" And immediately after saying this, he turned round and walked along with me; his friends likewise followed him.

And I in turn having addressed him, said, "What is there important?"

And he replied, "I was instructed," says he "by Corinthus the Socratic in Argos, that I ought not to despise or treat with indifference those who array themselves in this dress,[211] but to show them all kindness, and to associate with them, as perhaps some advantage would spring from the intercourse either to some such man or to myself. It is good, moreover, for both, if either the one or the other be benefited. On this account, therefore, whenever I see any one in such costume, I gladly approach him, and now, for the same reason, have I willingly accosted you; and these accompany me, in the expectation of hearing for themselves something profitable from you."

"But who are you, most excellent man?" So I replied to him in jest.[212]

Then he told me frankly both his name and his family. "Trypho," says he, "I am called; and I am a Hebrew of the circumcision, and having escaped from the war[213] lately carried on there, I am spending my days in Greece, and chiefly at Corinth."

"And in what," said I, "would you be profited by philosophy so much as by your own lawgiver and the prophets?"

---

[210] This Xystus, on the authority of Eusebius. (iv. 18), was at Ephesus. There, Philostratus mentions, Apollonius was wont to have disputations. —*Otto.*

[211] Eusebius (iv. 11): "Justin, in philosopher's garb, preached the word of God."

[212] In jest, no doubt, because quoting a line from Homer, Iliad ii. 123, *τίς δὲ σύ ἐσσι, χαταθνηῶν ἀνθρώπων.*

[213] The war instigated by Bar Cochba.

"Why not?" he replied. "Do not the philosophers turn every discourse on God? and do not questions continually arise to them about His unity and providence? Is not this truly the duty of philosophy, to investigate the Deity?"

"Assuredly," said I, "so we too have believed. But the most[214] have not taken thought of this, whether there be one or more gods, and whether they have a regard for each one of us or no, as if this knowledge contributed nothing to our happiness; nay, they moreover attempt to persuade us that God takes care of the universe with its genera and species, but not of me and you, and each individually, since otherwise we would surely not need to pray to Him night and day. But it is not difficult to understand the upshot of this; for fearlessness and license in speaking result to such as maintain these opinions, doing and saying whatever they choose, neither dreading punishment nor hoping for any benefit from God. For how could they? They affirm that the same things shall always happen; and, further, that I and you shall again live in like manner, having become neither better men nor worse. But there are some others,[215] who, having supposed the soul to be immortal and immaterial, believe that though they have committed evil they will not suffer punishment (for that which is immaterial is insensible), and that the soul, in consequence of its immortality, needs nothing from God."

And he, smiling gently, said, "Tell us your opinion of these matters, and what idea you entertain respecting God, and what your philosophy is."

Chapter II: *Justin describes his studies in philosophy.*

"I will tell you," said I, "what seems to me; for philosophy is, in fact, the greatest possession, and most honorable before God,[216] to whom it leads us and alone commends us; and these are truly holy men who have bestowed attention on philosophy. What philosophy is, however, and the reason why it has been sent down to men, have escaped the observation of most; for there would be neither Platonists,

---

[214] The opinions of Stoics. —*Otto.*

[215] The Platonists.

[216] *ᾧ* some omit, and put *θεῷ* of previous clause in this clause, reading so: "Philosophy is the greatest possession, and most honorable, and introduces us to God," etc.

nor Stoics, nor Peripatetics, nor Theoretics,[217] nor Pythagoreans, this knowledge being *one*.[218] I wish to tell you why it has become many-headed.

It has happened that those who first handled it [i.e., philosophy], and who were therefore esteemed illustrious men, were succeeded by those who made no investigations concerning truth, but only admired the perseverance and self-discipline of the former, as well as the novelty of the doctrines; and each thought that to be true which he learned from his teacher: then, moreover, those latter persons handed down to *their* successors such things, and others similar to them; and this system was called by the name of him who was styled the father of the doctrine.

Being at first desirous of personally conversing with one of these men, I surrendered myself to a certain Stoic; and having spent a considerable time with him, when I had not acquired any further knowledge of God (for he did not know himself, and said such instruction was unnecessary), I left him and betook myself to another, who was called a Peripatetic, and as *he* fancied, shrewd. And this man, after having entertained me for the first few days, requested me to settle the fee, in order that our intercourse might not be unprofitable. Him, too, for this reason I abandoned, believing him to be no philosopher at all.

But when my soul was eagerly desirous to hear the peculiar and choice philosophy, I came to a Pythagorean, very celebrated—a man who thought much of his own wisdom.

And then, when I had an interview with him, willing to become his hearer and disciple, he said, "What then? Are you acquainted with music, astronomy, and geometry? Do you expect to perceive any of those things which conduce to a happy life, if you have not been first informed on those points which wean the soul from sensible objects, and render it fitted for objects which appertain to the mind, so that it can contemplate that which is honorable in its essence and that which is good in its essence?"

---

[217] Maranus thinks that those who are different from the masters of philosophy are called *Theoretics*. I do not know whether they may be better designated *Skeptics* or *Pyrrhonists*. —*Otto*.

[218] Julian, *Orat.* vi., says: "Let no one divide our philosophy into many parts, or cut it into many parts, and especially let him not make many out of *one*: for as truth is one, so also is philosophy."

Having commended many of these branches of learning, and telling me that they were necessary, he dismissed me when I confessed to him my ignorance. Accordingly I took it rather impatiently, as was to be expected when I failed in my hope, the more so because I deemed the man had some knowledge; but reflecting again on the space of time during which I would have to linger over those branches of learning, I was not able to endure longer procrastination.

In my helpless condition it occurred to me to have a meeting with the Platonists, for their fame was great. I thereupon spent as much of my time as possible with one who had lately settled in our city,[219]—a sagacious man, holding a high position among the Platonists,—and I progressed, and made the greatest improvements daily. And the perception of immaterial things quite overpowered me, and the contemplation of ideas furnished my mind with wings,[220] so that in a little while I supposed that I had become wise; and such was my stupidity, I expected forthwith to look upon God, for this is the end of Plato's philosophy."

Chapter III: *Justin narrates the manner of his conversion.*

"And while I was thus disposed, when I wished at one period to be filled with great quietness, and to shun the path of men, I used to go into a certain field not far from the sea. And when I was near that spot one day, which having reached I purposed to be by myself, a certain old man, by no means contemptible in appearance, exhibiting meek and venerable manners, followed me at a little distance. And when I turned round to him, having halted, I fixed my eyes rather keenly on him.

"And he said, 'Do you know me?'

"I replied in the negative.

" 'Why, then,' said he to me, 'do you so look at me?'

" 'I am astonished,' I said, 'because you have chanced to be in my company in the same place; for I had not expected to see any man here.'

"And he says to me, 'I am concerned about some of my household. These are gone away from me; and therefore have I come to

---

[219] Either Flavia Neapolis is indicated, or Ephesus. —*Otto*.

[220] Narrating his progress in the study of Platonic philosophy, he elegantly employs this trite phrase of Plato's. —*Otto*.

make personal search for them, if, perhaps, they shall make their appearance somewhere.

" 'But why are you here?' said he to me.

" 'I delight,' said I, 'in such walks, where my attention is not distracted, for converse with myself is uninterrupted; and such places are most fit for philology.'[221]

" 'Are you, then, a philologian,'[222] said he, 'but no lover of deeds or of truth? and do you not aim at being a practical man so much as being a sophist?'

" 'What greater work,' said I, 'could one accomplish than this, to show the reason which governs all, and having laid hold of it, and being mounted upon it, to look down on the errors of others, and their pursuits? But without philosophy and right reason, prudence would not be present to any man. Wherefore it is necessary for every man to philosophize, and to esteem this the greatest and most honorable work; but other things only of second-rate or third-rate importance, though, indeed, if they be made to depend on philosophy, they are of moderate value, and worthy of acceptance; but deprived of it, and not accompanying it, they are vulgar and coarse to those who pursue them.'

" 'Does philosophy, then, make happiness?' said he, interrupting.

" 'Assuredly,' I said, 'and it alone.'

" 'What, then, is philosophy?' he says; 'and what is happiness? Pray tell me, unless something hinders you from saying.'

" 'Philosophy, then,' said I, 'is the knowledge of that which really exists, and a clear perception of the truth; and happiness is the reward of such knowledge and wisdom.'

" 'But what do you call God?' said he.

" 'That which always maintains the same nature, and in the same manner, and is the cause of all other things—that, indeed, is God.' So I answered him; and he listened to me with pleasure, and thus again interrogated me:

" 'Is not knowledge a term common to different matters? For in arts of all kinds, he who knows any one of them is called a skillful man in

[221] Philology, used here to denote the exercise of the *reason*.

[222] Philology, used here to denote the exercise of *speech*. The twofold use of λόγος—*oratio* and *ratio*—ought to be kept in view. The old man uses it in the former, Justin in the latter sense.

the art of generalship, or of ruling, or of healing equally. But in divine and human affairs it is not so. Is there a knowledge which affords understanding of human and divine things, and then a thorough acquaintance with the divinity and the righteousness of them?'

" 'Assuredly,' I replied.

" 'What, then? Is it in the same way we know man and God, as we know music, and arithmetic, and astronomy, or any other similar branch?'

" 'By no means,' I replied.

" 'You have not answered me correctly, then,' he said; 'for some [branches of knowledge] come to us by learning, or by some employment, while of others we have knowledge by sight. Now, if one were to tell you that there exists in India an animal with a nature unlike all others, but of such and such a kind, multiform and various, you would not know it before you saw it; but neither would you be competent to give any account of it, unless you should hear from one who had seen it.'

" 'Certainly not,' I said.

" 'How then,' he said, 'should the philosophers judge correctly about God, or speak any truth, when they have no knowledge of Him, having neither seen Him at any time, nor heard Him?'

" 'But, father,' said I, 'the Deity cannot be seen merely by the eyes, as other living beings can, but is discernible to the mind alone, as Plato says; and I believe him.'"

Chapter IV: *The soul of itself cannot see God.*

" 'Is there then,' says he, 'such and so great power in our mind? Or can a man not perceive by sense sooner? Will the mind of man see God at any time, if it is uninstructed by the Holy Spirit?'

" 'Plato indeed says,' replied I, 'that the mind's eye is of such a nature, and has been given for this end, that we may see that very Being when the mind is pure itself, who is the cause of all discerned by the mind, having no color, no form, no greatness—nothing, indeed, which the bodily eye looks upon; but It is something of this sort, he goes on to say, that is beyond all essence, unutterable and inexplicable, but alone honorable and good, coming suddenly into souls well-dispositioned, on account of their affinity to and desire of seeing Him.'

" 'What affinity, then,' replied he, 'is there between us and God? Is the soul also divine and immortal, and a part of that very regal mind? And even as that sees God, so also is it attainable by us to conceive of the Deity in our mind, and thence to become happy?'

" 'Assuredly,' I said.

" 'And do all the souls of all living beings comprehend Him?' he asked; 'or are the souls of men of one kind and the souls of horses and of asses of another kind?'

" No; but the souls which are in all are similar,' I answered.

" 'Then,' says he, 'shall both horses and asses see, or have they seen at some time or other, God?'

" 'No,' I said; 'for the majority of men will not, saving such as shall live justly, purified by righteousness, and by every other virtue.'

" 'It is not, therefore,' said he, 'on account of his affinity, that a man sees God, nor because he has a mind, but because he is temperate and righteous?'

" 'Yes,' said I; 'and because he has that whereby he perceives God.'

" 'What then? Do goats or sheep injure any one?'

" 'No one in any respect,' I said.

" 'Therefore these animals will see [God] according to your account,' says he.

" 'No; for their body being of such a nature, is an obstacle to them.'

"He rejoined, 'If these animals could assume speech, be well assured that they would with greater reason ridicule our body; but let us now dismiss this subject, and let it be conceded to you as you say. Tell me, however, this: Does the soul see [God] so long as it is in the body, or after it has been removed from it?'

" 'So long as it is in the form of a man, it is possible for it,' I continue, 'to attain to this by means of the mind; but especially when it has been set free from the body, and being apart by itself, it gets possession of that which it was wont continually and wholly to love.'

" 'Does it remember this, then [the sight of God], when it is again in the man?'

" 'It does not appear to me so,' I said.

" 'What, then, is the advantage to those who have seen [God]? or what has he who has seen more than he who has not seen, unless he remember this fact, that he *has* seen?'

" 'I cannot tell,' I answered.

" 'And what do those suffer who are judged to be unworthy of this spectacle?' said he.

" 'They are imprisoned in the bodies of certain wild beasts, and this is their punishment.'

" 'Do they know, then, that it is for this reason they are in such forms, and that they have committed some sin?'

" 'I do not think so.'

" 'Then these reap no advantage from their punishment, as it seems: moreover, I would say that they are not punished unless they are conscious of the punishment.'

" 'No indeed.'

" 'Therefore souls neither see God nor transmigrate into other bodies; for they would know that so they are punished, and they would be afraid to commit even the most trivial sin afterwards. But that they can perceive that God exists, and that righteousness and piety are honorable, I also quite agree with you,' said he.

" 'You are right,' I replied."

Chapter V: *The soul is not in its own nature immortal.*

" 'These philosophers know nothing, then, about these things; for they cannot tell what a soul is.'

" 'It does not appear so.'

" 'Nor ought it to be called immortal; for if it is immortal, it is plainly unbegotten.'

" 'It is both unbegotten and immortal, according to some who are styled Platonists.'

" 'Do you say that the world is also unbegotten?'

" 'Some say so. I do not, however, agree with them.'

" 'You are right; for what reason has one for supposing that a body so solid, possessing resistance, composite, changeable, decaying, and renewed every day, has not arisen from some cause? But if the world is begotten, souls also are necessarily begotten; and perhaps at one time they were not in existence, for they were made on account of men and other living creatures, if you will say that they have been begotten wholly apart, and not along with their respective bodies.'

" 'This seems to be correct.'

" 'They are not, then, immortal?'

" 'No; since the world has appeared to us to be begotten.'

" 'But I do not say, indeed, that all souls die; for that were truly a piece of good fortune to the evil. What then? The souls of the pious remain in a better place, while those of the unjust and wicked are in a worse, waiting for the time of judgment. Thus some which have appeared worthy of God never die; but others are punished so long as God wills them to exist and to be punished.'

" 'Is what you say, then, of a like nature with that which Plato in *Timaeus* hints about the world, when he says that it is indeed subject to decay, inasmuch as it has been created, but that it will neither be dissolved nor meet with the fate of death on account of the will of God? Does it seem to you the very same can be said of the soul, and generally of all things? For those things which exist after[223] God, or shall at any time exist,[224] these have the nature of decay, and are such as may be blotted out and cease to exist; for God alone is unbegotten and incorruptible, and therefore He is God, but all other things after Him are created and corruptible. For this reason souls both die and are punished: since, if they were unbegotten, they would neither sin, nor be filled with folly, nor be cowardly, and again ferocious; nor would they willingly transform into swine, and serpents, and dogs; and it would not indeed be just to compel them, if they be unbegotten. For that which is unbegotten is similar to, equal to, and the same with that which is unbegotten; and neither in power nor in honor should the one be preferred to the other, and hence there are not many things which are unbegotten: for if there were some difference between them, you would not discover the cause of the difference, though you searched for it; but after letting the mind ever wander to infinity, you would at length, wearied out, take your stand on one Unbegotten, and say that this is the Cause of all. Did such escape

[223] "Beside."

[224] Otto says: If the old man begins to speak here, then *ἔχει* must be read for *ἔχειν*. The received text makes it appear that Justin continues a quotation, or the substance of it, from Plato.

the observation of Plato and Pythagoras, those wise men,' I said, 'who have been as a wall and fortress of philosophy to us?'"

Chapter VI: *These things were unknown to Plato and other philosophers.*

" 'It makes no matter to me,' said he, 'whether Plato or Pythagoras, or, in short, any other man held such opinions. For the truth is so; and you would perceive it from this. The soul assuredly is or has life. If, then, it is life, it would cause something else, and not itself, to live, even as motion would move something else than itself. Now, that the soul lives, no one would deny. But if it lives, it lives not as being life, but as the partaker of life; but that which partakes of anything, is different from that of which it does partake. Now the soul partakes of life, since God wills it to live. Thus, then, it will not even partake [of life] when God does not will it to live. For to live is not its attribute, as it is God's; but as a man does not live always, and the soul is not for ever conjoined with the body, since, whenever this harmony must be broken up, the soul leaves the body, and the man exists no longer; even so, whenever the soul must cease to exist, the spirit of life is removed from it, and there is no more soul, but it goes back to the place from whence it was taken.'"

Chapter VII: *The knowledge of truth to be sought from the Jewish prophets alone.*

" 'Should anyone, then, employ a teacher?' I say, 'or whence may anyone be helped, if not even in them there is truth?'

" 'There existed, long before this time, certain men more ancient than all those who are esteemed philosophers, both righteous and beloved by God, who spoke by the Divine Spirit, and foretold events which would take place, and which are now taking place. They are called prophets. These alone both saw and announced the truth to men, neither reverencing nor fearing any man, not influenced by a desire for glory, but speaking those things alone which they saw and which they heard, being filled with the Holy Spirit. Their writings are still extant, and he who has read them is very much helped in his knowledge of the beginning and end of things, and of those matters which the philosopher ought to know, provided he has believed them. For they did not use demonstration in their treatises, seeing that they were witnesses to the truth above all demonstration, and worthy of belief; and those events which have happened, and those which are happening, compel you to assent to the utterances made by them, although, indeed, they were entitled to credit on account of the miracles which they performed, since they both glorified the Creator, the God and Father of all things, and proclaimed His Son, the Christ [sent] by Him: which, indeed, the false prophets, who are filled with the lying unclean spirit, neither have done nor do, but venture to work certain wonderful deeds for the purpose of astonishing men, and glorify the spirits and demons of error. But pray that, above all things, the gates of light may be opened to you; for these things cannot be perceived or understood by all, but only by the man to whom God and His Christ have imparted wisdom.'"

Chapter VIII: *Justin by his colloquy is kindled with love to Christ.*

"When he had spoken these and many other things, which there is no time for mentioning at present, he went away, bidding me attend to them; and I have not seen him since. But straightway a flame was kindled in my soul; and a love of the prophets, and of those men who are friends of Christ, possessed me; and whilst revolving his words in my mind, I found this philosophy alone to be safe and profitable. Thus, and for this reason, I am a philosopher. Moreover, I would wish that all, making a resolution similar to my own, do not keep themselves away from the words of the Savior. For they possess a terrible power in themselves, and are sufficient to inspire those who turn aside from the path of rectitude with awe; while the sweetest rest is afforded those who make a diligent practice of them. If, then, you have any concern for yourself, and if you are eagerly looking for salvation, and if you believe in God, you may—since you are not indifferent to the matter[225]—become acquainted with the Christ of God, and, after being initiated,[226] live a happy life."

---

[225] According to one interpretation, this clause is applied to God: "If you believe in God, seeing He is not indifferent to the matter," etc. Maranus says that it means: A Jew who reads so much of Christ in the Old Testament cannot be indifferent to the things which pertain to Him.

[226] Literally: having become perfect. Some refer the words to the perfection of character; some to initiation by baptism.

When I had said this, my beloved friend,[227] those who were with Trypho laughed; but he, smiling, says, "I approve of your other remarks, and admire the eagerness with which you study divine things; but it were better for you still to abide in the philosophy of Plato, or of some other man, cultivating endurance, self-control, and moderation, rather than be deceived by false words, and follow the opinions of men of no reputation. For if you remain in that mode of philosophy, and live blamelessly, a hope of a better destiny were left to you; but when you have forsaken God, and reposed confidence in man, what safety still awaits you? If, then, you are willing to listen to me (for I have already considered you a friend), first be circumcised, then observe what ordinances have been enacted with respect to the Sabbath, and the feasts, and the new moons of God; and, in a word, do all things which have been written in the law: and then perhaps you shall obtain mercy from God. But Christ—if He has indeed been born, and exists anywhere—is unknown, and does not even know Himself, and has no power until Elias come to anoint Him, and make Him manifest to all. And you, having accepted a groundless report, invent a Christ for yourselves, and for His sake are inconsiderately perishing."

Chapter IX: *The Christians have not believed groundless stories.*

"I excuse and forgive you, my friend," I said. "For you know not what you say, but have been persuaded by teachers who do not understand the Scriptures; and you speak, like a diviner, whatever comes into your mind. But if you are willing to listen to an account of Him, how we have not been deceived, and shall not cease to confess Him,—although men's reproaches be heaped upon us, although the most terrible tyrant compel us to deny Him,—I shall prove to you as you stand here that we have not believed empty fables, or words without any foundation but words filled with the Spirit of God, and big with power, and flourishing with grace."

Then again those who were in his company laughed, and shouted in an unseemly manner. Then I rose up and was about to leave; but he, taking hold of my garment, said I should not accomplish that[228] until I had performed what I promised.

---

[227] Latin version, "beloved Pompeius."

[228] According to another reading, "I did not *leave*."

" 'Let not, then, your companions be so tumultuous, or behave so disgracefully,' I said. 'But if they wish, let them listen in silence; or, if some better occupation prevent them, let them go away; while we, having retired to some spot, and resting there, may finish the discourse.'

It seemed good to Trypho that we should do so; and accordingly, having agreed upon it, we retired to the middle space of the Xystus. Two of his friends, when they had ridiculed and made game of our zeal, went off. And when we were come to that place, where there are stone seats on both sides, those with Trypho, having seated themselves on the one side, conversed with each other, some one of them having thrown in a remark about the war waged in Judaea."

Chapter X: *Trypho blames the Christians for this alone— the non-observance of the law.*

And when they ceased, I again addressed them thus:

"Is there any other matter, my friends, in which we are blamed, than this, that we live not after the law, and are not circumcised in the flesh as your forefathers were, and do not observe sabbaths as you do? Are our lives and customs also slandered among you? And I ask this: have you also believed concerning us, that we eat men; and that after the feast, having extinguished the lights, we engage in promiscuous concubinage? Or do you condemn us in this alone, that we adhere to such tenets, and believe in an opinion, untrue, as you think?"

"This is what we are amazed at," said Trypho, "but those things about which the multitude speak are not worthy of belief; for they are most repugnant to human nature. Moreover, I am aware that your precepts in the so-called Gospel are so wonderful and so great, that I suspect no one can keep them; for I have carefully read them. But this is what we are most at a loss about: that you, professing to be pious, and supposing yourselves better than others, are not in any particular separated from them, and do not alter your mode of living from the nations, in that you observe no festivals or sabbaths, and do not have the rite of circumcision; and further, resting your hopes on a man that was crucified, you yet expect to obtain some good thing from God, while you do not obey His commandments. Have you not read, that that soul shall be cut off from his people who shall not have been circumcised on the eighth day? And this has been ordained for strangers and for slaves equally. But you, despising this covenant rashly, reject the consequent duties, and attempt to persuade yourselves that you know God, when, however, you perform none of those things which they do who fear God. If, therefore, you can defend yourself on these points, and make it manifest in what way you hope for anything whatsoever, even though you do not observe the law, this we would very gladly hear from you, and we shall make other similar investigations."

Chapter XI: *Justin argues the law abrogated by Christ; the New Testament promised and given by God.*

"There will be no other God, O Trypho, nor was there from eternity any other existing" (I thus addressed him), "but He who made and disposed all this universe. Nor do we think that there is one God for us, another for you, but that He alone is God who led your fathers out from Egypt with a strong hand and a high arm. Nor have we trusted in any other (for there is no other), but in Him in whom you also have trusted, the God of Abraham, and of Isaac, and of Jacob. But we do not trust through Moses or through the law; for then we would do the same as yourselves. But now[229]—(for I have read that there shall be a final law, and a covenant, the chiefest of all, which it is now incumbent on all men to observe, as many as are seeking after the inheritance of God. For the law promulgated on Horeb is now old, and belongs to yourselves alone; but *this* is for all universally. Now, law placed against law has abrogated that which is before it, and a covenant which comes after in like manner has put an end to the previous one; and an eternal and final law—namely, Christ—has been given to us, and the covenant is trustworthy, after which there shall be no law, no commandment, no ordinance. Have you not read this which Isaiah says:

> ***Hearken unto Me, hearken unto Me, my people; and, ye kings, give ear unto Me: for a law shall go forth from Me, and My judgment shall be for a light to the nations. My righteousness***

[229] Editors suppose that Justin inserts a long parenthesis here, form "for" to "Egypt." It is more natural to take this as an anacoluthon. Justin was going to say, "But now we trust through Christ," but feels such a statement requires a preliminary explanation.

> ***approaches swiftly, and My salvation shall go forth, and nations shall trust in Mine arm?***[230]

And by Jeremiah, concerning this same new covenant, He thus speaks:

> ***Behold, the days come, saith the Lord, that I will make a new covenant with the house of Israel and with the house of Judah; not according to the covenant which I made with their fathers, in the day that I took them by the hand, to bring them out of the land of Egypt.***[231]

If, therefore, God proclaimed a new covenant which was to be instituted, and this for a light of the nations, we see and are persuaded that men approach God, leaving their idols and other unrighteousness, through the name of Him who was crucified, Jesus Christ, and abide by their confession even unto death, and maintain piety. Moreover, by the works and by the attendant miracles, it is possible for all to understand that He is the new law, and the new covenant, and the expectation of those who out of every people wait for the good things of God. For the true spiritual Israel, and descendants of Judah, Jacob, Isaac, and Abraham (who in uncircumcision was approved of and blessed by God on account of his faith, and called the father of many nations), are we who have been led to God through this crucified Christ, as shall be demonstrated while we proceed."

Chapter XII: *The Jews violate the eternal law, and interpret ill that of Moses.*

"I also adduced another passage in which Isaiah exclaims:

> ***Hear My words, and your soul shall live; and I will make an everlasting covenant with you, even the sure mercies of David. Behold, I have given Him for a witness to the people: nations which know not Thee shall call on Thee; peoples who know not***

---

[230] According to the LXX, Isaiah 51:4, 5. {See also Isaiah 2:3; Psalm 67:4.}

[231] Jeremiah 31:31, 32. {See also Jeremiah 32:40; Isaiah 55:3.}

> ***Thee shall escape to Thee, because of thy God, the Holy One of Israel; for He has glorified Thee.***[232]

This same law you have despised, and His new holy covenant you have slighted; and now you neither receive it, nor repent of your evil deeds. '***For your ears are closed, your eyes are blinded, and the heart is hardened***,' Jeremiah[233] has cried; yet not even then do you listen. The Lawgiver is present, yet you do not see Him; to the poor the Gospel is preached, the blind see, yet you do not understand. You have now need of a second circumcision, though you glory greatly in the flesh. The new law requires you to keep perpetual sabbath, and you, because you are idle for one day, suppose you are pious, not discerning why this has been commanded you; and if you eat unleavened bread, you say the will of God has been fulfilled. The Lord our God does not take pleasure in such observances: if there is any perjured person or a thief among you, let him cease to be so; if any adulterer, let him repent; then he has kept the sweet and true sabbaths of God. If anyone has impure hands, let him wash and be pure."

Chapter XIII: *Isaiah teaches that sins are forgiven through Christ's blood.*

"For Isaiah did not send you to a bath, there to wash away murder and other sins, which not even all the water of the sea were sufficient to purge; but, as might have been expected, this was that saving bath of the olden time which followed[234] those who repented, and who no longer were purified by the blood of goats and of sheep, or by the ashes of an heifer, or by the offerings of fine flour, but by faith through the blood of Christ, and through His death, who died for this very reason, as Isaiah himself said, when he spake thus:

> ***The Lord shall make bare His holy arm in the eyes of all the nations, and all the nations and the ends of the earth shall see the***

---

[232] Isaiah 55:3 ff., according to LXX. {Isaiah 55:3-5.}

[233] Not in Jeremiah; some would insert, in place of Jeremiah, Isaiah or John. {See also Isaiah 59:10; Matthew 13:15; Acts 28:27.}

[234] Corinthians 10:4. Otto reads: which he mentioned and which was for those who repented. {Citation to Corinthians seems in error.}

salvation of God. Depart ye, depart ye, depart ye,[235] *go ye out from thence, and touch no unclean thing; go ye out of the midst of her, be ye clean that bear the vessels of the Lord, for*[236] *ye go not with haste. For the Lord shall go before you; and the Lord, the God of Israel, shall gather you together. Behold, my servant shall deal prudently; and He shall be exalted, and be greatly glorified. As many were astonished at Thee, so Thy form and Thy glory shall be marred more than men. So shall many nations be astonished at Him, and the kings shall shut their mouths; for that which had not been told them concerning Him shall they see, and that which they had not heard shall they consider.*

Lord, who hath believed our report? and to whom is the arm of the Lord revealed? We have announced Him as a child before Him, as a root in a dry ground. He hath no form or comeliness, and when we saw Him He had no form or beauty; but His form is dishonored, and fails more than the sons of men. He is a man in affliction, and acquainted with bearing sickness, because His face has been turned away; He was despised, and we esteemed Him not. He bears our sins, and is distressed for us; and we esteemed Him to be in toil and in affliction, and in evil treatment. But He was wounded for our transgressions, He was bruised for our iniquities; the chastisement of our peace was upon Him. With His stripes we are healed. All we, like sheep, have gone astray. Every man has turned to his own way; and the Lord laid on Him our iniquities, and by reason of His oppression He opens not His mouth. He was brought as a sheep to the slaughter; and as a lamb before her shearer is dumb, so He openeth not His mouth. In His humiliation His judgment was taken away. And who shall declare His generation? For His life is taken from the earth. Because of the transgressions of my people He came unto death. And I will give the wicked for His grave, and the rich for His death, because He committed no iniquity, and deceit was not found in His mouth. And the Lord wills to purify Him from affliction. If he has been given for sin, your soul shall see a long-lived seed. And the Lord wills to take His soul away from trouble, to show Him light, and to form Him in understanding, to justify the righteous One who serves many well. And He shall bear our sins; therefore He shall inherit many, and shall divide the spoil of the strong, because

---

[235] Three times in Justin, not in LXX.

[236] Deviating slightly from LXX, omitting a clause.

His soul was delivered to death; and He was numbered with the transgressors, and He bare the sins of many, and was delivered for their transgression.

Sing, O barren, who barest not; break forth and cry aloud, thou who dost not travail in pain: for more are the children of the desolate than the children of the married wife. For the Lord said, Enlarge the place of thy tent and of thy curtains; fix them, spare not, lengthen thy cords, and strengthen thy stakes; stretch forth to thy right and thy left; and thy seed shall inherit the Gentiles, and thou shalt make the desolate cities to be inherited. Fear not because thou art ashamed, neither be thou confounded because thou hast been reproached; for thou shalt forget everlasting shame, and shalt not remember the reproach of thy widowhood, because the Lord has made a name for Himself, and He who has redeemed thee shall be called through the whole earth the God of Israel. The Lord has called thee as a woman forsaken and grieved in spirit, as[237] a woman forsaken and grieved in spirit, not as a woman hated from her youth."[238]

Chapter XIV: *Righteousness is not placed in Jewish rites, but in the conversion of the heart given in baptism by Christ.*

"By reason, therefore, of this laver of repentance and knowledge of God, which has been ordained on account of the transgression of God's people, as Isaiah cries, we have believed, and testify that that very baptism which he announced is alone able to purify those who have repented; and this is the water of life. But the cisterns which you have dug for yourselves are broken and profitless to you. For what is the use of that baptism which cleanses the flesh and body alone? Baptize the soul from wrath and from covetousness, from envy, and from hatred; and, lo! the body is pure. For this is the symbolic significance of unleavened bread, that you do not commit the old deeds of wicked leaven. But you have understood all things in a carnal sense, and you suppose it to be piety if you do such things, while your souls are filled with deceit, and, in short, with every wickedness. Accordingly, also, after the seven days of eating unleavened bread, God commanded them to mingle new leaven, that is, the performance of other works, and not the

[237] LXX. *"not as,"* etc.

[238] Isaiah 52:10 ff., following the LXX on to 54:6.

imitation of the old and evil works. And because this is what this new Lawgiver demands of you, I shall again refer to the words which have been quoted by me, and to others also which have been passed over. They are related by Isaiah to the following effect:

> ***Hearken to me, and your soul shall live; and I will make with you an everlasting covenant, even the sure mercies of David. Behold, I have given Him for a witness to the people, a leader and commander to the nations. Nations which know not Thee shall call on Thee; and peoples who know not Thee shall escape unto Thee, because of Thy God, the Holy One of Israel, for He has glorified Thee. Seek ye God; and when you find Him, call on Him, so long as He may be nigh you. Let the wicked forsake his ways, and the unrighteous man his thoughts; and let him return unto the Lord, and he will obtain mercy, because He will abundantly pardon your sins. For my thoughts are not as your thoughts, neither are my ways as your ways; but as far removed as the heavens are from the earth, so far is my way removed from your way, and your thoughts from my thoughts. For as the snow or the rain descends from heaven, and shall not return till it waters the earth, and makes it bring forth and bud, and gives seed to the sower and bread for food, so shall My Word be that goeth forth out of My mouth: it shall not return until it shall have accomplished all that I desired, and I shall make My commandments prosperous. For ye shall go out with joy, and be taught with gladness. For the mountains and the hills shall leap while they expect you, and all the trees of the fields shall applaud with their branches: and instead of the thorn shall come up the cypress, and instead of the brier shall come up the myrtle. And the Lord shall be for a name, and for an everlasting sign, and He shall not fail!***[239]

Of these and such like words written by the prophets, O Trypho," said I, "some have reference to the first advent of Christ, in which He is preached as inglorious, obscure, and of mortal appearance; but others had reference to His second advent, when He shall appear in glory and above the clouds; and your nation shall see and know Him whom they have pierced, as Hosea, one of the twelve prophets, and Daniel, foretold."

---

[239] Isaiah 55:3 to end.

Chapter XV: ***In what the true fasting consists.***

"Learn, therefore, to keep the true fast of God, as Isaiah says, that you may please God. Isaiah has cried thus:

> ***Shout vehemently, and do not spare: lift up thy voice as with a trumpet, and show My people their transgressions, and the house of Jacob their sins. They seek Me from day to day, and desire to know My ways, as a nation that did righteousness, and forsook not the judgment of God. They ask of Me now righteous judgment, and desire to draw near to God, saying, Wherefore have we fasted, and Thou seest not? and afflicted our souls, and Thou hast not known? Because in the days of your fasting you find your own pleasure, and oppress all those who are subject to you. Behold, ye fast for strifes and debates, and smite the humble with your fists. Why do ye fast for Me, as today, so that your voice is heard aloud? This is not the fast which I have chosen, the day in which a man shall afflict his soul. And not even if you bend your neck like a ring, or clothe yourself in sackcloth and ashes, shall you call this a fast, and a day acceptable to the Lord. This is not the fast which I have chosen, saith the Lord; but loose every unrighteous bond, dissolve the terms of wrongous covenants, let the oppressed go free, and avoid every iniquitous contract. Deal thy bread to the hungry, and lead the homeless poor under thy dwelling; if thou seest the naked, clothe him; and do not hide thyself from thine own flesh. Then shall thy light break forth as the morning, and thy garments[240] shall rise up quickly: and thy righteousness shall go before thee, and the glory of God shall envelope thee. Then shalt thou cry, and the Lord shall hear thee: while thou art speaking, He will say, Behold, I am here. And if thou take away from thee the yoke, and the stretching out of the hand, and the word of murmuring; and shalt give heartily thy bread to the hungry, and shalt satisfy the afflicted soul; then shall thy light arise in the darkness, and thy darkness shall be as the noon-day: and thy God shall be with thee continually, and thou shalt be satisfied according as thy soul desireth, and thy bones shall become fat, and shall be as a watered garden, and as a fountain of water, or as a land where water fails not.***[241]

---

[240] *ἱμάτια*; some read *ἰάματα*, as in LXX, "the health," the better reading probably.

[241] Isaiah 58:1-12.

Circumcise, therefore, the foreskin of your heart, as the words of God in all these passages demand."

Chapter XVI: *Circumcision given as a sign, that the Jews might be driven away for their evil deeds done to Christ and the Christians.*

"And God himself proclaimed by Moses, speaking thus: ***'And circumcise the hardness of your hearts, and no longer stiffen the neck. For the Lord your God is both Lord of lords, and a great, mighty, and terrible God, who regardeth not persons, and taketh not rewards.'***[242] And in Leviticus: ***'Because they have transgressed against Me, and despised Me, and because they have walked contrary to Me, I also walked contrary to them, and I shall cut them off in the land of their enemies. Then shall their uncircumcised heart be turned.'***[243] For the circumcision according to the flesh, which is from Abraham, was given for a sign; that you may be separated from other nations, and from us; and that you alone may suffer that which you now justly suffer; and that your land may be desolate, and your cities burned with fire; and that strangers may eat your fruit in your presence, and not one of you may go up to Jerusalem.[244] For you are not recognized among the rest of men by any other mark than your fleshly circumcision. For none of you, I suppose, will venture to say that God neither did nor does foresee the events, which are future, nor fore-ordained His deserts for each one. Accordingly, these things have happened to you in fairness and justice, for you have slain the Just One, and His prophets before Him; and now you reject those who hope in Him, and in Him who sent Him—God the Almighty and Maker of all things—cursing in your synagogues those that believe on Christ. For you have not the power to lay hands upon us, on account of those who now have the mastery. But as often as you could, you did so. Wherefore God, by Isaiah, calls to you, saying,

---

[242] Deuteronomy 10:16 f {and verse 17. See also Deuteronomy 7:21; Leviticus 26:41; Jeremiah 4:4; Daniel 2:47; 2 Chronicles 19:7; Romans 2:29; Colossians 2:11}

[243] Leviticus 26:40, 41.

[244] See *Apol.* i. 47. The Jews were prohibited by law from entering Jerusalem on pain of death. And so Justin sees in circumcision their own punishment.

> ***Behold how the righteous man perished, and no one regards it. For the righteous man is taken away from before iniquity. His grave shall be in peace, he is taken away from the midst. Draw near hither, ye lawless children, seed of the adulterers, and children of the whore. Against whom have you sported yourselves, and against whom have you opened the mouth, and against whom have you loosened the tongue?"***[245]

Chapter XVII: *The Jews sent persons through the whole earth to spread calumnies on Christians.*

"For other nations have not inflicted on us and on Christ this wrong to such an extent as you have, who in very deed are the authors of the wicked prejudice against the Just One, and us who hold by Him. For after that you had crucified Him, the only blameless and righteous Man,—through whose stripes those who approach the Father by Him are healed,—when you knew that He had risen from the dead and ascended to heaven, as the prophets foretold He would, you not only did not repent of the wickedness which you had committed, but at that time you selected and sent out from Jerusalem chosen men through all the land to tell that the godless heresy of the Christians had sprung up, and to publish those things which all they who knew us not speak against us. So that you are the cause not only of your own unrighteousness, but in fact of that of all other men. And Isaiah cries justly: ***'By reason of you, My name is blasphemed among the Gentiles.'***[246] And:

> ***Woe unto their soul! because they have devised an evil device against themselves, saying, Let us bind the righteous, for he is distasteful to us. Therefore they shall eat the fruit of their doings. Woe unto the wicked! evil shall be rendered to him according to the works of his hands.***[247]

And again, in other words:[248]

---

[245] Isaiah 57:1-4.

[246] Isaiah 52:5.

[247] {Isaiah 3:9-11. The clause "bind the righteous, for he is distasteful to us" or a similar phrase does not appear in all translations. Compare OSB to KJV.}

[248] Isaiah 3:9 ff. {This citation is an error. See Isaiah 5:19-20.}

> ***Woe unto them that draw their iniquity as with a long cord, and their transgressions as with the harness of a heifer's yoke: who say, Let his speed come near; and let the counsel of the Holy One of Israel come, that we may know it. Woe unto them that call evil good, and good evil; that put light for darkness, and darkness for light; that put bitter for sweet, and sweet for bitter!***[249]

Accordingly, you displayed great zeal in publishing throughout all the land bitter and dark and unjust things against the only blameless and righteous Light sent by God. For He appeared distasteful to you when He cried among you, '***It is written, My house is the house of prayer; but ye have made it a den of thieves!***'[250] He overthrew also the tables of the money-changers in the temple, and exclaimed, '***Woe unto you, Scribes and Pharisees, hypocrites! because ye pay tithe of mint and rue, but do not observe the love of God and justice. Ye whited sepulchers! appearing beautiful outward, but are within full of dead men's bones.***'[251] And to the Scribes, '***Woe unto you, Scribes! for ye have the keys, and ye do not enter in yourselves, and them that are entering in ye hinder; ye blind guides!***'"[252]

Chapter XVIII: *Christians would observe the law, if they did not know why it was instituted.*

"For since you have read, O Trypho, as you yourself admitted, the doctrines taught by our Savior, I do not think that I have done foolishly in adding some short utterances of His to the prophetic statements. Wash therefore, and be now clean, and put away iniquity from your souls, as God bids you be washed in this laver, and be circumcised with the true circumcision. For we too would observe the fleshly circumcision, and the Sabbaths, and in short all the feasts, if we did not know for what reason they were enjoined you,—namely, on account of your transgressions and the hardness of your hearts. For if we patiently endure all things

---

[249] Isaiah 5:18-20.

[250] Matthew 21:13. {See Isaiah 56:7.}

[251] This and the following quotation taken promiscuously from Matthew 23 and Luke 11. {See Matthew 23:23, 27, 29: and Luke 11:52.}

[252] {See Luke 11:52, said to the lawyers.}

contrived against us by wicked men and demons, so that even amid cruelties unutterable, death and torments, we pray for mercy to those who inflict such things upon us, and do not wish to give the least retort to anyone, even as the new Lawgiver commanded us: how is it, Trypho, that we would not observe those rites which do not harm us,—I speak of fleshly circumcision, and Sabbaths, and feasts?"

Chapter XIX: *Circumcision unknown before Abraham. The law was given by Moses on account of the hardness of their hearts.*

"It is this about which we are at a loss, and with reason, because, while you endure such things, you do not observe all the other customs which we are now discussing."

"This circumcision is not, however, necessary for all men, but for you alone, in order that, as I have already said, you may suffer these things which you now justly suffer. Nor do we receive that useless baptism of cisterns, for it has nothing to do with this baptism of life. Wherefore also God has announced that you have forsaken Him, the living fountain, and digged for yourselves broken cisterns which can hold no water. Even you, who are the circumcised according to the flesh, have need of our circumcision; but we, having the latter, do not require the former. For if it were necessary, as you suppose, God would not have made Adam uncircumcised; would not have had respect to the gifts of Abel when, being uncircumcised, he offered sacrifice; and would not have been pleased with the uncircumcision of Enoch, who was not found, because God had translated him. Lot, being uncircumcised, was saved from Sodom, the angels themselves and the Lord sending him out. Noah was the beginning of our race; yet, uncircumcised, along with his children he went into the ark. Melchizedek, the priest of the Most High, was uncircumcised; to whom also Abraham, the first who received circumcision after the flesh, gave tithes, and he blessed him: after whose order God declared, by the mouth of David, that He would establish the everlasting Priest. Therefore to you alone this circumcision was necessary, in order that the people may be no people, and the nation no nation; as also Hosea,[253] one of the twelve prophets, declares. Moreover, all those righteous men already mentioned, though they kept no

[253] Hosea 1 and 2. {See Hosea 1:9.}

Sabbaths, were pleasing to God; and after them Abraham with all his descendants until Moses, under whom your nation appeared unrighteous and ungrateful to God, making a calf in the wilderness: wherefore God, accommodating Himself to that nation, enjoined them also to offer sacrifices, as if to His name, in order that you might not serve idols. Which precept, however, you have not observed; nay, you sacrificed your children to demons. And you were commanded to keep Sabbaths, that you might retain the memorial of God. For His word makes this announcement, saying, '***That ye may know that I am God who redeemed you.***'"[254]

Chapter XX: *Why choice of meats was prescribed.*

"Moreover, you were commanded to abstain from certain kinds of food, in order that you might keep God before your eyes while you ate and drank, seeing that you were prone and very ready to depart from His knowledge, as Moses also affirms: '***The people ate and drank, and rose up to play.***'[255] And again: '***Jacob ate, and was satisfied, and waxed fat; and he who was beloved kicked: he waxed fat, he grew thick, he was enlarged, and he forsook God who had made him.***'[256] For it was told you by Moses in the book of Genesis, that God granted to Noah, being a just man, to eat of every animal, but not of flesh with the blood, which is dead."[257]

And as he {Trypho} was ready to say, "as the green herbs," I anticipated him:

"Why do you not receive this statement, 'as the green herbs,' in the sense in which it was given by God, to wit, that just as God has granted the herbs for sustenance to man, even so has He given the animals for the diet of flesh? But, you say, a distinction was laid down thereafter to Noah, because we do not eat certain herbs. As you interpret it, the thing is incredible. And first I shall not occupy myself with this, though able to say and to hold that every vegetable is food, and fit to

---

[254] Ezekiel 20:12.
[255] Exodus 32:6. {See also 1 Corinthians 10:7.}
[256] Deuteronomy 32:15.
[257] *νεχριμαῖον*, or "dieth of itself;" com. reading was *ἐχριμαῖον*, which was supposed to be derived from *ἐχρίπτω*, and to mean "which ought to be cast out:" the above was suggested by H. Stephanus.

be eaten. But although we discriminate between green herbs, not eating all, we refrain from eating some, not because they are common or unclean, but because they are bitter, or deadly, or thorny. But we lay hands on and take of all herbs which are sweet, very nourishing and good, whether they are marine or land plants. Thus also God by the mouth of Moses commanded you to abstain from unclean and improper[258] and violent animals: when, moreover, though you were eating manna in the desert, and were seeing all those wondrous acts wrought for you by God, you made and worshipped the golden calf.[259] Hence He cries continually, and justly, '***They are foolish children, in whom is no faith.***'"[260]

Chapter XXI: *Sabbaths were instituted on account of the people's sins, and not for a work of righteousness.*

"Moreover, that God enjoined you to keep the Sabbath, and impose on you other precepts for a sign, as I have already said, on account of your unrighteousness, and that of your fathers,—as He declares that for the sake of the nations, lest His name be profaned among them, therefore He permitted some of you to remain alive,—these words of His can prove to you: they are narrated by Ezekiel thus:

> ***I am the Lord your God; walk in My statutes, and keep My judgments, and take no part in the customs of Egypt; and hallow My Sabbaths; and they shall be a sign between Me and you, that ye may know that I am the Lord your God. Notwithstanding ye rebelled against Me, and your children walked not in My statutes, neither kept My judgments to do them: which if a man do, he shall live in them. But they polluted My Sabbaths. And I said that I would pour out My fury upon them in the wilderness, to accomplish My anger upon them; yet I did it not; that My name might not be altogether profaned in the sight of the heathen. I led them out before their eyes, and I lifted up Mine hand unto them in the wilderness, that I would scatter them among the heathen, and***

---

[258] *ἄδιχος χαὶ παράνομος.*

[259] "The reasoning of S. Justin is not quite clear to interpreters. As we abstain from some herbs, not because they are forbidden by law, but because they are deadly; so the law of abstinence from improper and violent animals was imposed not on Noah, but on you as a yoke on account of your sins."—*Maranus.*

[260] Deuteronomy 32:6, 20. {See also Matthew 17:17.}

disperse them through the countries; because they had not executed My judgments, but had despised My statutes, and polluted My Sabbaths, and their eyes were after the devices of their fathers. Wherefore I gave them also statutes which were not good, and judgments whereby they shall not live. And I shall pollute them in their own gifts, that I may destroy all that openeth the womb, when I pass through them."[261]

Chapter XXII: *So also were sacrifices and oblations.*

"And that you may learn that it was for the sins of your own nation, and for their idolatries, and not because there was any necessity for such sacrifices, that they were likewise enjoined, listen to the manner in which He speaks of these by Amos, one of the twelve, saying:

'Woe unto you that desire the day of the Lord! to what end is this day of the Lord for you? It is darkness and not light, as when a man flees from the face of a lion, and a bear meets him; and he goes into his house, and leans his hands against the wall, and the serpent bites him. Shall not the day of the Lord be darkness and not light, even very dark, and no brightness in it? I have hated, I have despised your feast-days, and I will not smell in your solemn assemblies: wherefore, though ye offer Me your burnt-offerings and sacrifices, I will not accept them; neither will I regard the peace-offerings of your presence. Take thou away from Me the multitude of thy songs and psalms; I will not hear thine instruments. But let judgment be rolled down as water, and righteousness as an impassable torrent. Have ye offered unto Me victims and sacrifices in the wilderness, O house of Israel? saith the Lord. And have ye taken up the tabernacle of Moloch, and the star of your god Raphan, the figures which ye made for yourselves? And I will carry you away beyond Damascus, saith the Lord, whose name is the Almighty God.

Woe to them that are at ease in Zion, and trust in the mountain of Samaria: those who are named among the chiefs have plucked away the first-fruits of the nations: the house of Israel have entered for themselves. Pass all of you unto Calneh, and see; and from thence go ye unto Hamath the great, and go down thence to Gath of the strangers, the noblest of all these kingdoms, if their

[261] Ezekiel 20:19-26.

> ***boundaries are greater than your boundaries. Ye who come to the evil day, who are approaching, and who hold to false Sabbaths; who lie on beds of ivory, and are at ease upon their couches; who eat the lambs out of the flock, and the sucking calves out of the midst of the herd; who applaud at the sound of the musical instruments; they reckon them as stable, and not as fleeting, who drink wine in bowls, and anoint themselves with the chief ointments, but they are not grieved for the affliction of Joseph. Wherefore now they shall be captives, among the first of the nobles who are carried away; and the house of evil-doers shall be removed, and the neighing of horses shall be taken away from Ephraim.***[262]

And again by Jeremiah: '***Collect your flesh, and sacrifices, and eat: for concerning neither sacrifices nor libations did I command your fathers in the day in which I took them by the hand to lead them out of Egypt.***'[263] And again by David, in the forty-ninth Psalm, He thus said:

> ***The God of gods, the Lord hath spoken, and called the earth, from the rising of the sun unto the going down thereof. Out of Zion is the perfection of His beauty. God, even our God, shall come openly, and shall not keep silence. Fire shall burn before Him, and it shall be very tempestuous round about Him. He shall call to the heavens above, and to the earth, that He may judge His people. Assemble to Him His saints; those that have made a covenant with Him by sacrifices. And the heavens shall declare His righteousness, for God is judge. Hear, O My people, and I will speak to thee; O Israel, and I will testify to thee: I am God, even thy God. I will not reprove thee for thy sacrifices; thy burnt-offerings are continually before me. I will take no bullocks out of thy house, nor he-goats out of thy folds: for all the beasts of the field are Mine, the herds and the oxen on the mountains. I know all the fowls of the heavens, and the beauty of the field is Mine. If I were hungry, I would not tell thee; for the world is Mine, and the fullness thereof. Will I eat the flesh of bulls, or drink the blood of goats? Offer unto God the sacrifice of praise, and pay thy vows unto the Most High, and call upon Me in the day of trouble, and I will deliver thee, and thou shalt glorify Me. But unto the wicked God saith, What hast***

---

[262] Amos 5:18 to end, 6:1-7.

[263] Jeremiah 7:21 {and 22}.

> ***thou to do to declare My statutes, and to take My covenant into thy mouth? But thou hast hated instruction, and cast My words behind thee. When thou sawest a thief, thou consentedst with him; and hast been partaker with the adulterer. Thy mouth has framed evil, and thy tongue has enfolded deceit. Thou sittest and speakest against thy brother; thou slanderest thine own mother's son. These things hast thou done, and I kept silence; thou thoughtest that I would be like thyself in wickedness. I will reprove thee, and set thy sins in order before thine eyes. Now consider this, ye that forget God, lest He tear you in pieces, and there be none to deliver. The sacrifice of praise shall glorify Me; and there is the way in which I shall show him My salvation.***[264]

Accordingly He neither takes sacrifices from you nor commanded them at first to be offered because they are needful to Him, but because of your sins. For indeed the temple, which is called the temple in Jerusalem, He admitted to be His house or court, not as though He needed it, but in order that you, in this view of it, giving yourselves to Him, might not worship idols. And that this is so, Isaiah says: '***What house have ye built Me? saith the Lord. Heaven is My throne, and earth is My footstool.***'"[265]

Chapter XXIII: *The opinion of the Jews regarding the law does an injury to God.*

"But if we do not admit this, we shall be liable to fall into foolish opinions, as if it were not the same God who existed in the times of Enoch and all the rest, who neither were circumcised after the flesh, nor observed Sabbaths, nor any other rites, seeing that Moses enjoined such observances; or that God has not wished each race of mankind continually to perform the same righteous actions: to admit which, seems to be ridiculous and absurd. Therefore we must confess that He, who is ever the same, has commanded these and such like institutions on account of sinful men, and we must declare Him to be benevolent, foreknowing, needing nothing, righteous and good. But if this be not so, tell me, sir, what you think of those matters which we are investigating."

---

[264] Psalm 50 (in E. V.). {Psalm 50 in OSB; Psalm 49 in KJV.}
[265] Isaiah 66:1.

And when no one responded: "Wherefore, Trypho, I will proclaim to you, and to those who wish to become proselytes, the divine message which I heard from that man.[266] Do you see that the elements are not idle, and keep no Sabbaths? Remain as you were born. For if there was no need of circumcision before Abraham, or of the observance of Sabbaths, of feasts and sacrifices, before Moses; no more need is there of them now, after that, according to the will of God, Jesus Christ the Son of God has been born without sin, of a virgin sprung from the stock of Abraham. For when Abraham himself was in uncircumcision, he was justified and blessed by reason of the faith which he reposed in God, as the Scripture tells. Moreover, the Scriptures and the facts themselves compel us to admit that He received circumcision for a sign, and not for righteousness. So that it was justly recorded concerning the people, that the soul which shall not be circumcised on the eighth day shall be cut off from his family. And, furthermore, the inability of the female sex to receive fleshly circumcision, proves that this circumcision has been given for a sign, and not for a work of righteousness. For God has given likewise to women the ability to observe all things which are righteous and virtuous; but we see that the bodily form of the male has been made different from the bodily form of the female; yet we know that neither of them is righteous or unrighteous merely for this cause, but [is considered righteous] by reason of piety and righteousness."

Chapter XXIV: *The Christians' circumcision far more excellent.*

"Now, sirs," I said, "it is possible for us to show how the eighth day possessed a certain mysterious import, which the seventh day did not possess, and which was promulgated by God through these rites. But lest I appear now to diverge to other subjects, understand what I say: the blood of that circumcision is obsolete, and we trust in the blood of salvation; there is now another covenant, and another law has gone forth from Zion. Jesus Christ circumcises all who will—as was declared above—with knives of stone;[267] that they may be a righteous nation, a people keeping faith, holding to the truth, and maintaining peace.[268] Come then

---

[266] The man he met by the sea-shore.
[267] Joshua 5:2. {See also Exodus 4:25.}
[268] {Isaiah 26:2-3.}

with me, all who fear God, who wish to see the good of Jerusalem. Come, let us go to the light of the Lord; for He has liberated His people, the house of Jacob. Come, all nations; let us gather ourselves together at Jerusalem, no longer plagued by war for the sins of her people. ***'For I was manifest to them that sought Me not; I was found of them that asked not for Me;'***[269] He exclaims by Isaiah:

> ***I said, Behold Me, unto nations which were not called by My name. I have spread out My hands all the day unto a disobedient and gainsaying people, which walked in a way that was not good, but after their own sins. It is a people that provoketh Me to my face."***[270]

Chapter XXV: *The Jews boast in vain that they are sons of Abraham.*

"Those who justify themselves, and say they are sons of Abraham, shall be desirous even in a small degree to receive the inheritance along with you;[271] as the Holy Spirit, by the mouth of Isaiah, cries, speaking thus while he personates them:

> ***Return from heaven, and behold from the habitation of Thy holiness and glory. Where is Thy zeal and strength? Where is the multitude of Thy mercy? for Thou hast sustained us, O Lord. For Thou art our Father, because Abraham is ignorant of us, and Israel has not recognized us. But Thou, O Lord, our Father, deliver us: from the beginning Thy name is upon us. O Lord, why hast Thou made us to err from Thy way? and hardened our hearts, so that we do not fear Thee? Return for Thy servants' sake, the tribes of Thine inheritance, that we may inherit for a little Thy holy mountain. We were as from the beginning, when Thou didst not bear rule over us, and when Thy name was not called upon us.***
>
> ***If Thou wilt open the heavens, trembling shall seize the mountains before Thee: and they shall be melted, as wax melts before the fire; and fire shall consume the adversaries, and Thy name shall be manifest among the adversaries; the nations shall***

---

[269] Isaiah 65:1. {See also Isaiah 63:19.}
[270] Isaiah 65:1-3.
[271] Other edd. have, "with us."

be put into disorder before Thy face. When Thou shall do glorious things, trembling shall seize the mountains before Thee. From the beginning we have not heard, nor have our eyes seen a God besides Thee: and Thy works,[272] the mercy which Thou shall show to those who repent. He shall meet those who do righteousness, and they shall remember Thy ways. Behold, Thou art wroth, and we were sinning. Therefore we have erred and become all unclean, and all our righteousness is as the rags of a woman set apart: and we have faded away like leaves by reason of our iniquities; thus the wind will take us away. And there is none that calleth upon Thy name, or remembers to take hold of Thee; for Thou hast turned away Thy face from us, and hast given us up on account of our sins. And now return, O Lord, for we are all Thy people. The city of Thy holiness has become desolate. Zion has become as a wilderness, Jerusalem a curse; the house, our holiness, and the glory which our fathers blessed, has been burned with fire; and all the glorious nations[273] have fallen along with it. And in addition to these [misfortunes], O Lord, Thou hast refrained Thyself, and art silent, and hast humbled us very much."[274]

And Trypho remarked, "What is this you say? that none of us shall inherit anything on the holy mountain of God?"

Chapter XXVI: No salvation to the Jews except through Christ.

And I replied, "I do not say so; but those who have persecuted and do persecute Christ, if they do not repent, shall not inherit anything on the holy mountain. But the Gentiles, who have believed on Him, and have repented of the sins which they have committed, they shall receive the inheritance along with the patriarchs and the prophets, and the just men who are descended from Jacob, even although they neither keep the Sabbath, nor are circumcised, nor observe the feasts. Assuredly they shall receive the holy inheritance of God. For God speaks by Isaiah thus:

[272] Otto reads: "Thy works which Thou shalt do to those who wait for mercy."
[273] Some suppose the correct reading to be, "our glorious institutions have," etc., ἔθη for ἔθνη.
[274] Isaiah 63:15 to end, and 64.

> **I, the Lord God, have called Thee in righteousness, and will hold Thine hand, and will strengthen Thee; and I have given Thee for a covenant of the people, for a light of the Gentiles, to open the eyes of the blind, to bring out them that are bound from the chains, and those who sit in darkness from the prison-house.**[275]

And again:

> ***Lift up a standard***[276] ***for the people; for, lo, the Lord has made it heard unto the end of the earth. Say ye to the daughters of Zion, Behold, thy Savior has come; having His reward, and His work before His face: and He shall call it a holy nation, redeemed by the Lord. And thou shalt be called a city sought out, and not forsaken.***
>
> ***Who is this that cometh from Edom? in red garments from Bosor? This that is beautiful in apparel, going up with great strength? I speak righteousness, and the judgment of salvation. Why are Thy garments red, and Thine apparel as from the trodden wine-press? Thou art full of the trodden grape. I have trodden the wine-press all alone, and of the people there is no man with Me; and I have trampled them in fury, and crushed them to the ground, and spilled their blood on the earth. For the day of retribution has come upon them, and the year of redemption is present. And I looked, and there was none to help; and I considered, and none assisted: and My arm delivered; and My fury came on them, and I trampled them in My fury, and spilled their blood on the earth."***[277]

Chapter XXVII: *Why God taught the same things by the prophets as by Moses.*

And Trypho said, "Why do you select and quote whatever you wish from the prophetic writings, but do not refer to those which expressly command the Sabbath to be observed? For Isaiah thus speaks:

---

[275] Isaiah 42:6, 7. {See also Isaiah 9:2, 43:1; 2 Timothy 2:26.}

[276] συσσεισμον, "a shaking," is the original reading; but LXX has *σύσσημον*, a standard or signal, and this most edd. adopt.

[277] Isaiah 62:10 to end, 63:1-6. {See also Lamentations 1:15; Isaiah 34:8, 40:10; Revelation 16:6.}

> ***If thou shalt turn away thy foot from the Sabbaths, so as not to do thy pleasure on the holy day, and shalt call the Sabbaths the holy delights of thy God; if thou shalt not lift thy foot to work, and shalt not speak a word from thine own mouth; then thou shalt trust in the Lord, and He shall cause thee to go up to the good things of the land; and He shall feed thee with the inheritance of Jacob thy father: for the mouth of the Lord hath spoken it.***"[278]

And I replied, "I have passed them by, my friends, not because such prophecies were contrary to me, but because you have understood, and do understand, that although God commands you by all the prophets to do the same things which He also commanded by Moses, it was on account of the hardness of your hearts, and your ingratitude towards Him, that He continually proclaims them, in order that, even in this way, if you repented, you might please Him, and neither sacrifice your children to demons, nor be partakers with thieves, nor lovers of gifts, nor hunters after revenge, nor fail in doing judgment for orphans, nor be inattentive to the justice due to the widow, nor have your hands full of blood.

> ***For the daughters of Zion have walked with a high neck, both sporting by winking with their eyes, and sweeping along their dresses.***[279] ***For they are all gone aside,***' He exclaims, '***they are all become useless. There is none that understands, there is not so much as one. With their tongues they have practiced deceit, their throat is an open sepulcher, the poison of asps is under their lips, destruction and misery are in their paths, and the way of peace they have not known.***[280]

So that, as in the beginning, these things were enjoined you because of your wickedness, in like manner because of your steadfastness in it, or rather your increased proneness to it, by means of the same precepts He calls you to a remembrance or knowledge of it. But you are a people hard-hearted and without understanding, both blind and lame, children in whom is no faith, as He Himself says, honoring Him only with your lips, far from Him in your hearts, teaching doctrines that are your own and not

---

[278] Isaiah 58:13, 14. {See also Isaiah 56:2; Deuteronomy 32:13.}
[279] Isaiah 3:16.
[280] Various passages strung together, comp. Rom. 3:10 and foll. verses. {See also Psalm 5:9, 10:7, 14:1, 62:4.}

His. For, tell me, did God wish the priests to sin when they offer the sacrifices on the Sabbaths? or those to sin, who are circumcised and do circumcise on the Sabbaths; since He commands that on the eighth day—even though it happen to be a Sabbath—those who are born shall be always circumcised? or could not the infants be operated upon one day previous or one day subsequent to the Sabbath, if He knew that it is a sinful act upon the Sabbaths? Or why did He not teach those—who are called righteous and pleasing to Him, who lived before Moses and Abraham, who were not circumcised in their foreskin, and observed no Sabbaths—to keep these institutions?"

Chapter XXVIII: *True righteousness is obtained by Christ.*

And Trypho replied, "We heard you adducing this consideration a little ago, and we have given it attention: for, to tell the truth, it is worthy of attention; and that answer which pleases most—namely, that so it seemed good to Him—does not satisfy me. For this is ever the shift to which those have recourse who are unable to answer the question."

Then I said, "Since I bring from the Scriptures and the facts themselves both the proofs and the inculcation of them, do not delay or hesitate to put faith in me, although I am an uncircumcised man; so short a time is left you in which to become proselytes. If Christ's coming shall have anticipated you, in vain you will repent, in vain you will weep; for He will not hear you. '***Break up your fallow ground,***' Jeremiah has cried to the people, '***and sow not among thorns. Circumcise yourselves to the Lord, and circumcise the foreskin of your heart.***'[281] Do not sow, therefore, among thorns, and in untilled ground, whence you can have no fruit. Know Christ; and behold the fallow ground, good, good and fat, is in your hearts. '***For, behold, the days come, saith the Lord, that I will visit all them that are circumcised in their foreskins; Egypt, and Judah,***[282] ***and Edom, and the sons of Moab. For all the nations are uncircumcised, and all the house of Israel are uncircumcised in their hearts.***'[283] Do you see how that God does not mean this circumcision which is given for a sign? For it is of no use to the Egyptians, or the sons of Moab, or the sons of

---

[281] Jeremiah 4:3 {and 4; see also Hosea 10:12}.
[282] So in A. V., but supposed to be Idumaea.
[283] Jeremiah 9:25 f {to 26).

Edom. But though a man be a Scythian or a Persian, if he has the knowledge of God and of His Christ, and keeps the everlasting righteous decrees, he is circumcised with the good and useful circumcision, and is a friend of God, and God rejoices in his gifts and offerings. But I will lay before you, my friends, the very words of God, when He said to the people by Malachi, one of the twelve prophets,

> ***I have no pleasure in you, saith the Lord; and I shall not accept your sacrifices at your hands: for from the rising of the sun unto its setting My name shall be glorified among the Gentiles; and in every place a sacrifice is offered unto My name, even a pure sacrifice: for My name is honored among the Gentiles, saith the Lord; but ye profane it.***[284]

And by David He said, '***A people whom I have not known, served Me; at the hearing of the ear they obeyed Me.***'"[285]

Chapter XXIX: *Christ is useless to those who observe the law.*

"Let us glorify God, all nations gathered together; for He has also visited us. Let us glorify Him by the King of glory, by the Lord of hosts. For He has been gracious towards the Gentiles also; and our sacrifices He esteems more grateful than yours. What need, then, have I of circumcision, who have been witnessed to by God? What need have I of that other baptism, who have been baptized with the Holy Ghost? I think that while I mention this I would persuade even those who are possessed of scanty intelligence. For these words have neither been prepared by me, nor embellished by the art of man; but David sung them, Isaiah preached them, Zechariah proclaimed them, and Moses wrote them. Are you acquainted with them, Trypho? They are contained in your Scriptures, or rather not yours, but ours. For we believe them; but you, though you read them, do not catch the spirit that is in them. Be not offended at, or reproach us with, the bodily uncircumcision with which God has created us; and think it not strange that we drink hot water on the Sabbaths, since God directs the government of the universe on this

---

[284] Malachi 1:10, etc. {through verse 12.}
[285] Psalm 18:43 {and 44}.

day equally as on all others; and the priests, as on other days, so on this, are ordered to offer sacrifices; and there are so many righteous men who have performed none of these legal ceremonies, and yet are witnessed to by God Himself."

Chapter XXX: *Christians possess the true righteousness.*

"But impute it to your own wickedness, that God even can be accused by those who have no understanding, of not having always instructed all in the same righteous statutes. For such institutions seemed to be unreasonable and unworthy of God to many men, who had not received grace to know that your nation were called to conversion and repentance of spirit,[286] while they were in a sinful condition and laboring under spiritual disease; and that the prophecy which was announced subsequent to the death of Moses is everlasting. And this is mentioned in the Psalm,[287] my friends. And that we, who have been made wise by them, confess that the statutes of the Lord are sweeter than honey and the honey-comb, is manifest from the fact that, though threatened with death, we do not deny His name. Moreover, it is also manifest to all, that we who believe in Him pray to be kept by Him from strange, i.e., from wicked and deceitful, spirits; as the word of prophecy, personating one of those who believe in Him, figuratively declares. For we do continually beseech God by Jesus Christ to preserve us from the demons which are hostile to the worship of God, and whom we of old time served, in order that, after our conversion by Him to God, we may be blameless. For we call Him Helper and Redeemer, the power of whose name even the demons do fear; and at this day, when they are exorcised in the name of Jesus Christ, crucified under Pontius Pilate, governor of Judaea, they are overcome. And thus it is manifest to all, that His Father has given Him so great power, by virtue of which demons are subdued to His name, and to the dispensation of His suffering."

---

[286] Or, "repentance of the Father;" *πατρός* for *πνεύματος*. Maranus explains the confusion on the ground of the similarity between the contractions for the words, *πρς* and *πνς*.

[287] Psalm 19.

Chapter XXXI: *If Christ's power be now so great, how much greater at the second advent!*

"But if so great a power is shown to have followed and to be still following the dispensation of His suffering, how great shall that be which shall follow His glorious advent! For He shall come on the clouds as the Son of man, so Daniel foretold, and His angels shall come with Him. These are the words:

> ***I beheld till the thrones were set; and the Ancient of days did sit, whose garment was white as snow, and the hair of His head like the pure wool. His throne was like a fiery flame, His wheels as burning fire. A fiery stream issued and came forth from before Him. Thousand thousands ministered unto Him, and ten thousand times ten thousand stood before Him. The books were opened, and the judgment was set. I beheld then the voice of the great words which the horn speaks: and the beast was beat down, and his body destroyed, and given to the burning flame. And the rest of the beasts were taken away from their dominion, and a period of life was given to the beasts until a season and time. I saw in the vision of the night, and, behold, one like the Son of man coming with the clouds of heaven; and He came to the Ancient of days, and stood before Him. And they who stood by brought Him near; and there were given Him power and kingly honor, and all nations of the earth by their families, and all glory, serve Him. And His dominion is an everlasting dominion, which shall not be taken away; and His kingdom shall not be destroyed. And my spirit was chilled within my frame, and the visions of my head troubled me. I came near unto one of them that stood by, and inquired the precise meaning of all these things. In answer he speaks to me, and showed me the judgment of the matters: These great beasts are four kingdoms, which shall perish from the earth, and shall not receive dominion for ever, even for ever and ever. Then I wished to know exactly about the fourth beast, which destroyed all [the others] and was very terrible, its teeth of iron, and its nails of brass; which devoured, made waste, and stamped the residue with its feet: also about the ten horns upon its head, and of the one which came up, by means of which three of the former fell. And that horn had eyes, and a mouth speaking great things; and its countenance excelled the rest. And I beheld that horn waging war against the saints, and prevailing against them, until the Ancient***

of days came; and He gave judgment for the saints of the Most High. And the time came, and the saints of the Most High possessed the kingdom. And it was told me concerning the fourth beast: There shall be a fourth kingdom upon earth, which shall prevail over all these kingdoms, and shall devour the whole earth, and shall destroy and make it thoroughly waste. And the ten horns are ten kings that shall arise; and one shall arise after them;[288] *and he shall surpass the first in evil deeds, and he shall subdue three kings, and he shall speak words against the Most High, and shall overthrow the rest of the saints of the Most High, and shall expect to change the seasons and the times. And it shall be delivered into his hands for a time, and times, and half a time. And the judgment sat, and they shall take away his dominion, to consume and to destroy it unto the end. And the kingdom, and the power, and the great places of the kingdoms under the heavens, were given to the holy people of the Most High, to reign in an everlasting kingdom: and all powers shall be subject to Him, and shall obey Him. Hitherto is the end of the matter. I, Daniel, was possessed with a very great astonishment, and my speech was changed in me; yet I kept the matter in my heart."*[289]

Chapter XXXII: *Trypho objecting that Christ is described as glorious by Daniel, Justin distinguishes two advents.*

And when I had ceased, Trypho said, "These and such like Scriptures, sir, compel us to wait for Him who, as Son of man, receives from the Ancient of days the everlasting kingdom. But this so-called Christ of yours was dishonorable and inglorious, so much so that the last curse contained in the law of God fell on him, for he was crucified."

Then I replied to him, "If, sirs, it were not said by the Scriptures which I have already quoted, that His form was inglorious, and His generation not declared, and that for His death the rich would suffer death, and with His stripes we should be healed, and that He would be led away like a sheep; and if I had not explained that there would be two advents of His,—one in which He was pierced by you; a second, when you shall know Him whom you have pierced, and your tribes shall mourn, each tribe by itself, the women apart, and the men apart,—then I must

---

[288] Literally, "And the ten horns, ten kings shall arise after them."

[289] Daniel 7:9-28.

have been speaking dubious and obscure things. But now, by means of the contents of those Scriptures esteemed holy and prophetic amongst you, I attempt to prove all [that I have adduced], in the hope that some one of you may be found to be of that remnant which has been left by the grace of the Lord of Sabaoth for the eternal salvation.

In order, therefore, that the matter inquired into may be plainer to you, I will mention to you other words also spoken by the blessed David, from which you will perceive that the Lord is called the Christ by the Holy Spirit of prophecy; and that the Lord, the Father of all, has brought Him again from the earth, setting Him at His own right hand, until He makes His enemies His footstool; which indeed happens from the time that our Lord Jesus Christ ascended to heaven, after He rose again from the dead, the times now running on to their consummation; and he whom Daniel foretells would have dominion for a time, and times, and an half, is even already at the door, about to speak blasphemous and daring things against the Most High. But you, being ignorant of how long he will have dominion, hold another opinion. For you interpret the 'time' as being a hundred years. But if this is so, the man of sin must, at the shortest, reign three hundred and fifty years, in order that we may compute that which is said by the holy Daniel—'and times'—to be *two* times only.

All this I have said to you in digression, in order that you at length may be persuaded of what has been declared against you by God, that you are foolish sons; and of this, '***Therefore, behold, I will proceed to take away this people, and shall take them away; and I will strip the wise of their wisdom, and will hide the understanding of their prudent men***;'[290] and may cease to deceive yourselves and those who hear you, and may learn of us, who have been taught wisdom by the grace of Christ. The words, then, which were spoken by David, are these:

> ***The Lord said unto My Lord, Sit Thou at My right hand, until I make Thine enemies Thy footstool. The Lord shall send the rod of Thy strength out of Sion: rule Thou also in the midst of Thine enemies. With Thee shall be, in the day, the chief of Thy power, in the beauties of Thy saints. From the womb, before the morning star, have I begotten Thee. The Lord hath sworn, and will not***

[290] Isaiah 29:14. {See also Jeremiah 49:7; Habakkuk 1:5.}

repent: Thou art a priest for ever after the order of Melchizedek. The Lord is at Thy right hand: He has crushed kings in the day of His wrath: He shall judge among the heathen, He shall fill [with] the dead bodies.[291] ***He shall drink of the brook in the way; therefore shall He lift up the head."***[292]

Chapter XXXIII: *Psalm 110 is not spoken of Hezekiah. He proves that Christ was first humble, then shall be glorious.*

"And," I continued, "I am not ignorant that you venture to expound this Psalm as if it referred to king Hezekiah; but that you are mistaken, I shall prove to you from these very words forthwith. ***'The Lord hath sworn, and will not repent,'***[293] it is said; and, ***'Thou art a priest forever, after the order of Melchizedek,'***[294] with what follows and precedes. Not even you will venture to object that Hezekiah was either a priest, or is the everlasting priest of God; but that this is spoken of our Jesus, these expressions show. But your ears are shut up, and your hearts are made dull.[295] For by this statement, ***'The Lord hath sworn, and will not repent: Thou art a priest for ever, after the order of Melchizedek,'***[296] with an oath God has shown Him (on account of your unbelief) to be the High Priest after the order of Melchizedek; i.e., as Melchizedek was described by Moses as the priest of the Most High, and he was a priest of those who were in uncircumcision, and blessed the circumcised Abraham who brought him tithes, so God has shown that His everlasting Priest, called also by the Holy Spirit Lord, would be Priest of those in uncircumcision. Those too in circumcision who approach Him, that is, believing Him and seeking blessings from Him, He will both receive and bless. And that He shall be first humble as a man, and then exalted, these words at the end of the Psalm show: ***'He shall drink of the brook in the way,'***[297] and then, ***'Therefore shall He lift up the head.'"***[298]

---

[291] *πληρώσει πτώματα*; Lat. Version, *implebit ruinas*. Thirlby suggested that an omission has taken place in the mss. by the transcriber's fault.

[292] Psalm 110.

[293] {Psalm 110: 4.}

[294] {Ibid.}

[295] *πεπήρωνται*. Maranus thinks *πεπωρονται* more probable, "hardened."

[296] {Psalm 110:4.}

[297] {Psalm 110:7.}

[298] {Ibid.}

Chapter XXXIV: *Nor does Psalm 72 apply to Solomon, whose faults Christians shudder at.*

"Further, to persuade you that you have not understood anything of the Scriptures, I will remind you of another Psalm, dictated to David by the Holy Spirit, which you say refers to Solomon, who was also your king. But it refers also to our Christ. But you deceive yourselves by the ambiguous forms of speech. For where it is said, '***The law of the Lord is perfect***,'[299] you do not understand it of the law which was to be after Moses, but of the law which was given by Moses, although God declared that He would establish a new law and a new covenant. And where it has been said, '***O God, give Thy judgment to the king***,'[300] since Solomon was king, you say that the Psalm refers to him, although the words of the Psalm expressly proclaim that reference is made to the everlasting King, i.e., to Christ. For Christ is King, and Priest, and God, and Lord, and angel, and man, and captain, and stone, and a Son born, and first made subject to suffering, then returning to heaven, and again coming with glory, and He is preached as having the everlasting kingdom: so I prove from all the Scriptures. But that you may perceive what I have said, I quote the words of the Psalm; they are these:

> ***O God, give Thy judgment to the king, and Thy righteousness unto the king's son, to judge Thy people with righteousness, and Thy poor with judgment. The mountains shall take up peace to the people, and the little hills righteousness. He shall judge the poor of the people, and shall save the children of the needy, and shall abase the slanderer. He shall co-endure with the sun, and before the moon unto all generations. He shall come down like rain upon the fleece, as drops falling on the earth. In His days shall righteousness flourish, and abundance of peace until the moon be taken away. And He shall have dominion from sea to sea, and from the rivers unto the ends of the earth. Ethiopians shall fall down before Him, and His enemies shall lick the dust. The kings of Tarshish and the isles shall offer gifts; the kings of Arabia and Seba shall offer gifts; and all the kings of the earth shall worship Him, and all the nations shall serve Him: for He has delivered the poor from the man of power, and the needy that hath no helper. He***

[299] {Psalm 19:7.}

[300] {Psalm 72:1.}

> ***shall spare the poor and needy, and shall save the souls of the needy: He shall redeem their souls from usury and injustice, and His name shall be honorable before them. And He shall live, and to Him shall be given of the gold of Arabia, and they shall pray continually for Him: they shall bless Him all the day. And there shall be a foundation on the earth, it shall be exalted on the tops of the mountains: His fruit shall be on Lebanon, and they of the city shall flourish like grass of the earth. His name shall be blessed for ever. His name shall endure before the sun; and all tribes of the earth shall be blessed in Him, all nations shall call Him blessed. Blessed be the Lord, the God of Israel, who only doeth wondrous things; and blessed be His glorious name for ever, and for ever and ever; and the whole earth shall be filled with His glory. Amen, amen.***[301]

And at the close of this Psalm which I have quoted, it is written, '***The hymns of David the son of Jesse are ended.***'[302] Moreover, that Solomon was a renowned and great king, by whom the temple called that at Jerusalem was built, I know; but that none of those things mentioned in the Psalm happened to him, is evident. For neither did all kings worship him; nor did he reign to the ends of the earth; nor did his enemies, falling before him, lick the dust. Nay, also, I venture to repeat what is written in the book of Kings as committed by him, how through a woman's influence he worshipped the idols of Sidon, which those of the Gentiles who know God, the Maker of all things through Jesus the crucified, do not venture to do, but abide every torture and vengeance even to the extremity of death, rather than worship idols, or eat meat offered to idols."

Chapter XXXV: *Heretics confirm the Catholics in the faith.*

And Trypho said, "I believe, however, that many of those who say that they confess Jesus, and are called Christians, eat meats offered to idols, and declare that they are by no means injured in consequence."

And I replied, "The fact that there are such men confessing themselves to be Christians, and admitting the crucified Jesus to be both

---

[301] Psalm 72.

[302] {Psalm 72:20.}

Lord and Christ, yet not teaching His doctrines, but those of the spirits of error, causes us who are disciples of the true and pure doctrine of Jesus Christ, to be more faithful and steadfast in the hope announced by Him. For what things He predicted would take place in His name, these we do see being actually accomplished in our sight. For he said, '***Many shall come in My name, clothed outwardly in sheep's clothing, but inwardly they are ravening wolves.***'"[303] And, '***There shall be schisms and heresies.***'[304] And, '***Beware of false prophets, who shall come to you clothed outwardly in sheep's clothing, but inwardly they are ravening wolves.***'[305] And, '***Many false Christs and false apostles shall arise, and shall deceive many of the faithful.***'[306]

There are, therefore, and there were many, my friends, who, coming forward in the name of Jesus, taught both to speak and act impious and blasphemous things; and these are called by us after the name of the men from whom each doctrine and opinion had its origin. (For some in one way, others in another, teach to blaspheme the Maker of all things, and Christ, who was foretold by Him as coming, and the God of Abraham, and of Isaac, and of Jacob, with whom we have nothing in common, since we know them to be atheists, impious, unrighteous, and sinful, and confessors of Jesus in name only, instead of worshippers of Him. Yet they style themselves Christians, just as certain among the Gentiles inscribe the name of God upon the works of their own hands, and partake in nefarious and impious rites.) Some are called Marcians, and some Valentinians, and some Basilidians, and some Saturnilians, and others by other names; each called after the originator of the individual opinion, just as each one of those who consider themselves philosophers, as I said before, thinks he must bear the name of the philosophy which he follows, from the name of the father of the particular doctrine.

So that, in consequence of these events, we know that Jesus foreknew what would happen after Him, as well as in consequence of many other events which He foretold would befall those who believed on and confessed Him, the Christ. For all that we suffer, even when killed by

---

[303] Matthew 7:15.

[304] 1 Corinthians 11:19. {See also Luke 2:35.}

[305] Matthew 7:15. {See also Jeremiah 5:31, 14:14; Lamentations 2:14; Matthew 24:11; Mark 13:22; Luke 6:26; 1 John 4:1.}

[306] Matthew 24:11. {See also Matthew 24:24; Mark 13:22.}

friends, He foretold would take place; so that it is manifest no word or act of His can be found fault with. Wherefore we pray for you and for all other men who hate us; in order that you, having repented along with us, may not blaspheme Him who, by His works, by the mighty deeds even now wrought through His name, by the words He taught, by the prophecies announced concerning Him, is the blameless, and in all things irreproachable, Christ Jesus; but, believing on Him, may be saved in His second glorious advent, and may not be condemned to fire by Him."

Chapter XXXVI: *Justin proves that Christ is called Lord of Hosts.*

Then he replied, "Let these things be so as you say—namely, that it was foretold Christ would suffer, and be called a stone; and after His first appearance, in which it had been announced He would suffer, would come in glory, and be Judge finally of all, and eternal King and Priest. Now show if this man be He of whom these prophecies were made."

And I said, "As you wish, Trypho, I shall come to these proofs which you seek in the fitting place; but now you will permit me first to recount the prophecies, which I wish to do in order to prove that Christ is called both God and Lord of hosts, and Jacob, in parable by the Holy Spirit; and your interpreters, as God says, are foolish, since they say that reference is made to Solomon and not to Christ, when he bore the ark of testimony into the temple which he built. The Psalm of David is this:

> ***The earth is the Lord's, and the fullness thereof; the world, and all that dwell therein. He hath founded it upon the seas, and prepared it upon the floods. Who shall ascend into the hill of the Lord? or who shall stand in His holy place? He that is clean of hands and pure of heart: who has not received his soul in vain, and has not sworn guilefully to his neighbor: he shall receive blessing from the Lord, and mercy from God his Savior. This is the generation of them that seek the Lord, that seek the face of the God of Jacob.***[307] ***Lift up your gates, ye rulers; and be ye lift up, ye everlasting doors; and the King of glory shall come in. Who is this King of glory? The Lord strong and mighty in battle. Lift up your gates, ye rulers; and be ye lift up, ye everlasting doors; and the***

---

[307] Maranus remarks from Thirlby: "As Justin wrote a little before, 'and is called Jacob in parable,' it seems to convince us that Justin wrote, 'thy face, O Jacob.'"

> ***King of glory shall come in. Who is this King of glory? The Lord of hosts, He is the King of glory.***[308]

Accordingly, it is shown that Solomon is not the Lord of hosts; but when our Christ rose from the dead and ascended to heaven, the rulers in heaven, under appointment of God, are commanded to open the gates of heaven, that He who is King of glory may enter in, and having ascended, may sit on the right hand of the Father until He make the enemies His footstool, as has been made manifest by another Psalm. For when the rulers of heaven saw Him of uncomely and dishonored appearance, and inglorious, not recognizing Him, they inquired, '***Who is this King of glory?***'[309] And the Holy Spirit, either from the person of His Father, or from His own person, answers them, '***The Lord of hosts, He is this King of glory.***'[310] For every one will confess that not one of those who presided over the gates of the temple at Jerusalem would venture to say concerning Solomon, though he was so glorious a king, or concerning the ark of testimony, '***Who is this King of glory?***'"

Chapter XXXVII: *The same is proved from other Psalms.*

"Moreover, in the diapsalm of the forty-sixth Psalm, reference is thus made to Christ:

> ***God went up with a shout, the Lord with the sound of a trumpet. Sing ye to our God, sing ye: sing to our King, sing ye; for God is King of all the earth: sing with understanding. God has ruled over the nations. God sits upon His holy throne. The rulers of the nations were assembled along with the God of Abraham, for the strong ones of God are greatly exalted on the earth.***[311]

And in the ninety-eighth Psalm, the Holy Spirit reproaches you, and predicts Him whom you do not wish to be king to be King and Lord, both of Samuel, and of Aaron, and of Moses, and, in short, of all the others. And the words of the Psalm are these:

---

[308] Psalm 24.

[309] {Psalm 24:10.}

[310] {*Ibid*}.

[311] Psalm 47:6-10. {Begins at Psalm 47:5 ends at 47:9.}

> ***The Lord has reigned, let the nations be angry: [it is] He who sits upon the cherubim, let the earth be shaken. The Lord is great in Zion, and He is high above all the nations. Let them confess Thy great name, for it is fearful and holy, and the honor of the King loves judgment. Thou hast prepared equity; judgment and righteousness hast Thou performed in Jacob. Exalt the Lord our God, and worship the footstool of His feet; for He is holy. Moses and Aaron among His priests, and Samuel among those who call upon His name. They called (says the Scripture) on the Lord, and He heard them. In the pillar of the cloud He spake to them; for[312] they kept His testimonies, and the commandment which he gave them. O Lord our God, Thou heardest them: O God, Thou wert propitious to them, and [yet] taking vengeance on all their inventions. Exalt the Lord our God, and worship at His holy hill; for the Lord our God is holy."***[313]

Chapter XXXVIII: *It is an annoyance to the Jew that Christ is said to be adored. Justin confirms it, however, from Psalm 45.*

And Trypho said, "Sir, it were good for us if we obeyed our teachers, who laid down a law that we should have no intercourse with any of you, and that we should not have even any communication with you on these questions. For you utter many blasphemies, in that you seek to persuade us that this crucified man was with Moses and Aaron, and spoke to them in the pillar of the cloud; then that he became man, was crucified, and ascended up to heaven, and comes again to earth, and ought to be worshipped."

Then I answered, "I know that, as the word of God says, this great wisdom of God, the Maker of all things, and the Almighty, is hid from you. Wherefore, in sympathy with you, I am striving to the utmost that you may understand these matters which to you are paradoxical; but if not, that I myself may be innocent in the day of judgment. For you shall hear other words which appear still more paradoxical; but be not confounded, nay, rather remain still more zealous hearers and investigators, despising the tradition of your teachers, since they are convicted by the Holy Spirit

---

[312] "For" wanting in both Codd.

[313] Psalm 99.

of inability to perceive the truths taught by God, and of preferring to teach their own doctrines. Accordingly, in the forty-fourth [forty-fifth] Psalm, these words are in like manner referred to Christ:

> ***My heart has brought forth a good matter; I tell my works to the King. My tongue is the pen of a ready writer. Fairer in beauty than the sons of men: grace is poured forth into Thy lips: therefore hath God blessed Thee for ever. Gird Thy sword upon Thy thigh, O mighty One. Press on in Thy fairness and in Thy beauty, and prosper and reign, because of truth, and of meekness, and of righteousness: and Thy right hand shall instruct Thee marvelously. Thine arrows are sharpened, O mighty One; the people shall fall under Thee; in the heart of the enemies of the King [the arrows are fixed]. Thy throne, O God, is for ever and ever: a scepter of equity is the scepter of Thy kingdom. Thou hast loved righteousness, and hast hated iniquity; therefore thy God[314] hath anointed Thee with the oil of gladness above Thy fellows. [He hath anointed Thee] with myrrh, and oil,[315] and cassia, from Thy garments; from the ivory palaces, whereby they made Thee glad. Kings' daughters are in Thy honor. The queen stood at Thy right hand, clad in garments[316] embroidered with gold. Hearken, O daughter, and behold, and incline thine ear, and forget thy people and the house of thy father: and the King shall desire thy beauty; because He is thy Lord, they shall worship Him also. And the daughter of Tyre [shall be there] with gifts. The rich of the people shall entreat Thy face. All the glory of the King's daughter [is] within, clad in embroidered garments of needlework. The virgins that follow her shall be brought to the King; her neighbors shall be brought unto Thee: they shall be brought with joy and gladness: they shall be led into the King's shrine. Instead of thy fathers, thy sons have been born: Thou shalt appoint them rulers over all the earth. I shall remember Thy name in every generation: therefore the people shall confess Thee for ever, and for ever and ever."***[317]

---

[314] Or, "God, thy God."

[315] *σγαχτη*.

[316] Literally, "garments of gold, variegated."

[317] {Psalm 45.}

Chapter XXXIX: *The Jews hate the Christians who believe this. How great the distinction is between both!*

"Now it is not surprising," I continued, "that you hate us who hold these opinions, and convict you of a continual hardness of heart.[318] For indeed Elijah, conversing with God concerning you, speaks thus: ***'Lord, they have slain Thy prophets, and digged down Thine altars: and I am left alone, and they seek my life.'***[319] And He answers him: ***'I have still seven thousand men who have not bowed the knee to Baal.'***[320] Therefore, just as God did not inflict His anger on account of those seven thousand men, even so He has now neither yet inflicted judgment, nor does inflict it, knowing that daily some [of you] are becoming disciples in the name of Christ, and quitting the path of error; who are also receiving gifts, each as he is worthy, illumined through the name of this Christ. For one receives the spirit of understanding, another of counsel, another of strength, another of healing, another of fore-knowledge, another of teaching, and another of the fear of God."

To this Trypho said to me, "I wish you knew that you are beside yourself, talking these sentiments."

And I said to him, "Listen, O friend,[321] for I am not mad or beside myself; but it was prophesied that, after the ascent of Christ to heaven, He would deliver[322] us from error and give us gifts. The words are these: ***'He ascended up on high; He led captivity captive; He gave gifts to men.'***[323] Accordingly, we who have received gifts from Christ, who has ascended up on high, prove from the words of prophecy that you, ***'the wise in yourselves, and the men of understanding in your own eyes,'***[324] are foolish, and honor God and His Christ by lip only. But we, who are instructed in the whole truth,[325] honor Them both in acts, and in knowledge, and in heart, even unto death. But you hesitate to confess that He is Christ, as the Scriptures and the events witnessed and done in His name prove, perhaps for this reason, lest you be persecuted by the

---

318 Literally, "of a hard-hearted opinion."

319 {1 Kings 19:10, 14. See also Acts 7:52; Revelation 18:24.}

320 1 Kings 19:14, 18.

321 *ὦ οὗτος.*

322 Literally, "carry us captive."

323 Psalm 68:{18-}19. {See also Judges 5:12.}

324 Isaiah 5:21. {See also Proverbs 3:7.}

325 Contrasting either Catholics with heretics, or Christians with Jews.

rulers, who, under the influence of the wicked and deceitful spirit, the serpent, will not cease putting to death and persecuting those who confess the name of Christ until He come again, and destroy them all, and render to each his deserts."

And Trypho replied, "Now, then, render us the proof that this man who you say was crucified and ascended into heaven is the Christ of God. For you have sufficiently proved by means of the Scriptures previously quoted by you, that it is declared in the Scriptures that Christ must suffer, and come again with glory, and receive the eternal kingdom over all the nations, every kingdom being made subject to Him: now show us that this man is He."

And I replied, "It has been already proved, sirs, to those who have ears, even from the facts which have been conceded by you; but that you may not think me at a loss, and unable to give proof of what you ask, as I promised, I shall do so at a fitting place. At present, I resume the consideration of the subject which I was discussing."

Chapter XL: *Justin returns to the Mosaic laws, and proves that they were figures of the things which pertain to Christ.*

"The mystery, then, of the lamb which God enjoined to be sacrificed as the passover, was a type of Christ; with whose blood, in proportion to their faith in Him, they anoint their houses, i.e., themselves, who believe on Him. For that the creation which God created—to wit, Adam—was a house for the spirit which proceeded from God, you all can understand. And that this injunction was temporary, I prove thus.

God does not permit the lamb of the passover to be sacrificed in any other place than where His name was named; knowing that the days will come, after the suffering of Christ, when even the place in Jerusalem shall be given over to your enemies, and all the offerings, in short, shall cease; and that lamb which was commanded to be wholly roasted was a symbol of the suffering of the Cross which Christ would undergo. For the lamb,[326] which is roasted, is roasted and dressed up in the form of the Cross. For one spit is transfixed right through from the lower parts up to

[326] Some think this particularly refers to the paschal lamb, others to any lamb which is roasted.

the head, and one across the back, to which are attached the legs of the lamb.

And the two goats which were ordered to be offered during the fast, of which one was sent away as the scape [goat], and the other sacrificed, were similarly declarative of the two appearances of Christ: the first, in which the elders of your people, and the priests, having laid hands on Him and put Him to death, sent Him away as the scape [goat]; and His second appearance, because in the same place in Jerusalem you shall recognize Him whom you have dishonored, and who was an offering for all sinners willing to repent, and keeping the fast which Isaiah speaks of, loosening the terms[327] of the violent contracts, and keeping the other precepts, likewise enumerated by him, and which I have quoted,[328] which those believing in Jesus do. And further, you are aware that the offering of the two goats, which were enjoined to be sacrificed at the fast, was not permitted to take place similarly anywhere else, but only in Jerusalem."

Chapter XLI: *The oblation of fine flour was a figure of the Eucharist.*

"And the offering of fine flour, sirs," I said, "which was prescribed to be presented on behalf of those purified from leprosy, was a type of the bread of the Eucharist, the celebration of which our Lord Jesus Christ prescribed, in remembrance of the suffering which He endured on behalf of those who are purified in soul from all iniquity, in order that we may at the same time thank God for having created the world, with all things therein, for the sake of man, and for delivering us from the evil in which we were, and for utterly overthrowing[329] principalities and powers by Him who suffered according to His will. Hence God speaks by the mouth of Malachi, one of the twelve [prophets], as I said before,[330] about the sacrifices at that time presented by you:

> ***I have no pleasure in you, saith the Lord; and I will not accept your sacrifices at your hands: for, from the rising of the sun unto the going down of the same, My name has been glorified among the***

[327] Literally, "cords."
[328] Chapter XV.
[329] Literally, "overthrowing with a perfect overthrow."
[330] Chapter XXVIII.

> ***Gentiles, and in every place incense is offered to My name, and a pure offering: for My name is great among the Gentiles, saith the Lord: but ye profane it.***[331]

[So] He then speaks of those Gentiles, namely us, who in every place offer sacrifices to Him, i.e., the bread of the Eucharist, and also the cup of the Eucharist, affirming both that we glorify His name, and that you profane [it]. The command of circumcision, again, bidding [them] always circumcise the children on the eighth day, was a type of the true circumcision, by which we are circumcised from deceit and iniquity through Him who rose from the dead on the first day after the Sabbath, [namely through] our Lord Jesus Christ. For the first day after the Sabbath, remaining the first[332] of all the days, is called, however, the eighth, according to the number of all the days of the cycle, and [yet] remains the first."

Chapter XLII: *The bells on the priest's robe were a figure of the apostles.*

"Moreover, the prescription that twelve bells[333] be attached to the [robe] of the high priest, which hung down to the feet, was a symbol of the twelve apostles, who depend on the power of Christ, the eternal Priest; and through their voice it is that all the earth has been filled with the glory and grace of God and of His Christ. Wherefore David also says: '***Their sound has gone forth into all the earth, and their words to the ends of the world.***'[334] And Isaiah speaks as if he were personating the apostles, when they say to Christ that they believe not in their own report, but in the power of Him who sent them. And so he says: '***Lord, who hath believed our report? and to whom is the arm of the Lord revealed? We have preached before Him as if [He were] a child, as if a root in a dry ground.***'[335] (And what follows in order of the prophecy

---

[331] Malachi 1:10-12. {See also Malachi 1:7; Psalm 113:3.}
[332] Or, "being the first."
[333] Exodus 28:33 gives no definite number of bells. Otto presumes Justin to have confounded the bells and the gems, which were twelve in number.
[334] Psalm 19:4. {See also Romans 10:18.}
[335] Isaiah 53:1, 2. {See following footnotes. See also Isaiah 11:1.}

already quoted.[336]) But when the passage speaks as from the lips of many, '***We have preached before Him***,'[337] and adds, '***as if a child***,'[338] it signifies that the wicked shall become subject to Him, and shall obey His command, and that all shall become as one child. Such a thing as you may witness in the body: although the members are enumerated as many, all are called *one*, and are a *body*. For, indeed, a commonwealth and a church,[339] though many individuals in number, are in fact as one, called and addressed by one appellation. And in short, sirs," said I, "by enumerating all the other appointments of Moses, I can demonstrate that they were types, and symbols, and declarations of those things which would happen to Christ, of those who it was foreknown were to believe in Him, and of those things which would also be done by Christ Himself. But since what I have now enumerated appears to me to be sufficient, I revert again to the order of the discourse."[340]

Chapter XLIII: *He concludes that the law had an end in Christ, who was born of the Virgin.*

"As, then, circumcision began with Abraham, and the Sabbath and sacrifices and offerings and feasts with Moses, and it has been proved they were enjoined on account of the hardness of your people's heart, so it was necessary, in accordance with the Father's will, that they should have an end in Him who was born of a virgin, of the family of Abraham and tribe of Judah, and of David; in Christ the Son of God, who was proclaimed as about to come to all the world, to be the everlasting law and the everlasting covenant, even as the aforementioned prophecies show. And we, who have approached God through Him, have received not carnal, but spiritual circumcision, which Enoch and those like him observed. And we have received it through baptism, since we were sinners, by God's mercy; and all men may equally obtain it.

---

[336] Chapter XIII.

[337] {This is not always found in other Bible translations. In the OSB it is rendered "We proclaim his presence."}

[338] {This is the rendering in the OSB. However, the phrase rendered here "as a child" is usually rendered as a "young" or "tender" "branch" or "plant" in other Bible translations. }

[339] *ἐχχλησία*. Lat. vers. has *conventus*.

[340] Literally, "to the discourse in order."

But since the mystery of His birth now demands our attention, I shall speak of it. Isaiah then asserted in regard to the generation of Christ, that it could not be declared by man, in words already quoted:[341] '***Who shall declare His generation? for His life is taken from the earth: for the transgressions of my people was He led***[342] ***to death.***'[343] The Spirit of prophecy thus affirmed that the generation of Him who was to die, that we sinful men might be healed by His stripes, was such as could not be declared.

Furthermore, that the men who believe in Him may possess the knowledge of the manner in which He came into the world,[344] the Spirit of prophecy by the same Isaiah foretold how it would happen thus:

> ***And the Lord spoke again to Ahaz, saying, Ask for thyself a sign from the Lord thy God, in the depth, or in the height. And Ahaz said, I will not ask, neither will I tempt the Lord. And Isaiah said, Hear then, O house of David; Is it a small thing for you to contend with men, and how do you contend with the Lord? Therefore the Lord Himself will give you a sign. Behold, the virgin shall conceive, and shall bear a son, and his name shall be called Immanuel. Butter and honey shall he eat, before he knows or prefers the evil, and chooses out the good;***[345] ***for before the child knows good or ill, he rejects evil***[346] ***by choosing out the good. For before the child knows how to call father or mother, he shall receive the power of Damascus and the spoil of Samaria in presence of the king of Assyria. And the land shall be forsaken,***[347] ***which thou shalt with difficulty endure in consequence of the presence of its two kings.***[348] ***But God shall bring on thee, and on thy people, and on the house***

---

[341] Chapter XIII.
[342] Or, "was I led."
[343] Isaiah 53:8.
[344] Literally, "He was in the world, being born."
[345] See Chapter LXVI.
[346] Literally, "disobeys evil" (*ἀπειθεῖ πονηρά*). Conjectural: *ἀπωθεῖ*; and *ἀπειθεῖ πονηρία*.
[347] The mss. of Justin read, "shall be taken:" *χαταληφθήσεται*. This is plainly a mistake for *χαταλειφθήσεται*; but whether the mistake is Justin's or the transcribers', it would be difficult to say, as Thirlby remarks.
[348] The rendering of this is doubtful: literally, "from the face of the two kings," and the words might go with "shall be forsaken."

> ***of thy father, days which have not yet come upon thee since the day in which Ephraim took away from Judah the king of Assyria.***[349]

Now it is evident to all, that in the race of Abraham according to the flesh no one has been born of a virgin, or is said to have been born [of a virgin], save this our Christ. But since you and your teachers venture to affirm that in the prophecy of Isaiah it is not said, '***Behold, the virgin shall conceive***,'[350] but, '*Behold, the young woman shall conceive, and bear a son*;'[351] and [since] you explain the prophecy as if [it referred] to Hezekiah, who was your king, I shall endeavor to discuss shortly this point in opposition to you, and to show that reference is made to Him who is acknowledged by us as Christ."

Chapter XLIV: *The Jews in vain promise themselves salvation, which cannot be obtained except through Christ.*

"For thus, so far as you are concerned, I shall be found in all respects innocent, if I strive earnestly to persuade you by bringing forward demonstrations. But if you remain hard-hearted, or weak in [forming] a resolution, on account of death, which is the lot of the Christians, and are unwilling to assent to the truth, you shall appear as the authors of your own [evils]. And you deceive yourselves while you fancy that, because you are the seed of Abraham after the flesh, therefore you shall fully inherit the good things announced to be bestowed by God through Christ. For no one, not even of them,[352] has anything to look for, but only those who in mind are assimilated to the faith of Abraham, and who have recognized all the mysteries: for I say,[353]

---

[349] Isaiah 7:10-17 with Isaiah 8:4 inserted. The last clause may also be translated, "in which He took away from Judah Ephraim, even the king of Assyria."

[350] {Isaiah 7:14.}

[351] {Italics added. This is not bolded by this editor because it is not consistent with the revealed Scripture, which is Saint Justin's point, as the Jews have substituted for "***the virgin***" the phrase "the *young woman*" (emphases added).}

[352] I.e., of Abraham's seed.

[353] Justin distinguishes between such essential acts as related to God's worship and the establishment of righteousness, and such ceremonial observances as had a mere temporary significance. The recognition of this distinction he alleges to be necessary to salvation: necessary in this sense, that justification must be placed not on the latter, but

that some injunctions were laid on you in reference to the worship of God and practice of righteousness; but some injunctions and acts were likewise mentioned in reference to the mystery of Christ, on account of[354] the hardness of your people's hearts. And that this is so, God makes known in Ezekiel, [when] He said concerning it: ***'If Noah and Jacob[355] and Daniel should beg either sons or daughters, the request would not be granted them.'***[356] And in Isaiah, of the very same matter He spake thus: ***'The Lord God said, they shall both go forth and look on the members [of the bodies] of the men that have transgressed. For their worm shall not die, and their fire shall not be quenched, and they shall be a gazing-stock to all flesh.'***[357] So that it becomes you to eradicate this hope from your souls, and hasten to know in what way forgiveness of sins, and a hope of inheriting the promised good things, shall be yours. But there is no other [way] than this,—to become acquainted with this Christ, to be washed in the fountain[358] spoken of by Isaiah for the remission of sins; and for the rest, to live sinless lives."

Chapter XLV: *Those who were righteous before and under the law shall be saved by Christ.*

And Trypho said, "If I seem to interrupt these matters, which you say must be investigated, yet the question which I mean to put is urgent. Suffer me first."

And I replied, "Ask whatever you please, as it occurs to you; and I shall endeavor, after questions and answers, to resume and complete the discourse."

Then he said, "Tell me, then, shall those who lived according to the law given by Moses, live in the same manner with Jacob, Enoch, and Noah, in the resurrection of the dead, or not?"

---

on the former; and without such recognition, a Jew would, as Justin says, rest his hopes on his noble descent from Abraham.

[354] More probably, "or an account of."

[355] In Bible, "Job;" Maranus prefers "Jacob," and thinks the mention of his name very suitable to disprove the arrogant claims of Jacob's posterity.

[356] Ezekiel 14:20. {See also Ezekiel 14:14, 16.}

[357] Isaiah 66:24.

[358] Some refer this to Christ's baptism. See Cyprian, *Adv. Jud.* 24.—*Otto.*

I replied to him, "When I quoted, sir, the words spoken by Ezekiel, that '***even if Noah and Daniel and Jacob were to beg sons and daughters, the request would not be granted them***,'[359] but that each one, that is to say, shall be saved by his own righteousness, I said also, that those who regulated their lives by the law of Moses would in like manner be saved. For what in the law of Moses is naturally good, and pious, and righteous, and has been prescribed to be done by those who obey it;[360] and what was appointed to be performed by reason of the hardness of the people's hearts; was similarly recorded, and done also by those who were under the law.

Since those who did that which is universally, naturally, and eternally good are pleasing to God, they shall be saved through this Christ in the resurrection equally with those righteous men who were before them, namely Noah, and Enoch, and Jacob, and whoever else there be, along with those who have known[361] this Christ, Son of God, who was before the morning star and the moon, and submitted to become incarnate, and be born of this Virgin of the family of David, in order that, by this dispensation, the serpent that sinned from the beginning, and the angels like him, may be destroyed, and that death may be contemned, and forever quit, at the second coming of the Christ Himself, those who believe in Him and live acceptably,—and be no more: when some are sent to be punished unceasingly into judgment and condemnation of fire; but others shall exist in freedom from suffering, from corruption, and from grief, and in immortality."

Chapter XLVI: *Trypho asks whether a man who keeps the law even now will be saved. Justin proves that it contributes nothing to righteousness.*

"But if some, even now, wish to live in the observance of the institutions given by Moses, and yet believe in this Jesus who was crucified, recognizing Him to be the Christ of God, and that it is given to Him to be absolute Judge of all, and that His is the everlasting kingdom, can they also be saved?" he inquired of me.

---

[359] Ezekiel 14:20. {See also Ezekiel 14:14, 16.}

[360] It, i.e., the law, or "what is the law," etc.

[361] Those who live after Christ.

And I replied, "Let us consider that also together, whether one may now observe all the Mosaic institutions."

And he answered, "No. For we know that, as you said, it is not possible either anywhere to sacrifice the lamb of the passover, or to offer the goats ordered for the fast; or, in short, [to present] all the other offerings."

And I said, "Tell [me] then yourself, I pray, some things which can be observed; for you will be persuaded that, though a man does not keep or has not performed the eternal[362] decrees, he may assuredly be saved."

Then he replied, "To keep the Sabbath, to be circumcised, to observe months, and to be washed if you touch anything prohibited by Moses, or after sexual intercourse."

And I said, "Do you think that Abraham, Isaac, Jacob, Noah, and Job, and all the rest before or after them equally righteous, also Sarah the wife of Abraham, Rebekah the wife of Isaac, Rachel the wife of Jacob, and Leah, and all the rest of them, until the mother of Moses the faithful servant, who observed none of these [statutes], will be saved?"

And Trypho answered, "Were not Abraham and his descendants circumcised?"

And I said, "I know that Abraham and his descendants were circumcised. The reason why circumcision was given to them I stated at length in what has gone before; and if what has been said does not convince you[363], let us again search into the matter. But you are aware that, up to Moses, no one in fact who was righteous observed any of these rites at all of which we are talking, or received one commandment to observe, except that of circumcision, which began from Abraham."

And he replied, "We know it, and admit that they are saved."

Then I returned answer, "You perceive that God by Moses laid all such ordinances upon you on account of the hardness of your people's hearts, in order that, by the large number of them, you might keep God continually, and in every action, before your eyes, and never begin to act unjustly or impiously. For He enjoined you to place around you [a fringe] of purple dye,[364] in order that you might not forget God; and He

---

[362] "Eternal," i.e., as the Jew thinks.

[363] Literally, "put you out of countenance."

[364] Numbers 15:38. {OSB and KJV have the color blue.}

commanded you to wear a phylactery,[365] certain characters, which indeed we consider holy, being engraved on very thin parchment; and by these means stirring you up[366] to retain a constant remembrance of God: at the same time, however, convincing you, that in your hearts you have not even a faint remembrance of God's worship. Yet not even so were you dissuaded from idolatry: for in the times of Elijah, when [God] recounted the number of those who had not bowed the knee to Baal, He said the number was seven thousand; and in Isaiah He rebukes you for having sacrificed your children to idols. But we, because we refuse to sacrifice to those to whom we were of old accustomed to sacrifice, undergo extreme penalties, and rejoice in death,—believing that God will raise us up by His Christ, and will make us incorruptible, and undisturbed, and immortal; and we know that the ordinances imposed by reason of the hardness of your people's hearts, contribute nothing to the performance of righteousness and of piety."

Chapter XLVII: *Justin communicates with Christians who observe the law. Not a few Catholics do otherwise.*

And Trypho again inquired, "But if someone, knowing that this is so, after he recognizes that this man is Christ, and has believed in and obeys Him, wishes, however, to observe these [institutions], will he be saved?"

I said, "In my opinion, Trypho, such an one will be saved, if he does not strive in every way to persuade other men,—I mean those Gentiles who have been circumcised from error by Christ, to observe the same things as himself, telling them that they will not be saved unless they do so. This you did yourself at the commencement of the discourse, when you declared that I would not be saved unless I observe these institutions."

Then he replied, "Why then have you said, 'In my opinion, such an one will be saved,' unless there are some[367] who affirm that such will not be saved?"

---

[365] Deuteronomy 6:6. {Correctly, 6:8. KJV has, "And thou shalt bind them for a sign upon thine hand, and they shall be as frontlets between thine eyes."}

[366] Literally, "importuning."

[367] Or, "Are there not some," etc.

"There are such people, Trypho," I answered; "and these do not venture to have any intercourse with or to extend hospitality to such persons; but I do not agree with them. But if some, through weak-mindedness, wish to observe such institutions as were given by Moses, from which they expect some virtue, but which we believe were appointed by reason of the hardness of the people's hearts, along with their hope in this Christ, and [wish to perform] the eternal and natural acts of righteousness and piety, yet choose to live with the Christians and the faithful, as I said before, not inducing them either to be circumcised like themselves, or to keep the Sabbath, or to observe any other such ceremonies, then I hold that we ought to join ourselves to such, and associate with them in all things as kinsmen and brethren. But if, Trypho," I continued, "some of your race, who say they believe in this Christ, compel those Gentiles who believe in this Christ to live in all respects according to the law given by Moses, or choose not to associate so intimately with them, I in like manner do not approve of them. But I believe that even those, who have been persuaded by them to observe the legal dispensation along with their confession of God in Christ, shall probably be saved. And I hold, further, that such as have confessed and known this man to be Christ, yet who have gone back from some cause to the legal dispensation, and have denied that this man is Christ, and have repented not before death, shall by no means be saved.

Further, I hold that those of the seed of Abraham who live according to the law, and do not believe in this Christ before death, shall likewise not be saved, and especially those who have anathematized and do anathematize this very Christ in the synagogues, and everything by which they might obtain salvation and escape the vengeance of fire.[368] For the goodness and the loving-kindness of God, and His boundless riches, hold righteous and sinless the man who, as Ezekiel[369] tells, repents of sins; and reckons sinful, unrighteous, and impious the man who fails away from piety and righteousness to unrighteousness and ungodliness.

---

[368] The text seems to be corrupt. Otto reads: "Do anathematize those who put their trust in this very Christ so as to obtain salvation," etc.

[369] Ezekiel 33:11-20.

Wherefore also our Lord Jesus Christ said, '*In whatsoever things I shall take you, in these I shall judge you*.'"[370]

Chapter XLVIII: *Before the divinity of Christ is proved, Trypho demands that it be settled that He is Christ.*

And Trypho said, "We have heard what you think of these matters. Resume the discourse where you left off, and bring it to an end. For some of it appears to me to be paradoxical, and wholly incapable of proof. For when you say that this Christ existed as God before the ages, then that He submitted to be born and become man, yet that He is not man of man, this [assertion] appears to me to be not merely paradoxical, but also foolish."

And I replied to this, "I know that the statement does appear to be paradoxical, especially to those of your race, who are ever unwilling to understand or to perform the [requirements] of God, but [ready to perform] those of your teachers, as God Himself declares.[371] Now assuredly, Trypho," I continued, "[the proof] that this man[372] is the Christ of God does not fail, though I be unable to prove that He existed formerly as Son of the Maker of all things, being God, and was born a man by the Virgin. But since I have certainly proved that this man is the Christ of God, whoever He be, even if I do not prove that He pre-existed, and submitted to be born a man of like passions with us, having a body, according to the Father's will; in this last matter alone is it just to say that I have erred, and not to deny that He is the Christ, though it should appear that He was born man of men, and [nothing more] is proved [than this], that He has become Christ by election. For there are some, my friends," I said, "of our race,[373] who admit that He is Christ, while holding Him to be man of men; with whom I do not agree, nor would I,[374] even

---

[370] Grabius thinks this taken from the Gospel according to the Hebrews. It is not in the New or Old Testament. {For this reason, this editor does not put this text in bold.}

[371] Comp. Isaiah 29:13. {See also Ezekiel 33:31; Mark 7:6.}

[372] Or, "such a man."

[373] Some read, "of your race," referring to the *Ebionites*. Maranus believes the reference is to the Ebionites., and supports in a long note the reading "our," inasmuch as Justin would be more likely to associate these Ebionites with Christians than with Jews, even though they were heretics.

[374] Langus translates: "Nor would, indeed, many who are of the same opinion as myself say so."

though most of those who have [now] the same opinions as myself should say so; since we were enjoined by Christ Himself to put no faith in human doctrines, but in those proclaimed by the blessed prophets and taught by Himself."

Chapter XLIX: *To those who object that Elijah has not yet come, he replies that he is the precursor of the first advent.*

And Trypho said, "Those who affirm him to have been a man, and to have been anointed by election, and then to have become Christ, appear to me to speak more plausibly than you who hold those opinions which you express. For we all expect that Christ will be a man [born] of men, and that Elijah when he comes will anoint him. But if this man appear to be Christ, he must certainly be known as man [born] of men; but from the circumstance that Elijah has not yet come, I infer that this man is not He [the Christ]."

Then I inquired of him, "Does not Scripture, in the book of Zechariah,[375] say that Elijah shall come before the great and terrible day of the Lord?"

And he answered, "Certainly."

"If therefore Scripture compels you to admit that two advents of Christ were predicted to take place,—one in which He would appear suffering, and dishonored, and without comeliness; but the other in which He would come glorious and Judge of all, as has been made manifest in many of the fore-cited passages,—shall we not suppose that the word of God has proclaimed that Elijah shall be the precursor of the great and terrible day, that is, of His second advent?"

"Certainly," he answered.

"And, accordingly, our Lord in His teaching," I continued, "proclaimed that this very thing would take place, saying that Elijah would also come. And we know that this shall take place when our Lord Jesus Christ shall come in glory from heaven; whose first manifestation the Spirit of God who was in Elijah preceded as herald in [the person of] John, a prophet among your nation; after whom no other prophet appeared among you. He cried, as he sat by the river Jordan:

---

[375] Malachi 4:5. {Saint Justin attributes this to Zechariah, but it is from Malachi.}

> ***'I baptize you with water to repentance; but He that is stronger than I shall come, whose shoes I am not worthy to bear: He shall baptize you with the Holy Ghost and with fire: whose fan is in His hand, and He will thoroughly purge His floor, and will gather the wheat into the barn; but the chaff He will burn up with unquenchable fire.'***[376]

And this very prophet your king Herod had shut up in prison; and when his birth-day was celebrated, and the niece[377] of the same Herod by her dancing had pleased him, he told her to ask whatever she pleased. Then the mother of the maiden instigated her to ask the head of John, who was in prison; and having asked it, [Herod] sent and ordered the head of John to be brought in on a charger. Wherefore also our Christ said, [when He was] on earth, to those who were affirming that Elijah must come before Christ: ***'Elijah shall come, and restore all things; but I say unto you, that Elijah has already come, and they knew him not, but have done to him whatsoever they chose.'***[378] And it is written, ***'Then the disciples understood that He spake to them about John the Baptist.'***"[379]

And Trypho said, "This statement also seems to me paradoxical; namely, that the prophetic Spirit of God, who was in Elijah, was also in John."

To this I replied, "Do you not think that the same thing happened in the case of Joshua the son of Nave (Nun), who succeeded to the command of the people after Moses, when Moses was commanded to lay his hands on Joshua, and God said to him, ***'I will take of the spirit which is in thee, and put it on him***?'"[380]

And he said, "Certainly."

"As therefore," I say, "while Moses was still among men, God took of the spirit which was in Moses and put it on Joshua, even so God was able to cause [the spirit] of Elijah to come upon John; in order that, as Christ at His first coming appeared inglorious, even so the first coming

---

[376] Matthew 3:11, 12.
[377] Literally, "cousin."
[378] Matthew 17:{11-}12.
[379] {Matthew 17:13.}
[380] Numbers 11:17, spoken of the seventy elders. Justin confuses what is said here with Numbers 27:18 and Deuteronomy 34:9.

of the spirit, which remained always pure in Elijah[381] like that of Christ, might be perceived to be inglorious. For the Lord said He would wage war against Amalek with concealed hand; and you will not deny that Amalek fell. But if it is said that only in the glorious advent of Christ war will be waged with Amalek, how great will the fulfillment[382] of Scripture be which says, '***God will wage war against Amalek with concealed hand***!'[383] You can perceive that the concealed power of God was in Christ the crucified, before whom demons, and all the principalities and powers of the earth, tremble."

Chapter L: *It is proved from Isaiah that John the Baptist is the precursor of Christ.*

And Trypho said, "You seem to me to have come out of a great conflict with many persons about all the points we have been searching into, and therefore quite ready to return answers to all questions put to you. Answer me then, first, how you can show that there is another God besides the Maker of all things; and then you will show, [further], that He submitted to be born of the Virgin."

I replied, "Give me permission first of all to quote certain passages from the prophecy of Isaiah, which refer to the office of forerunner discharged by John the Baptist and prophet before this our Lord Jesus Christ."

"I grant it," said he.

Then I said, "Isaiah thus foretold John's forerunning: '***And Hezekiah said to Isaiah, Good is the word of the Lord which He spake: Let there be peace and righteousness in my days.***'[384] And,

> ***Encourage the people; ye priests, speak to the heart of Jerusalem, and encourage her, because her humiliation is accomplished. Her sin is annulled; for she has received of the Lord's hand double for her sins. A voice of one crying in the wilderness, Prepare the ways of the Lord; make straight the paths of our God. Every valley shall***

---

[381] The meaning is, that no division of person took place. Elijah remained the same after as before his spirit was shed on John.

[382] Literally, "fruit."

[383] {Compare Exodus 17:9-13.}

[384] Isaiah 39:8.

be filled up, and every mountain and hill shall be brought low: and the crooked shall be made straight, and the rough way shall be plain ways; and the glory of the Lord shall be seen, and all flesh shall see the salvation of God: for the Lord hath spoken it. A voice of one saying, Cry; and I said, What shall I cry? All flesh is grass, and all the glory of man as the flower of grass. The grass has withered, and the flower of it has fallen away; but the word of the Lord endureth for ever. Thou that bringest good tidings to Zion, go up to the high mountain; thou that bringest good tidings to Jerusalem, lift up thy voice with strength. Lift ye up, be not afraid; tell the cities of Judah, Behold your God! Behold, the Lord comes with strength, and [His] arm comes with authority. Behold, His reward is with Him, and His work before Him. As a shepherd He will tend His flock, and will gather the lambs with [His] arm, and cheer on her that is with young. Who has measured the water with [his] hand, and the heaven with a span, and all the earth with [his] fist? Who has weighed the mountains, and [put] the valleys into a balance? Who has known the mind of the Lord? And who has been His counselor, and who shall advise Him? Or with whom did He take counsel, and he instructed Him? Or who showed Him judgment? Or who made Him to know the way of understanding? All the nations are reckoned as a drop of a bucket, and as a turning of a balance, and shall be reckoned as spittle. But Lebanon is not sufficient to burn, nor the beasts sufficient for a burnt-offering; and all the nations are considered nothing, and for nothing."[385]

Chapter LI: *It is proved that Isaiah's prophecy has been fulfilled.*

And when I ceased, Trypho said, "All the words of the prophecy you repeat, sir, are ambiguous, and have no force in proving what you wish to prove."

Then I answered, "If the prophets had not ceased, so that there were no more in your nation, Trypho, after this John, it is evident that what I say in reference to Jesus Christ might be regarded perhaps as ambiguous. But if John came first calling on men to repent, and Christ, while [John] still sat by the river Jordan, having come, put an end to his prophesying and baptizing, and preached also Himself, saying that the

[385] Isaiah 40:1-17.

kingdom of heaven is at hand, and that He must suffer many things from the scribes and Pharisees, and be crucified, and on the third day rise again, and would appear again in Jerusalem, and would again eat and drink with His disciples; and foretold that in the interval between His [first and second] advent, as I previously said,[386] priests and false prophets would arise in His name, which things do actually appear; then how can they be ambiguous, when you may be persuaded by the facts? Moreover, He referred to the fact that there would be no longer in your nation any prophet, and to the fact that men recognized how that the New Testament, which God formerly announced [His intention of] promulgating, was then present, i.e., Christ Himself; and in the following terms: ***'The law and the prophets were until John the Baptist; from that time the kingdom of heaven suffereth violence, and the violent take it by force. And if you can[387] receive it, he is Elijah, who was to come. He that hath ears to hear, let him hear.'"***[388]

Chapter LII: *Jacob predicted two advents of Christ.*

"And it was prophesied by Jacob the patriarch that there would be two advents of Christ, and that in the first He would suffer, and that after He came there would be neither prophet nor king in your nation (I proceeded), and that the nations who believed in the suffering Christ would look for His future appearance. And for this reason the Holy Spirit had uttered these truths in a parable, and obscurely: for," I added, "it is said,

> ***Judah, thy brethren have praised thee: thy hands [shall be] on the neck of thine enemies; the sons of thy father shall worship thee. Judah is a lion's whelp; from the germ, my son, thou art sprung up. Reclining, he lay down like a lion, and like [a lion's] whelp: who shall raise him up? A ruler shall not depart from Judah, or a leader from his thighs, until that which is laid up in store for him shall come; and he shall be the desire of nations, binding his foal to the vine, and the foal of his ass to the tendril of the vine. He shall***

---

[386] Chapter XXV.

[387] "Are willing."

[388] Matthew 11:12-15. {See Luke 16:16; see also Matthew 13:9; Revelation 2:7; and Malachi 4:6 for the end of the prophets.}

> ***wash his garments in wine, and his vesture in the blood of the grape. His eyes shall be bright with[389] wine, and his teeth white like milk.***[390]

Moreover, that in your nation there never failed either prophet or ruler, from the time when they began until the time when this Jesus Christ appeared and suffered, you will not venture shamelessly to assert, nor can you prove it. For though you affirm that Herod, after[391] whose [reign] He suffered, was an Ashkelonite, nevertheless you admit that there was a high priest in your nation; so that you then had one who presented offerings according to the law of Moses, and observed the other legal ceremonies; also [you had] prophets in succession until John, (even then, too, when your nation was carried captive to Babylon, when your land was ravaged by war, and the sacred vessels carried off); there never failed to be a prophet among you, who was lord, and leader, and ruler of your nation. For the Spirit which was in the prophets anointed your kings, and established them. But after the manifestation and death of our Jesus Christ in your nation, there was and is nowhere any prophet: nay, further, you ceased to exist under your own king, your land was laid waste, and forsaken like a lodge in a vineyard; and the statement of Scripture, in the mouth of Jacob, '***And He shall be the desire of nations***,'[392] meant symbolically His two advents, and that the nations would believe in Him; which facts you may now at length discern. For those out of all the nations who are pious and righteous through the faith of Christ, look for His future appearance."

Chapter LIII: *Jacob predicted that Christ would ride on an ass, and Zechariah confirms it.*

"And that expression, '***binding his foal to the vine, and the ass's foal to the vine tendril***,'[393] was a declaring beforehand both of the works wrought by Him at His first advent, and also of that belief in Him which

---

[389] Or, "in comparison of."
[390] Genesis 49:8-12.
[391] *ἀφ' οὗ*; many translated "under whom," as if *ἐφ' ου*. This would be erroneous. Conjectured also *ἔφυγε* for *ἔπαθεν*.
[392] {Cf. Haggai 2:7.}
[393] {Genesis 49:11.}

the nations would repose. For they were like an unharnessed foal, which was not bearing a yoke on its neck, until this Christ came, and sent His disciples to instruct them; and they bore the yoke of His word, and yielded the neck to endure all [hardships], for the sake of the good things promised by Himself, and expected by them. And truly our Lord Jesus Christ, when He intended to go into Jerusalem, requested His disciples to bring Him a certain ass, along with its foal, which was bound in an entrance of a village called Bethphage; and having seated Himself on it, He entered into Jerusalem. And as this was done by Him in the manner in which it was prophesied in precise terms that it would be done by the Christ, and as the fulfillment was recognized, it became a clear proof that He was the Christ.

And though all this happened and is proved from Scripture, you are still hard-hearted. Nay, it was prophesied by Zechariah, one of the twelve [prophets], that such would take place, in the following words: '***Rejoice greatly, daughter of Zion; shout, and declare, daughter of Jerusalem; behold, thy King shall come to thee, righteous, bringing salvation, meek, and lowly, riding on an ass, and the foal of an ass.***'[394] Now, that the Spirit of prophecy, as well as the patriarch Jacob, mentioned both an ass and its foal, which would be used by Him; and, further, that He, as I previously said, requested His disciples to bring both beasts; [this fact] was a prediction that you of the synagogue, along with the Gentiles, would believe in Him. For as the unharnessed colt was a symbol of the Gentiles even so the harnessed ass was a symbol of your nation. For you possess the law which was imposed [upon you] by the prophets.

Moreover, the prophet Zechariah foretold that this same Christ would be smitten, and His disciples scattered: which also took place. For after His crucifixion, the disciples that accompanied Him were dispersed, until He rose from the dead, and persuaded them that so it had been prophesied concerning Him, that He would suffer; and being thus persuaded, they went into all the world, and taught these truths. Hence also we are strong in His faith and doctrine, since we have [this our] persuasion both from the prophets, and from those who throughout the world are seen to be worshippers of God in the name of that crucified One. The following is said, too, by Zechariah: '***O sword, rise up against***

[394] Zechariah 9:9.

My Shepherd, and against the man of My people, saith the Lord of hosts. Smite the Shepherd, and His flock shall be scattered.'"[395]

Chapter LIV: *What the blood of the grape signifies.*

"And that expression which was committed to writing[396] by Moses, and prophesied by the patriarch Jacob, namely, '***He shall wash His garments with wine, and His vesture with the blood of the grape,***'[397] signified that He would wash those that believe in Him with His own blood. For the Holy Spirit called those who receive remission of sins through Him, His garments; amongst whom He is always present in power, but will be manifestly present at His second coming. That the Scripture mentions the blood of the grape has been evidently designed, because Christ derives blood not from the seed of man, but from the power of God. For as God, and not man, has produced the blood of the vine, so also [the Scripture] has predicted that the blood of Christ would be not of the seed of man, but of the power of God. But this prophecy, sirs, which I repeated, proves that Christ is not man of men, begotten in the ordinary course of humanity."

Chapter LV: *Trypho asks that Christ be proved God, but without metaphor. Justin promises to do so.*

And Trypho answered, "We shall remember this your exposition, if you strengthen [your solution of] this difficulty by other arguments: but now resume the discourse, and show us that the Spirit of prophecy admits another God besides the Maker of all things, taking care not to speak of the sun and moon, which, it is written,[398] God has given to the nations to worship as gods; and oftentimes the prophets, employing[399] this manner of speech, say that '***thy God is a God of gods, and a Lord of lords,***'[400] adding frequently, '***the great and strong and terrible [God].***'[401]

[395] Zechariah 13:7.
[396] Literally, "inquired into."
[397] {Genesis 49:11.}
[398] Deuteronomy 4:19, an apparent misinterpretation of the passage.
[399] "Or, misusing."
[400] {Deuteronomy 10:17; Daniel 2:47.}
[401] {Deuteronomy 10:17.}

For such expressions are used, not as if they really were gods, but because the Scripture is teaching us that the true God, who made all things, is Lord alone of those who are reputed gods and lords. And in order that the Holy Spirit may convince [us] of this, He said by the holy David, '***The gods of the nations, reputed gods, are idols of demons, and not gods***;'[402] and He denounces a curse on those who worship them."

And I replied, "I would not bring forward these proofs, Trypho, by which I am aware those who worship these [idols] and such like are condemned, but such [proofs] as no one could find any objection to. They will appear strange to you, although you read them every day; so that even from this fact[403] we understand that, because of your wickedness, God has withheld from you the ability to discern the wisdom of His Scriptures; yet [there are] some exceptions, to whom, according to the grace of His long-suffering, as Isaiah said, He has left a seed of[404] salvation, lest your race be utterly destroyed, like Sodom and Gomorrah. Pay attention, therefore, to what I shall record out of the holy Scriptures, which[405] do not need to be expounded, but only listened to."

Chapter LVI: *God who appeared to Moses is distinguished from God the Father.*

"Moses, then, the blessed and faithful servant of God, declares that He who appeared to Abraham under the oak in Mamre is God, sent with the two angels in His company to judge Sodom by Another who remains ever in the supercelestial places, invisible to all men, holding personal intercourse with none, whom we believe to be Maker and Father of all things; for he speaks thus:

> ***God appeared to him under the oak in Mamre, as he sat at his tent-door at noontide. And lifting up his eyes, he saw, and behold, three men stood before him; and when he saw them, he ran to***

---

[402] Psalm 96:5. {This verse is not so rendered in all Bible translations. Compare OSB with KJV.}

[403] Com. reading "you;" evidently wrong.

[404] Literally "for."

[405] Two constructions, "which" referring either to Scripture as whole, or to what he records from them. Last more probable.

> ***meet them from the door of his tent; and he bowed himself toward the ground, and said;"***[406]

(and so on;)[407] "***Abraham got up early in the morning to the place where he stood before the Lord: and he looked toward Sodom and Gomorrah, and toward the adjacent country, and beheld, and, lo, a flame went up from the earth, like the smoke of a furnace.'"***[408]

And when I had made an end of quoting these words, I asked them if they had understood them.

And they said they had understood them, but that the passages adduced brought forward no proof that there is any other God or Lord, or that the Holy Spirit says so, besides the Maker of all things.

Then I replied, "I shall attempt to persuade you, since you have understood the Scriptures, [of the truth] of what I say, that there is, and that there is said to be, another God and Lord subject to[409] the Maker of all things; who is also called an Angel, because He announces to men whatsoever the Maker of all things—above whom there is no other God—wishes to announce to them." And quoting once more the previous passage, I asked Trypho, "Do you think that God appeared to Abraham under the oak in Mamre, as the Scripture asserts?"

He said, "Assuredly."

"Was He one of those three," I said, "whom Abraham saw, and whom the Holy Spirit of prophecy describes as men?"

He said, "No; but God appeared to him, before the vision of the three. Then those three whom the Scripture calls men, were angels; two of them sent to destroy Sodom, and one to announce the joyful tidings to Sarah, that she would bear a son; for which cause he was sent, and having accomplished his errand, went away."[410]

"How then," said I, "does the one of the three, who was in the tent, and who said, '***I shall return to thee hereafter, and Sarah shall have a son,***'[411] appear to have returned when Sarah had begotten a son, and to

---

[406] Genesis 18:1,2.

[407] Genesis 19:27, 28; "and so on" inserted probably not by Justin, but by some copyist, as is evident from succeeding words.

[408] {Genesis 19:27-28.}

[409] Some, "besides;" but probably as above.

[410] Or, "going away, departed."

[411] Genesis 18:10.

be there declared, by the prophetic word, God? But that you may clearly discern what I say, listen to the words expressly employed by Moses; they are these:

> ***And Sarah saw the son of Hagar the Egyptian bond-woman, whom she bore to Abraham, sporting with Isaac her son, and said to Abraham, Cast out this bond-woman and her son; for the son of this bond-woman shall not share the inheritance of my son Isaac. And the matter seemed very grievous in Abraham's sight, because of his son. But God said to Abraham, Let it not be grievous in thy sight because of the son, and because of the bond-woman. In all that Sarah hath said unto thee, hearken to her voice; for in Isaac shall thy seed be called.***[412]

Have you perceived, then, that He who said under the oak that He would return, since He knew it would be necessary to advise Abraham to do what Sarah wished him, came back as it is written; and is God, as the words declare, when they so speak: '***God said to Abraham, Let it not be grievous in thy sight because of the son, and because of the bond-woman***?'"[413] I inquired.

And Trypho said, "Certainly; but you have not proved from this that there is another God besides Him who appeared to Abraham, and who also appeared to the other patriarchs and prophets. You have proved, however, that we were wrong in believing that the three who were in the tent with Abraham were all angels."

I replied again, "If I could not have proved to you from the Scriptures that one of those three is God, and is called Angel,[414] because, as I already said, He brings messages to those to whom God the Maker of all things wishes [messages to be brought], then in regard to Him who appeared to Abraham on earth in human form in like manner as the two angels who came with Him, and who was God even before the creation of

---

[412] Genesis 21:9-12.

[413] {Genesis 21:12.}

[414] Or, "Messenger." In the various passages in which Justin assigns the reason for Christ being called angel or messenger, Justin uses also the verb *ἄγγελος* to convey message, announce. The similarity between *ἄγγελος* and *ἀγγέλλω* cannot be retained in English, and therefore the point of Justin's remarks is lost to the English reader.

the world, it were reasonable for you to entertain the same belief as is entertained by the whole of your nation."

"Assuredly," he said, "for up to this moment this has been our belief."

Then I replied, "Reverting to the Scriptures, I shall endeavor to persuade you, that He who is said to have appeared to Abraham, and to Jacob, and to Moses, and who is called God, is distinct from Him who made all things,—numerically, I mean, not [distinct] in will. For I affirm that He has never at any time done anything which He who made the world—above whom there is no other God—has not wished Him both to do and to engage Himself with."

And Trypho said, "Prove now that this is the case, that we also may agree with you. For we do not understand you to affirm that He has done or said anything contrary to the will of the Maker of all things."

Then I said, "The Scripture just quoted by me will make this plain to you. It is thus: ***'The sun was risen on the earth, and Lot entered into Segor (Zoar); and the Lord rained on Sodom sulfur and fire from the Lord out of heaven, and overthrew these cities and all the neighborhood.'***"[415]

Then the fourth of those who had remained with Trypho said, "It[416] must therefore necessarily be said that one of the two angels who went to Sodom, and is named by Moses in the Scripture Lord, is different from Him who also is God and appeared to Abraham."

"It is not on this ground solely," I said, "that it must be admitted absolutely that some other one is called Lord by the Holy Spirit besides Him who is considered Maker of all things; not solely [for what is said] by Moses, but also [for what is said] by David. For there is written by him: ***'The Lord says to my Lord, Sit on My right hand, until I make Thine enemies Thy footstool,'***[417] as I have already quoted. And again, in other words: ***'Thy throne, O God, is for ever and ever. A scepter of equity is the scepter of Thy kingdom: Thou hast loved righteousness and hated iniquity: therefore God, even Thy God, hath anointed Thee with the oil of gladness above Thy fellows.'***[418] If, therefore, you assert that the Holy

[415] Genesis 19:23 {-25}.

[416] Or, "We must of necessity think that, besides the one of the two angels who came down to Sodom, and whom the Scripture by Moses calls Lord, God Himself appeared to Abraham."

[417] Psalm 110:1.

[418] Psalm 45:6, 7.

Spirit calls some other one God and Lord, besides the Father of all things and His Christ, answer me; for I undertake to prove to you from Scriptures themselves, that He whom the Scripture calls Lord is not one of the two angels that went to Sodom, but He who was with them, and is called God, that appeared to Abraham."

And Trypho said, "Prove this; for, as you see, the day advances, and we are not prepared for such perilous replies; since never yet have we heard any man investigating, or searching into, or proving these matters; nor would we have tolerated your conversation, had you not referred everything to the Scriptures: for you are very zealous in adducing proofs from them; and you are of opinion that there is no God above the Maker of all things."

Then I replied, "You are aware, then, that the Scripture says, ***'And the Lord said to Abraham, Why did Sarah laugh, saying, Shall I truly conceive? for I am old. Is anything impossible with God? At the time appointed shall I return to thee according to the time of life, and Sarah shall have a son.'***[419] And after a little interval: ***'And the men rose up from thence, and looked towards Sodom and Gomorrah; and Abraham went with them, to bring them on the way. And the Lord said, I will not conceal from Abraham, my servant, what I do.'***[420] And again, after a little, it thus says:

> ***The Lord said, The cry of Sodom and Gomorrah is great,***[421] ***and their sins are very grievous. I will go down now, and see whether they have done altogether according to their cry which has come unto me; and if not, that I may know. And the men turned away thence, and went to Sodom. But Abraham was standing before the Lord; and Abraham drew near, and said, Wilt Thou destroy the righteous with the wicked?"***[422]

(and so on,[423] for I do not think fit to write over again the same words, having written them all before, but shall of necessity give those by which I established the proof to Trypho and his companions. Then I proceeded to

[419] Genesis 18:13, 14. {See also Matthew 3:9.}
[420] Genesis 18:16, 17. {See also Psalm 25:14; John 15:15. Cf. Acts 20:27}
[421] Literally, "is multiplied."
[422] Genesis 18:20-23.
[423] Comp. {previous note to Chapter LVI}.

what follows, in which these words are recorded:) "'***And the Lord went His way as soon as He had left communing with Abraham; and [Abraham] went to his place. And there came two angels to Sodom at even. And Lot sat in the gate of Sodom;***'[424] and what follows until, '***But the men put forth their hands, and pulled Lot into the house to them, and shut to the door of the house;***'[425] and what follows till,

> ***And the angels laid hold on his hand, and on the hand of his wife, and on the hands of his daughters, the Lord being merciful to him. And it came to pass, when they had brought them forth abroad, that they said, Save, save thy life. Look not behind thee, nor stay in all the neighborhood; escape to the mountain, lest thou be taken along with [them]. And Lot said to them, I beseech [Thee], O Lord, since Thy servant hath found grace in Thy sight, and Thou hast magnified Thy righteousness, which Thou showest towards me in saving my life; but I cannot escape to the mountain, lest evil overtake me, and I die. Behold, this city is near to flee unto, and it is small: there I shall be safe, since it is small; and any soul shall live. And He said to him, Behold, I have accepted thee***[426] ***also in this matter, so as not to destroy the city for which thou hast spoken. Make haste to save thyself there; for I shall not do anything till thou be come thither. Therefore he called the name of the city Segor (Zoar). The sun was risen upon the earth; and Lot entered into Segor (Zoar). And the Lord rained on Sodom and Gomorrah sulfur and fire from the Lord out of heaven; and He overthrew these cities, and all the neighborhood.***"[427]

And after another pause I added: "And now have you not perceived, my friends, that one of the three, who is both God and Lord, and ministers to Him who is in the heavens, is Lord of the two angels? For when [the angels] proceeded to Sodom, He remained behind, and communed with Abraham in the words recorded by Moses; and when He departed after the conversation, Abraham went back to his place. And when he came [to Sodom], the two angels no longer conversed with Lot, but Himself, as the Scripture makes evident; and He is the Lord who received commission

---

[424] Genesis 18:33, 19:1.

[425] Genesis 19:10.

[426] Literally, "I have admired the face."

[427] Genesis 19:16-25.

from the Lord who [remains] in the heavens, i.e., the Maker of all things, to inflict upon Sodom and Gomorrah the [judgments] which the Scripture describes in these terms: '***The Lord rained down upon Sodom and Gomorrah sulfur and fire from the Lord out of heaven.***'"[428]

Chapter LVII: *The Jew objects, why is He said to have eaten, if He be God? Answer of Justin.*

Then Trypho said when I was silent, "That Scripture compels us to admit this, is manifest; but there is a matter about which we are deservedly at a loss—namely, about what was said to the effect that [the Lord] ate what was prepared and placed before him by Abraham; and you would admit this."

I answered, "It is written that they ate; and if we believe[429] that it is said the three ate, and not the two alone—who were really angels, and are nourished in the heavens, as is evident to us, even though they are not nourished by food similar to that which mortals use—(for, concerning the sustenance of manna which supported your fathers in the desert, Scripture speaks thus, that they ate angels' food): [if we believe that three ate], then I would say that the Scripture which affirms they ate bears the same meaning as when we would say about fire that it has devoured all things; yet it is not certainly understood that they ate, masticating with teeth and jaws. So that not even here should we be at a loss about anything, if we are acquainted even slightly with figurative modes of expression, and able to rise above them."

And Trypho said, "It is possible that [the question] about the mode of eating may be thus explained: [the mode, that is to say,] in which it is written, they took and ate what had been prepared by Abraham: so that you may now proceed to explain to us how this God who appeared to Abraham, and is minister to God the Maker of all things, being born of the Virgin, became man, of like passions with all, as you said previously."

Then I replied, "Permit me first, Trypho, to collect some other proofs on this head, so that you, by the large number of them, may be persuaded of [the truth of] it, and thereafter I shall explain what you ask."

---

[428] {Genesis 19:24.}

[429] Literally, "hear."

And he said, "Do as seems good to you; for I shall be thoroughly pleased."

Chapter LVIII: *The same is proved from the visions which appeared to Jacob.*

Then I continued, "I purpose to quote to you Scriptures, not that I am anxious to make merely an artful display of words; for I possess no such faculty, but God's grace alone has been granted to me to the understanding of His Scriptures, of which grace I exhort all to become partakers freely and bounteously, in order that they may not, through want of it,[430] incur condemnation in the judgment which God the Maker of all things shall hold through my Lord Jesus Christ."

And Trypho said, "What you do is worthy of the worship of God; but you appear to me to feign ignorance when you say that you do not possess a store of artful words."

I again replied, "Be it so, since you think so; yet I am persuaded that I speak the truth.[431] But give me your attention, that I may now rather adduce the remaining proofs."

"Proceed," said he.

And I continued: "It is again written by Moses, my brethren, that He who is called God and appeared to the patriarchs is called both Angel and Lord, in order that from this you may understand Him to be minister to the Father of all things, as you have already admitted, and may remain firm, persuaded by additional arguments. The word of God, therefore, [recorded] by Moses, when referring to Jacob the grandson of Abraham, speaks thus:

> ***And it came to pass, when the sheep conceived, that I saw them with my eyes in the dream: And, behold, the he-goats and the rams which leaped upon the sheep and she-goats were spotted with white, and speckled and sprinkled with a dun color. And the Angel of God said to me in the dream, Jacob, Jacob. And I said, What is it, Lord? And He said, Lift up thine eyes, and see that the he-goats and rams leaping on the sheep and she-goats are spotted with white, speckled, and sprinkled with a dun color. For I have***

[430] Literally, "for this sake."
[431] Or, "speak otherwise."

> ***seen what Laban doeth unto thee. I am the God who appeared to thee in Bethel,[432] where thou anointedst a pillar and vowedst a vow unto Me. Now therefore arise, and get thee out of this land, and depart to the land of thy birth, and I shall be with thee.[433]***

And again, in other words, speaking of the same Jacob, it thus says:

> ***And having risen up that night, he took the two wives, and the two women-servants, and his eleven children, and passed over the ford Jabbok; and he took them and went over the brook, and sent over all his belongings. But Jacob was left behind alone, and an Angel[434] wrestled with him until morning. And He saw that He is not prevailing against him, and He touched the broad part of his thigh; and the broad part of Jacob's thigh grew stiff while he wrestled with Him. And He said, Let Me go, for the day breaketh. But he said, I will not let Thee go, except Thou bless me. And He said to him, What is thy name? And he said, Jacob. And He said, Thy name shall be called no more Jacob, but Israel shall be thy name; for thou hast prevailed with God, and with men shalt be powerful. And Jacob asked Him, and said, Tell me Thy name. But He said, Why dost thou ask after My name? And He blessed him there. And Jacob called the name of that place Peniel,[435] for I saw God face to face, and my soul rejoiced.[436]***

And again, in other terms, referring to the same Jacob, it says the following:

> ***And Jacob came to Luz, in the land of Canaan, which is Bethel, he and all the people that were with him. And there he built an altar, and called the name of that place Bethel; for there God appeared to him when he fled from the face of his brother Esau. And Deborah, Rebekah's nurse, died, and was buried beneath Bethel under an oak: and Jacob called the name of it The Oak of Sorrow. And God appeared again to Jacob in Luz, when he came out from Mesopotamia in Syria, and He blessed him. And God said to him,***

---

[432] Literally, "in the place of God."
[433] Genesis 31:10-13.
[434] Some read, "a man."
[435] Literally, "the face of God."
[436] Genesis 32:22-30.

> ***Thy name shall be no more called Jacob, but Israel shall be thy name.***[437]

He is called God, and He is and shall be God." And when all had agreed on these grounds, I continued: "Moreover, I consider it necessary to repeat to you the words which narrate how He who is both Angel and God and Lord, and who appeared as a man to Abraham, and who wrestled in human form with Jacob, was seen by him when he fled from his brother Esau. They are as follows:

> ***And Jacob went out from the well of the oath,***[438] ***and went toward Charran.***[439] ***And he lighted on a spot, and slept there, for the sun was set; and he gathered of the stones of the place, and put them under his head. And he slept in that place; and he dreamed, and, behold, a ladder was set up on the earth, whose top reached to heaven; and the angels of God ascended and descended upon it. And the Lord stood***[440] ***above it, and He said, I am the Lord, the God of Abraham thy father, and of Isaac; be not afraid: the land whereon thou liest, to thee will I give it, and to thy seed; and thy seed shall be as the dust of the earth, and shall be extended to the west, and south, and north, and east: and in thee, and in thy seed, shall all families of the earth be blessed. And, behold, I am with thee, keeping thee in every way wherein thou goest, and will bring thee again into this land; for I will not leave thee, until I have done all that I have spoken to thee of. And Jacob awaked out of his sleep, and said, Surely the Lord is in this place, and I knew it not. And he was afraid, and said, How dreadful is this place! this is none other than the house of God, and this is the gate of heaven. And Jacob rose up in the morning, and took the stone which he had placed under his head, and he set it up for a pillar, and poured oil upon the top of it; and Jacob called the name of the place The House of God, and the name of the city formerly was Ulammaus."***[441]

---

[437] Genesis 35:6-10.
[438] Or, "Beersheba."
[439] So LXX and N.T.; Heb, "Haran."
[440] Literally, "was set up."
[441] Genesis 28:10-19.

Chapter LIX: *God distinct from the Father conversed with Moses.*

When I had spoken these words, I continued: "Permit me, further, to show you from the book of Exodus how this same One, who is both Angel, and God, and Lord, and man, and who appeared in human form to Abraham and Isaac,[442] appeared in a flame of fire from the bush, and conversed with Moses."

And after they said they would listen cheerfully, patiently, and eagerly, I went on: "These words are in the book which bears the title of Exodus: '***And after many days the king of Egypt died, and the children of Israel groaned by reason of the works***;'[443] and so on until,

> ***Go and gather the elders of Israel, and thou shalt say unto them, The Lord God of your fathers, the God of Abraham, the God of Isaac, and the God of Jacob, hath appeared to me, saying, I am surely beholding you, and the things which have befallen you in Egypt.***"[444]

In addition to these words, I went on: "Have you perceived, sirs, that this very God whom Moses speaks of as an Angel that talked to him in the flame of fire, declares to Moses that He is the God of Abraham, of Isaac, and of Jacob?"

Chapter LX: *Opinions of the Jews with regard to Him who appeared in the bush.*

Then Trypho said, "We do not perceive this from the passage quoted by you, but [only this], that it was an angel who appeared in the flame of fire, but God who conversed with Moses; so that there were really two persons in company with each other, an angel and God, that appeared in that vision."

I again replied, "Even if this were so, my friends, that an angel and God were together in the vision seen by Moses, yet, as has already been proved to you by the passages previously quoted, it will not be the

---

[442] Some conjecture "Jacob," others insert "Jacob" after "Isaac." {See OSB Genesis 26:2, where it says, "Then the Lord appeared to him," referring to Isaac. KJV (same). See also Genesis 26:24 (also referring to Isaac)}.

[443] Exodus 2:23.

[444] Exodus 3:16.

Creator of all things that is the God that said to Moses that He was the God of Abraham, and the God of Isaac, and the God of Jacob, but it will be He who has been proved to you to have appeared to Abraham, ministering to the will of the Maker of all things, and likewise carrying into execution His counsel in the judgment of Sodom; so that, even though it be as you say, that there were two—an angel and God—he who has but the smallest intelligence will not venture to assert that the Maker and Father of all things, having left all supercelestial matters, was visible on a little portion of the earth."

And Trypho said, "Since it has been previously proved that He who is called God and Lord, and appeared to Abraham, received from the Lord, who is in the heavens, that which He inflicted on the land of Sodom, even although an angel had accompanied the God who appeared to Moses, we shall perceive that the God who communed with Moses from the bush was not the Maker of all things, but He who has been shown to have manifested Himself to Abraham and to Isaac and to Jacob; who also is called and is perceived to be the Angel of God the Maker of all things, because He publishes to men the commands of the Father and Maker of all things."

And I replied, "Now assuredly, Trypho, I shall show that, in the vision of Moses, this same One alone who is called an Angel, and who is God, appeared to and communed with Moses. For the Scripture says thus:

> ***The Angel of the Lord appeared to him in a flame of fire from the bush; and he sees that the bush burns with fire, but the bush was not consumed. And Moses said, I will turn aside and see this great sight, for the bush is not burnt. And when the Lord saw that he is turning aside to behold, the Lord called to him out of the bush.***[445]

In the same manner, therefore, in which the Scripture calls Him who appeared to Jacob in the dream an Angel, then [says] that the same Angel who appeared in the dream spoke to him,[446] saying, '***I am the God that appeared to thee when thou didst flee from the face of Esau thy***

---

[445] Exodus 3:2-4.

[446] Genesis 35:7.

brother;'[447] and [again] says that, in the judgment which befell Sodom in the days of Abraham, the Lord had inflicted the punishment[448] of the Lord who [dwells] in the heavens;—even so here, the Scripture, in announcing that the Angel of the Lord appeared to Moses, and in afterwards declaring him to be Lord and God, speaks of the same One, whom it declares by the many testimonies already quoted to be minister to God, who is above the world, above whom there is no other [God]."

Chapter LXI: *Wisdom is begotten of the Father, as fire from fire.*

"I shall give you another testimony, my friends," said I, "from the Scriptures, that God begat before all creatures a Beginning,[449] [who was] a certain rational power [proceeding] from Himself, who is called by the Holy Spirit, now the Glory of the Lord, now the Son, again Wisdom, again an Angel, then God, and then Lord and Logos; and on another occasion He calls Himself Captain, when He appeared in human form to Joshua the son of Nave (Nun). For He can be called by all those names, since He ministers to the Father's will, and since He was begotten of the Father by an act of will;[450] just as we see[451] happening among ourselves: for when we give out some word, we beget the word; yet not by abscission, so as to lessen the word[452] [which remains] in us, when we give it out: and just as we see also happening in the case of a fire, which is not lessened when it has kindled [another], but remains the same; and that which has been kindled by it likewise appears to exist by itself, not diminishing that from which it was kindled. The Word of Wisdom, who is Himself this God begotten of the Father of all things, and Word, and Wisdom, and Power, and the Glory of the Begetter, will bear evidence to me, when He speaks by Solomon the following:

---

[447] {Genesis 35:7.}

[448] Literally, "judgment."

[449] Or, "in the beginning, before all creatures."

[450] The act of will or volition is on the part of the Father.

[451] Or, "Do we not see," etc.

[452] The word λόγος, translated "word," means both the thinking power or reason which proclaims ideas and the expression of these ideas. And Justin passes here from the one meaning to the other. When we utter a thought, the utterance of it does not diminish the power of the thought in us, though in one sense the thought has gone away from us.

> ***If I shall declare to you what happens daily, I shall call to mind events from everlasting, and review them. The Lord made me the beginning of His ways for His works. From everlasting He established me in the beginning, before He had made the earth, and before He had made the deeps, before the springs of the waters had issued forth, before the mountains had been established. Before all the hills He begets me. God made the country, and the desert, and the highest inhabited places under the sky. When He made ready the heavens, I was along with Him, and when He set up His throne on the winds: when He made the high clouds strong, and the springs of the deep safe, when He made the foundations of the earth, I was with Him arranging. I was that in which He rejoiced; daily and at all times I delighted in His countenance, because He delighted in the finishing of the habitable world, and delighted in the sons of men. Now, therefore, O son, hear me. Blessed is the man who shall listen to me, and the mortal who shall keep my ways, watching[453] daily at my doors, observing the posts of my ingoings. For my outgoings are the outgoings of life, and [my] will has been prepared by the Lord. But they who sin against me, trespass against their own souls; and they who hate me love death.***"[454]

Chapter LXII: *The words "Let Us make man" agree with the testimony of Proverbs.*

"And the same sentiment was expressed, my friends, by the word of God [written] by Moses, when it indicated to us, with regard to Him whom it has pointed out,[455] that God speaks in the creation of man with the very same design, in the following words:

> ***Let Us make man after our image and likeness. And let them have dominion over the fish of the sea, and over the fowl of the heaven,***

---

[453] The mss. of Justin read "sleeping," but this is regarded as the mistake of some careless transcriber.

[454] Proverbs 8:21 ff {thru verse 36}.

[455] Justin, since he is of opinion that the Word is the beginning of the universe, thinks that by these words, "in the beginning," Moses indicated the Word, like many other writers. Hence also he says in *Ap*. i. 23, that Moses declares the Word "to be begotten first by God." If this explanation does not satisfy, read, "with regard to Him whom I have pointed out" (Maranus).

> ***and over the cattle, and over all the earth, and over all the creeping things that creep on the earth. And God created man: after the image of God did He create him; male and female created He them. And God blessed them, and said, Increase and multiply, and fill the earth, and have power over it.***[456]

And that you may not change the [force of the] words just quoted, and repeat what your teachers assert,—either that God said to Himself, '***Let Us make***,'[457] just as we, when about to do something, oftentimes say to ourselves, 'Let us make;'[458] or that God spoke to the elements, to wit, the earth and other similar substances of which we believe man was formed, '***Let Us make***,'—I shall quote again the words narrated by Moses himself, from which we can indisputably learn that [God] conversed with someone who was numerically distinct from Himself, and also a rational Being. These are the words: '***And God said, Behold, Adam has become as one of Us, to know good and evil.***'[459] In saying, therefore, '***as one of Us***,' [Moses] has declared that [there is a certain] number of persons associated with one another, and that they are at least two. For I would not say that the dogma of that heresy[460] which is said to be among you[461] is true, or that the teachers of it can prove that [God] spoke to angels, or that the human frame was the workmanship of angels. But this Offspring, which was truly brought forth from the Father, was with the Father before all the creatures, and the Father communed with Him; even as the Scripture by Solomon has made clear, that He whom Solomon calls Wisdom, was begotten as a Beginning before all His creatures and as

---

[456] Genesis 1:26, 28 {actually 1:26-28).

[457] {Genesis 1:26.}

[458] {Here, Saint Justin's intimation seems to be: Might we, when we utter such words, be subconsciously acknowledging that we as individuals act with the grace of God, with our Lord by our side even, and not that we act alone completely of our own accord?}

[459] Genesis 3:22.

[460] Heresy or sect.

[461] Or, "among us." Maranus pronounces against this latter reading for the following reason: (1.) The Jews had their own heresies which supplied many things to the Christian heresies, especially to Meander and Saturnius. (2.) The sect which Justin here refutes was of opinion that God spoke to angels. But those angels, as Meander and Saturnius invented, "exhorted themselves, saying, Let us make," etc. (3.) The expression *διδάσχαλοι* suits the rabbis well. So Justin frequently calls them. (4.) Those teachers seem for no other cause to have put the words in the angels' mouths, than to eradicate the testimony by which they proved divine persons.

Offspring by God, who has also declared this same thing in the revelation made by Joshua the son of Nave (Nun). Listen, therefore, to the following from the book of Joshua, that what I say may become manifest to you; it is this:

> ***And it came to pass, when Joshua was near Jericho, he lifted up his eyes, and sees a man standing over against him. And Joshua approached to Him, and said, Art thou for us, or for our adversaries? And He said to him, I am Captain of the Lord's host: now have I come. And Joshua fell on his face on the ground, and said to Him, Lord, what commandest Thou Thy servant? And the Lord's Captain says to Joshua, Loose the shoes off thy feet; for the place whereon thou standest is holy ground.***
>
> ***And Jericho was shut up and fortified, and no one went out of it. And the Lord said to Joshua, Behold, I give into thine hand Jericho, and its king, [and] its mighty men."***[462]

Chapter LXIII: *It is proved that this God was incarnate.*

And Trypho said, "This point has been proved to me forcibly, and by many arguments, my friend. It remains, then, to prove that He submitted to become man by the Virgin, according to the will of His Father; and to be crucified, and to die. Prove also clearly, that after this He rose again and ascended to heaven."

I answered, "This, too, has been already demonstrated by me in the previously quoted words of the prophecies, my friends; which, by recalling and expounding for your sakes, I shall endeavor to lead you to agree with me also about this matter. The passage, then, which Isaiah records, '***Who shall declare His generation? for His life is taken away from the earth,***'[463]—does it not appear to you to refer to One who, not having descent from men, was said to be delivered over to death by God for the transgressions of the people?—of whose blood, Moses (as I mentioned before), when speaking in parable, said, that He would wash His garments in the blood of the grape; since His blood did not spring from the seed of man, but from the will of God. And then, what is said by David, '***In the splendors of Thy holiness have I begotten Thee from the***

[462] Joshua 5:13 ad fin., and 6:1, 2.
[463] Isaiah 53:8.

womb, before the morning star. The Lord hath sworn, and will not repent, Thou art a priest forever, after the order of Melchizedek,'[464]—does this not declare to you[465] that [He was] from of old,[466] and that the God and Father of all things intended Him to be begotten by a human womb? And speaking in other words, which also have been already quoted, [he says]:

> ***Thy throne, O God, is for ever and ever: a scepter of rectitude is the scepter of Thy kingdom. Thou hast loved righteousness, and hast hated iniquity: therefore God, even thy God, hath anointed Thee with the oil of gladness above Thy fellows. [He hath anointed Thee] with myrrh, and oil, and cassia from Thy garments, from the ivory palaces, whereby they made Thee glad. Kings' daughters are in Thy honor. The queen stood at Thy right hand, clad in garments embroidered with gold.***[467] ***Hearken, O daughter, and behold, and incline thine ear, and forget thy people and the house of thy father; and the King shall desire thy beauty: because He is thy Lord, and thou shalt worship Him.***[468]

Therefore these words testify explicitly that He is witnessed to by Him who established these things,[469] as deserving to be worshipped, as God and as Christ. Moreover, that the word of God speaks to those who believe in Him as being one soul, and one synagogue, and one church, as to a daughter; that it thus addresses the church which has sprung from His name and partakes of His name (for we are all called Christians), is distinctly proclaimed in like manner in the following words, which teach us also to forget [our] old ancestral customs, when they speak thus:[470] ***'Hearken, O daughter, and behold, and incline thine ear; forget thy people and the house of thy father, and the King shall desire thy beauty: because He is thy Lord, and thou shalt worship Him.'"***[471]

---

[464] Psalm 110:3, 4.
[465] Or, "to us."
[466] *ἄνωθεν*; in Latin vers. *antiquitus*, which Maranus prefers.
[467] Literally, "garments of gold, variegated."
[468] Psalm 45:6-11.
[469] The incarnation, etc.
[470] "Being so" literally.
[471] {Psalm 45:10-11.}

Chapter LXIV: *Justin adduces other proofs to the Jew, who denies that he needs this Christ.*

Here Trypho said, "Let Him be recognized as Lord and Christ and God, as the Scriptures declare, by you of the Gentiles, who have from His name been all called Christians; but we who are servants of God that made this same [Christ], do not require to confess or worship Him."

To this I replied, "If I were to be quarrelsome and light-minded like you, Trypho, I would no longer continue to converse with you, since you are prepared not to understand what has been said, but only to return some captious answer;[472] but now, since I fear the judgment of God, I do not state an untimely opinion concerning any one of your nation, as to whether or not some of them may be saved by the grace of the Lord of Sabaoth. Therefore, although you act wrongfully, I shall continue to reply to any proposition you shall bring forward, and to any contradiction which you make; and, in fact, I do the very same to all men of every nation, who wish to examine along with me, or make inquiry at me, regarding this subject. Accordingly, if you had bestowed attention on the Scriptures previously quoted by me, you would already have understood, that those who are saved of your own nation are saved through this [Man], and partake of His lot; and you would not certainly have asked me about this matter. I shall again repeat the words of David previously quoted by me, and beg of you to comprehend them, and not to act wrongfully, and stir each other up to give merely some contradiction. The words which David speaks, then, are these:

> ***The Lord has reigned; let the nations be angry: [it is] He who sits upon the cherubim; let the earth be shaken. The Lord is great in Zion; and He is high above all the nations. Let them confess Thy great name, for it is fearful and holy; and the honor of the king loves judgment. Thou hast prepared equity; judgment and righteousness hast Thou performed in Jacob. Exalt the Lord our God, and worship the footstool of His feet; for He is holy. Moses and Aaron among His priests, and Samuel among them that call upon His name; they called on the Lord, and He heard them. In the pillar of the cloud He spake to them; for they kept His testimonies and His commandments which He gave them.***[473]

---

[472] Literally, "but only sharpen yourselves to say something."

[473] Psalm 99:1-7.

And from the other words of David, also previously quoted, which you foolishly affirm refer to Solomon, [because] inscribed for Solomon, it can be proved that they do not refer to Solomon, and that this [Christ] existed before the sun, and that those of your nation who are saved shall be saved through Him. [The words] are these:

> ***O God, give Thy judgment to the king, and Thy righteousness unto the king's son. He shall judge***[474] ***Thy people with righteousness, and Thy poor with judgment. The mountains shall take up peace to the people, and the little hills righteousness. He shall judge the poor of the people, and shall save the children of the needy, and shall abase the slanderer: and He shall co-endure with the sun, and before the moon unto all generations;***[475]

and so on until,

> ***His name endureth before the sun, and all tribes of the earth shall be blessed in Him. All nations shall call Him blessed. Blessed be the Lord, the God of Israel, who only doeth wondrous things: and blessed be His glorious name for ever and ever: and the whole earth shall be filled with His glory. Amen, Amen.***[476]

And you remember from other words also spoken by David, and which I have mentioned before, how it is declared that He would come forth from the highest heavens, and again return to the same places, in order that you may recognize Him as God coming forth from above, and man living among men; and [how it is declared] that He will again appear, and they who pierced Him shall see Him, and shall bewail Him. [The words] are these:

> ***The heavens declare the glory of God, and the firmament showeth His handiwork. Day unto day uttereth speech, and night unto night showeth knowledge. They are not speeches or words whose voices are heard. Their sound has gone out through all the earth, and their words to the ends of the world. In the sun has He set His habitation; and He, like a bridegroom going forth from His***

---

[474] Or, to judge" as in Chapter XXXIV.

[475] {Psalm 72:1-5.}

[476] Psalm 72:1, etc. {Actually, Psalm 72:17-19.}

chamber, will rejoice as a giant to run his race: from the highest heaven is His going forth, and He returns to the highest heaven, and there is not one who shall be hidden from His heat."[477]

Chapter LXV: *The Jew objects that God does not give His glory to another. Justin explains the passage.*

And Trypho said, "Being shaken[478] by so many Scriptures, I know not what to say about the Scripture which Isaiah writes, in which God says that He gives not His glory to another, speaking thus: ***'I am the Lord God; this is my name; my glory will I not give to another, nor my virtues.'***"[479]

And I answered, "If you spoke these words, Trypho, and then kept silence in simplicity and with no ill intent, neither repeating what goes before nor adding what comes after, you must be forgiven; but if [you have done so] because you imagined that you could throw doubt on the passage, in order that I might say the Scriptures contradicted each other, you have erred. But I shall not venture to suppose or to say such a thing; and if a Scripture which appears to be of such a kind be brought forward, and if there be a pretext [for saying] that it is contrary [to some other], since I am entirely convinced that no Scripture contradicts another, I shall admit rather that I do not understand what is recorded, and shall strive to persuade those who imagine that the Scriptures are contradictory, to be rather of the same opinion as myself. With what intent, then, you have brought forward the difficulty, God knows. But I shall remind you of what the passage says, in order that you may recognize even from this very [place] that God gives glory to His Christ alone.

And I shall take up some short passages, sirs, those which are in connection with what has been said by Trypho, and those which are also joined on in consecutive order. For I will not repeat those of another section, but those which are joined together in one. Do you also give me your attention. [The words] are these:

---

[477] Psalm 19:1-6.
[478] Literally, "importuned."
[479] Isaiah 42:8. {See also Isaiah 48:11.}

> ***Thus saith the Lord, the God that created the heavens, and made[480] them fast, that established the earth, and that which is in it; and gave breath to the people upon it, and spirit to them who walk therein: I the Lord God have called Thee in righteousness, and will hold Thine hand, and will strengthen Thee; and I have given Thee for a covenant of the people, for a light of the Gentiles, to open the eyes of the blind, to bring out them that are bound from the chains, and those who sit in darkness from the prison-house. I am the Lord God; this is my name: my glory will I not give to another, nor my virtues to graven images. Behold, the former things are come to pass; new things which I announce, and before they are announced they are made manifest to you. Sing unto the Lord a new song: His sovereignty [is] from the end of the earth. [Sing], ye who descend into the sea, and continually sail[481] [on it]; ye islands, and inhabitants thereof. Rejoice, O wilderness, and the villages thereof, and the houses; and the inhabitants of Cedar shall rejoice, and the inhabitants of the rock shall cry aloud from the top of the mountains: they shall give glory to God; they shall publish His virtues among the islands. The Lord God of hosts shall go forth, He shall destroy war utterly, He shall stir up zeal, and He shall cry aloud to the enemies with strength."***[482]

And when I repeated this, I said to them, "Have you perceived, my friends, that God says He will give Him whom He has established as a light of the Gentiles, glory, and to no other; and not, as Trypho said, that God was retaining the glory to Himself?"

Then Trypho answered, "We have perceived this also; pass on therefore to the remainder of the discourse."

Chapter LXVI: *He proves from Isaiah that God was born from a virgin.*

And I, resuming the discourse where I had left off[483] at a previous stage, when proving that He was born of a virgin, and that His birth of a

[480] Literally, "fixed."
[481] Or, "ye islands which sail on it;" or without "continually."
[482] Isaiah 42:5-13.
[483] Chapter XLIII.

virgin had been predicted by Isaiah, quoted again the same prophecy. It is as follows:

> ***And the Lord spoke again to Ahaz, saying, Ask for thyself a sign from the Lord thy God, in the depth or in the height. And Ahaz said I will not ask, neither will I tempt the Lord. And Isaiah said, Hear then, O house of David; Is it no small thing for you to contend with men? And how do you contend with the Lord? Therefore the Lord Himself will give you a sign; Behold, the virgin shall conceive, and shall bear a Son, and they shall call His name Immanuel. Butter and honey shall He eat; before He knows or prefers the evil He will choose out the good. For before the Child knows ill or good, He rejects evil by choosing out the good. For before the Child knows how to call father or mother, He shall receive the power of Damascus, and the spoil of Samaria, in presence of the king of Assyria. And the land shall be forsaken, which[484] thou shalt with difficulty endure in consequence of the presence of its two kings. But God shall bring on thee, and on thy people, and on the house of thy father, days which have not yet come upon thee since the day in which Ephraim took away from Judah the king of Assyria."[485]***

And I continued: "Now it is evident to all, that in the race of Abraham according to the flesh no one has been born of a virgin, or is said to have been born [of a virgin], save this our Christ."

Chapter LXVII: *Trypho compares Jesus with Perseus; and would prefer [to say] that He was elected [to be Christ] on account of observance of the law. Justin speaks of the law as formerly.*

And Trypho answered, "The Scripture has not, '***Behold, the virgin shall conceive, and bear a Son***,'[486] but, '*Behold, the young woman shall conceive, and bear a son*,' and so on, as you quoted. But the whole prophecy refers to Hezekiah, and it is proved that it was fulfilled in him, according to the terms of this prophecy. Moreover, in the fables of those

---

[484] ἤν, which is in Chapter XLIII, is here omitted, but ought to be inserted without doubt.

[485] Isaiah 7:10-17, with Isaiah 8:4 inserted between verse 16 and 17.

[486] {Isaiah 7:14. This is a repetitive argument from Trypho that Saint Justin previously addressed.}

who are called Greeks, it is written that Perseus was begotten of Danae, who was a virgin; he who was called among them Zeus having descended on her in the form of a golden shower. And you ought to feel ashamed when you make assertions similar to theirs, and rather [should] say that this Jesus was born man of men. And if you prove from the Scriptures that He is the Christ, and that on account of having led a life conformed to the law, and perfect, He deserved the honor of being elected to be Christ, [it is well]; but do not venture to tell monstrous phenomena, lest you be convicted of talking foolishly like the Greeks."

Then I said to this, "Trypho, I wish to persuade you, and all men in short, of this, that even though you talk worse things in ridicule and in jest, you will not move me from my fixed design; but I shall always adduce from the words which you think can be brought forward [by you] as proof [of your own views], the demonstration of what I have stated along with the testimony of the Scriptures. You are not, however, acting fairly or truthfully in attempting to undo those things in which there has been constantly agreement between us; namely, that certain commands were instituted by Moses on account of the hardness of your people's hearts. For you said that, by reason of His living conformably to law, He was elected and became Christ, if indeed He were proved to be so."

And Trypho said, "You admitted[487] to us that He was both circumcised, and observed the other legal ceremonies ordained by Moses."

And I replied, "I have admitted it, and do admit it: yet I have admitted that He endured all these not as if He were justified by them, but completing the dispensation which His Father, the Maker of all things, and Lord and God, wished Him [to complete]. For I admit that He endured crucifixion and death, and the incarnation, and the suffering of as many afflictions as your nation put upon Him. But since again you dissent from that to which you but lately assented, Trypho, answer me: Are those righteous patriarchs who lived before Moses, who observed none of those [ordinances] which, the Scripture shows, received the

---

[487] We have not seen that Justin admitted this; but it is not to be supposed that the passage where he did admit it has been lost, as Perionius suspected; for sometimes Justin refers to passages at other places, which he did not relate in their own place.—*Maranus*. {Saint Justin seems to have been familiar with the Gospel of Saint Luke, so his acknowledgment of Christ's circumcision is not surprising. See Luke 2:21, where His circumcision is implied.}

commencement of [their] institution from Moses, saved, [and have they attained to] the inheritance of the blessed?"

And Trypho said, "The Scriptures compel me to admit it."

"Likewise I again ask you," said I, "did God enjoin your fathers to present the offerings and sacrifices because He had need of them, or because of the hardness of their hearts and tendency to idolatry?"

"The latter," said he, "the Scriptures in like manner compel us to admit."

"Likewise," said I, "did not the Scriptures predict that God promised to dispense a new covenant besides that which [was dispensed] in the mountain Horeb?"

This, too, he replied, had been predicted.

Then I said again, "Was not the old covenant laid on your fathers with fear and trembling, so that they could not give ear to God?"

He admitted it.

"What then?" said I: "God promised that there would be another covenant, not like that old one, and said that it would be laid on them without fear, and trembling, and lightnings, and that it would be such as to show what kind of commands and deeds God knows to be eternal and suited to every nation, and what commandments He has given, suiting them to the hardness of your people's hearts, as He exclaims also by the prophets."

"To this also," said he, "those who are lovers of truth and not lovers of strife must assuredly assent."

Then I replied, "I know not how you speak of persons very fond of strife, [since] you yourself oftentimes were plainly acting in this very manner, frequently contradicting what you had agreed to."

Chapter LXVIII: *He complains of the obstinacy of Trypho; he answers his objection; he convicts the Jews of bad faith.*

And Trypho said, "You endeavor to prove an incredible and well-nigh impossible thing; [namely], that God endured to be born and become man."

"If I undertook," said I, "to prove this by doctrines or arguments of man, you should not bear with me. But if I quote frequently Scriptures, and so many of them, referring to this point, and ask you to comprehend them, you are hard-hearted in the recognition of the mind and will of

God. But if you wish to remain forever so, I would not be injured at all; and forever retaining the same [opinions] which I had before I met with you, I shall leave you."

And Trypho said, "Look, my friend, you made yourself master of these [truths] with much labor and toil. And we accordingly must diligently scrutinize all that we meet with, in order to give our assent to those things which the Scriptures compel us [to believe]."

Then I said to this, "I do not ask you not to strive earnestly by all means, in making an investigation of the matters inquired into; but [I ask you], when you have nothing to say, not to contradict those things which you said you had admitted."

And Trypho said, "So we shall endeavor to do."

I continued again: "In addition to the questions I have just now put to you, I wish to put more: for by means of these questions I shall strive to bring the discourse to a speedy termination."

And Trypho said, "Ask the questions."

Then I said, "Do you think that any other one is said to be worthy of worship and called Lord and God in the Scriptures, except the Maker of all, and Christ, who by so many Scriptures was proved to you to have become man?"

And Trypho replied, "How can we admit this, when we have instituted so great an inquiry as to whether there is any other than the Father alone?"

Then I again said, "I must ask you this also, that I may know whether or not you are of a different opinion from that which you admitted some time ago."[488]

He replied, "It is not, sir."

Then again I, "Since you certainly admit these things, and since Scripture says, '***Who shall declare His generation?***'[489] ought you not now to suppose that He is not the seed of a human race?"

And Trypho said, "How then does the Word say to David, that out of his loins God shall take to Himself a Son, and shall establish His kingdom, and shall set Him on the throne of His glory?"

And I said, "Trypho, if the prophecy which Isaiah uttered, '***Behold, the virgin shall conceive,***'[490] is said not to the house of David, but to

---

[488] *τίως*: Vulg. *παρὰ Θεῷ, vitiose.—Otto.*

[489] {Isaiah 53:8.}

another house of the twelve tribes, perhaps the matter would have some difficulty; but since this prophecy refers to the house of David, Isaiah has explained how that which was spoken by God to David in mystery would take place. But perhaps you are not aware of this, my friends, that there were many sayings written obscurely, or parabolically, or mysteriously, and symbolical actions, which the prophets who lived after the persons who said or did them expounded."

"Assuredly," said Trypho.

"If therefore, I shall show that this prophecy of Isaiah refers to our Christ, and not to Hezekiah, as you say, shall I not in this matter, too, compel you not to believe your teachers, who venture to assert that the explanation which your seventy elders that were with Ptolemy the king of the Egyptians gave, is untrue in certain respects? For some statements in the Scriptures, which appear explicitly to convict them of a foolish and vain opinion, these they venture to assert have not been so written. But other statements, which they fancy they can distort and harmonize with human actions,[491] these, they say, refer not to this Jesus Christ of ours, but to him of whom they are pleased to explain them. Thus, for instance, they have taught you that this Scripture which we are now discussing refers to Hezekiah, in which, as I promised, I shall show they are wrong. And since they are compelled, they agree that some Scriptures which we mention to them, and which expressly prove that Christ was to suffer, to be worshipped, and [to be called] God, and which I have already recited to you, do refer indeed to Christ, but they venture to assert that this man is not Christ. But they admit that He will come to suffer, and to reign, and to be worshipped, and to be God;[492] and this opinion I shall in like manner show to be ridiculous and silly. But since I am pressed to answer first to what was said by you in jest, I shall make answer to it, and shall afterwards give replies to what follows."

---

[490] {Isaiah 7:14.}

[491] The text is corrupt, and various emendations have been proposed.

[492] Or, "and to be worshipped as God."

Chapter LXIX: *The devil, since he emulates the truth, has invented fables about Bacchus, Hercules, and Aesculapius.*

"Be well assured, then, Trypho," I continued, "that I am established in the knowledge of and faith in the Scriptures by those counterfeits which he who is called the devil is said to have performed among the Greeks; just as some were wrought by the Magi in Egypt, and others by the false prophets in Elijah's days. For when they tell that Bacchus, son of Jupiter, was begotten by [Jupiter's] intercourse with Semele, and that he was the discoverer of the vine; and when they relate, that being torn in pieces, and having died, he rose again, and ascended to heaven; and when they introduce wine[493] into his mysteries, do I not perceive that [the devil] has imitated the prophecy announced by the patriarch Jacob, and recorded by Moses? And when they tell that Hercules was strong, and travelled over all the world, and was begotten by Jove of Alcmene, and ascended to heaven when he died, do I not perceive that the Scripture which speaks of Christ, ***'strong as a giant to run his race,'***[494] has been in like manner imitated? And when he [the devil] brings forward Aesculapius as the raiser of the dead and healer of all diseases, may I not say that in this matter likewise he has imitated the prophecies about Christ? But since I have not quoted to you such Scripture as tells that Christ will do these things, I must necessarily remind you of one such: from which you can understand, how that to those destitute of a knowledge of God, I mean the Gentiles, who, ***'having eyes, saw not, and having a heart, understood not,'***[495] worshipping the images of wood, [how even to them] Scripture prophesied that they would renounce these [vanities], and hope in this Christ. It is thus written:

> ***Rejoice, thirsty wilderness: let the wilderness be glad, and blossom as the lily: the deserts of the Jordan shall both blossom and be glad: and the glory of Lebanon was given to it, and the honor of Carmel. And my people shall see the exaltation of the***

---

[493] Or, "an ass." The ass was sacred to Bacchus; and many fluctuate between *οἶνον* and *ὄνον*.

[494] Psalm 19:5. {St. Paul remarks a number of times about running a race. See, e.g., 1 Corinthians 9:24; 2 Timothy 4:7; Hebrews 12:1.}

[495] {Compare Psalm 115: 2, 5; with Isaiah 6:10; Jeremiah 5:21; Ezekiel 12:2; Matthew 13:15; Mark 8:18; John 12:40; Acts 28:27; and Romans 11:8.}

> ***Lord, and the glory of God. Be strong, ye careless hands and enfeebled knees. Be comforted, ye faint in soul: be strong, fear not. Behold, our God gives, and will give, retributive judgment. He shall come and save us. Then the eyes of the blind shall be opened, and the ears of the deaf shall hear. Then the lame shall leap as an hart, and the tongue of the stammerers shall be distinct: for water has broken forth in the wilderness, and a valley in the thirsty land; and the parched ground shall become pools, and a spring of water shall [rise up] in the thirsty land.***[496]

The spring of living water which gushed forth from God in the land destitute of the knowledge of God, namely the land of the Gentiles, was this Christ, who also appeared in your nation, and healed those who were maimed, and deaf, and lame in body from their birth, causing them to leap, to hear, and to see, by His word. And having raised the dead, and causing them to live, by His deeds He compelled the men who lived at that time to recognize Him. But though they saw such works, they asserted it was magical art. For they dared to call Him a magician, and a deceiver of the people. Yet He wrought such works, and persuaded those who were [destined to] believe on Him; for even if anyone be laboring under a defect of body, yet be an observer of the doctrines delivered by Him, He shall raise him up at His second advent perfectly sound, after He has made him immortal, and incorruptible, and free from grief."

Chapter LXX: *So also the mysteries of Mithras are distorted from the prophecies of Daniel and Isaiah.*

"And when those who record the mysteries of Mithras say that he was begotten of a rock, and call the place where those who believe in him are initiated a cave, do I not perceive here that the utterance of Daniel, that a stone without hands was cut out of a great mountain, has been imitated by them, and that they have attempted likewise to imitate the whole of Isaiah's[497] words?[498] For they[499] contrived that the words of

---

[496] Isaiah 35:1-7.

[497] The text here has *ταὺτα ποιῆσαι ὁμοίως*. Maranus suggests *Ἡσαίου* for *ποιῆσαι*; and so we have translated.

[498] Maranus says: Justin says that the priests of Mithras imitated all the words of Isaiah about to be quoted; and to prove it, is content with a single example, namely, the precepts of righteousness, which they were wont to relate to them, as in these words of

righteousness be quoted also by them.[500] But I must repeat to you the words of Isaiah referred to, in order that from them you may know that these things are so. They are these:

> ***Hear, ye that are far off, what I have done; those that are near shall know my might. The sinners in Zion are removed; trembling shall seize the impious. Who shall announce to you the everlasting place? The man who walks in righteousness, speaks in the right way, hates sin and unrighteousness, and keeps his hands pure from bribes, stops the ears from hearing the unjust judgment of blood, closes the eyes from seeing unrighteousness: he shall dwell in the lofty cave of the strong rock. Bread shall be given to him, and his water [shall be] sure. Ye shall see the King with glory, and your eyes shall look far off. Your soul shall pursue diligently the fear of the Lord. Where is the scribe? where are the counselors? where is he that numbers those who are nourished,—the small and great people? with whom they did not take counsel, nor knew the depth of the voices, so that they heard not. The people who are become depreciated, and there is no understanding in him who hears.***[501]

Now it is evident, that in this prophecy [allusion is made] to the bread which our Christ gave us to eat,[502] in remembrance of His being made flesh for the sake of His believers, for whom also He suffered; and to the cup which He gave us to drink,[503] in remembrance of His own blood, with giving of thanks. And this prophecy proves that we shall behold this very King with glory; and the very terms of the prophecy declare loudly, that the people foreknown to believe in Him were foreknown to pursue

---

Isaiah: "He who walks in righteousness," etc. Justin omitted many other passages, as easy and obvious. For since Mithras is the same as fire, it manifestly answers to the fire of which Isaiah speaks. And since Justin reminded them who are initiated, that they are said to be initiated by Mithras himself, it was not necessary to remind them of the words of Isaiah are imitated in this: "You shall see the King with glory." Bread and water are referred to by Isaiah: so also in these mysteries of Mithras, Justin testifies that bread and a cup of water are placed before them (*Apol.* i.).

[499] I.e., the devils.

[500] I.e., the priests of Mithras.

[501] Isaiah 33:13-19.

[502] Literally, "to do" *ποςρῖρ*.

[503] Literally, "to do" *ποςρῖρ*.

diligently the fear of the Lord. Moreover, these Scriptures are equally explicit in saying, that those who are reputed to know the writings of the Scriptures, and who hear the prophecies, have no understanding. And when I hear, Trypho," said I, "that Perseus was begotten of a virgin, I understand that the deceiving serpent counterfeited also this."

Chapter LXXI: *The Jews reject the interpretation of the LXX, from which, moreover, they have taken away some passages.*

"But I am far from putting reliance in your teachers, who refuse to admit that the interpretation made by the seventy elders who were with Ptolemy [king] of the Egyptians is a correct one; and they attempt to frame another. And I wish you to observe, that they have altogether taken away many Scriptures from the translations effected by those seventy elders who were with Ptolemy, and by which this very man who was crucified is proved to have been set forth expressly as God, and man, and as being crucified, and as dying; but since I am aware that this is denied by all of your nation, I do not address myself to these points, but I proceed[504] to carry on my discussions by means of those passages which are still admitted by you. For you assent to those which I have brought before your attention, except that you contradict the statement, '***Behold, the virgin shall conceive***,'[505] and say it ought to be read, '*Behold, the young woman shall conceive*.' And I promised to prove that the prophecy referred, not, as you were taught, to Hezekiah, but to this Christ of mine: and now I shall go to the proof."

Here Trypho remarked, "We ask you first of all to tell us some of the Scriptures which you allege have been completely cancelled."

Chapter LXXII: *Passages have been removed by the Jews from Esdras and Jeremiah.*

And I said, "I shall do as you please. From the statements, then, which Esdras made in reference to the law of the passover, they have taken away the following:

[504] Or, "profess."
[505] {Isaiah 7:14.}

> *And Esdras said to the people, This passover is our Savior and our refuge. And if you have understood, and your heart has taken it in, that we shall humble Him on a standard, and*[506] *thereafter hope in Him, then this place shall not be forsaken forever, says the God of hosts. But if you will not believe Him, and will not listen to His declaration, you shall be a laughing-stock to the nations.*[507]

And from the sayings of Jeremiah they have cut out the following: ***'I [was] like a lamb that is brought to the slaughter: they devised a device against me, saying,*** *Come, let us lay on wood on His bread,* ***and let us blot Him out from the land of the living; and His name shall no more be remembered.'***[508]

And since this passage from the sayings of Jeremiah is still written in some copies [of the Scriptures] in the synagogues of the Jews (for it is only a short time since they were cut out), and since from these words it is demonstrated that the Jews deliberated about the Christ Himself, to crucify and put Him to death, He Himself is both declared to be led as a sheep to the slaughter, as was predicted by Isaiah, and is here represented as a harmless lamb; but being in a difficulty about them, they give themselves over to blasphemy.

And again, from the sayings of the same Jeremiah these have been cut out: *'The Lord God remembered His dead people of Israel who lay in the graves; and He descended to preach to them His own salvation.'"*[509]

Chapter LXXIII: *The words "From the wood" have been cut out of Psalm 96.*

"And from the ninety-fifth (ninety-sixth) Psalm they have taken away this short saying of the words of David: *'From the wood.'*[510] For

---

[506] Or, "even if we."

[507] It is not known where this passage comes from. {Hence, the text has not been put in bold italics. Nor could it be found in a recent search of multiple Bible versions.}

[508] Jeremiah 11:19.

[509] This is wanting in our Scriptures: it is cited by Irenaeus iii. 20 under the name of Isaiah, and in iv. 22 under that of Jeremiah.—*Maranus*. {Hence, the text has not been put in bold italics.}

[510] These words were not taken away by the Jews, but added by some Christians.—*Otto*.

when the passage said, '*Tell ye among the nations, the Lord hath reigned from the wood*,' they have left, '***Tell ye among the nations, the Lord hath reigned.***'[511] Now no one of your people has ever been said to have reigned as God and Lord among the nations, with the exception of Him only who was crucified, of whom also the Holy Spirit affirms in the same Psalm that He was raised again, and freed from [the grave], declaring that there is none like Him among the gods of the nations: for they are idols of demons. But I shall repeat the whole Psalm to you, that you may perceive what has been said. It is thus:

> ***Sing unto the Lord a new song; sing unto the Lord, all the earth. Sing unto the Lord, and bless His name; show forth His salvation from day to day. Declare His glory among the nations, His wonders among all people. For the Lord is great, and greatly to be praised: He is to be feared above all the gods. For all the gods of the nations are demons; but the Lord made the heavens. Confession and beauty are in His presence; holiness and magnificence are in His sanctuary. Bring to the Lord, O ye countries of the nations, bring to the Lord glory and honor, bring to the Lord glory in His name. Take sacrifices, and go into His courts; worship the Lord in His holy temple. Let the whole earth be moved before Him: tell ye among the nations, the Lord hath reigned.***[512] ***For He hath established the world, which shall not be moved; He shall judge the nations with equity. Let the heavens rejoice, and the earth be glad; let the sea and its fullness shake. Let the fields and all therein be joyful. Let all the trees of the wood be glad before the Lord: for He comes, for He comes to judge the earth. He shall judge the world with righteousness, and the people with His truth."***[513]

Here Trypho remarked, "Whether [or not] the rulers of the people have erased any portion of the Scriptures, as you affirm, God knows; but it seems incredible."

"Assuredly," said I, "it does seem incredible. For it is more horrible than the calf which they made, when satisfied with manna on the

---

[511] {Psalm 96:10.}

[512] It is strange that "from the wood" is not added; but the audacity of the copyists in such matters is well known.—*Maranus*.

[513] {Psalm 96.}

earth; or than the sacrifice of children to demons; or than the slaying of the prophets. But," said I, "you appear to me not to have heard the Scriptures which I said they had stolen away. For such as have been quoted are more than enough to prove the points in dispute, besides those which are retained by us,[514] and shall yet be brought forward."

Chapter LXXIV: *The beginning of Psalm 96 is attributed to the Father [by Trypho]. But [it refers] to Christ by these words: "Tell ye among the nations that the Lord," etc.*

Then Trypho said, "We know that you quoted these because we asked you. But it does not appear to me that this Psalm which you quoted last from the words of David refers to any other than the Father and Maker of the heavens and earth. You, however, asserted that it referred to Him who suffered, whom you also are eagerly endeavoring to prove to be Christ."

And I answered, "Attend to me, I beseech you, while I speak of the statement which the Holy Spirit gave utterance to in this Psalm; and you shall know that I speak not sinfully, and that we[515] are not really bewitched; for so you shall be enabled of yourselves to understand many other statements made by the Holy Spirit. '***Sing unto the Lord a new song; sing unto the Lord, all the earth: sing unto the Lord, and bless His name; show forth His salvation from day to day, His wonderful works among all people.***'[516] He bids the inhabitants of all the earth, who have known the mystery of this salvation, i.e., the suffering of Christ, by which He saved them, sing and give praises to God the Father of all things, and recognize that He is to be praised and feared, and that He is the Maker of heaven and earth, who effected this salvation in behalf of the human race, who also was crucified and was dead, and who was deemed worthy by Him (God) to reign over all the earth. As [is clearly seen[517]] also by the land into which [He said] He would bring [your fathers]; [for He thus speaks]:[518]

---

[514] Many think, "you."

[515] In text, "you." Maranus suggests, as far better, "we."

[516] {Psalm 96:1-3.}

[517] Something is here wanting; the suggested reading of Maranus has been adopted.

[518] Deuteronomy 31:16-18.

> ***This people [shall go a whoring after other gods], and shall forsake Me, and shall break My covenant which I made with them in that day; and I will forsake them, and will turn away My face from them; and they shall be devoured,[519] and many evils and afflictions shall find them out; and they shall say in that day, Because the Lord my God is not amongst us, these misfortunes have found us out. And I shall certainly turn away My face from them in that day, on account of all the evils which they have committed, in that they have turned to other gods."[520]***

Chapter LXXV: *It is proved that Jesus was the name of God in the book of Exodus.*

"Moreover, in the book of Exodus we have also perceived that the name of God Himself which, He says, was not revealed to Abraham or to Jacob, was Jesus, and was declared mysteriously through Moses. Thus it is written:

> ***And the Lord spake to Moses, Say to this people, Behold, I send My angel before thy face, to keep thee in the way, to bring thee into the land which I have prepared for thee. Give heed to Him, and obey Him; do not disobey Him. For He will not draw back from you; for My name is in Him.***[521]

Now understand that He who led your fathers into the land is called by this name Jesus, and first called Auses (Oshea). For if you shall understand this, you shall likewise perceive that the name of Him who said to Moses, '***for My name is in Him***,'[522] was Jesus. For, indeed, He was also called Israel, and Jacob's name was changed to this also. Now Isaiah shows that those prophets who are sent to publish tidings from God are called His angels and apostles. For Isaiah says in a certain place, '***Send me.***'[523] And that the prophet whose name was changed, Jesus [Joshua], was strong and great, is manifest to all. If, then, we know that God revealed Himself in so many forms to Abraham, and to Jacob, and to

---

[519] Literally, "for food."
[520] The first conference seems to have ended hereabout.
[521] Exodus 23:20, 21. {See also Psalm 91:11.}
[522] {Exodus 23:21.}
[523] Isaiah 6:8.

Moses, how are we at a loss, and do not believe that, according to the will of the Father of all things, it was possible for Him to be born man of the Virgin, especially after we have such[524] Scriptures, from which it can be plainly perceived that He became so according to the will of the Father?"

Chapter LXXVI: *From other passages the same majesty and government of Christ are proved.*

"For when Daniel speaks of '***one like unto the Son of man***'[525] who received the everlasting kingdom, does he not hint at this very thing? For he declares that, in saying '***like unto the Son of man***,' He appeared, and was man, but not of human seed. And the same thing he proclaimed in mystery when he speaks of this stone which was cut out without hands. For the expression '***it was cut out without hands***'[526] signified that it is not a work of man, but [a work] of the will of the Father and God of all things, who brought Him forth. And when Isaiah says, '***Who shall declare His generation?***'[527] he meant that His descent could not be declared. Now no one who is a man of men has a descent that cannot be declared. And when Moses says that He will wash His garments in the blood of the grape, does not this signify what I have now often told you is an obscure prediction, namely, that He had blood, but not from men; just as not man, but God, has begotten the blood of the vine? And when Isaiah calls Him the Angel of mighty counsel, did he not foretell Him to be the Teacher of those truths which He did teach when He came [to earth]? For He alone taught openly those mighty counsels which the Father designed both for all those who have been and shall be well-pleasing to Him, and also for those who have rebelled against His will, whether men or angels, when He said: '***They shall come from the east [and from the west***[528]***], and shall sit down with Abraham, and Isaac, and Jacob, in the kingdom of heaven: but the children of the kingdom shall be cast out into outer darkness.***'[529] And, '***Many shall say to Me in that day, Lord, Lord, have we not eaten, and drunk, and prophesied, and cast out***

---

[524] Or, "so many."
[525] {See Daniel 7:13}
[526] {Daniel 2:34, 45. See also 2 Corinthians 5:1.}
[527] {Isaiah 53:8.}
[528] Not in all edd.
[529] Matthew 8:11 {-12}.

demons in Thy name? And I will say to them, Depart from Me.'[530] Again, in other words, by which He shall condemn those who are unworthy of salvation, He said, '***Depart into outer darkness, which the Father has prepared for Satan and his, angels.'***[531] And again, in other words, He said, '***I give unto you power to tread on serpents, and on scorpions, and on scolopendras, and on all the might of the enemy.'***[532]

And now we, who believe on our Lord Jesus, who was crucified under Pontius Pilate, when we exorcise all demons and evil spirits, have them subjected to us. For if the prophets declared obscurely that Christ would suffer, and thereafter be Lord of all, yet that [declaration] could not be understood by any man until He Himself persuaded the apostles that such statements were expressly related in the Scriptures. For He exclaimed before His crucifixion: '***The Son of man must suffer many things, and be rejected by the scribes and Pharisees, and be crucified, and on the third day rise again.'***[533] And David predicted that He would be born from the womb before sun and moon,[534] according to the Father's will, and made Him known, being Christ, as God strong and to be worshipped."

Chapter LXXVII: *He returns to explain the prophecy of Isaiah.*

Then Trypho said, "I admit that such and so great arguments are sufficient to persuade one; but I wish [you] to know that I ask you for the proof which you have frequently proposed to give me. Proceed then to make this plain to us, that we may see how you prove that that [passage] refers to this Christ of yours. For we assert that the prophecy relates to Hezekiah."

And I replied, "I shall do as you wish. But show me yourselves first of all how it is said of Hezekiah, that before he knew how to call father or mother, he received the power of Damascus and the spoils of Samaria in the presence of the king of Assyria. For it will not be conceded to you, as

---

[530] Matthew 7:22 {-23; see also Psalm 5:5}.

[531] Matthew 25:41.

[532] Luke 10:19 {See also Mark 16:18.}.

[533] Luke 9:22. {See also Matthew 16:21; 20:18-19.}

[534] Justin puts "sun and moon" instead of "Lucifer." Maranus says, David did predict, not that Christ would be born of Mary before sun and moon, but that it would happen before the sun and moon that he would be born of a virgin.

you wish to explain it, that Hezekiah waged war with the inhabitants of Damascus and Samaria in presence of the king of Assyria. ***'For before the child knows how to call father or mother,'***[535] the prophetic word said, ***'He shall take the power of Damascus and spoils of Samaria in presence of the king of Assyria.'***[536] For if the Spirit of prophecy had not made the statement with an addition, ***'Before the child knows how to call father or mother, he shall take the power of Damascus and spoils of Samaria,'***[537] but had only said, *'And shall bear a son, and he shall take the power of Damascus and spoils of Samaria,'* then you might say that God foretold that he would take these things, since He foreknew it. But now the prophecy has stated it with this addition: ***'Before the child knows how to call father or mother, he shall take the power of Damascus and spoils of Samaria.'***[538]

And you cannot prove that such a thing ever happened to any one among the Jews. But we are able to prove that it happened in the case of our Christ. For at the time of His birth, Magi who came from Arabia worshipped Him, coming first to Herod, who then was sovereign in your land, and whom the Scripture calls king of Assyria on account of his ungodly and sinful character. For you know," continued I, "that the Holy Spirit oftentimes announces such events by parables and similitudes; just as He did towards all the people in Jerusalem, frequently saying to them, ***'Thy father is an Amorite, and thy mother a Hittite.'"***[539]

Chapter LXXVIII: *He proves that this prophecy harmonizes with Christ alone, from what is afterwards written.*

"Now this king Herod, at the time when the Magi came to him from Arabia, and said they knew from a star which appeared in the heavens that a King had been born in your country, and that they had come to worship Him, learned from the elders of your people that it was thus written regarding Bethlehem in the prophet: ***'And thou, Bethlehem, in the land of Judah, art by no means least among the princes of Judah;***

---

[535] {Isaiah 8:4.}
[536] {Ibid.}
[537] {Ibid.}
[538] {Ibid.}
[539] Ezekiel 16:3.

for out of thee shall go forth the leader who shall feed my people.'[540] Accordingly the Magi from Arabia came to Bethlehem and worshipped the Child, and presented Him with gifts, gold and frankincense, and myrrh; but returned not to Herod, being warned in a revelation after worshipping the Child in Bethlehem. And Joseph, the spouse of Mary, who wished at first to put away his betrothed Mary, supposing her to be pregnant by intercourse with a man, i.e., from fornication, was commanded in a vision not to put away his wife; and the angel who appeared to him told him that what is in her womb is of the Holy Ghost. Then he was afraid, and did not put her away; but on the occasion of the first census which was taken in Judaea, under Cyrenius, he went up from Nazareth, where he lived, to Bethlehem, to which he belonged, to be enrolled; for his family was of the tribe of Judah, which then inhabited that region. Then along with Mary he is ordered to proceed into Egypt, and remain there with the Child until another revelation warn them to return into Judaea. But when the Child was born in Bethlehem, since Joseph could not find a lodging in that village, he took up his quarters in a certain cave near the village; and while they were there Mary brought forth the Christ and placed Him in a manger, and here the Magi who came from Arabia found Him. I have repeated to you," I continued, "what Isaiah foretold about the sign which foreshadowed the cave; but for the sake of those who have come with us today, I shall again remind you of the passage."

Then I repeated the passage from Isaiah which I have already written, adding that, by means of those words, those who presided over the mysteries of Mithras were stirred up by the devil to say that in a place, called among them a cave, they were initiated by him.[541] "So Herod, when the Magi from Arabia did not return to him, as he had asked them to do, but had departed by another way to their own country, according to the commands laid on them; and when Joseph, with Mary and the Child, had now gone into Egypt, as it was revealed to them to do; as he did not know the Child whom the Magi had gone to worship,

---

[540] Micah 5:2. {OSB Micah 5:1. This verse does not have the last clause which includes "feed my people." Leaders are often commanded to feed His people. Compare 2 Samuel 5:2, 7:7; and 1 Chronicles 11:2, 17:6. Of course, Jesus would literally and miraculously feed people. See, e.g., Matthew 14:15-21; Mark 6:35-44; Luke 9:12-17; John 6:5-14.}

[541] Text has, by "them;" but Maranus says the artifice lay in the priest's compelling the initiated to say that Mithras himself was the initiator of the cave.

ordered simply the whole of the children then in Bethlehem to be massacred.

And Jeremiah prophesied that this would happen, speaking by the Holy Ghost thus: ***'A voice was heard in Ramah, lamentation and much wailing, Rachel weeping for her children; and she would not be comforted, because they are not.'***[542] Therefore, on account of the voice which would be heard from Ramah, i.e., from Arabia (for there is in Arabia at this very time a place called Rama), wailing would come on the place where Rachel the wife of Jacob called Israel, the holy patriarch, has been buried, i.e., on Bethlehem; while the women weep for their own slaughtered children, and have no consolation by reason of what has happened to them.

For that expression of Isaiah, ***'He shall take the power of Damascus and spoils of Samaria,'***[543] foretold that the power of the evil demon that dwelt in Damascus should be overcome by Christ as soon as He was born; and this is proved to have happened. For the Magi, who were held in bondage[544] for the commission of all evil deeds through the power of that demon, by coming to worship Christ, show that they have revolted from that dominion which held them captive; and this [dominion] the Scripture has showed us to reside in Damascus. Moreover, that sinful and unjust power is termed well in parable, Samaria.[545] And none of you can deny that Damascus was, and is, in the region of Arabia, although now it belongs to what is called Syrophoenicia.

Hence it would be becoming for you, sirs, to learn what you have not perceived, from those who have received grace from God, namely, from us Christians; and not to strive in every way to maintain your own doctrines, dishonoring those of God. Therefore also this grace has been transferred to us, as Isaiah says, speaking to the following effect:

> ***This people draws near to Me, they honor Me with their lips, but their heart is far from Me; but in vain they worship Me, teaching the commands and doctrines of men. Therefore, behold, I will***

---

[542] Jeremiah 31:15. {See also Matthew 2:17-18.}

[543] {Isaiah 8:4.}

[544] Literally, "spoiled."

[545] Justin thinks the "spoils of Samaria" denote spoils of Satan; Tertullian thinks that they are spoils of Christ.

> ***proceed[546] to remove this people, and I shall remove them; and I shall take away the wisdom of their wise men, and bring to nothing the understanding of the prudent men."[547]***

Chapter LXXIX: *He proves against Trypho that the wicked angels have revolted from God.*

On this, Trypho, who was somewhat angry, but respected the Scriptures, as was manifest from his countenance, said to me, "The utterances of God are holy, but your expositions are mere contrivances, as is plain from what has been explained by you; nay, even blasphemies, for you assert that angels sinned and revolted from God."

And I, wishing to get him to listen to me, answered in milder tones, thus: "I admire, sir, this piety of yours; and I pray that you may entertain the same disposition towards Him to whom angels are recorded to minister, as Daniel says; for [one] like the Son of man is led to the Ancient of days, and every kingdom is given to Him for ever and ever. But that you may know, sir," continued I, "that it is not our audacity which has induced us to adopt this exposition, which you reprehend, I shall give you evidence from Isaiah himself; for he affirms that evil angels have dwelt and do dwell in Tanis, in Egypt. These are [his] words:

> ***Woe to the rebellious children! Thus saith the Lord, You have taken counsel, but not through Me; and [made] agreements, but not through My Spirit, to add sins to sins; who have sinned[548] in going down to Egypt (but they have not inquired at Me), that they may be assisted by Pharaoh, and be covered with the shadow of the Egyptians. For the shadow of Pharaoh shall be a disgrace to you, and a reproach to those who trust in the Egyptians; for the princes in Tanis[549] are evil angels. In vain will they labor for a people which will not profit them by assistance, but [will be] for a disgrace and a reproach [to them].[550]***

---

[546] Literally, "add."
[547] Isaiah 29:13, 14. {See also Jeremiah 49:7; Ezekiel 33:31; Mark 7:6.}
[548] LXX "who walk," *πορευόμενοι* for *πονηρευόμενοι*.
[549] In E. V. "Zoan."
[550] Isaiah 30:1-5.

And, further, Zechariah tells, as you yourself have related, that the devil stood on the right hand of Joshua the priest, to resist him; and [the Lord] said, '***The Lord, who has taken***[551] ***Jerusalem, rebuke thee.***'[552] And again, it is written in Job,[553] as you said yourself, how that the angels came to stand before the Lord, and the devil came with them. And we have it recorded by Moses in the beginning of Genesis, that the serpent beguiled Eve, and was cursed. And we know that in Egypt there were magicians who emulated[554] the mighty power displayed by God through the faithful servant Moses. And you are aware that David said, '***The gods of the nations are demons.***'"[555]

Chapter LXXX: *The opinion of Justin with regard to the reign of a thousand years. Several Catholics reject it.*

And Trypho to this replied, "I remarked to you sir, that you are very anxious to be safe in all respects, since you cling to the Scriptures. But tell me, do you really admit that this place, Jerusalem, shall be rebuilt; and do you expect your people to be gathered together, and made joyful with Christ and the patriarchs, and the prophets, both the men of our nation, and other proselytes who joined them before your Christ came? or have you given way, and admitted this in order to have the appearance of worsting us in the controversies?"

Then I answered, "I am not so miserable a fellow, Trypho, as to say one thing and think another. I admitted to you formerly,[556] that I and many others are of this opinion, and [believe] that such will take place, as you assuredly are aware;[557] but, on the other hand, I signified to you that many who belong to the pure and pious faith, and are true Christians, think otherwise. Moreover, I pointed out to you that some who are called Christians, but are godless, impious heretics, teach doctrines that are in every way blasphemous, atheistical, and foolish.

---

[551] *ἐχδεξάμενος*; in Chapter CXV, *inf.* It is ἐχλεξάμενος.
[552] Zechariah 3:1. {This is actually verse 3:2.}
[553] Job 1:6.
[554] Maranus suggests the insertion of *ἐποίησαν* or *ἐπείρασαν* before *ἐξιοοῦσθαι.*
[555] Psalm 96:5.
[556] Justin made no previous allusion to this point, so far as we know from the writing preserved.
[557] Or, "so as to thoroughly believe that such will take place" (after "opinion").

But that you may know that I do not say this before you alone, I shall draw up a statement, so far as I can, of all the arguments which have passed between us; in which I shall record myself as admitting the very same things which I admit to you. For I choose to follow not men or men's doctrines, but God and the doctrines [delivered] by Him. For if you have fallen in with some who are called Christians, but who do not admit this [truth],[558] and venture to blaspheme the God of Abraham, and the God of Isaac, and the God of Jacob; who say there is no resurrection of the dead, and that their souls, when they die, are taken to heaven; do not imagine that they are Christians, even as one, if he would rightly consider it, would not admit that the Sadducees, or similar sects of Genistae, Meristae,[559] Galilaeans, Hellenists,[560] Pharisees, Baptists, are Jews (do not hear me impatiently when I tell you what I think), but are [only] called Jews and children of Abraham, worshipping God with the lips, as God Himself declared, but the heart was far from Him. But I and others, who are right-minded Christians on all points, are assured that there will be a resurrection of the dead, and a thousand years[561] in Jerusalem, which will then be built, adorned, and enlarged, [as] the prophets Ezekiel and Isaiah and others declare."

---

[558] I.e., resurrection.

[559] Maranus says, Hieron, thinks *Genistae* were so called because they were sprung from Abraham (*γένος*), the *Meristae* so called because they separated the Scriptures. Josephus bears testimony to the fact that the sects of Jews differed in regard to fate and providence; the Pharisees submitting that all things indeed to God, with the exception of human wills; the Essenes making no exceptions, and submitting all to God. I believe therefore that the *Genistae* were so called because they believed the world to be in general governed by God; the *Meristae*, because they believed that a fate or providence belonged to each man.

[560] Otto says, the author and chief of this sect of *Galilaeans* was Judas Galilaeus, who, after the exile of king Archelaus, when the Romans wished to raise a tax in Judaea, excited his countrymen to the retaining of their former liberty.—The *Hellenists*, or rather *Hellenaeans*. No one mentions this sect but Justin; perhaps *Herodians* or *Hillelaeans* (from R. Hillel).

[561] We have translated the text of Justin as it stands. Commentators make the sense, "and that there will be a thousand years in Jerusalem," or, "that the saints will live a thousand years in Jerusalem."

Chapter LXXXI: *He endeavors to prove this opinion from Isaiah and the Apocalypse.*

"For Isaiah spake thus concerning this space of a thousand years:

> ***For there shall be the new heaven and the new earth, and the former shall not be remembered, or come into their heart; but they shall find joy and gladness in it, which things I create. For, Behold, I make Jerusalem a rejoicing, and My people a joy; and I shall rejoice over Jerusalem, and be glad over My people. And the voice of weeping shall be no more heard in her, or the voice of crying. And there shall be no more there a person of immature years, or an old man who shall not fulfill his days.***[562] ***For the young man shall be an hundred years old;***[563] ***but the sinner who dies an hundred years old,***[564] ***he shall be accursed. And they shall build houses, and shall themselves inhabit them; and they shall plant vines, and shall themselves eat the produce of them, and drink the wine. They shall not build, and others inhabit; they shall not plant, and others eat. For according to the days of the tree of life shall be the days of my people; the works of their toil shall abound.***[565] ***Mine elect shall not toil fruitlessly, or beget children to be cursed; for they shall be a seed righteous and blessed by the Lord, and their offspring with them. And it shall come to pass, that before they call I will hear; while they are still speaking, I shall say, What is it? Then shall the wolves and the lambs feed together, and the lion shall eat straw like the ox; but the serpent [shall eat] earth as bread. They shall not hurt or maltreat each other on the holy mountain, saith the Lord.***[566]

Now we have understood that the expression used among these words, ***'According to the days of the tree [of life***[567]***] shall be the days of my people; the works of their toil shall abound'***[568] obscurely predicts a thousand years. For as Adam was told that in the day he ate of the tree

---

[562] Literally, "time."

[563] Literally, "the son of an hundred years."

[564] Literally, "the son of an hundred years."

[565] Or, as in margin of A. V., "they shall make the works of their toil continue long," so reading *παλαιώσουσιν* for *πλεονάσουσιν*: thus also LXX.

[566] Isaiah 65:17 to end.

[567] These words are not found in the mss.

[568] {Isaiah 65:22.}

he would die, we know that he did not complete a thousand years. We have perceived, moreover, that the expression, '***The day of the Lord is as a thousand years***,'[569] is connected with this subject. And further, there was a certain man with us, whose name was John, one of the apostles of Christ, who prophesied, by a revelation that was made to him, that those who believed in our Christ would dwell[570] a thousand years in Jerusalem; and that thereafter the general, and, in short, the eternal resurrection and judgment of all men would likewise take place. Just as our Lord also said, '***They shall neither marry nor be given in marriage, but shall be equal to the angels, the children of the God of the resurrection.***'"[571]

Chapter LXXXII: *The prophetical gifts of the Jews were transferred to the Christians.*

"For the prophetical gifts remain with us, even to the present time. And hence you ought to understand that [the gifts] formerly among your nation have been transferred to us. And just as there were false prophets contemporaneous with your holy prophets, so are there now many false teachers amongst us, of whom our Lord forewarned us to beware; so that in no respect are we deficient, since we know that He foreknew all that would happen to us after His resurrection from the dead and ascension to heaven. For He said we would be put to death, and hated for His name's sake; and that many false prophets and false Christs would appear in His name, and deceive many: and so has it come about. For many have taught godless, blasphemous, and unholy doctrines, forging them in His name; have taught, too, and even yet are teaching, those things which proceed from the unclean spirit of the devil, and which were put into their hearts. Therefore we are most anxious that you be persuaded not to be misled by such persons, since we know that everyone who can speak the truth, and yet speaks it not, shall be judged by God, as God testified by Ezekiel, when He said, '***I have made thee a watchman to the house of Judah. If the sinner sin, and thou warn***

---

[569] Psalm 90:4; 2 Peter 3:8.
[570] Literally, "make."
[571] Luke 20:35 {-36}.

him not, he himself shall die in his sin; but his blood will I require at thine hand. But if thou warn him, thou shalt be innocent.'[572]

And on this account we are, through fear, very earnest in desiring to converse [with men] according to the Scriptures, but not from love of money, or of glory, or of pleasure. For no man can convict us of any of these [vices]. No more do we wish to live like the rulers of your people, whom God reproaches when He says, '***Your rulers are companions of thieves, lovers of bribes, followers of the rewards.***'[573] Now, if you know certain amongst us to be of this sort, do not for their sakes blaspheme the Scriptures and Christ, and do not assiduously strive to give falsified interpretations."

Chapter LXXXIII: *It is proved that the Psalm, "The Lord said to My Lord," etc., does not suit Hezekiah.*

"For your teachers have ventured to refer the passage, '***The Lord says to my Lord, Sit at my right hand, till I make Thine enemies Thy footstool,***'[574] to Hezekiah; as if he were requested to sit on the right side of the temple, when the king of Assyria sent to him and threatened him; and he was told by Isaiah not to be afraid. Now we know and admit that what Isaiah said took place; that the king of Assyria desisted from waging war against Jerusalem in Hezekiah's days, and the angel of the Lord slew about 185,000 of the host of the Assyrians. But it is manifest that the Psalm does not refer to him. For thus it is written,

> ***The Lord says to my Lord, Sit at My right hand, till I make Thine enemies Thy footstool. He shall send forth a rod of power over***[575] ***Jerusalem, and it shall rule in the midst of Thine***[576] ***enemies. In the splendor of the saints before the morning star have I begotten Thee. The Lord hath sworn, and will not repent, Thou art a priest for ever after the order of Melchizedek.***[577]

---

[572] Ezekiel 3:17, 18, 19.

[573] Isaiah 1:23.

[574] {Psalm 110:1.}

[575] ἐπί, but afterwards εἰς. Maranus thinks ἐπί is the insertion of some copyist.

[576] Or better, "His." This quotation from Psalm 110 is put very differently from the previous quotation of the same Psalm in Chapter XXXII.

[577] {Psalm 110:1-4.}

Who does not admit, then, that Hezekiah is no priest for ever after the order of Melchizedek? And who does not know that he is not the redeemer of Jerusalem? And who does not know that he neither sent a rod of power into Jerusalem, nor ruled in the midst of his enemies; but that it was God who averted from him the enemies, after he mourned and was afflicted? But our Jesus, who has not yet come in glory, has sent into Jerusalem a rod of power, namely, the word of calling and repentance [meant] for all nations over which demons held sway, as David says, '***The gods of the nations are demons.***'[578] And His strong word has prevailed on many to forsake the demons whom they used to serve, and by means of it to believe in the Almighty God because the gods of the nations are demons.[579] And we mentioned formerly that the statement, '***In the splendor of the saints before the morning star have I begotten Thee from the womb***,'[580] is made to Christ."

Chapter LXXXIV: *That prophecy, "Behold, a virgin," etc., suits Christ alone.*

"Moreover, the prophecy, '***Behold, the virgin shall conceive, and bear a son***,'[581] was uttered respecting Him. For if He to whom Isaiah referred was not to be begotten of a virgin, of whom[582] did the Holy Spirit declare, '***Behold, the Lord Himself shall give us a sign: behold, the virgin shall conceive, and bear a son***?'[583] For if He also were to be begotten of sexual intercourse, like all other first-born sons, why did God say that He would give a sign which is not common to all the first-born sons? But that which is truly a sign, and which was to be made trustworthy to mankind,—namely, that the first-begotten of all creation should become incarnate by the Virgin's womb, and be a child,—this he anticipated by the Spirit of prophecy, and predicted it, as I have repeated to you, in various ways; in order that, when the event should take place, it might be known as the operation of the power and will of the Maker of all things;

---

578 {Psalm 96:5.}

579 This last clause is thought to be an interpolation.

580 {Psalm 110:3. This has been translated quite differently in various Bible translations.}

581 {Isaiah 7:14.}

582 Or, "why was it."

583 {Isaiah 7:14.}

just as Eve was made from one of Adam's ribs, and as all living beings were created in the beginning by the word of God.

But you in these matters venture to pervert the expositions which your elders that were with Ptolemy king of Egypt gave forth, since you assert that the Scripture is not so as they have expounded it, but says, 'Behold, the young woman shall conceive,' as if great events were to be inferred if a woman should beget from sexual intercourse: which indeed all young women, with the exception of the barren, do; but even these, God, if He wills, is able to cause [to bear]. For Samuel's mother, who was barren, brought forth by the will of God; and so also the wife of the holy patriarch Abraham; and Elisabeth, who bore John the Baptist, and other such. So that you must not suppose that it is impossible for God to do anything He wills. And especially when it was predicted that this would take place, do not venture to pervert or misinterpret the prophecies, since you will injure yourselves alone, and will not harm God."

Chapter LXXXV: *He proves that Christ is the Lord of Hosts from Psalm 24, and from his authority over demons.*

"Moreover, some of you venture to expound the prophecy which runs, '***Lift up your gates, ye rulers; and be ye lift up, ye everlasting doors, that the King of glory may enter***,'[584] as if it referred likewise to Hezekiah, and others of you [expound it] of Solomon; but neither to the latter nor to the former, nor, in short, to any of your kings, can it be proved to have reference, but to this our Christ alone, who appeared without comeliness, and inglorious, as Isaiah and David and all the Scriptures said; who is the Lord of hosts, by the will of the Father who conferred on Him [the dignity]; who also rose from the dead, and ascended to heaven, as the Psalm and the other Scriptures manifested when they announced Him to be Lord of hosts; and of this you may, if you will, easily be persuaded by the occurrences which take place before your eyes. For every demon, when exorcised in the name of this very Son of God—who is the First-born of every creature, who became man by the Virgin, who suffered, and was crucified under Pontius Pilate by your nation, who died, who rose from the dead, and ascended into heaven—is overcome and subdued. But though you exorcise any demon in the name of any of

[584] Psalm 24:7.

those who were amongst you—either kings, or righteous men, or prophets, or patriarchs—it will not be subject to you. But if any of you exorcise it in [the name of] the God of Abraham, and the God of Isaac, and the God of Jacob, it will perhaps be subject to you.

Now assuredly your exorcists, I have said,[585] make use of craft when they exorcise, even as the Gentiles do, and employ fumigations and incantations.[586] But that they are angels and powers whom the word of prophecy by David [commands] to lift up the gates, that He who rose from the dead, Jesus Christ, the Lord of hosts, according to the will of the Father, might enter, the word of David has likewise showed; which I shall again recall to your attention for the sake of those who were not with us yesterday, for whose benefit, moreover, I sum up many things I said yesterday.

And now, if I say this to you, although I have repeated it many times, I know that it is not absurd so to do. For it is a ridiculous thing to see the sun, and the moon, and the other stars, continually keeping the same course, and bringing round the different seasons; and to see the computer who may be asked how many are twice two, because he has frequently said that they are four, not ceasing to say again that they are four; and equally so other things, which are confidently admitted, to be continually mentioned and admitted in like manner; yet that he who founds his discourse on the prophetic Scriptures should leave them and abstain from constantly referring to the same Scriptures, because it is thought he can bring forth something better than Scripture. The passage, then, by which I proved that God reveals that there are both angels and hosts in heaven is this: '***Praise the Lord from the heavens: praise Him in the highest. Praise Him, all His angels: praise Him, all His hosts.***'"[587]

Then one of those who had come with them on the second day, whose name was Mnaseas, said, "We are greatly pleased that you undertake to repeat the same things on our account."

And I said, "Listen, my friends, to the Scripture which induces me to act thus. Jesus commanded [us] to love even [our] enemies, as was

---

[585] Chapter LXXVI.

[586] *χατάδεσμοι*, by some thought to be verses by which evil spirits, once expelled, were kept from returning. Plato (*Rep.*) speaks of incantations by which demons were summoned to the help of those who practiced such rites; but Justin refers to them only as being expelled. Others regard them as drugs.

[587] Psalm 148:1, 2.

predicted by Isaiah in many passages, in which also is contained the mystery of our own regeneration, as well, in fact, as the regeneration of all who expect that Christ will appear in Jerusalem, and by their works endeavor earnestly to please Him. These are the words spoken by Isaiah:

> ***Hear the word of the Lord, ye that tremble at His word. Say, our brethren, to them that hate you and detest you, that the name of the Lord has been glorified. He has appeared to your joy, and they shall be ashamed. A voice of noise from the city, a voice from the temple,[588] a voice of the Lord who rendereth recompense to the proud. Before she that travailed brought forth, and before the pains of labor came, she brought forth a male child. Who hath heard such a thing? and who hath seen such a thing? has the earth brought forth in one day? and has she produced a nation at once? for Zion has travailed and borne her children. But I have given such an expectation even to her that does not bring forth, said the Lord. Behold, I have made her that begetteth, and her that is barren, saith the Lord. Rejoice, O Jerusalem, and hold a joyous assembly, all ye that love her. Be glad, all ye that mourn for her, that ye may suck and be filled with the breast of her consolation, that having suck ye may be delighted with the entrance of His glory."[589]***

Chapter LXXXVI: *There are various figures in the Old Testament of the wood of the Cross by which Christ reigned.*

And when I had quoted this, I added, "Hear, then, how this Man, of whom the Scriptures declare that He will come again in glory after His crucifixion, was symbolized both by the tree of life, which was said to have been planted in paradise, and by those events which should happen to all the just. Moses was sent with a rod to effect the redemption of the people; and with this in his hands at the head of the people, he divided the sea. By this he saw the water gushing out of the rock; and when he cast a tree into the waters of Marah, which were bitter, he made them sweet. Jacob, by putting rods into the water-troughs, caused the sheep of his uncle to conceive, so that he should obtain their young. With his rod the same Jacob boasts that he had crossed the river. He said he had

---

[588] In both mss. "people."
[589] Isaiah 66:5-11.

seen a ladder, and the Scripture has declared that God stood above it. But that this was not the Father, we have proved from the Scriptures.

And Jacob, having poured oil on a stone in the same place, is testified to by the very God who appeared to him, that he had anointed a pillar to the God who appeared to him. And that the stone symbolically proclaimed Christ, we have also proved by many Scriptures; and that the unguent, whether it was of oil, or of stacte, or of any other compounded sweet balsams, had reference to Him, we have also proved,[590] inasmuch as the word says: ***'Therefore God, even Thy God, hath anointed Thee with the oil of gladness above Thy fellows.'***[591] For indeed all kings and anointed persons obtained from Him their share in the names of kings and anointed: just as He Himself received from the Father the titles of King, and Christ, and Priest, and Angel, and such like other titles which He bears or did bear. Aaron's rod, which blossomed, declared him to be the high priest. Isaiah prophesied that a rod would come forth from the root of Jesse, [and this was] Christ.

And David says that the righteous man is ***'like the tree that is planted by the channels of waters, which should yield its fruit in its season, and whose leaf should not fade.'***[592] Again, the righteous is said to flourish like the palm-tree. God appeared from a tree to Abraham, as it is written, near the oak in Mamre. The people found seventy willows and twelve springs after crossing the Jordan.[593] David affirms that God comforted him with a rod and staff. Elisha, by casting a stick[594] into the river Jordan, recovered the iron part of the axe with which the sons of the prophets had gone to cut down trees to build the house in which they wished to read and study the law and commandments of God; even as our Christ, by being crucified on the tree, and by purifying [us] with water, has redeemed us, though plunged in the direst offences which we have committed, and has made [us] a house of prayer and adoration. Moreover, it was a rod that pointed out Judah to be the father of Tamar's sons by a great mystery."

---

[590] In Chapter LXIII, probably, where the same Psalm is quoted.

[591] Psalm 45:7.

[592] Psalm 1:3.

[593] The Red Sea, not the Jordan.

[594] Literally, "a tree."

Chapter LXXXVII: *Trypho maintains in objection these words: "And shall rest on Him," etc. They are explained by Justin.*

Hereupon Trypho, after I had spoken these words, said, "Do not now suppose that I am endeavoring, by asking what I do ask, to overturn the statements you have made; but I wish to receive information respecting those very points about which I now inquire. Tell me, then, how, when the Scripture asserts by Isaiah,

> ***There shall come forth a rod from the root of Jesse; and a flower shall grow up from the root of Jesse; and the Spirit of God shall rest upon Him, the spirit of wisdom and understanding, the spirit of counsel and might, the spirit of knowledge and piety: and the spirit of the fear of the Lord shall fill Him*:**[595]

(now you admitted to me," continued he, "that this referred to Christ, and you maintain Him to be pre-existent God, and having become incarnate by God's will, to be born man by the Virgin:) how He can be demonstrated to have been pre-existent, who is filled with the powers of the Holy Ghost, which the Scripture by Isaiah enumerates, as if He were in lack of them?"

Then I replied, "You have inquired most discreetly and most prudently, for truly there does seem to be a difficulty; but listen to what I say, that you may perceive the reason of this also. The Scripture says that these enumerated powers of the Spirit have come on Him, not because He stood in need of them, but because they would rest in Him, i.e., would find their accomplishment in Him, so that there would be no more prophets in your nation after the ancient custom: and this fact you plainly perceive. For after Him no prophet has arisen among you.

Now, that [you may know that] your prophets, each receiving some one or two powers from God, did and spoke the things which we have learned from the Scriptures, attend to the following remarks of mine. Solomon possessed the spirit of wisdom, Daniel that of understanding and counsel, Moses that of might and piety, Elijah that of fear, and Isaiah that of knowledge; and so with the others: each possessed one power, or one joined alternately with another; also Jeremiah, and the twelve [prophets], and David, and, in short, the rest

---

[595] Isaiah 11:1 {-2}. {See also Isaiah 4:2; Zechariah 3:8, 6:12; Revelation 5:5.}

who existed amongst you. Accordingly He[596] rested, i.e., ceased, when *He* came, after whom, in the times of this dispensation wrought out by Him amongst men,[597] it was requisite that such gifts should cease from you; and having received their rest in Him, should again, as had been predicted, become gifts which, from the grace of His Spirit's power, He imparts to those who believe in Him, according as He deems each man worthy thereof. I have already said, and do again say, that it had been prophesied that this would be done by Him after His ascension to heaven. It is accordingly said,[598] '***He ascended on high, He led captivity captive, He gave gifts unto the sons of men.***'[599] And again, in another prophecy it is said: '***And it shall come to pass after this, I will pour out My Spirit on all flesh, and on My servants, and on My handmaids, and they shall prophesy.***'"[600]

Chapter LXXXVIII: *Christ has not received the Holy Spirit on account of poverty.*

"Now, it is possible to see amongst us women and men who possess gifts of the Spirit of God; so that it was prophesied that the powers enumerated by Isaiah would come upon Him, not because He needed power, but because these would not continue after Him. And let this be a proof to you, namely, what I told you was done by the Magi from Arabia, who as soon as the Child was born came to worship Him, for even at His birth He was in possession of His power; and as He grew up like all other men, by using the fitting means, He assigned its own [requirements] to each development, and was sustained by all kinds of nourishment, and waited for thirty years, more or less, until John appeared before Him as the herald of His approach, and preceded Him in the way of baptism, as I have already shown. And then, when Jesus had gone to the river Jordan, where John was baptizing, and when He had stepped into the water, a fire[601] was kindled in the Jordan; and when He

---

[596] He, that is, the Spirit. The following "He" is Christ.

[597] Or, "wrought out amongst His People." So Otto.

[598] Literally, "He said accordingly." Psalm 68:18.

[599] {Psalm 68:18; see also Judges 5:12.}

[600] Joel 2:28 {-29; this prophecy is cited in Acts 2:17; cf. Isaiah 44:3}.

[601] Justin learned this either from tradition or from apocryphal books. Mention is made of a fire both in the Ebionite Gospel and in another publication called *Pauli Praedicatio*, the

came out of the water, the Holy Ghost lighted on Him like a dove, [as] the apostles of this very Christ of ours wrote.

Now, we know that he did not go to the river because He stood in need of baptism, or of the descent of the Spirit like a dove; even as He submitted to be born and to be crucified, not because He needed such things, but because of the human race, which from Adam had fallen under the power of death and the guile of the serpent, and each one of which had committed personal transgression. For God, wishing both angels and men, who were endowed with free-will, and at their own disposal, to do whatever He had strengthened each to do, made them so, that if they chose the things acceptable to Himself, He would keep them free from death and from punishment; but that if they did evil, He would punish each as He sees fit. For it was not His entrance into Jerusalem sitting on an ass, which we have showed was prophesied, that empowered Him to be Christ, but it furnished men with a proof that He is the Christ; just as it was necessary in the time of John that men have proof, that they might know who is Christ. For when John remained[602] by the Jordan, and preached the baptism of repentance, wearing only a leathern girdle and a vesture made of camels' hair, eating nothing but locusts and wild honey, men supposed him to be Christ; but he cried to them, '***I am not the Christ, but the voice of one crying; for He that is stronger than I shall come, whose shoes I am not worthy to bear.***'[603]

And when Jesus came to the Jordan, He was considered to be the son of Joseph the carpenter; and He appeared without comeliness, as the Scriptures declared; and He was deemed a carpenter (for He was in the habit of working as a carpenter when among men, making ploughs and yokes; by which He taught the symbols of righteousness and an active life); but then the Holy Ghost, and for man's sake, as I formerly stated, lighted on Him in the form of a dove, and there came at the same instant from the heavens a voice, which was uttered also by David when he spoke, personating Christ, what the Father would say to Him: '***Thou art***

---

readers and users of which denied that the rite of baptism had been duly performed, unless *quam mox in aquam descenderunt, statim super ignis appareat*. {Online translation renders: "As soon as the water went down immediately appear on Fire."}

[602] Literally, "gat."

[603] {See Matthew 3:11; Mark 1:7; Luke 3:16. See also Malachi 3:1; Matthew 3:3; Mark 1:3; Luke 3:4.}

My Son: this day have I begotten Thee;'[604] [the Father] saying that His generation would take place for men, at the time when they would become acquainted with Him: ***'Thou art My Son; this day have I begotten thee.'"***[605]

Chapter LXXXIX: *The Cross alone is offensive to Trypho on account of the curse, yet it proves that Jesus is Christ.*

Then Trypho remarked, "Be assured that all our nation waits for Christ; and we admit that all the Scriptures which you have quoted refer to Him. Moreover, I do also admit that the name of Jesus, by which the son of Nave (Nun) was called, has inclined me very strongly to adopt this view. But whether Christ should be so shamefully crucified, this we are in doubt about. For whosoever is crucified is said in the law to be accursed, so that I am exceedingly incredulous on this point. It is quite clear, indeed, that the Scriptures announce that Christ had to suffer; but we wish to learn if you can prove it to us whether it was by the suffering cursed in the law."

I replied to him, "If Christ was not to suffer, and the prophets had not foretold that He would be led to death on account of the sins of the people, and be dishonored and scourged, and reckoned among the transgressors, and as a sheep be led to the slaughter, whose generation, the prophet says, no man can declare, then you would have good cause to wonder. But if these are to be characteristic of Him and mark Him out to all, how is it possible for us to do anything else than believe in Him most confidently? And will not as many as have understood the writings of the prophets, whenever they hear merely that He was crucified, say that this is He and no other?"

Chapter XC: *The stretched-out hands of Moses signified beforehand the Cross.*

"Bring us on, then," said [Trypho], "by the Scriptures, that we may also be persuaded by you; for we know that He should suffer and be

---

[604] Psalm 2:7.

[605] The repetition seems quite superfluous. {At Christ's baptism, of course, a voice from Heaven said, "This is my beloved Son, in Whom I am well pleased." Matthew 3:17. See also Mark 1:11; Luke 3:22.}

led as a sheep. But prove to us whether He must be crucified and die so disgracefully and so dishonorably by the death cursed in the law. For we cannot bring ourselves even to think of this."

"You know," said I, "that what the prophets said and did they veiled by parables and types, as you admitted to us; so that it was not easy for all to understand the most [of what they said], since they concealed the truth by these means, that those who are eager to find out and learn it might do so with much labor."

They answered, "We admitted this."

"Listen, therefore," say I, "to what follows; for Moses first exhibited this seeming curse of Christ's by the signs which he made."

"Of what [signs] do you speak?" said he.

"When the people," replied I, "waged war with Amalek, and the son of Nave (Nun) by name Jesus (Joshua), led the fight, Moses himself prayed to God, stretching out both hands, and Hur with Aaron supported them during the whole day, so that they might not hang down when he got wearied. For if he gave up any part of this sign, which was an imitation of the Cross, the people were beaten, as is recorded in the writings of Moses; but if he remained in this form, Amalek was proportionally defeated, and he who prevailed prevailed by the Cross. For it was not because Moses so prayed that the people were stronger, but because, while one who bore the name of Jesus (Joshua) was in the forefront of the battle, he himself made the sign of the Cross. For who of you knows not that the prayer of one who accompanies it with lamentation and tears, with the body prostrate, or with bended knees, propitiates God most of all? But in such a manner neither he nor any other one, while sitting on a stone, prayed. Nor even the stone symbolized Christ, as I have shown."

Chapter XCI: *The Cross was foretold in the blessings of Joseph, and in the serpent that was lifted up.*

"And God by Moses shows in another way the force of the mystery of the Cross, when He said in the blessing wherewith Joseph was blessed,

> ***From the blessing of the Lord is his land; for the seasons of heaven, and for the dews, and for the deep springs from beneath, and for***

> ***the seasonable fruits of the sun,***[606] ***and for the coming together of the months, and for the heights of the everlasting mountains, and for the heights of the hills, and for the ever-flowing rivers, and for the fruits of the fatness of the earth; and let the things accepted by Him who appeared in the bush come on the head and crown of Joseph. Let him be glorified among his brethren;***[607] ***his beauty is [like] the firstling of a bullock; his horns the horns of an unicorn: with these shall he push the nations from one end of the earth to another.***[608]

Now, no one could say or prove that the horns of an unicorn represent any other fact or figure than the type which portrays the Cross. For the one beam is placed upright, from which the highest extremity is raised up into a horn, when the other beam is fitted on to it, and the ends appear on both sides as horns joined on to the one horn. And the part which is fixed in the center, on which are suspended those who are crucified, also stands out like a horn; and it also looks like a horn conjoined and fixed with the other horns. And the expression, '***With these shall he push as with horns the nations from one end of the earth to another***,'[609] is indicative of what is now the fact among all the nations. For some out of all the nations, through the power of this mystery, having been so pushed, that is, pricked in their hearts, have turned from vain idols and demons to serve God.

But the same figure is revealed for the destruction and condemnation of the unbelievers; even as Amalek was defeated and Israel victorious when the people came out of Egypt, by means of the type of the stretching out of Moses' hands, and the name of Jesus (Joshua), by which the son of Nave (Nun) was called. And it seems that the type and sign, which was erected to counteract the serpents which bit Israel, was intended for the salvation of those who believe that death was declared to come thereafter on the serpent through Him that would be crucified, but salvation to those who had been bitten by him and had

---

[606] There is a variety of reading here: either *ἀβύσσου πηγῶν χάτωθενχαθαρῶν* or *ἀβύσου πηγῶν χάτωθεν χαὶ χαθ'*, which we prefer.

[607] The translation in the text is a rendering of the Septuagint. The mss. of Justin read: "Being glorified as the first-born among the brethren."

[608] Deuteronomy 33:13-17.

[609] {Deuteronomy 33:17.}

betaken themselves to Him that sent His Son into the world to be crucified. For the Spirit of prophecy by Moses did not teach us to believe in the serpent, since it shows us that he was cursed by God from the beginning; and in Isaiah tells us that he shall be put to death as an enemy by the mighty sword, which is Christ."

Chapter XCII: *Unless the scriptures be understood through God's great grace, God will not appear to have taught always the same righteousness.*

"Unless, therefore, a man by God's great grace receives the power to understand what has been said and done by the prophets, the appearance of being able to repeat the words or the deeds will not profit him, if he cannot explain the argument of them. And will they not assuredly appear contemptible to many, since they are related by those who understood them not? For if one should wish to ask you why, since Enoch, Noah with his sons, and all others in similar circumstances, who neither were circumcised nor kept the Sabbath, pleased God, God demanded by other leaders, and by the giving of the law after the lapse of so many generations, that those who lived between the times of Abraham and of Moses be justified by circumcision, and that those who lived after Moses be justified by circumcision and the other ordinances—to wit, the Sabbath, and sacrifices, and libations,[610] and offerings; [God will be slandered] unless you show, as I have already said, that God who foreknew was aware that your nation would deserve expulsion from Jerusalem, and that none would be permitted to enter into it.

(For[611] you are not distinguished in any other way than by the fleshly circumcision, as I remarked previously. For Abraham was declared by God to be righteous, not on account of circumcision, but on account of faith. For before he was circumcised the following statement was made regarding him: '***Abraham believed God, and it was accounted unto him for righteousness.***'[612] And we, therefore, in the uncircumcision of our flesh, believing God through Christ, and having that circumcision which is

---

[610] Or, "ashes," *σποδῶν* for *σπονδῶν*.

[611] We have adopted the parenthesis inserted by Maranus. Langus would insert before it, *τί ἕξετε ἀποχρίνασθαι;* "What will you have to answer?"

[612] Genesis 15:6. {See also Psalm 106:31; Galatians 3:6.}

of advantage to us who have acquired it—namely, that of the heart—we hope to appear righteous before and well-pleasing to God: since already we have received His testimony through the words of the prophets.)

[And, further, God will be slandered unless you show] that you were commanded to observe the Sabbath, and to present offerings, and that the Lord submitted to have a place called by the name of God, in order that, as has been said, you might not become impious and godless by worshipping idols and forgetting God, as indeed you do always appear to have been.

(Now, that God enjoined the ordinances of Sabbaths and offerings for these reasons, I have proved in what I previously remarked; but for the sake of those who came today, I wish to repeat nearly the whole.) For if this is not the case, God will be slandered,[613] as having no foreknowledge, and as not teaching all men to know and to do the same acts of righteousness (for many generations of men appear to have existed before Moses); and the Scripture is not true which affirms that '***God is true and righteous, and all His ways are judgments, and there is no unrighteousness in Him.***'[614] But since the Scripture is true, God is always willing that such even as you be neither foolish nor lovers of yourselves, in order that you may obtain the salvation of Christ,[615] who pleased God, and received testimony from Him, as I have already said, by alleging proof from the holy words of prophecy."

Chapter XCIII: *The same kind of righteousness is bestowed on all. Christ comprehends it in two precepts.*

"For [God] sets before every race of mankind that which is always and universally just, as well as all righteousness; and every race knows that adultery, and fornication, and homicide,[616] and such like, are sinful; and though they all commit such practices, yet they do not escape from the knowledge that they act unrighteously whenever they so do, with the exception of those who are possessed with an unclean spirit, and who have been debased by education, by wicked customs, and by sinful

[613] We have supplied this phrase twice above.

[614] {This may be a collection of Scriptural fragments. See Psalm 92:15; see also Ephesians 4:24.}

[615] Literally, salvation along with Christ, that is, by the aid of Christ.

[616] *ἀνδρομανία* is read in mss. for *ἀνδροφονία*.

institutions, and who have lost, or rather quenched and put under, their natural ideas. For we may see that such persons are unwilling to submit to the same things which they inflict upon others, and reproach each other with hostile consciences for the acts which they perpetrate.

And hence I think that our Lord and Savior Jesus Christ spoke well when He summed up all righteousness and piety in two commandments. They are these: ***'Thou shalt love the Lord thy God with all thy heart, and with all thy strength, and thy neighbor as thyself.'***[617] For the man who loves God with all the heart, and with all the strength, being filled with a God-fearing mind, will reverence no other god; and since God wishes it, he would reverence that angel who is beloved by the same Lord and God. And the man who loves his neighbor as himself will wish for him the same good things that he wishes for himself, and no man will wish evil things for himself. Accordingly, he who loves his neighbor would pray and labor that his neighbor may be possessed of the same benefits as himself. Now nothing else is neighbor to man than that similarly-affectioned and reasonable being—man. Therefore, since all righteousness is divided into two branches, namely, in so far as it regards God and men, whoever, says the Scripture, loves the Lord God with all the heart, and all the strength, and his neighbor as himself, would be truly a righteous man.

But you were never shown to be possessed of friendship or love either towards God, or towards the prophets, or towards yourselves, but, as is evident, you are ever found to be idolaters and murderers of righteous men, so that you laid hands even on Christ Himself; and to this very day you abide in your wickedness, execrating those who prove that this man who was crucified by you is the Christ. Nay, more than this, you suppose that He was crucified as hostile to and cursed by God, which supposition is the product of your most irrational mind. For though you have the means of understanding that this man is Christ from the signs given by Moses, yet you will not; but, in addition, fancying that we can have no arguments, you put whatever question comes into your minds, while you yourselves are at a loss for arguments whenever you meet with some firmly established Christian."

---

[617] Matthew 22:37 {and Matthew 22:39. See also Leviticus 19:18; Mark 12:30-31; Romans 13:9.}

Chapter XCIV: *In what sense he who hangs on a tree is cursed.*

"For tell me, was it not God who commanded by Moses that no image or likeness of anything which was in heaven above or which was on the earth should be made, and yet who caused the brazen serpent to be made by Moses in the wilderness, and set it up for a sign by which those bitten by serpents were saved? Yet is He free from unrighteousness. For by this, as I previously remarked, He proclaimed the mystery, by which He declared that He would break the power of the serpent which occasioned the transgression of Adam, and [would bring] to them that believe on Him [who was foreshadowed] by this sign, i.e., Him who was to be crucified, salvation from the fangs of the serpent, which are wicked deeds, idolatries, and other unrighteous acts. Unless the matter be so understood, give me a reason why Moses set up the brazen serpent for a sign, and bade those that were bitten gaze at it, and the wounded were healed; and this, too, when he had himself commanded that no likeness of anything whatsoever should be made."

On this, another of those who came on the second day said, "You have spoken truly: we cannot give a reason. For I have frequently interrogated the teachers about this matter, and none of them gave me a reason: therefore continue what you are speaking; for we are paying attention while you unfold the mystery, on account of which the doctrines of the prophets are falsely slandered."

Then I replied, "Just as God commanded the sign to be made by the brazen serpent, and yet He is blameless; even so, though a curse lies in the law against persons who are crucified, yet no curse lies on the Christ of God, by whom all that have committed things worthy of a curse are saved."

Chapter XCV: *Christ took upon Himself the curse due to us.*

"For the whole human race will be found to be under a curse. For it is written in the law of Moses, '***Cursed is every one that continueth not in all things that are written in the book of the law to do them.***'[618] And no one has accurately done all, nor will you venture to deny this; but

---

[618] Deuteronomy 27:26. {See also Deuteronomy 28:15; Leviticus 26:14 et seq.; Jeremiah 11:3.}

some more and some less than others have observed the ordinances enjoined. But if those who are under this law appear to be under a curse for not having observed all the requirements, how much more shall all the nations appear to be under a curse who practice idolatry, who seduce youths, and commit other crimes?

If, then, the Father of all wished His Christ for the whole human family to take upon Him the curses of all, knowing that, after He had been crucified and was dead, He would raise Him up, why do you argue about Him, who submitted to suffer these things according to the Father's will, as if He were accursed, and do not rather bewail yourselves? For although His Father caused Him to suffer these things in behalf of the human family, yet you did not commit the deed as in obedience to the will of God. For you did not practice piety when you slew the prophets.

And let none of you say: If His Father wished Him to suffer this, in order that by His stripes the human race might be healed, we have done no wrong. If, indeed, you repent of your sins, and recognize Him to be Christ, and observe His commandments, then you may assert this; for, as I have said before, remission of sins shall be yours. But if you curse Him and them that believe on Him, and, when you have the power, put them to death, how is it possible that requisition shall not be made of you, as of unrighteous and sinful men, altogether hard-hearted and without understanding, because you laid your hands on Him?"

Chapter XCVI: *That curse was a prediction of the things which the Jews would do.*

"For the statement in the law, '***Cursed is every one that hangeth on a tree***,'[619] confirms our hope which depends on the crucified Christ, not because He who has been crucified is cursed by God, but because God foretold that which would be done by you all, and by those like to you, who do not know[620] that this is He who existed before all, who is the eternal Priest of God, and King, and Christ. And you clearly see that this has come to pass. For you curse in your synagogues all those who are

---

[619] Deuteronomy 21:23. {See also Joshua 8:29; Galatians 3:13.}

[620] We read *ἐπισταμένων* for *ἐπιστάμενον*. Otherwise to be translated: "God foretold that which you did not know," etc.

called[621] from Him Christians; and other nations effectively carry out the curse, putting to death those who simply confess themselves to be Christians; to all of whom we say, You are our brethren; rather recognize the truth of God. And while neither they nor you are persuaded by us, but strive earnestly to cause us to deny the name of Christ, we choose rather and submit to death, in the full assurance that all the good which God has promised through Christ He will reward us with. And in addition to all this we pray for you, that Christ may have mercy upon you. For He taught us to pray for our enemies also, saying, ***'Love your enemies; be kind and merciful, as your heavenly Father is.'***[622] For we see that the Almighty God is kind and merciful, causing His sun to rise on the unthankful and on the righteous, and sending rain on the holy and on the wicked; all of whom He has taught us He will judge."

Chapter XCVII: *Other predictions of the Cross of Christ.*

"For it was not without design that the prophet Moses, when Hur and Aaron upheld his hands, remained in this form until evening. For indeed the Lord remained upon the tree almost until evening, and they buried Him at eventide; then on the third day He rose again. This was declared by David thus: ***'With my voice I cried to the Lord, and He heard me out of His holy hill. I laid me down, and slept; I awaked, for the Lord sustained me.'***[623] And Isaiah likewise mentions concerning Him the manner in which He would die, thus: ***'I have spread out My hands unto a people disobedient, and gainsaying, that walk in a way which is not good.'***[624] And that He would rise again, Isaiah himself said: ***'His burial has been taken away from the midst, and I will give the rich for His death.'***[625] And again, in other words, David in the twenty-first[626] Psalm thus refers to the suffering and to the Cross in a parable of mystery: ***'They pierced my hands and my feet; they counted all my bones. They considered and gazed on me; they parted my garments among***

---

[621] *λεγομένων* for *γενομένων*.

[622] Luke 6:35 {-36}. {See also Psalm 37:26-27.}

[623] Psalm 3:4, 5.

[624] Isaiah 65:2; comp. also Romans 10:21.

[625] Isaiah 53:9.

[626] That is, Psalm 22:16-18.

themselves, and cast lots upon my vesture.'[627] For when they crucified Him, driving in the nails, they pierced His hands and feet; and those who crucified Him parted His garments among themselves, each casting lots for what he chose to have, and receiving according to the decision of the lot. And this very Psalm you maintain does not refer to Christ; for you are in all respects blind, and do not understand that no one in your nation who has been called King or Christ has ever had his hands or feet pierced while alive, or has died in this mysterious fashion—to wit, by the Cross—save this Jesus alone."

Chapter XCVIII: *Predictions of Christ in Psalm 22.*

"I shall repeat the whole Psalm, in order that you may hear His reverence to the Father, and how He refers all things to Him, and prays to be delivered by Him from this death; at the same time declaring in the Psalm who they are that rise up against Him, and showing that He has truly become man capable of suffering. It is as follows:

> ***O God, my God, attend to me: why hast Thou forsaken me? The words of my transgressions are far from my salvation. O my God, I will cry to Thee in the day-time, and Thou wilt not hear; and in the night-season, and it is not for want of understanding in me. But Thou, the Praise of Israel, inhabitest the holy place. Our fathers trusted in Thee; they trusted, and Thou didst deliver them. They cried unto Thee, and were delivered: they trusted in Thee, and were not confounded. But I am a worm, and no man; a reproach of men, and despised of the people. All they that see me laughed me to scorn; they spake with the lips, they shook the head: He trusted on the Lord: let Him deliver him, let Him save him, since he desires Him. For Thou art He that took me out of the womb; my hope from the breasts of my mother: I was cast upon Thee from the womb. Thou art my God from my mother's belly: be not far from me, for trouble is near; for there is none to help. Many calves have compassed me; fat bulls have beset me round. They opened their mouth upon me, as a ravening and roaring lion. All my bones are poured out and dispersed like water. My heart has become like wax melting in the midst of my belly. My strength is***

[627] {Psalm 22:16-18. See also the Gospels, where these prophecies are fulfilled: Matthew 27:35-36; Mark 15:24-25; Luke 23:33-34; John 19:23-24.}

dried up like a potsherd; and my tongue has cleaved to my throat; and Thou hast brought me into the dust of death. For many dogs have surrounded me; the assembly of the wicked have beset me round. They pierced my hands and my feet, they did tell all my bones. They did look and stare upon me; they parted my garments among them, and cast lots upon my vesture. But do not Thou remove Thine assistance from me, O Lord: give heed to help me; deliver my soul from the sword, and my[628] only-begotten from the hand of the dog. Save me from the lion's mouth, and my humility from the horns of the unicorns. I will declare Thy name to my brethren; in the midst of the Church will I praise Thee. Ye that fear the Lord, praise Him: all ye the seed of Jacob, glorify Him. Let all the seed of Israel fear Him."[629]

Chapter XCIX: *In the commencement of the Psalm are Christ's dying words.*

And when I had said these words, I continued: "Now I will demonstrate to you that the whole Psalm refers thus to Christ, by the words which I shall again explain. What is said at first—***'O God, my God, attend to me: why hast Thou forsaken me?'***[630]—announced from the beginning that which was to be said in the time of Christ. For when crucified, He spake: ***'O God, my God, why hast Thou forsaken me?'***[631] And what follows: ***'The words of my transgressions are far from my salvation. O my God, I will cry to Thee in the day-time, and Thou wilt not hear; and in the night-season, and it is not for want of understanding in me.'***[632] These, as well as the things which He was to do, were spoken. For on the day on which He was to be crucified, having taken three of His disciples to the hill called Olivet, situated opposite to the temple in Jerusalem, He prayed in these words: ***'Father, if it be possible, let this cup pass from me.'***[633] And again He prayed: ***'Not as I***

[628] Probably should be "Thy."
[629] Psalm 22.
[630] {Psalm 22:1.}
[631] {Matthew 27:46; see also Psalm 22:1.}
[632] {See Psalm 22:1-2.}
[633] Matthew 26:39. {See also Matthew 20:22.}

will, but as Thou wilt;'[634] showing by this that He had become truly a suffering man.

But lest anyone should say, He did not know then that He had to suffer, He adds immediately in the Psalm: ***'And it is not for want of understanding in me.'***[635] Even as there was no ignorance on God's part when He asked Adam where he was, or asked Cain where Abel was; but [it was done] to convince each what kind of man he was, and in order that through the record [of Scripture] we might have a knowledge of all: so likewise Christ declared that ignorance was not on His side, but on theirs, who thought that He was not the Christ, but fancied they would put Him to death, and that He, like some common mortal, would remain in Hades."

Chapter C: *In what sense Christ is [called] Jacob, and Israel, and Son of Man.*

"Then what follows—***'But Thou, the praise of Israel, inhabitest the holy place'***[636]—declared that He is to do something worthy of praise and wonderment, being about to rise again from the dead on the third day after the crucifixion; and this He has obtained from the Father. For I have showed already that Christ is called both Jacob and Israel; and I have proved that it is not in the blessing of Joseph and Judah alone that what relates to Him was proclaimed mysteriously, but also in the Gospel it is written that He said: ***'All things are delivered unto me by My Father;'***[637] and, ***'No man knoweth the Father but the Son; nor the Son but the Father, and they to whom the Son will reveal Him.'***[638]

Accordingly He revealed to us all that we have perceived by His grace out of the Scriptures, so that we know Him to be the first-begotten of God, and to be before all creatures; likewise to be the Son of the patriarchs, since He assumed flesh by the Virgin of their family, and submitted to become a man without comeliness, dishonored, and subject to suffering. Hence, also, among His words He said, when He was

---

[634] Ibid.

[635] {Psalm 22:3; not all Bible translations render it so. Compare the OSB to the KJV, for example.}

[636] {Psalm 22:3 or 4 depending on the Bible translation.}

[637] {Matthew 11:27; see also Matthew 28:18.}

[638] Matthew 11:27. {See also John 1:18.}

discoursing about His future sufferings: ***'The Son of man must suffer many things, and be rejected by the Pharisees and scribes, and be crucified, and on the third day rise again.'***[639] He said then that He was the Son of man, either because of His birth by the Virgin, who was, as I said, of the family of David and Jacob, and Isaac, and Abraham; or because Adam[640] was the father both of Himself and of those who have been first enumerated from whom Mary derives her descent. For we know that the fathers of women are the fathers likewise of those children whom their daughters bear. For [Christ] called one of His disciples—previously known by the name of Simon—Peter; since he recognized Him to be Christ the Son of God, by the revelation of His Father: and since we find it recorded in the memoirs of His apostles that He is the Son of God, and since we call Him the Son, we have understood that He proceeded before all creatures from the Father by His power and will (for He is addressed in the writings of the prophets in one way or another as Wisdom, and the Day,[641] and the East, and a Sword, and a Stone, and a Rod, and Jacob, and Israel); and that He became man by the Virgin, in order that the disobedience which proceeded from the serpent might receive its destruction in the same manner in which it derived its origin.

For Eve, who was a virgin and undefiled, having conceived the word of the serpent, brought forth disobedience and death. But the Virgin Mary received faith and joy, when the angel Gabriel announced the good tidings to her that the Spirit of the Lord would come upon her, and the power of the Highest would overshadow her: wherefore also the Holy Thing begotten of her is the Son of God;[642] and she replied, ***'Be it unto me according to thy word.'***[643] And by her has He been born, to whom we have proved so many Scriptures refer, and by whom God destroys both the serpent and those angels and men who are like him; but works deliverance from death to those who repent of their wickedness and believe upon Him."

---

[639] Matthew 16:21. {See also Matthew 20:18-19; Luke 9:22.}

[640] The text is, *αὖτν τδν 'Αβραὰμ πατέρα.* Thirlby proposed *αὐτδμ τὺ Αδὰμ*; Maranus changed this into, *αὖτοῦ τδν 'Αδὰμ πατέρα.*

[641] It is not easy, says Maranus, to say in what Scripture Christ is so called. Perhaps Justin had in his mind the passage, "This is the *day* which the Lord hath made" (Psalm 118:24). Clem. Alex. teaches that Christ is here referred to.

[642] Luke 1:35. See Meyer *in loc.*

[643] Luke 1:38.

Chapter CI: *Christ refers all things to the Father.*

"Then what follows of the Psalm is this, in which He says: ***'Our fathers trusted in Thee; they trusted, and Thou didst deliver them. They cried unto Thee, and were not confounded. But I am a worm, and no man; a reproach of men, and despised of the people;'***[644] which show that He admits them to be His fathers, who trusted in God and were saved by Him, who also were the fathers of the Virgin, by whom He was born and became man; and He foretells that He shall be saved by the same God, but boasts not in accomplishing anything through His own will or might. For when on earth He acted in the very same manner, and answered to one who addressed Him as ***'Good Master:' 'Why callest thou me good? One is good, my Father who is in heaven.'***[645] But when He says, ***'I am a worm, and no man; a reproach of men, and despised of the people,'***[646] He prophesied the things which do exist, and which happen to Him. For we who believe on Him are everywhere a reproach, ***'despised of the people;'*** for, rejected and dishonored by your nation, He suffered those indignities which you planned against Him.

And the following: ***'All they that see me laughed me to scorn; they spake with the lips, they shook the head: He trusted in the Lord; let Him deliver him, since he desires Him;'***[647] this likewise He foretold should happen to Him. For they that saw Him crucified shook their heads each one of them, and distorted their lips, and twisting their noses to each other,[648] they spake in mockery the words which are recorded in the memoirs of His apostles: ***'He said he was the Son of God: let him come down; let God save him.'"***[649]

Chapter CII: *The prediction of the events which happened to Christ when He was born. Why God permitted it.*

"And what follows—

---

[644] {Psalm 22:5-6; see also Psalm 25:2; Job 25:6.}
[645] Luke 18:18 {-19}. {See also Matthew 19:16-17.}
[646] {Psalm 22:6.}
[647] {See Matthew 27:39-40; Mark 15:29-30; Luke 23:35-37; Psalm 22:7-8.}
[648] The text is corrupt, and the meaning is doubtful. Otto translates: *naribus inter se certantes.*
[649] {Matthew 27:40.}

> ***My hope from the breasts of my mother. On Thee have I been cast from the womb; from my mother's belly Thou art my God: for there is no helper. Many calves have compassed me; fat bulls have beset me round. They opened their mouth upon me, as a ravening and a roaring lion. All my bones are poured out and dispersed like water. My heart has become like wax melting in the midst of my belly. My strength is become dry like a potsherd; and my tongue has cleaved to my throat***[650]

—foretold what would come to pass; for the statement, '***My hope from the breasts of my mother***,'[651] [is thus explained]. As soon as He was born in Bethlehem, as I previously remarked, king Herod, having learned from the Arabian Magi about Him, made a plot to put Him to death; and by God's command Joseph took Him with Mary and departed into Egypt. For the Father had decreed that He whom He had begotten should be put to death, but not before He had grown to manhood, and proclaimed the word which proceeded from Him.

But if any of you say to us, Could not God rather have put Herod to death? I return answer by anticipation: Could not God have cut off in the beginning the serpent, so that he exist not, rather than have said, '***And I will put enmity between him and the woman, and between his seed and her seed***?'[652] Could He not have at once created a multitude of men? But yet, since He knew that it would be good, He created both angels and men free to do that which is righteous, and He appointed periods of time during which He knew it would be good for them to have the exercise of free-will; and because He likewise knew it would be good, He made general and particular judgments; each one's freedom of will, however, being guarded.

Hence Scripture says the following, at the destruction of the tower, and division and alteration of tongues: '***And the Lord said, Behold, the people is one, and they have all one language; and this they have begun to do: and now nothing will be restrained from them of all which they have attempted to do.***'[653] And the statement, '***My strength is***

---

[650] {Psalm 22:9-15.}
[651] {Psalm 22:9.}
[652] Genesis 3:15.
[653] Genesis 11:6. {See also Acts 17:26.}

become dry like a potsherd, and my tongue has cleaved to my throat,'[654] was also a prophecy of what would be done by Him according to the Father's will. For the power of His strong word, by which He always confuted the Pharisees and scribes, and, in short, all your nation's teachers that questioned Him, had a cessation like a plentiful and strong spring, the waters of which have been turned off, when He kept silence, and chose to return no answer to anyone in the presence of Pilate; as has been declared in the memoirs of His apostles, in order that what is recorded by Isaiah might have efficacious fruit, where it is written, ***'The Lord gives me a tongue, that I may know when I ought to speak.'***[655]

Again, when He said, ***'Thou art my God; be not far from me,'***[656] He taught that all men ought to hope in God who created all things, and seek salvation and help from Him alone; and not suppose, as the rest of men do, that salvation can be obtained by birth, or wealth, or strength, or wisdom.

And such have ever been your practices: at one time you made a calf, and always you have shown yourselves ungrateful, murderers of the righteous, and proud of your descent. For if the Son of God evidently states that He can be saved, [neither][657] because He is a son, nor because He is strong or wise, but that without God He cannot be saved, even though He be sinless, as Isaiah declares in words to the effect that even in regard to His very language He committed no sin (for He committed no iniquity or guile with His mouth), how do you or others who expect to be saved without this hope, suppose that you are not deceiving yourselves?"

Chapter CIII: *The Pharisees are the bulls: the roaring lion is Herod or the devil.*

"Then what is next said in the Psalm—***'For trouble is near, for there is none to help me. Many calves have compassed me; fat bulls have beset me round. They opened their mouth upon me as a ravening and roaring lion. All my bones are poured out and dispersed like water,'***[658]—was likewise a prediction of the events which happened to

---

[654] {Psalm 22:15.}
[655] Isaiah 50:4.
[656] {Psalm 22:10-11; see also Psalm 46:1.}
[657] Not found in mss.
[658] {Psalm 22:11-14.}

Him. For on that night when some of your nation, who had been sent by the Pharisees, and scribes, and teachers,[659] came upon Him from the Mount[660] of Olives, those whom Scripture called butting and prematurely destructive calves surrounded Him.

And the expression, '***Fat bulls have beset me round***,'[661] He spoke beforehand of those who acted similarly to the calves, when He was led before your teachers. And the Scripture described them as bulls, since we know that bulls are authors of calves' existence. As therefore the bulls are the begetters of the calves, so your teachers were the cause why their children went out to the Mount of Olives to take Him and bring Him to them.

And the expression, '***For there is none to help***,'[662] is also indicative of what took place. For there was not even a single man to assist Him as an innocent person.

And the expression, '***They opened their mouth upon me like a roaring lion***,'[663] designates him who was then king of the Jews, and was called Herod, a successor of the Herod who, when Christ was born, slew all the infants in Bethlehem born about the same time, because he imagined that amongst them He would assuredly be of whom the Magi from Arabia had spoken; for he was ignorant of the will of Him that is stronger than all, how He had commanded Joseph and Mary to take the Child and depart into Egypt, and there to remain until a revelation should again be made to them to return into their own country.

And there they did remain until Herod, who slew the infants in Bethlehem, was dead, and Archelaus had succeeded him. And he died before Christ came to the dispensation on the Cross which was given Him by His Father.

And when Herod succeeded Archelaus, having received the authority which had been allotted to him, Pilate sent to him by way of compliment Jesus bound; and God foreknowing that this would happen,

---

[659] *χαι τῶν διδασχάλων*, adopted instead of *χατὰ τὴν διδασχαλίαν*, "according to their instructions."

[660] *ἀπδ τοῦ ὅρους*. Justin seems to have supposed that the Jews came on Christ from some point of the hill while he was in the valley below. *'Γπὶ τοῦ ὅρους* and *ἐπὶ τδ ὅρος* have been suggested.

[661] {See Psalm 22:12.}

[662] {Psalm 22:11.}

[663] {Psalm 22:13.}

had thus spoken: *'**And they brought Him to the Assyrian, a present to the king.**'*[664] Or He meant the devil by the lion roaring against Him: whom Moses calls the serpent, but in Job and Zechariah he is called the devil, and by Jesus is addressed as Satan, showing that a compounded name was acquired by him from the deeds which he performed. For 'Sata' in the Jewish and Syrian tongue means apostate; and 'Nas' is the word from which he is called by interpretation the *serpent*, i.e., according to the interpretation of the Hebrew term, from both of which there arises the single word *Satanas*. For this devil, when [Jesus] went up from the river Jordan, at the time when the voice spake to Him, *'**Thou art my Son: this day have I begotten Thee**,'*[665] is recorded in the memoirs of the apostles to have come to Him and tempted Him, even so far as to say to Him, *'**Worship me**;'*[666] and Christ answered him, *'**Get thee behind me, Satan: thou shalt worship the Lord thy God, and Him only shalt thou serve.**'*[667] For as he had deceived Adam, so he hoped[668] that he might contrive some mischief against Christ also.

Moreover, the statement, *'**All my bones are poured out**[669] **and dispersed like water; my heart has become like wax, melting in the midst of my belly**,'*[670] was a prediction of that which happened to Him on that night when men came out against Him to the Mount of Olives to seize Him. For in the memoirs which I say were drawn up by His apostles and those who followed them, [it is recorded] that His sweat fell down like drops of blood while He was praying, and saying, *'**If it be possible, let this cup pass**:'*[671] His heart and also His bones trembling; His heart being like wax melting in His belly: in order that we may perceive that the Father wished His Son really[672] to undergo such sufferings for our sakes,

---

[664] Hosea 10:6.

[665] Psalm 2:7; comp. Matthew 3:17. {See above text, Ch. LXXXVIII and accompanying notes.}

[666] {Matthew 4:9.}

[667] Matthew 4:9, 10. {See also Deuteronomy 6:13, 10, 12; Psalm 63:11; 1 Samuel 7:3.}

[668] Literally, "said,"

[669] Maranus says it is hardly to be doubted that Justin read, "I am poured out like water," etc.

[670] {Psalm 22:14.}

[671] Luke 22:44, 42. {Verse 44 refers to Christ's sweat. Verse 42 refers to His statement.}

[672] Justin refers to the opinion of the Docetes {*sic* Docetists}, that Christ suffered in appearance merely, and not in reality.

and may not say that He, being the Son of God, did not feel what was happening to Him and inflicted on Him.

Further, the expression, '***My strength is dried up like a potsherd, and my tongue has cleaved to my throat,***'[673] was a prediction, as I previously remarked, of that silence, when He who convicted all your teachers of being unwise returned no answer at all."

Chapter CIV: *Circumstances of Christ's death are predicted in Psalm 22.*

"And the statement,

> **Thou hast brought me into the dust of death; for many dogs have surrounded me: the assembly of the wicked have beset me round. They pierced my hands and my feet. They did tell all my bones. They did look and stare upon me. They parted my garments among them, and cast lots upon my vesture,**[674]

—was a prediction, as I said before, of the death to which the synagogue of the wicked would condemn Him, whom He calls both dogs and hunters, declaring that those who hunted Him were both gathered together and assiduously striving to condemn Him. And this is recorded to have happened in the memoirs of His apostles. And I have shown that, after His crucifixion, they who crucified Him parted His garments among them."

Chapter CV: *Psalm 22 also predicts the crucifixion and the subject of the last prayers of Christ on Earth.*

"And what follows of the Psalm,—'***But Thou, Lord, do not remove Thine assistance from me; give heed to help me. Deliver my soul from the sword, and my***[675] ***only-begotten from the hand of the dog; save me from the lion's mouth, and my humility from the horns of the unicorns,***'[676]—was also information and prediction of the events which

---

[673] {Psalm 22:15.}
[674] {Psalm 22:15-18.}
[675] See note on Chapter XCVIII.
[676] {Psalm 22:19-21.}

should befall Him. For I have already proved that He was the only-begotten of the Father of all things, being begotten in a peculiar manner Word and Power by Him, and having afterwards become man through the Virgin, as we have learned from the memoirs. Moreover, it is similarly foretold that He would die by crucifixion. For the passage, '***Deliver my soul from the sword, and my***[677] ***only-begotten from the hand of the dog; save me from the lion's mouth, and my humility from the horns of the unicorns***,'[678] is indicative of the suffering by which He should die, i.e., by crucifixion. For the '***horns of the, unicorns***,'[679] I have already explained to you, are the figure of the Cross only. And the prayer that His soul should be saved from the sword, and lion's mouth, and hand of the dog, was a prayer that no one should take possession of His soul: so that, when we arrive at the end of life, we may ask the same petition from God, who is able to turn away every shameless evil angel from taking our souls.

And that the souls survive, I have shown[680] to you from the fact that the soul of Samuel was called up by the witch, as Saul demanded. And it appears also, that all the souls of similar righteous men and prophets fell under the dominion of such powers, as is indeed to be inferred from the very facts in the case of that witch. Hence also God by His Son teaches[681] us for whose sake these things seem to have been done, always to strive earnestly, and at death to pray that our souls may not fall into the hands of any such power. For when Christ was giving up His spirit on the Cross, He said, '***Father, into Thy hands I commend my spirit***,'[682] as I have learned also from the memoirs. For He exhorted His disciples to surpass the pharisaic way of living, with the warning, that if they did not, they might be sure they could not be saved; and these words are recorded in the memoirs: '***Unless your righteousness exceed that of the scribes and Pharisees, ye shall not enter into the kingdom of heaven.***'"[683]

---

[677] {Psalm 22:20.}

[678] {Psalm 22:20-21.}

[679] {Psalm 22:21.}

[680] This demonstration is not given.

[681] Sylburg proposed *διχαίους γίνεσθαι* for *δί οὓς γιν.*, "to strive earnestly to become righteous, and at death to pray."

[682] Luke 23:46. {See also Mark 15:37; 1 Peter 2-23.}

[683] Matthew 5:20.

Chapter CVI: *Christ's resurrection is foretold in the conclusion of Psalm 22.*

"The remainder of the Psalm makes it manifest that He knew His Father would grant to Him all things which He asked, and would raise Him from the dead; and that He urged all who fear God to praise Him because He had compassion on all races of believing men, through the mystery of Him who was crucified; and that He stood in the midst of His brethren the apostles (who repented of their flight from Him when He was crucified, after He rose from the dead, and after they were persuaded by Himself that, before His passion He had mentioned to them that He must suffer these things, and that they were announced beforehand by the prophets), and when living with them sang praises to God, as is made evident in the memoirs of the apostles. The words are the following: '***I will declare Thy name to my brethren; in the midst of the church will I praise Thee. Ye that fear the Lord, praise Him; all ye, the seed of Jacob, glorify Him. Let all the seed of Israel fear Him.***'[684]

And when it is said that He changed the name of one of the apostles to Peter; and when it is written in the memoirs of Him that this so happened, as well as that He changed the names of other two brothers, the sons of Zebedee, to Boanerges, which means sons of thunder; this was an announcement of the fact that it was He by whom Jacob was called Israel, and Oshea called Jesus (Joshua), under whose name the people who survived of those that came from Egypt were conducted into the land promised to the patriarchs.

And that He should arise like a star from the seed of Abraham, Moses showed before hand when he thus said, '***A star shall arise from Jacob, and a leader from Israel***;'[685] and another Scripture says, '***Behold a man; the East is His name.***'[686] Accordingly, when a star rose in heaven at the time of His birth, as is recorded in the memoirs of His apostles, the Magi from Arabia, recognizing the sign by this, came and worshipped Him."

---

[684] {Psalm 22:22-23.}

[685] Numbers 24:17.

[686] Zechariah 6:12 (according to LXX). {The Orthodox Study Bible translates this "Orient" but acknowledges other variants as "Dayspring" and "Sunshine" and that the Hebrew is rendered "Branch" as in the KJV. The OSB translates Zechariah 3:8 as "Dayspring" and the KJV as "Branch."}

Chapter CVII: *The same is taught from the history of Jonah.*

"And that He would rise again on the third day after the crucifixion, it is written[687] in the memoirs that some of your nation, questioning Him, said, '***Show us a sign***;'[688] and He replied to them, '***An evil and adulterous generation seeketh after a sign; and no sign shall be given them, save the sign of Jonah.***'[689] And since He spoke this obscurely, it was to be understood by the audience that after His crucifixion He should rise again on the third day.

And He showed that your generation was more wicked and more adulterous than the city of Nineveh; for the latter, when Jonah preached to them, after he had been cast up on the third day from the belly of the great fish, that after three (in other versions, forty)[690] days they should all perish, proclaimed a fast of all creatures, men and beasts, with sackcloth, and with earnest lamentation, with true repentance from the heart, and turning away from unrighteousness, in the belief that God is merciful and kind to all who turn from wickedness; so that the king of that city himself, with his nobles also, put on sackcloth and remained fasting and praying, and obtained their request that the city should not be overthrown.

But when Jonah was grieved that on the (fortieth) third day, as he proclaimed, the city was not overthrown, by the dispensation of a gourd[691] springing up from the earth for him, under which he sat and was shaded from the heat (now the gourd had sprung up suddenly, and Jonah had neither planted nor watered it, but it had come up all at once to afford him shade), and by the other dispensation of its withering away, for which Jonah grieved, [God] convicted him of being unjustly displeased because the city of Nineveh had not been overthrown, and said,

> ***Thou hast had pity on the gourd, for that which thou hast not labored, neither madest it grow; which came up in a night, and perished in a night. And shall I not spare Nineveh, the great city, wherein dwell more than six score thousand persons that cannot***

---

[687] Matthew 12:38 f.

[688] {Matthew 12:38; see also Matthew 16:1; Luke 11:16; 1 Corinthians 1:22.}

[689] {Matthew 12:39.}

[690] In the LXX, only *three* days are recorded, though in the Hebrew and other versions *forty*. The parenthetic clause is probably the work of a transcriber.

[691] Read *χιχυῶνα* for *σιχυῶνα*.

***discern between their right hand and their left hand; and also much cattle*?"[692]**

Chapter CVIII: *The resurrection of Christ did not convert the Jews. But through the whole world they have sent men to accuse Christ.*

"And though all the men of your nation knew the incidents in the life of Jonah, and though Christ said amongst you that He would give the sign of Jonah, exhorting you to repent of your wicked deeds at least after He rose again from the dead, and to mourn before God as did the Ninevites, in order that your nation and city might not be taken and destroyed, as they have been destroyed; yet you not only have not repented, after you learned that He rose from the dead, but, as I said before[693] you have sent chosen and ordained men throughout all the world to proclaim that a godless and lawless heresy had sprung from one Jesus, a Galilaean deceiver, whom we crucified, but His disciples stole Him by night from the tomb, where He was laid when unfastened from the Cross, and now deceive men by asserting that He has risen from the dead and ascended to Heaven.

Moreover, you accuse Him of having taught those godless, lawless, and unholy doctrines which you mention to the condemnation of those who confess Him to be Christ, and a Teacher from and Son of God. Besides this, even when your city is captured, and your land ravaged, you do not repent, but dare to utter imprecations on Him and all who believe in Him. Yet we do not hate you or those who, by your means, have conceived such prejudices against us; but we pray that even now all of you may repent and obtain mercy from God, the compassionate and long-suffering Father of all."

Chapter CIX: *The conversion of the Gentiles has been predicted by Micah.*

"But that the Gentiles would repent of the evil in which they led erring lives, when they heard the doctrine preached by His apostles from Jerusalem, and which they learned[694] through them, suffer me to show

---

[692] Jonah 4:10 {-11}.

[693] Chapter XVII.

[694] Read *μαθόντα* for *παθόντα*.

you by quoting a short statement from the prophecy of Micah, one of the twelve [minor prophets]. This is as follows:

> ***And in the last days the mountain of the Lord shall be manifest, established on the top of the mountains; it shall be exalted above the hills, and people shall flow unto it.*[695] *And many nations shall go, and say, Come, let us go up to the mountain of the Lord, and to the house of the God of Jacob; and they shall enlighten us in His way, and we shall walk in His paths: for out of Zion shall go forth the law, and the word of the Lord from Jerusalem. And He shall judge among many peoples, and shall rebuke strong nations afar off; and they shall beat their swords into ploughshares, and their spears into sickles: nation shall not lift up a sword against nation, neither shall they learn war any more. And each man shall sit under his vine and under his fig tree; and there shall be none to terrify: for the mouth of the Lord of hosts hath spoken it. For all people will walk in the name of their gods; but we will walk in the name of the Lord our God for ever. And it shall come to pass in that day, that I will assemble her that is afflicted, and gather her that is driven out, and whom I had plagued; and I shall make her that is afflicted a remnant, and her that is oppressed a strong nation. And the Lord shall reign over them in Mount Zion from henceforth, and even for ever."***[696]

Chapter CX: *A portion of the prophecy already fulfilled in the Christians: the rest shall be fulfilled at the second advent.*

And when I had finished these words, I continued: "Now I am aware that your teachers, sirs, admit the whole of the words of this passage to refer to Christ; and I am likewise aware that they maintain He has not yet come; or if they say that He has come, they assert that it is not known who He is; but when He shall become manifest and glorious, then it shall be known who He is. And then, they say, the events mentioned in this passage shall happen, just as if there was no fruit as yet from the words of the prophecy.

O unreasoning men! understanding not what has been proved by all these passages, that two advents of Christ have been announced: the

---

695 Literally, "the people shall place a river in it."
696 Micah 4:1 ff.

one, in which He is set forth as suffering, inglorious, dishonored, and crucified; but the other, in which He shall come from Heaven with glory, when the man of apostasy,[697] who speaks strange things against the Most High, shall venture to do unlawful deeds on the earth against us the Christians, who, having learned the true worship of God from the law, and the word which went forth from Jerusalem by means of the apostles of Jesus, have fled for safety to the God of Jacob and God of Israel; and we who were filled with war, and mutual slaughter, and every wickedness, have each through the whole earth changed our warlike weapons,—our swords into ploughshares, and our spears into implements of tillage,—and we cultivate piety, righteousness, philanthropy, faith, and hope, which we have from the Father Himself through Him who was crucified; and sitting each under his vine, i.e., each man possessing his own married wife. For you are aware that the prophetic word says, '***And his wife shall be like a fruitful vine***.'[698]

Now it is evident that no one can terrify or subdue us who have believed in Jesus over all the world. For it is plain that, though beheaded, and crucified, and thrown to wild beasts, and chains, and fire, and all other kinds of torture, we do not give up our confession; but the more such things happen, the more do others and in larger numbers become faithful, and worshippers of God through the name of Jesus. For just as if one should cut away the fruit-bearing parts of a vine, it grows up again, and yields other branches flourishing and fruitful; even so the same thing happens with us. For the vine planted by God and Christ the Savior is His people.

But the rest of the prophecy shall be fulfilled at His second coming. For the expression, '***He that is afflicted [and driven out]***,'[699] i.e., from the world, [implies] that, so far as you and all other men have it in your power, each Christian has been driven out not only from his own property, but even from the whole world; for you permit no Christian to live.

But you say that the same fate has befallen your own nation. Now, if you have been cast out after defeat in battle, you have suffered such treatment justly indeed, as all the Scriptures bear witness; but we,

---

[697] 2 Thessalonians 2:3; and see Chapter XXXII.

[698] Psalm 128:3.

[699] {See Micah 4:6.}

though we have done no such [evil acts] after we knew the truth of God, are testified to by God, that, together with the most righteous, and only spotless and sinless Christ, we are taken away out of the earth. For Isaiah cries, '***Behold how the righteous perishes, and no man lays it to heart; and righteous men are taken away, and no man considers it.***'"[700]

Chapter CXI: *The two advents were signified by the two goats. Other figures of the first advent, in which the Gentiles are freed by the blood of Christ.*

"And that it was declared by symbol, even in the time of Moses, that there would be two advents of this Christ, as I have mentioned previously, [is manifest] from the symbol of the goats presented for sacrifice during the fast. And again, by what Moses and Joshua did, the same thing was symbolically announced and told beforehand. For the one of them, stretching out his hands, remained till evening on the hill, his hands being supported; and this reveals a type of no other thing than of the Cross: and the other, whose name was altered to Jesus (Joshua), led the fight, and Israel conquered. Now this took place in the case of both those holy men and prophets of God, that you may perceive how one of them could not bear up both the mysteries: I mean, the type of the Cross and the type of the Name. For this is, was, and shall be the strength of Him alone, whose Name every power dreads, being very much tormented because they shall be destroyed by Him. Therefore our suffering and crucified Christ was not cursed by the law, but made it manifest that He alone would save those who do not depart from His faith.

And the blood of the passover, sprinkled on each man's door-posts and lintel, delivered those who were saved in Egypt, when the first-born of the Egyptians were destroyed. For the passover was Christ, who was afterwards sacrificed, as also Isaiah said, '***He was led as a sheep to the slaughter.***'[701] And it is written, that on the day of the passover you seized Him, and that also during the passover you crucified Him. And as the blood of the passover saved those who were in Egypt, so also the blood of Christ will deliver from death those who have believed.

---

[700] Isaiah 57:1.

[701] Isaiah 53:7. {See also Acts 8:32.}

Would God, then, have been deceived if this sign had not been above the doors? I do not say that; but I affirm that He announced beforehand the future salvation for the human race through the blood of Christ. For the sign of the scarlet thread, which the spies, sent to Jericho by Joshua, son of Nave (Nun), gave to Rahab the harlot, telling her to bind it to the window through which she let them down to escape from their enemies, also manifested the symbol of the blood of Christ, by which those who were at one time harlots and unrighteous persons out of all nations are saved, receiving remission of sins, and continuing no longer in sin."

Chapter CXII: *The Jews expound these signs jejunely and feebly, and take up their attention only with insignificant matters.*

"But you, expounding these things in a low [and earthly] manner, impute much weakness to God, if you thus listen to them merely, and do not investigate the force of the words spoken. Since even Moses would in this way be considered a transgressor: for he enjoined that no likeness of anything in heaven, or on earth, or in the sea, be made; and then he himself made a brazen serpent and set it on a standard, and bade those who were bitten look at it: and they were saved when they looked at it. Will the serpent, then, which (I have already said) God had in the beginning cursed and cut off by the great sword, as Isaiah says,[702] be understood as having preserved at that time the people? and shall we receive these things in the foolish acceptation of your teachers, and [regard] them not as signs? And shall we not rather refer the standard to the resemblance of the crucified Jesus, since also Moses by his outstretched hands, together with him who was named Jesus (Joshua), achieved a victory for your people? For in this way we shall cease to be at a loss about the things which the lawgiver did, when he, without forsaking God, persuaded the people to hope in a beast through which transgression and disobedience had their origin. And this was done and said by the blessed prophet with much intelligence and mystery; and there is nothing said or done by any one of the prophets, without exception, which one can justly reprehend, if he possess the knowledge which is in them.

---

[702] Isaiah 37:3.

But if your teachers only expound to you why female camels are spoken of in this passage, and are not in that; or why so many measures of fine flour and so many measures of oil [are used] in the offerings; and do so in a low and sordid manner, while they never venture either to speak of or to expound the points which are great and worthy of investigation, or command you to give no audience to us while we expound them, and to come not into conversation with us; will they not deserve to hear what our Lord Jesus Christ said to them: ***'Whited sepulchers, which appear beautiful outward, and within are full of dead men's bones; which pay tithe of mint, and swallow a camel: ye blind guides!'***[703] If, then, you will not despise the doctrines of those who exalt themselves and wish to be called Rabbi, Rabbi, and come with such earnestness and intelligence to the words of prophecy as to suffer the same inflictions from your own people which the prophets themselves did, you cannot receive any advantage whatsoever from the prophetic writings."

Chapter CXIII: *Joshua was a figure of Christ.*

"What I mean is this. Jesus (Joshua), as I have now frequently remarked, who was called Oshea, when he was sent to spy out the land of Canaan, was named by Moses Jesus (Joshua). Why he did this you neither ask, nor are at a loss about it, nor make strict inquiries. Therefore Christ has escaped your notice; and though you read, you understand not; and even now, though you hear that Jesus is our Christ, you consider not that the name was bestowed on Him not purposelessly nor by chance.

But you make a theological discussion as to why one *'α'* was added to Abraham's first name; and as to why one *'ρ'* was added to Sarah's name, you use similar high-sounding disputations.[704] But why do you not similarly investigate the reason why the name of Oshea the son of Nave (Nun), which his father gave him, was changed to Jesus (Joshua)? But since not only was his name altered, but he was also appointed successor to Moses, being the only one of his contemporaries who came out from Egypt, he led the surviving people into the Holy Land; and as he, not Moses, led the people into the Holy Land, and as he distributed it by

---

[703] Matthew 23:27, 23, 24. {See also Psalm 5:9; Luke 11:44; cf. Mark 7:4.}
[704] According to the LXX, *Σάρα* was altered to *Σάῤῥα*, and to *Ἄβραμ*.

lot to those who entered along with him, so also Jesus the Christ will turn again the dispersion of the people, and will distribute the good land to each one, though not in the same manner. For the former gave them a temporary inheritance, seeing he was neither Christ who is God, nor the Son of God; but the latter, after the holy resurrection,[705] shall give us the eternal possession. The former, after he had been named Jesus (Joshua), and after he had received strength from His Spirit, caused the sun to stand still.

For I have proved that it was Jesus who appeared to and conversed with Moses, and Abraham, and all the other patriarchs without exception, ministering to the will of the Father; who also, I say, came to be born man by the Virgin Mary, and lives forever. For the latter is He after[706] whom and by whom the Father will renew both the heaven and the earth; this is He who shall shine an eternal light in Jerusalem; this is he who is the king of Salem after the order of Melchizedek, and the eternal Priest of the Most High. The former is said to have circumcised the people a second time with knives of stone (which was a sign of this circumcision with which Jesus Christ Himself has circumcised us from the idols made of stone and of other materials), and to have collected together those who were circumcised from the uncircumcision, i.e., from the error of the world, in every place by the knives of stone, to wit, the words of our Lord Jesus. For I have shown that Christ was proclaimed by the prophets in parables a Stone and a Rock. Accordingly the knives of stone we shall take to mean His words, by means of which so many who were in error have been circumcised from uncircumcision with the circumcision of the heart, with which God by Jesus commanded those from that time to be circumcised who derived their circumcision from Abraham, saying that Jesus (Joshua) would circumcise a second time with knives of stone those who entered into that holy land."

---

[705] Or, "resurrection of the saints."

[706] Justin seems to mean that the renewal of heaven and earth dates from the incarnation of Christ.

Chapter CXIV: *Some rules for discerning what is said about Christ. The circumcision of the Jews is very different from that which Christians receive.*

"For the Holy Spirit sometimes brought about that something, which was the type of the future, should be done clearly; sometimes He uttered words about what was to take place, as if it was then taking place, or had taken place. And unless those who read perceive this art, they will not be able to follow the words of the prophets as they ought.

For example's sake, I shall repeat some prophetic passages, that you may understand what I say. When He speaks by Isaiah, '***He was led as a sheep to the slaughter, and like a lamb before the shearer***,'[707] He speaks as if the suffering had already taken place. And when He says again, '***I have stretched out my hands to a disobedient and gainsaying people***;'[708] and when He says, '***Lord, who hath believed our report***?'[709]—the words are spoken as if announcing events which had already come to pass. For I have shown that Christ is oftentimes called a Stone in parable, and in figurative speech Jacob and Israel. And again, when He says, '***I shall behold the heavens, the works of Thy fingers***,'[710] unless I understand His method of using words,[711] I shall not understand intelligently, but just as your teachers suppose, fancying that the Father of all, the unbegotten God, has hands and feet, and fingers, and a soul, like a composite being; and they for this reason teach that it was the Father Himself who appeared to Abraham and to Jacob.

Blessed therefore are we who have been circumcised the second time with knives of stone. For your first circumcision was and is performed by iron instruments, for you remain hard-hearted; but our circumcision, which is the second, having been instituted after yours, circumcises us from idolatry and from absolutely every kind of wickedness by sharp stones, i.e., by the words [preached] by the apostles of the corner-stone cut out without hands. And our hearts are thus circumcised from evil, so that we are happy to die for the name of the

---

[707] Isaiah 53:7. {See also Acts 8:32.}

[708] Isaiah 65:2.

[709] Isaiah 53:1.

[710] Psalm 8:3.

[711] Literally, "the operation of His words." Editors have changed *τῶν λόγων* into *τὸν λόγον* or *τοῦ λόγου*; but there is no need of change.

good Rock, which causes living water to burst forth for the hearts of those who by Him have loved the Father of all, and which gives those who are willing to drink of the water of life.

But you do not comprehend me when I speak these things; for you have not understood what it has been prophesied that Christ would do, and you do not believe us who draw your attention to what has been written. For Jeremiah thus cries: ***'Woe unto you! because you have forsaken the living fountain, and have digged for yourselves broken cisterns that can hold no water. Shall there be a wilderness where Mount Zion is, because I gave Jerusalem a bill of divorce in your sight?'"***[712]

Chapter CXV: *Prediction about the Christians in Zechariah. The malignant way which the Jews have in disputations.*

"But you ought to believe Zechariah when he shows in parable the mystery of Christ, and announces it obscurely. The following are his words:

> ***Rejoice, and be glad, O daughter of Zion: for, lo, I come, and I shall dwell in the midst of thee, saith the Lord. And many nations shall be added to the Lord in that day. And they shall be my people, and I will dwell in the midst of thee; and they shall know that the Lord of hosts hath sent me unto thee. And the Lord shall inherit Judah his portion in the holy land, and He shall choose Jerusalem again. Let all flesh fear before the Lord, for He is raised up out of His holy clouds. And He showed me Jesus (Joshua) the high priest standing before the angel [of the Lord***[713]***]; and the devil stood at his right hand to resist him. And the Lord said to the devil, The Lord who hath chosen Jerusalem rebuke thee. Behold, is not this a brand plucked out of the fire?"***[714]

As Trypho was about to reply and contradict me, I said, "Wait and hear what I say first: for I am not to give the explanation which you suppose, as if there had been no priest of the name of Joshua (Jesus) in

---

[712] Jeremiah 2:13. {This citation is to the first sentence only. Compare Jeremiah 2:31, 3:2, 8}
[713] Omitted by Justin in this place.
[714] Zechariah 2:10-13, 3:1, 2.

the land of Babylon, where your nation were prisoners. But even if I did, I have shown that if there[715] was a priest named Joshua (Jesus) in your nation, yet the prophet had not seen him in his revelation, just as he had not seen either the devil or the angel of the Lord by eyesight, and in his waking condition, but in a trance, at the time when the revelation was made to him.

But I now say, that as [Scripture] said that the Son of Nave (Nun) by the name Jesus (Joshua) wrought powerful works and exploits which proclaimed beforehand what would be performed by our Lord; so I proceed now to show that the revelation made among your people in Babylon in the days of Jesus (Joshua) the priest, was an announcement of the things to be accomplished by our Priest, who is God, and Christ the Son of God the Father of all."

"Indeed, I wondered," continued I, "why a little ago you kept silence while I was speaking, and why you did not interrupt me when I said that the son of Nave (Nun) was the only one of contemporaries who came out of Egypt that entered the Holy Land along with the men described as younger than that generation. For you swarm and light on sores like flies. For though one should speak ten thousand words well, if there happen to be one little word displeasing to you, because not sufficiently intelligible or accurate, you make no account of the many good words, but lay hold of the little word, and are very zealous in setting it up as something impious and guilty; in order that, when you are judged with the very same judgment by God, you may have a much heavier account to render for your great audacities, whether evil actions, or bad interpretations which you obtain by falsifying the truth. For with what judgment you judge, it is righteous that you be judged withal."

Chapter CXVI: *It is shown how this prophecy suits the Christians.*

"But to give you the account of the revelation of the holy Jesus Christ, I take up again my discourse, and I assert that even that revelation was made for us who believe on Christ the High Priest, namely this crucified One; and though we lived in fornication and all kinds of filthy conversation, we have by the grace of our Jesus, according to His Father's will, stripped ourselves of all those filthy wickednesses with which we

[715] The reading suggested by Maranus, *εί μὲν ήν*.

were imbued. And though the devil is ever at hand to resist us, and anxious to seduce all to himself, yet the Angel of God, i.e., the Power of God sent to us through Jesus Christ, rebukes him, and he departs from us. And we are just as if drawn out from the fire, when purified from our former sins, and [rescued] from the affliction and the fiery trial by which the devil and all his coadjutors try us; out of which Jesus the Son of God has promised again to deliver us,[716] and invest us with prepared garments, if we do His commandments; and has undertaken to provide an eternal kingdom [for us].

For just as that Jesus (Joshua), called by the prophet a priest, evidently had on filthy garments because he is said to have taken a harlot for a wife,[717] and is called a brand plucked out of the fire, because he had received remission of sins when the devil that resisted him was rebuked; even so we, who through the name of Jesus have believed as one man in God the Maker of all, have been stripped, through the name of His first-begotten Son, of the filthy garments, i.e., of our sins; and being vehemently inflamed by the word of His calling, we are the true high priestly race of God, as even God Himself bears witness, saying that in every place among the Gentiles sacrifices are presented to Him well-pleasing and pure. Now God receives sacrifices from no one, except through His priests."

Chapter CXVII: *Malachi's prophecy concerning the sacrifices of the Christians. It cannot be taken as referring to the prayers of Jews of the dispersion.*

"Accordingly, God, anticipating all the sacrifices which we offer through this name, and which Jesus the Christ enjoined us to offer, i.e., in the Eucharist of the bread and the cup, and which are presented by Christians in all places throughout the world, bears witness that they are well-pleasing to Him. But He utterly rejects those presented by you and by those priests of yours, saying, '***And I will not accept your sacrifices at***

---

[716] Maranus changed *ἀποσπᾷ* into *ἀποσπᾶν*, an emendation adopted in our translation. Otto retains the reading of the mss. "out of which Jesus the Son of God again snatches us. He promised that He would clothe us with," etc.

[717] Justin either confuses Joshua son of Josedech with Hosea the prophet, or he refers to the Jewish tradition that "filthy garments" signified either an illicit marriage, or sins of the people, or the squalor of captivity.

your hands; for from the rising of the sun to its setting my name is glorified among the Gentiles (He says); but ye profane it.'[718]

Yet even now, in your love of contention, you assert that God does not accept the sacrifices of those who dwelt then in Jerusalem, and were called Israelites; but says that He is pleased with the prayers of the individuals of that nation then dispersed, and calls their prayers sacrifices. Now, that prayers and giving of thanks, when offered by worthy men, are the only perfect and well-pleasing sacrifices to God, I also admit. For such alone Christians have undertaken to offer, and in the remembrance effected by their solid and liquid food, whereby the suffering of the Son of God[719] which He endured is brought to mind, whose name the high priests of your nation and your teachers have caused to be profaned and blasphemed over all the earth. But these filthy garments, which have been put by you on all who have become Christians by the name of Jesus, God shows shall be taken away from us, when He shall raise all men from the dead, and appoint some to be incorruptible, immortal, and free from sorrow in the everlasting and imperishable kingdom; but shall send others away to the everlasting punishment of fire.

But as to you and your teachers deceiving yourselves when you interpret what the Scripture says as referring to those of your nation then in dispersion, and maintain that their prayers and sacrifices offered in every place are pure and well-pleasing, learn that you are speaking falsely, and trying by all means to cheat yourselves: for, first of all, not even now does your nation extend from the rising to the setting of the sun, but there are nations among which none of your race ever dwelt. For there is not one single race of men, whether barbarians, or Greeks, or whatever they may be called, nomads, or vagrants, or herdsmen living in tents, among whom prayers and giving of thanks are not offered through the name of the crucified Jesus. And then,[720] as the Scriptures show, at the time when Malachi wrote this, your dispersion over all the earth, which now exists, had not taken place.

---

[718] Malachi 1:10-12.
[719] Or, "God of God."
[720] *εἶτα δὲ* for *είδότες*.

Chapter CXVIII: *He exhorts to repentance before Christ comes; in whom Christians, since they believe, are far more religious than Jews.*

"So that you ought rather to desist from the love of strife, and repent before the great day of judgment come, wherein all those of your tribes who have pierced this Christ shall mourn, as I have shown has been declared by the Scriptures. And I have explained that the Lord swore, '***after the order of Melchizedek,***'[721] and what this prediction means; and the prophecy of Isaiah which says, '***His burial is taken away from the midst,***'[722] I have already said, referred to the future burying and rising again of Christ; and I have frequently remarked that this very Christ is the Judge of all the living and the dead.

And Nathan likewise, speaking to David about Him, thus continued: '***I will be His Father, and He shall be my Son; and My mercy shall I not take away from Him, as I did from them that went before Him; and I will establish Him in My house, and in His kingdom for ever.***'[723] And Ezekiel says, '***There shall be no other prince in the house but He.***'[724] For He is the chosen Priest and eternal King, the Christ, inasmuch as He is the Son of God; and do not suppose that Isaiah or the other prophets speak of sacrifices of blood or libations being presented at the altar on His second advent, but of true and spiritual praises and giving of thanks. And we have not in vain believed in Him, and have not been led astray by those who taught us such doctrines; but this has come to pass through the wonderful foreknowledge of God, in order that we, through the calling of the new and eternal covenant, that is, of Christ, might be found more intelligent and God-fearing than yourselves, who are considered to be lovers of God and men of understanding, but are not.

Isaiah, filled with admiration of this, said: '***And kings shall shut their mouths: for those to whom no announcement has been made in regard to Him***[725] ***shall see; and those who heard not shall understand.***

---

[721] Psalm 110:4.

[722] Isaiah 53:8.

[723] 2 Samuel 7:14 {-16}.

[724] Ezekiel 44:3.

[725] The mss. read "them." Otto has changed it to "Him."

Lord, who hath believed our report? and to whom is the arm of the Lord revealed?'"[726]

"And in repeating this, Trypho," I continued, "as far as is allowable, I endeavor to do so for the sake of those who came with you today, yet briefly and concisely."

Then he replied, "You do well; and though you repeat the same things at considerable length, be assured that I and my companions listen with pleasure."

Chapter CXIX: *Christians are the holy people promised to Abraham. They have been called like Abraham.*

Then I said again, "Would you suppose, sirs, that we could ever have understood these matters in the Scriptures, if we had not received grace to discern by the will of Him whose pleasure it was? in order that the saying of Moses[727] might come to pass,

> ***They provoked me with strange [gods], they provoked me to anger with their abominations. They sacrificed to demons whom they knew not; new gods that came newly up, whom their fathers knew not. Thou hast forsaken God that begat thee, and forgotten God that brought thee up. And the Lord saw, and was jealous, and was provoked to anger by reason of the rage of His sons and daughters: and He said, I will turn My face away from them, and I will show what shall come on them at the last; for it is a very froward generation, children in whom is no faith. They have moved Me to jealousy with that which is not God, they have provoked Me to anger with their idols; and I will move them to jealousy with that which is not a nation, I will provoke them to anger with a foolish people. For a fire is kindled from Mine anger, and it shall burn to Hades. It shall consume the earth and her increase, and set on fire the foundations of the mountains; I will heap mischief on them.***[728]

And after that Righteous One was put to death, we flourished as another people, and shot forth as new and prosperous corn; as the prophets said,

---

[726] Isaiah 52:15, 53:1.
[727] Literally, "in the time of Moses."
[728] Deuteronomy 32:16-23.

'And many nations shall betake themselves to the Lord in that day for a people: and they shall dwell in the midst of all the earth.'[729] But we are not only a people, but also a holy people, as we have shown already.[730] ***'And they shall call them the holy people, redeemed by the Lord.'***[731] Therefore we are not a people to be despised, nor a barbarous race, nor such as the Carian and Phrygian nations; but God has even chosen us and He has become manifest to those who asked not after Him. ***'Behold, I am God,'*** He says, ***'to the nation which called not on My name.'***[732] For this is that nation which God of old promised to Abraham, when He declared that He would make him a father of many nations; not meaning, however, the Arabians, or Egyptians, or Idumaeans, since Ishmael became the father of a mighty nation, and so did Esau; and there is now a great multitude of Ammonites. Noah, moreover, was the father of Abraham, and in fact of all men; and others were the progenitors of others.

What larger measure of grace, then, did Christ bestow on Abraham? This, namely, that He called him with His voice by the like calling, telling him to quit the land wherein he dwelt. And He has called all of us by that voice, and we have left already the way of living in which we used to spend our days, passing our time in evil after the fashions of the other inhabitants of the earth; and along with Abraham we shall inherit the holy land, when we shall receive the inheritance for an endless eternity, being children of Abraham through the like faith. For as he believed the voice of God, and it was imputed to him for righteousness, in like manner we having believed God's voice spoken by the apostles of Christ, and promulgated to us by the prophets, have renounced even to death all the things of the world. Accordingly, He promises to him a nation of similar faith, God-fearing, righteous, and delighting the Father; but it is not you, ***'in whom is no faith.'***"[733]

Chapter CXX: *Christians were promised to Isaac, Jacob, and Judah.*

"Observe, too, how the same promises are made to Isaac and to Jacob. For thus He speaks to Isaac: ***"And in thy seed shall all the nations***

---

[729] Zechariah 2:11.
[730] See Chapter CX.
[731] Isaiah 62:12.
[732] Isaiah 65:1.
[733] {Deuteronomy 32:20; see also Matthew 17:17.}

of the earth be blessed.'[734] And to Jacob: ***'And in thee and in thy seed shall all families of the earth be blessed.'***[735] He says that neither to Esau nor to Reuben, nor to any other; only to those of whom the Christ should arise, according to the dispensation, through the Virgin Mary. But if you would consider the blessing of Judah, you would perceive what I say. For the seed is divided from Jacob, and comes down through Judah, and Phares, and Jesse, and David. And this was a symbol of the fact that some of your nation would be found children of Abraham, and found, too, in the lot of Christ; but that others, who are indeed children of Abraham, would be like the sand on the sea-shore, barren and fruitless, much in quantity, and without number indeed, but bearing no fruit whatever, and only drinking the water of the sea.

And a vast multitude in your nation are convicted of being of this kind, imbibing doctrines of bitterness and godlessness, but spurning the word of God. He speaks therefore in the passage relating to Judah: ***'A prince shall not fail from Judah, nor a ruler from his thighs, till that which is laid up for him come; and He shall be the expectation of the nations.'***[736] And it is plain that this was spoken not of Judah, but of Christ. For all we out of all nations do expect not Judah, but Jesus, who led your fathers out of Egypt. For the prophecy referred even to the advent of Christ: ***'Till He come for whom this is laid up, and He shall be the expectation of nations.'***[737]

Jesus came, therefore, as we have shown at length, and is expected again to appear above the clouds; whose name you profane, and labor hard to get it profaned over all the earth. It were possible for me, sirs," I continued, "to contend against you about the reading which you so interpret, saying it is written, '*Till the things laid up for Him come*;' though the Seventy have not so explained it, but thus, ***'Till He comes for whom this is laid up.'***[738] But since what follows indicates that the reference is to Christ (for it is, ***'and He shall be the expectation of nations'***),[739] I do not proceed to have a mere verbal controversy with you,

[734] Genesis 26:4. {See also Genesis 12:3, 28:14.}
[735] Genesis 28:14. {See also Genesis 12:3, 26:4.}
[736] Genesis 49:10. {See also Isaiah 2:2.}
[737] Genesis 49:10.
[738] Ibid.
[739] Ibid.

as I have not attempted to establish proof about Christ from the passages of Scripture which are not admitted by you which I quoted from the words of Jeremiah the prophet, and Esdras, and David; but from those which are even now admitted by you, which had your teachers comprehended, be well assured they would have deleted them, as they did those about the death of Isaiah, whom you sawed asunder with a wooden saw. And this was a mysterious type of Christ being about to cut your nation in two, and to raise those worthy of the honor to the everlasting kingdom along with the holy patriarchs and prophets; but He has said that He will send others to the condemnation of the unquenchable fire along with similar disobedient and impenitent men from all the nations. ***'For they shall come,'*** He said, ***'from the west and from the east, and shall sit down with Abraham, and Isaac, and Jacob in the kingdom of heaven; but the children of the kingdom shall be cast out into outer darkness.'***[740]

And I have mentioned these things, taking nothing whatever into consideration, except the speaking of the truth, and refusing to be coerced by anyone, even though I should be forthwith torn in pieces by you. For I gave no thought to any of my people, that is, the Samaritans, when I had a communication in writing with Caesar,[741] but stated that they were wrong in trusting to the magician Simon of their own nation, who, they say, is God above all power, and authority, and might."

Chapter CXXI: *From the fact that the Gentiles believe in Jesus, it is evident that He is Christ.*

And as they kept silence, I went on: "[The Scripture], speaking by David about this Christ, my friends, said no longer that ***'****in His seed****'*** the nations should be blessed, but ***'in Him.'*** So it is here: ***'His name shall rise up for ever above the sun; and in Him shall all nations be blessed.'***[742] But if all nations are blessed in Christ, and we of all nations believe in Him, then He is indeed the Christ, and we are those blessed by Him. God formerly gave the sun as an object of worship,[743] as it is written, but no

---

[740] Matthew 8:11 {-12}.

[741] The *Apology*, I, Chapter XXVI; and II Chapter XV.

[742] Psalm 72:17. {See also Jeremiah 4:2. Compare Genesis 12:3.}

[743] So Justin concludes from Deuteronomy 4:19; comp. Chapter LV.

one ever was seen to endure death on account of his faith in the sun; but for the name of Jesus you may see men of every nation who have endured and do endure all sufferings, rather than deny Him. For the word of His truth and wisdom is more ardent and more light-giving than the rays of the sun, and sinks down into the depths of heart and mind. Hence also the Scripture said, '***His name shall rise up above the sun.***'[744] And again, Zechariah says, '***His name is the East.***'[745] And speaking of the same, he says that '***each tribe shall mourn.***'[746] But if He so shone forth and was so mighty in His first advent (which was without honor and comeliness, and very contemptible), that in no nation He is unknown, and everywhere men have repented of the old wickedness in each nation's way of living, so that even demons were subject to His name, and all powers and kingdoms feared His name more than they feared all the dead, shall He not on His glorious advent destroy by all means all those who hated Him, and who unrighteously departed from Him, but give rest to His own, rewarding them with all they have looked for?

To us, therefore, it has been granted to hear, and to understand, and to be saved by this Christ, and to recognize all the [truths revealed] by the Father. Wherefore He said to Him: '***It is a great thing for Thee to be called My servant, to raise up the tribes of Jacob, and turn again the dispersed of Israel. I have appointed Thee for a light to the Gentiles, that Thou mayest be their salvation unto the end of the earth.***'"[747]

Chapter CXXII: *The Jews understand this of the proselytes without reason.*

"You think that these words refer to the stranger[748] and the proselytes, but in fact they refer to us who have been illumined by Jesus. For Christ would have borne witness even to them; but now you are become ***twofold more the children of hell,***[749] as He said Himself. Therefore what was written by the prophets was spoken not of those persons, but of us, concerning whom the Scripture speaks: '***I will lead the***

---

[744] {Psalm 72:17.}
[745] Zechariah 6:12. {See Ch. C, CVI, and discussion in n. 686, above.}
[746] Zechariah 12:12.
[747] Isaiah 49:6.
[748] *Γηόρα* or *Γειόρα*. Found in LXX, Exodus 12:19 and Isaiah 14:1.
[749] Matthew 23:15.

blind by a way which they knew not; and they shall walk in paths which they have not known. And I am witness, saith the Lord God, and My servant whom I have chosen.'[750]

To whom, then, does Christ bear witness? Manifestly to those who have believed. But the proselytes not only do not believe, but twofold more than yourselves blaspheme His name, and wish to torture and put to death us who believe in Him; for in all points they strive to be like you.

And again in other words He cries: '***I the Lord have called Thee in righteousness, and will hold Thine hand, and will strengthen Thee, and will give Thee for a covenant of the people, for a light of the Gentiles, to open the eyes of the blind, to bring out the prisoners from their bonds.***'[751] These words, indeed, sirs, refer also to Christ, and concern the enlightened nations; or will you say again, He speaks to them of the law and the proselytes?"

Then some of those who had come on the second day cried out as if they had been in a theatre, "But what? does He not refer to the law, and to those illumined by it? Now these are proselytes."

"No," I said, looking towards Trypho, "since, if the law were able to enlighten the nations and those who possess it, what need is there of a new covenant? But since God announced beforehand that He would send a new covenant, and an everlasting law and commandment, we will not understand this of the old law and its proselytes, but of Christ and His proselytes, namely us Gentiles, whom He has illumined, as He says somewhere: '***Thus saith the Lord, In an acceptable time have I heard Thee, and in a day of salvation have I helped Thee, and I have given Thee for a covenant of the people, to establish the earth, and to inherit the deserted.***'[752]

What, then, is Christ's inheritance? Is it not the nations? What is the covenant of God? Is it not Christ? As He says in another place: '***Thou art my Son; this day have I begotten Thee. Ask of Me, and I shall give Thee the nations for Thine inheritance, and the uttermost parts of the earth for Thy possession.***'"[753]

---

[750] Isaiah 42:16; 43:10.

[751] Isaiah 42:6. {Actually a collection of verses, including Isaiah 42:6, 7, 49:6.}

[752] Isaiah 49:8.

[753] Psalm 2:7 {-8}.

Chapter CXXIII: *Ridiculous interpretations of the Jews. Christians are the true Israel.*

"As, therefore, all these latter prophecies refer to Christ and the nations, you should believe that the former refer to Him and them in like manner. For the proselytes have no need of a covenant, if, since there is one and the same law imposed on all that are circumcised, the Scripture speaks about them thus: ***'And the stranger shall also be joined with them, and shall be joined to the house of Jacob***;'[754] and because the proselyte, who is circumcised that he may have access to the people, becomes like one of themselves,[755] while we who have been deemed worthy to be called a people are yet Gentiles, because we have not been circumcised. Besides, it is ridiculous for you to imagine that the eyes of the proselytes are to be opened while your own are not, and that you be understood as blind and deaf while they are enlightened.

And it will be still more ridiculous for you, if you say that the law has been given to the nations, but you have not known it. For you would have stood in awe of God's wrath, and would not have been lawless, wandering sons; being much afraid of hearing God always say, ***'Children in whom is no faith. And who are blind, but my servants? and deaf, but they that rule over them? And the servants of God have been made blind. You see often, but have not observed; your ears have been opened, and you have not heard.'***[756]

Is God's commendation of you honorable? and is God's testimony seemly for His servants? You are not ashamed though you often hear these words. You do not tremble at God's threats, for you are a people foolish and hard-hearted. ***'Therefore, behold, I will proceed to remove this people,' saith the Lord; and I will remove them, and destroy the wisdom of the wise, and hide the understanding of the prudent.'***[757] Deservedly too: for you are neither wise nor prudent, but crafty and unscrupulous; wise only to do evil, but utterly incompetent to know the hidden counsel of God, or the faithful covenant of the Lord, or to find out the everlasting paths. ***'Therefore, saith the Lord, I will raise up to Israel***

---

[754] Isaiah 14:1.

[755] Literally, "a native of the land."

[756] Deuteronomy 32:20; Isaiah 42:19 {-20}.

[757] Isaiah 29:14. {See also Jeremiah 49:7; Habakkuk 1:5.}

and to Judah the seed of men and the seed of beasts.'[758] And by Isaiah He speaks thus concerning another Israel: '***In that day shall there be a third Israel among the Assyrians and the Egyptians, blessed in the land which the Lord of Sabaoth hath blessed, saying, blessed shall My people in Egypt and in Assyria be, and Israel Mine inheritance.***'[759]

Since then God blesses this people, and calls them Israel, and declares them to be His inheritance, how is it that you repent not of the deception you practice on yourselves, as if you alone were the Israel, and of executing the people whom God has blessed? For when He speaks to Jerusalem and its environs, He thus added: '***And I will beget men upon you, even my people Israel; and they shall inherit you, and you shall be a possession for them; and you shall be no longer bereaved of them.***'"[760]

"What, then?" says Trypho; "are you Israel? and speaks He such things of you?"

"If, indeed," I replied to him, "we had not entered into a lengthy discussion on these topics, I might have doubted whether you ask this question in ignorance; but since we have brought the matter to a conclusion by demonstration and with your assent, I do not believe that you are ignorant of what I have just said, or desire again mere contention, but that you are urging me to exhibit the same proof to these men."

And in compliance with the assent expressed in his eyes, I continued: "Again in Isaiah, if you have ears to hear it, God, speaking of Christ in parable, calls Him Jacob and Israel. He speaks thus:

> ***Jacob is My servant, I will uphold Him; Israel is Mine elect, I will put my Spirit upon Him, and He shall bring forth judgment to the Gentiles. He shall not strive, nor cry, neither shall any one hear His voice in the street: a bruised reed He shall not break, and smoking flax He shall not quench; but He shall bring forth judgment to truth: He shall shine,***[761] ***and shall not be broken till He have set judgment on the earth. And in His name shall the Gentiles trust.***[762]

---

[758] Jeremiah 31:27. {See also Ezekiel 36:9; Zechariah 10:9.}

[759] Isaiah 19:24 {-25}.

[760] Ezekiel 36:12. {Compare Jeremiah 15:7.}

[761] LXX, *ἀναλάμψει*, as above. The reading of the text is *ἀναλήψει*.

[762] Isaiah 42:1-4.

As therefore from the one man Jacob, who was surnamed Israel, all your nation has been called Jacob and Israel; so we from Christ, who begat us unto God, like Jacob, and Israel, and Judah, and Joseph, and David, are called and are the true sons of God, and keep the commandments of Christ."

Chapter CXXIV: *Christians are the sons of God.*

And when I saw that they were perturbed because I said that we are the sons of God, I anticipated their questioning, and said, "Listen, sirs, how the Holy Ghost speaks of this people, saying that they are all sons of the Highest; and how this very Christ will be present in their assembly, rendering judgment to all men. The words are spoken by David, and are, according to your version of them, thus:

> ***God standeth in the congregation of gods; He judgeth among the gods. How long do ye judge unjustly, and accept the persons of the wicked? Judge for the orphan and the poor, and do justice to the humble and needy. Deliver the needy, and save the poor out of the hand of the wicked. They know not, neither have they understood; they walk on in darkness: all the foundations of the earth shall be shaken. I said, Ye are gods, and are all children of the Most High. But ye die like men, and fall like one of the princes. Arise, O God! judge the earth, for Thou shalt inherit all nations.***[763]

But in the version of the Seventy it is written, '***Behold, ye die like men, and fall like one of the princes,***'[764] in order to manifest the disobedience of men,—I mean of Adam and Eve,—and the fall of one of the princes, i.e., of him who was called the serpent, who fell with a great overthrow, because he deceived Eve. But as my discourse is not intended to touch on this point, but to prove to you that the Holy Ghost reproaches men because they were made like God, free from suffering and death, provided that they kept His commandments, and were deemed deserving of the name of His sons, and yet they, becoming like Adam and Eve, work

---

[763] Psalm 82.

[764] In the text there is certainly no distinction given. But if we read *ώς ἄνθρωπος* {(Hebrew)} "as a man," in the first quotation we shall be able to follow Justin's argument. {See Psalm 82:7; see also Job 21:32.}

out death for themselves; let the interpretation of the Psalm be held just as you wish, yet thereby it is demonstrated that all men are deemed worthy of becoming gods, and of having power to become sons of the Highest; and shall be each by himself judged and condemned like Adam and Eve. Now I have proved at length that Christ is called God."

Chapter CXXV: *He explains what force the word Israel has, and how it suits Christ.*

"I wish, sirs," I said, "to learn from you what is the force of the name Israel." And as they were silent, I continued: "I shall tell you what I know: for I do not think it right, when I know, not to speak; or, suspecting that you do know, and yet from envy or from voluntary ignorance deceive yourselves,[765] to be continually solicitous; but I speak all things simply and candidly, as my Lord said: '***A sower went forth to sow the seed; and some fell by the wayside; and some among thorns, and some on stony ground, and some on good ground.***'[766] I must speak, then, in the hope of finding good ground somewhere; since that Lord of mine, as One strong and powerful, comes to demand back His own from all, and will not condemn His steward if He recognizes that he, by the knowledge that the Lord is powerful and has come to demand His own, has given it to every bank, and has not digged for any cause whatsoever.

Accordingly the name Israel signifies this, A man who overcomes power; for *Isra* is a man overcoming, and *El* is power. And that Christ would act so when He became man was foretold by the mystery of Jacob's wrestling with Him who appeared to him, in that He ministered to the will of the Father, yet nevertheless is God, in that He is the first-begotten of all creatures. For when He became man, as I previously remarked, the devil came to Him—i.e., that power which is called the serpent and Satan—tempting Him, and striving to effect His downfall by asking Him to worship him. But He destroyed and overthrew the devil, having proved him to be wicked, in that he asked to be worshipped as God, contrary to the Scripture; who is an apostate from the will of God. For He answers him, '***It is written, Thou shalt worship the Lord thy God,***

---

[765] The reading here is *ἐπίσταμαι*, which is generally abandoned for *ἀπατᾶν ἑαυτούς*.

[766] Matthew 13:3 {-8}. {See also Luke 8:5-8.}

and Him only shall thou serve.'[767] Then, overcome and convicted, the devil departed at that time. But since our Christ was to be numbed, i.e., by pain and experience of suffering, He made a previous intimation of this by touching Jacob's thigh, and causing it to shrink. But Israel was His name from the beginning, to which He altered the name of the blessed Jacob when He blessed him with His own name, proclaiming thereby that all who through Him have fled for refuge to the Father, constitute the blessed Israel.

But you, having understood none of this, and not being prepared to understand, since you are the children of Jacob after the fleshly seed, expect that you shall be assuredly saved. But that you deceive yourselves in such matters, I have proved by many words."

Chapter CXXVI: *The various names of Christ according to both natures. It is shown that He is God, and appeared to the patriarchs.*

"But if you knew, Trypho," continued I, "who He is that is called at one time the Angel of great counsel, and a Man by Ezekiel, and like the Son of man by Daniel, and a Child by Isaiah, and Christ and God to be worshipped by David, and Christ and a Stone by many, and Wisdom by Solomon, and Joseph and Judah and a Star by Moses, and the East by Zechariah, and the Suffering One and Jacob and Israel by Isaiah again, and a Rod, and Flower, and Corner-Stone, and Son of God, you would not have blasphemed Him who has now come, and been born, and suffered, and ascended to heaven; who shall also come again, and then your twelve tribes shall mourn. For if you had understood what has been written by the prophets, you would not have denied that He was God, Son of the only, unbegotten, unutterable God.

For Moses says somewhere in Exodus the following: '***The Lord spoke to Moses, and said to him, I am the Lord, and I appeared to Abraham, to Isaac, and to Jacob, being their God; and My name I revealed not to them, and I established My covenant with them.***'[768] And thus again he says, '***A man wrestled with Jacob***,'[769] and asserts it was God; narrating that Jacob said, '***I have seen God face to face, and my life***

---

[767] Matthew 4:10. {See also Deuteronomy 6:13; 1 Samuel 7:3.}
[768] Exodus 6:2 {-4}.
[769] Genesis 32:24, 30.

is preserved.'[770] And it is recorded that he called the place where He wrestled with him, appeared to and blessed him, the Face of God (Peniel). And Moses says that God appeared also to Abraham near the oak in Mamre, when he was sitting at the door of his tent at mid-day. Then he goes on to say: ***'And he lifted up his eyes and looked, and, behold, three men stood before him; and when he saw them, he ran to meet them.'***[771] After a little, one of them promises a son to Abraham: ***'Wherefore did Sarah laugh, saying, Shall I of a surety bear a child, and I am old? Is anything impossible with God? At the time appointed I will return, according to the time of life, and Sarah shall have a son. And they went away from Abraham.'***[772] Again he speaks of them thus: ***'And the men rose up from thence, and looked toward Sodom.'***[773] Then to Abraham He who was and is again speaks: ***'I will not hide from Abraham, my servant, what I intend to do.'"***[774]

And what follows in the writings of Moses I quoted and explained; "from which I have demonstrated," I said, "that He who is described as God appeared to Abraham, to Isaac, and to Jacob, and the other patriarchs, was appointed under the authority of the Father and Lord, and ministers to His will."

Then I went on to say what I had not said before: "And so, when the people desired to eat flesh, and Moses had lost faith in Him, who also there is called the Angel, and who promised that God would give them to satiety, He who is both God and the Angel, sent by the Father, is described as saying and doing these things. For thus the Scripture says: ***'And the Lord said to Moses, Will the Lord's hand not be sufficient? thou shall know now whether My word shall conceal thee or not.'***[775] And again, in other words, it thus says: ***'But the Lord spoke unto me, Thou shalt not go over this Jordan: the Lord thy God, who goeth before thy face, He shall cut off the nations.'"***[776]

---

[770] {Genesis 32:30.}
[771] Genesis 18:2.
[772] Genesis 18:13 {-16}.
[773] Genesis 18:16.
[774] Genesis 18:17. {See also Psalm 25:14; John 15:15; Acts 20:27.}
[775] Numbers 11:23.
[776] Deuteronomy 31:2 {-3}.

Chapter CXXVII: *These passages of Scripture do not apply to the Father, but to the Word.*

"These and other such sayings are recorded by the lawgiver and by the prophets; and I suppose that I have stated sufficiently, that wherever[777] God says, '***God went up from Abraham***,'[778] or, '***The Lord spake to Moses***,'[779] and '***The Lord came down to behold the tower which the sons of men had built***,'[780] or when '***God shut Noah into the ark***,'[781] you must not imagine that the unbegotten God Himself came down or went up from any place. For the ineffable Father and Lord of all neither has come to any place, nor walks, nor sleeps, nor rises up, but remains in His own place, wherever that is, quick to behold and quick to hear, having neither eyes nor ears, but being of indescribable might; and He sees all things, and knows all things, and none of us escapes His observation; and He is not moved or confined to a spot in the whole world, for He existed before the world was made.

How, then, could He talk with any one, or be seen by any one, or appear on the smallest portion of the earth, when the people at Sinai were not able to look even on the glory of Him who was sent from Him; and Moses himself could not enter into the tabernacle which he had erected, when it was filled with the glory of God; and the priest could not endure to stand before the temple when Solomon conveyed the ark into the house in Jerusalem which he had built for it? Therefore neither Abraham, nor Isaac, nor Jacob, nor any other man, saw the Father and ineffable Lord of all, and also of Christ, but [saw] Him who was according to His will His Son, being God, and the Angel because He ministered to His will; whom also it pleased Him to be born man by the Virgin; who also was fire when He conversed with Moses from the bush. Since, unless we thus comprehend the Scriptures, it must follow that the Father and Lord of all had not been in heaven when what Moses wrote took place: '***And the Lord rained upon Sodom fire and brimstone from the Lord out of heaven***;'[782] and again, when it is thus said by David: '***Lift up your gates,***

---

[777] *ὅταν που* instead of *ὅταν μου*.
[778] Genesis 18:22.
[779] Exodus 6:29. {See also Exodus 6:2.}
[780] Genesis 11:5. {Compare Genesis 18:21.}
[781] Genesis 7:16.
[782] Genesis 19:24. {See also Deuteronomy 29:23; Jeremiah 20:16}

ye rulers; and be ye lift up, ye everlasting gates; and the King of glory shall enter;'[783] and again, when He says: ***'The Lord says to my Lord, Sit at My right hand, till I make Thine enemies Thy footstool.'***"[784]

Chapter CXXVIII: *The Word is sent not as an inanimate power, but as a Person begotten of the Father's substance.*

"And that Christ being Lord, and God the Son of God, and appearing formerly in power as Man, and Angel, and in the glory of fire as at the bush, so also was manifested at the judgment executed on Sodom, has been demonstrated fully by what has been said."

Then I repeated once more all that I had previously quoted from Exodus, about the vision in the bush, and the naming of Joshua (Jesus), and continued:

"And do not suppose, sirs, that I am speaking superfluously when I repeat these words frequently: but it is because I know that some wish to anticipate these remarks, and to say that the power sent from the Father of all which appeared to Moses, or to Abraham, or to Jacob, is called an Angel because He came to men (for by Him the commands of the Father have been proclaimed to men); is called Glory, because He appears in a vision sometimes that cannot be borne; is called a Man, and a human being, because He appears arrayed in such forms as the Father pleases; and they call Him the Word, because He carries tidings from the Father to men: but maintain that this power is indivisible and inseparable from the Father, just as they say that the light of the sun on earth is indivisible and inseparable from the sun in the heavens; as when it sinks, the light sinks along with it; so the Father, when He chooses, say they, causes His power to spring forth, and when He chooses, He makes it return to Himself. In this way, they teach, He made the angels. But it is proved that there are angels who always exist, and are never reduced to that form out of which they sprang. And that this power which the prophetic word calls God, as has been also amply demonstrated, and Angel, is not numbered [as different] in name only like the light of the sun but is indeed something numerically distinct, I have discussed briefly in what has gone before; when I asserted that this power was begotten

[783] Psalm 24:7. {See also Psalm 97:6. Haggai 2:7.}

[784] Psalm 110:1.

from the Father, by His power and will, but not by abscission, as if the essence of the Father were divided; as all other things partitioned and divided are not the same after as before they were divided: and, for the sake of example, I took the case of fires kindled from a fire, which we see to be distinct from it, and yet that from which many can be kindled is by no means made less, but remains the same."

Chapter CXXIX: *That is confirmed from other passages of Scripture.*

"And now I shall again recite the words which I have spoken in proof of this point. When Scripture says, '***The Lord rained fire from the Lord out of heaven***,'[785] the prophetic word indicates that there were two in number: One upon the earth, who, it says, descended to behold the cry of Sodom; Another in heaven, who also is Lord of the Lord on earth, as He is Father and God; the cause of His power and of His being Lord and God. Again, when the Scripture records that God said in the beginning, '***Behold, Adam has become like one of Us***,'[786] this phrase, '***like one of Us***,' is also indicative of number; and the words do not admit of a figurative meaning, as the sophists endeavor to affix on them, who are able neither to tell nor to understand the truth.

And it is written in the book of Wisdom:

> ***If I should tell you daily events, I would be mindful to enumerate them from the beginning. The Lord created me the beginning of His ways for His works. From everlasting He established Me in the beginning, before He formed the earth, and before He made the depths, and before the springs of waters came forth, before the mountains were settled; He begets Me before all the hills.***"[787]

When I repeated these words, I added: "You perceive, my hearers, if you bestow attention, that the Scripture has declared that this Offspring was begotten by the Father before all things created; and that

[785] {Genesis 19:24.}

[786] Genesis 3:22.

[787] Proverbs 8:22 {-25}. {But not the first sentence quoted; compare Isaiah 40:21, 41:26, 48:3, 5, 16. See also Job 15:7.}

which is begotten is numerically distinct from that which begets, any one will admit."

Chapter CXXX: *He returns to the conversion of the Gentiles, and shows that it was foretold.*

And when all had given assent, I said: "I would now adduce some passages which I had not recounted before. They are recorded by the faithful servant Moses in parable, and are as follows: '***Rejoice, O ye heavens, with Him, and let all the angels of God worship Him***;'"[788] and I added what follows of the passage:

> "***Rejoice, O ye nations, with His people, and let all the angels of God be strengthened in Him: for the blood of His sons He avenges, and will avenge, and will recompense His enemies with vengeance, and will recompense those that hate Him; and the Lord will purify the land of His people.***[789]

And by these words He declares that we, the nations, rejoice with His people,—to wit, Abraham, and Isaac, and Jacob, and the prophets, and, in short, all of that people who are well-pleasing to God, according to what has been already agreed on between us. But we will not receive it of all your nation; since we know from Isaiah[790] that the members of those who have transgressed shall be consumed by the worm and unquenchable fire, remaining immortal; so that they become a spectacle to all flesh.

But in addition to these, I wish, sirs," said I, "to add some other passages from the very words of Moses, from which you may understand that God has from of old dispersed all men according to their kindreds and tongues; and out of all kindreds has taken to Himself your kindred, a useless, disobedient, and faithless generation; and has shown that those who were selected out of every nation have obeyed His will through Christ,—whom He calls also Jacob, and names Israel,—and these, then, as I mentioned fully previously, must be Jacob and Israel. For when He says, '***Rejoice, O ye nations, with His people***,'[791] He allots the same inheritance

---

[788] Deuteronomy 32:43. {Compare Romans 15:10.}

[789] {Deuteronomy 32:43.}

[790] Isaiah 66:24.

[791] {Deuteronomy 32:43.}

to them, and does not call them by the same name;[792] but when He says that they as Gentiles rejoice with His people, He calls them Gentiles to reproach you. For even as you provoked Him to anger by your idolatry, so also He has deemed those who were idolaters worthy of knowing His will, and of inheriting His inheritance."

Chapter CXXXI: *How much more faithful to God the Gentiles are who are converted to Christ than the Jews.*

"But I shall quote the passage by which it is made known that God divided all the nations. It is as follows:

> ***Ask thy father, and he will show thee; thine elders, and they will tell thee; when the Most High divided the nations, as He dispersed the sons of Adam. He set the bounds of the nations according to the numbers of the children of Israel; and the Lord's portion became His people Jacob, and Israel was the lot of His inheritance."***[793]

And having said this, I added: "The Seventy have translated it, '***He set the bounds of the nations according to the number of the angels of God.***'[794] But because my argument is again in nowise weakened by this, I have adopted your exposition.

And you yourselves, if you will confess the truth, must acknowledge that we, who have been called by God through the despised and shameful mystery of the Cross (for the confession of which, and obedience to which, and for our piety, punishments even to death have been inflicted on us by demons, and by the host of the devil, through the aid ministered to them by you), and endure all torments rather than deny Christ even by word, through whom we are called to the salvation prepared beforehand by the Father, are more faithful to God than you, who were redeemed from Egypt with a high hand and a visitation of great glory, when the sea was parted for you, and a passage left dry, in which

---

[792] The reading is "and calls them by the same name." But the whole argument shows that the Jews and Gentiles are distinguished by name.

[793] Deuteronomy 32:7 {-9}.

[794] {Deuteronomy 32:8. Saint Justin's point may be seen when comparing different translations of the Bible. Compare, e.g., OSB and KJV.}

[God] slew those who pursued you with a very great equipment, and splendid chariots, bringing back upon them the sea which had been made a way for your sakes; on whom also a pillar of light shone, in order that you, more than any other nation in the world, might possess a peculiar light, never-failing and never-setting; for whom He rained manna as nourishment, fit for the heavenly angels, in order that you might have no need to prepare your food; and the water at Marah was made sweet; and a sign of Him that was to be crucified was made, both in the matter of the serpents which bit you, as I already mentioned (God anticipating before the proper times these mysteries, in order to confer grace upon you, to whom you are always convicted of being thankless), as well as in the type of the extending of the hands of Moses, and of Oshea being named Jesus (Joshua); when you fought against Amalek: concerning which God enjoined that the incident be recorded, and the name of Jesus laid up in your understandings; saying that this is He who would blot out the memorial of Amalek from under heaven.

Now it is clear that the memorial of Amalek remained after the son of Nave (Nun): but He makes it manifest that through Jesus, who was crucified, of whom also those symbols were fore-announcements of all that would happen to Him, the demons would be destroyed, and would dread His name, and that all principalities and kingdoms would fear Him; and that they who believe in Him out of all nations would be shown as God-fearing and peaceful men; and the facts already quoted by me, Trypho, indicate this.

Again, when you desired flesh, so vast a quantity of quails was given you, that they could not be told; for whom also water gushed from the rock; and a cloud followed you for a shade from heat, and covering from cold, declaring the manner and signification of another and new heaven; the latchets of your shoes did not break, and your shoes waxed not old, and your garments wore not away, but even those of the children grew along with them."

Chapter CXXXII: *How great the power was of the name of Jesus in the Old Testament.*

"Yet after this you made a calf, and were very zealous in committing fornication with the daughters of strangers, and in serving idols. And again, when the land was given up to you with so great a display of power, that you witnessed the sun stand still in the heavens by the order of that man whose name was Jesus (Joshua), and not go down for thirty-six hours, as well as all the other miracles which were wrought for you as time served;[795] and of these it seems good to me now to speak of another, for it conduces to your hereby knowing Jesus, whom we also know to have been Christ the Son of God, who was crucified, and rose again, and ascended to heaven, and will come again to judge all men, even up to Adam himself.

You are aware, then," I continued, "that when the ark of the testimony was seized by the enemies of Ashdod,[796] and a terrible and incurable malady had broken out among them, they resolved to place it on a cart to which they yoked cows that had recently calved, for the purpose of ascertaining by trial whether or not they had been plagued by God's power on account of the ark, and if God wished it to be taken back to the place from which it had been carried away. And when they had done this, the cows, led by no man, went not to the place whence the ark had been taken, but to the fields of a certain man whose name was Oshea, the same as his whose name was altered to Jesus (Joshua), as has been previously mentioned, who also led the people into the land and meted it out to them: and when the cows had come into these fields they remained there, showing to you thereby that they were guided by the name of power;[797] just as formerly the people who survived of those that came out of Egypt, were guided into the land by him who had received the name Jesus (Joshua), who before was called Oshea."

Chapter CXXXIII: *The hard-heartedness of the Jews, for whom the Christians pray.*

"Now, although these and all other such unexpected and marvelous works were wrought amongst and seen by you at different times, yet you are convicted by the prophets of having gone to such a length as offering your own children to demons; and besides all this, of having dared to do such things against Christ; and you still dare to do

[795] The anacoluthon is in the original. {I.e., a syntactical inconsistency, incoherence, or shift of syntax within a sentence.}
[796] See 1 Samuel 5.
[797] Or, "by the power of the name."

them: for all which may it be granted to you to obtain mercy and salvation from God and His Christ. For God, knowing before that you would do such things, pronounced this curse upon you by the prophet Isaiah:

> ***Woe unto their soul! they have devised evil counsel against themselves, saying, Let us bind the righteous man, for he is distasteful to us. Therefore they shall eat the fruit of their own doings. Woe to the wicked! evil, according to the works of his hands, shall befall him. O my people, your exactors glean you, and those who extort from you shall rule over you. O my people, they who call you blessed cause you to err, and disorder the way of your paths. But now the Lord shall assist[798] His people to judgment, and He shall enter into judgment with the elders of the people and the princes thereof. But why have you burnt up My vineyard? and why is the spoil of the poor found in your houses? Why do you wrong My people, and put to shame the countenance of the humble?[799]***

Again, in other words, the same prophet spake to the same effect:

> ***Woe unto them that draw their iniquity as with a long cord, and their transgressions as with the harness of an heifer's yoke: who say, Let His speed come near, and let the counsel of the Holy One of Israel come, that we may know it. Woe unto them that call evil good, and good evil! that put light for darkness, and darkness for light! that put bitter for sweet, and sweet for bitter! Woe unto them that are wise in their own eyes, and prudent in their own sight! Woe unto those that are mighty among you, who drink wine, who are men of strength, who mingle strong drink! who justify the wicked for a reward, and take away justice from the righteous! Therefore, as the stubble shall be burnt by the coal of fire, and utterly consumed by the burning flame, their root shall be as wool, and their flower shall go up like dust. For they would not have the law of the Lord of Sabaoth, but despised[800] the word of the Lord, the Holy One of Israel. And the Lord of Sabaoth was very angry, and laid His hands upon them, and smote them; and He***

[798] {An early version reads, "sist."}
[799] Isaiah 3:9-15.
[800] Literally, "provoked."

> ***was provoked against the mountains, and their carcasses were in the midst like dung on the road. And for all this they have not repented,***[801] ***but their hand is still high.***[802]

For verily your hand is high to commit evil, because ye slew the Christ, and do not repent of it; but so far from that, ye hate and murder us who have believed through Him in the God and Father of all, as often as ye can; and ye curse Him without ceasing, as well as those who side with Him; while all of us pray for you, and for all men, as our Christ and Lord taught us to do, when He enjoined us to pray even for our enemies, and to love them that hate us, and to bless them that curse us."

Chapter CXXXIV: *The marriages of Jacob are a figure of the Church.*

"If, then, the teaching of the prophets and of Himself moves you, it is better for you to follow God than your imprudent and blind masters, who even till this time permit each man to have four or five wives; and if anyone see a beautiful woman and desire to have her, they quote the doings of Jacob [called] Israel, and of the other patriarchs, and maintain that it is not wrong to do such things; for they are miserably ignorant in this matter. For, as I before said, certain dispensations of weighty mysteries were accomplished in each act of this sort. For in the marriages of Jacob I shall mention what dispensation and prophecy were accomplished, in order that you may thereby know that your teachers never looked at the divine motive which prompted each act, but only at the groveling and corrupting passions.

Attend therefore to what I say. The marriages of Jacob were types of that which Christ was about to accomplish. For it was not lawful for Jacob to marry two sisters at once. And he serves Laban for [one of] the daughters; and being deceived in [the obtaining of] the younger, he again served seven years. Now Leah is your people and synagogue; but Rachel is our Church. And for these, and for the servants in both, Christ even now serves. For while Noah gave to the two sons the seed of the third as servants, now on the other hand Christ has come to restore both

---

[801] Literally, "turned away."
[802] Isaiah 5:18-25.

the free sons and the servants amongst them, conferring the same honor on all of them who keep His commandments; even as the children of the free women and the children of the bond women born to Jacob were all sons, and equal in dignity. And it was foretold what each should be according to rank and according to fore-knowledge.

Jacob served Laban for speckled and many-spotted sheep; and Christ served, even to the slavery of the Cross, for the various and many-formed races of mankind, acquiring them by the blood and mystery of the Cross. Leah was weak-eyed; for the eyes of your souls are excessively weak. Rachel stole the gods of Laban, and has hid them to this day; and we have lost our paternal and material gods. Jacob was hated for all time by his brother; and we now, and our Lord Himself, are hated by you and by all men, though we are brothers by nature. Jacob was called Israel; and Israel has been demonstrated to be the Christ, who is, and is called, Jesus."

Chapter CXXXV: *Christ is king of Israel, and Christians are the Israelitic race.*

"And when Scripture says, '***I am the Lord God, the Holy One of Israel, who have made known Israel your King,***'[803] will you not understand that truly Christ is the everlasting King? For you are aware that Jacob the son of Isaac was never a king. And therefore Scripture again, explaining to us, says what king is meant by Jacob and Israel:

> ***Jacob is my Servant, I will uphold Him; and Israel is Mine Elect, My soul shall receive Him. I have given Him My Spirit; and He shall bring forth judgment to the Gentiles. He shall not cry, and His voice shall not be heard without. The bruised reed He shall not break, and the smoking flax He shall not quench, until He shall bring forth judgment to victory. He shall shine, and shall not be broken, until He set judgment on the earth. And in His name shall the Gentiles trust.***[804]

Then is it Jacob the patriarch in whom the Gentiles and yourselves shall trust? or is it not Christ? As, therefore, Christ is the Israel and the Jacob,

---

[803] Isaiah 43:15.
[804] Isaiah 42:1-4.

even so we, who have been quarried out from the belly of Christ, are the true Israelitic race. But let us attend rather to the very word:

> ***And I will bring forth,*'** He says, '***the seed out of Jacob, and out of Judah: and it shall inherit My holy mountain; and Mine Elect and My servants shall possess the inheritance, and shall dwell there; and there shall be folds of flocks in the thicket, and the valley of Achor shall be a resting-place of cattle for the people who have sought Me. But as for you, who forsake Me, and forget My holy mountain, and prepare a table for demons, and fill out drink for the demon, I shall give you to the sword. You shall all fall with a slaughter; for I called you, and you hearkened not, and did evil before Me, and did choose that wherein I delighted not.***[805]

Such are the words of Scripture; understand, therefore, that the seed of Jacob now referred to is something else, and not, as may be supposed, spoken of your people. For it is not possible for the seed of Jacob to leave an entrance for the descendants of Jacob, or for [God] to have accepted the very same persons whom He had reproached with unfitness for the inheritance, and promise it to them again; but as there the prophet says, '***And now, O house of Jacob, come and let us walk in the light of the Lord; for He has sent away His people, the house of Jacob, because their land was full, as at the first, of soothsayers and divinations;***'[806] even so it is necessary for us here to observe that there are two seeds of Judah, and two races, as there are two houses of Jacob: the one begotten by blood and flesh, the other by faith and the Spirit."

Chapter CXXXVI: *The Jews, in rejecting Christ, rejected God who sent him.*

"For you see how He now addresses the people, saying a little before: '***As the grape shall be found in the cluster, and they will say, Destroy it not, for a blessing is in it; so will I do for My servant's sake: for His sake I will not destroy them all.***'[807] And thereafter He adds: '***And***

---

[805] Isaiah 65:9-12.

[806] Isaiah 2:5 {-6}.

[807] Isaiah 65:8 f.

I shall bring forth the seed out of Jacob, and out of Judah.'[808] It is plain then that if He thus be angry with them, and threaten to leave very few of them, He promises to bring forth certain others, who shall dwell in His mountain. But these are the persons whom He said He would sow and beget. For you neither suffer Him when He calls you, nor hear Him when He speaks to you, but have done evil in the presence of the Lord.

But the highest pitch of your wickedness lies in this, that you hate the Righteous One, and slew Him; and so treat those who have received from Him all that they are and have, and who are pious, righteous, and humane. Therefore '***woe unto their soul***,' says the Lord, '***for they have devised an evil counsel against themselves***,[809] *saying, Let us take away the righteous, for he is distasteful to us.*' For indeed you are not in the habit of sacrificing to Baal, as were your fathers, or of placing cakes in groves and on high places for the host of heaven: but you have not accepted God's Christ. For he who knows not Him, knows not the will of God; and he who insults and hates Him, insults and hates Him that sent Him. And whoever believes not in Him, believes not the declarations of the prophets, who preached and proclaimed Him to all."

Chapter CXXXVII: *He exhorts the Jews to be converted.*

"Say no evil thing, my brothers, against Him that was crucified, and treat not scornfully the stripes wherewith all may be healed, even as we are healed. For it will be well if, persuaded by the Scriptures, you are circumcised from hard-heartedness: not that circumcision which you have from the tenets that are put into you; for that was given for a sign, and not for a work of righteousness, as the Scriptures compel you [to admit]. Assent, therefore, and pour no ridicule on the Son of God; obey not the Pharisaic teachers, and scoff not at the King of Israel, as the rulers of your synagogues teach you to do after your prayers: for if he that touches those who are not pleasing[810] to God, is as one that touches the apple of God's eye, how much more so is he that touches His beloved! And that this is He, has been sufficiently demonstrated."

---

[808] {Isaiah 65:9.}

[809] Isaiah 3:9. {Compare, below, nn. 811, 812.}

[810] Zechariah 2:8.

And as they kept silence, I continued: "My friends, I now refer to the Scriptures as the Seventy have interpreted them; for when I quoted them formerly as you possess them, I made proof of you [to ascertain] how you were disposed. For, mentioning the Scripture which says, '***Woe unto them! for they have devised evil counsel against themselves, saying***'[811] (as the Seventy have translated, I continued): '*Let us take away the righteous, for he is distasteful to us;*'[812] whereas at the commencement of the discussion I added what your version has: '*Let us bind the righteous, for he is distasteful to us.*' But you had been busy about some other matter, and seem to have listened to the words without attending to them.

But now, since the day is drawing to a close, for the sun is about to set, I shall add one remark to what I have said, and conclude. I have indeed made the very same remark already, but I think it would be right to bestow some consideration on it again."

Chapter CXXXVIII: *Noah is a figure of Christ, who has regenerated us by water, and faith, and wood [i.e., the Cross].*

"You know, then, sirs," I said, "that God has said in Isaiah to Jerusalem: '*I saved thee in the deluge of Noah.*'[813] By this which God said was meant that the mystery of saved men appeared in the deluge. For righteous Noah, along with the other mortals at the deluge, i.e., with his own wife, his three sons and their wives, being eight in number, were a symbol of the eighth day, wherein Christ appeared when He rose from the dead, forever the first in power. For Christ, being the first-born of every creature, became again the chief of another race regenerated by Himself through water, and faith, and wood, containing the mystery of

---

[811] Isaiah 3:9.

[812] {See OSB Isaiah 3:10: "'Let us hand over the righteous man, for he is burdensome for us.' They shall eat the fruit of their doings."" Compare KJV: "Say ye to the righteous, that it shall be well with him, for they shall eat the fruit of their doings." See also Isaiah 5:23, 57:1.}

[813] Isaiah 54:9 comes nearer to these words than any other passage; but still the exact quotation is not in Isaiah, or in any part of Scripture. {See also Genesis 8:21. This quotation is actually a paraphrase of Isaiah and so is not in boldface. Isaiah 54:9 states: "For this is like the waters of Noah to Me; For as I have sworn That the waters of Noah would no longer cover the earth, So have I sworn That I would not be angry with you, nor rebuke you."}

the Cross; even as Noah was saved by wood when he rode over the waters with his household. Accordingly, when the prophet says, '*I saved thee in the times of Noah*,'[814] as I have already remarked, he addresses the people who are equally faithful to God, and possess the same signs. For when Moses had the rod in his hands, he led your nation through the sea. And you believe that this was spoken to your nation only, or to the land. But the whole earth, as the Scripture says, was inundated, and the water rose in height fifteen cubits above all the mountains: so that it is evident this was not spoken to the land, but to the people who obeyed Him: for whom also He had before prepared a resting-place in Jerusalem, as was previously demonstrated by all the symbols of the deluge; I mean, that by water, faith, and wood, those who are afore-prepared, and who repent of the sins which they have committed, shall escape from the impending judgment of God."

Chapter CXXXIX: *The blessings, and also the curse, pronounced by Noah were prophecies of the future.*

"For another mystery was accomplished and predicted in the days of Noah, of which you are not aware. It is this: in the blessings wherewith Noah blessed his two sons, and in the curse pronounced on his son's son. For the Spirit of prophecy would not curse the son that had been by God blessed along with [his brothers]. But since the punishment of the sin would cleave to the whole descent of the son that mocked at his father's nakedness, he made the curse originate with *his* son. Now, in what he said, he foretold that the descendants of Shem would keep in retention the property and dwellings of Canaan: and again that the descendants of Japheth would take possession of the property of which Shem's descendants had dispossessed Canaan's descendants; and spoil the descendants of Shem, even as they plundered the sons of Canaan. And listen to the way in which it has so come to pass. For you, who have derived your lineage from Shem, invaded the territory of the sons of Canaan by the will of God; and you possessed it. And it is manifest that the sons of Japheth, having invaded you in turn by the judgment of God, have taken your land from you, and have possessed it. Thus it is written:

---

[814] {See Isaiah 54:9 and prior note.}

> ***And Noah awoke from the wine, and knew what his younger son had done unto him; and he said, Cursed be Canaan, the servant; a servant shall he be unto his brethren. And he said, Blessed be the Lord God of Shem; and Canaan shall be his servant. May the Lord enlarge Japheth, and let him dwell in the houses of Shem; and let Canaan be his servant.***[815]

Accordingly, as two peoples were blessed,—those from Shem, and those from Japheth,—and as the offspring of Shem were decreed first to possess the dwellings of Canaan, and the offspring of Japheth were predicted as in turn receiving the same possessions, and to the two peoples there was the one people of Canaan handed over for servants; so Christ has come according to the power given Him from the Almighty Father, and summoning men to friendship, and blessing, and repentance, and dwelling together, has promised, as has already been proved, that there shall be a future possession for all the saints in this same land. And hence all men everywhere, whether bond or free, who believe in Christ, and recognize the truth in His own words and those of His prophets, know that they shall be with Him in that land, and inherit everlasting and incorruptible good."

Chapter CXL: *In Christ all are free. The Jews hope for salvation in vain because they are sons of Abraham.*

"Hence also Jacob, as I remarked before, being himself a type of Christ, had married the two handmaids of his two free wives, and of them begat sons, for the purpose of indicating beforehand that Christ would receive even all those who amongst Japheth's race are descendants of Canaan, equally with the free, and would have the children fellow-heirs. And we are such; but you cannot comprehend this, because you cannot drink of the living fountain of God, but of broken cisterns which can hold no water, as the Scripture says.[816] But they are cisterns broken, and holding no water, which your own teachers have digged, as the Scripture also expressly asserts, '***teaching for doctrines the commandments of men.***'[817] And besides, they beguile themselves and you, supposing that

[815] Genesis 9:24-27.

[816] Jeremiah 2:13.

[817] Isaiah 29:13. {See also Mark 7:7.}

the everlasting kingdom will be assuredly given to those of the dispersion who are of Abraham after the flesh, although they be sinners, and faithless, and disobedient towards God, which the Scriptures have proved is not the case. For if so, Isaiah would never have said this: '***And unless the Lord of Sabaoth had left us a seed, we would have been like Sodom and Gomorrah.***'[818] And Ezekiel:

> ***'Even if Noah, and Jacob, and Daniel were to pray for sons or daughters, their request should not be granted.'***[819] ***But neither shall the father perish for the son, nor the son for the father; but every one for his own sin, and each shall be saved for his own righteousness.***[820]

And again Isaiah says: '***They shall look on the carcasses***[821] ***of them that have transgressed: their worm shall not cease, and their fire shall not be quenched; and they shall be a spectacle to all flesh.***'[822] And our Lord, according to the will of Him that sent Him, who is the Father and Lord of all, would not have said, '***They shall come from the east, and from the west, and shall sit down with Abraham, and Isaac, and Jacob in the kingdom of heaven. But the children of the kingdom shall be cast out into outer darkness.***'[823] Furthermore, I have proved in what has preceded,[824] that those who were foreknown to be unrighteous, whether men or angels, are not made wicked by God's fault, but each man by his own fault is what he will appear to be."

Chapter CXLI: *Free-will in men and angels.*

"But that you may not have a pretext for saying that Christ must have been crucified, and that those who transgressed must have been among your nation, and that the matter could not have been otherwise, I said briefly by anticipation, that God, wishing men and angels to follow

---

[818] Isaiah 1:9. {See also Romans 9:29.}
[819] Ezekiel 14:18, 20. {See also Ezekiel 14:14.}
[820] Ezekiel 18:20. {Some is a paraphrase.}
[821] Literally, "limbs."
[822] Isaiah 66:24.
[823] Matthew 8:11 {-12}.
[824] Chapter LXXXVIII, CII.

His will, resolved to create them free to do righteousness; possessing reason, that they may know by whom they are created, and through whom they, not existing formerly, do now exist; and with a law that they should be judged by Him, if they do anything contrary to right reason: and of ourselves we, men and angels, shall be convicted of having acted sinfully, unless we repent beforehand.

But if the word of God foretells that some angels and men shall be certainly punished, it did so because it foreknew that they would be unchangeably [wicked], but not because God had created them so. So that if they repent, all who wish for it can obtain mercy from God: and the Scripture foretells that they shall be blessed, saying, '***Blessed is the man to whom the Lord imputeth not sin***;'[825] that is, having repented of his sins, that he may receive remission of them from God; and not as you deceive yourselves, and some others who resemble you in this, who say, that even though they be sinners, but know God, the Lord will not impute sin to them.

We have as proof of this the one fall of David, which happened through his boasting, which was forgiven then when he so mourned and wept, as it is written. But if even to such a man no remission was granted before repentance, and only when this great king, and anointed one, and prophet, mourned and conducted himself so, how can the impure and utterly abandoned, if they weep not, and mourn not, and repent not, entertain the hope that the Lord will not impute to them sin?

And this one fall of David, in the matter of Uriah's wife, proves, sirs," I said, "that the patriarchs had many wives, not to commit fornication, but that a certain dispensation and all mysteries might be accomplished by them; since, if it were allowable to take any wife, or as many wives as one chooses, and how he chooses, which the men of your nation do over all the earth, wherever they sojourn, or wherever they have been sent, taking women under the name of marriage, much more would David have been permitted to do this."

When I had said this, dearest Marcus Pompeius, I came to an end.

---

[825] Psalm 32:2.

Chapter CXLII: *The Jews return thanks, and leave Justin.*

Then Trypho, after a little delay, said, "You see that it was not intentionally that we came to discuss these points. And I confess that I have been particularly pleased with the conference; and I think that these are of quite the same opinion as myself. For we have found more than we expected, and more than it was possible to have expected. And if we could do this more frequently, we should be much helped in the searching of the Scriptures themselves. But since," he said, "you are on the eve of departure, and expect daily to set sail, do not hesitate to remember us as friends when you are gone."

"For my part," I replied, "if I had remained, I would have wished to do the same thing daily. But now, since I expect, with God's will and aid, to set sail, I exhort you to give all diligence in this very great struggle for your own salvation, and to be earnest in setting a higher value on the Christ of the Almighty God than on your own teachers."

After this they left me, wishing me safety in my voyage, and from every misfortune. And I, praying for them, said, "I can wish no better thing for you, sirs, than this, that, recognizing in this way that intelligence is given to every man, you may be of the same opinion as ourselves, and believe that Jesus is the Christ of God."[826]

---

[826] This last sentence is very dubious. For *παντὶ ἀνθρώπινον νοῦν* read *παντί ἀνθρώπῳ τόν νοῦν*. For *ποιήσητε* read *πιοεύσητε*. And lastly, for *τὸ ἡμῶν* read *τὸν 'Ιησῦν*.

The Discourse to the Greeks

Chapter I: *Justin justifies his departure from Greek customs.*

Do not suppose, ye Greeks, that my separation from your customs is unreasonable and unthinking; for I found in them nothing that is holy or acceptable to God. For the very compositions of your poets are monuments of madness and intemperance. For anyone who becomes the scholar of your most eminent instructor, is more beset by difficulties than all men besides.

For first they say that Agamemnon, abetting the extravagant lust of his brother, and his madness and unrestrained desire, readily gave even his daughter to be sacrificed, and troubled all Greece that he might rescue Helen, who had been ravished by the leprous[827] shepherd. But when in the course of the war they took captives, Agamemnon was himself taken captive by Chryseis, and for Briseis' sake kindled a feud with the son of Thetis. And Pelides himself, who crossed the river,[828] overthrew Troy, and subdued Hector, this your hero became the slave of Polyxena, and was conquered by a dead Amazon; and putting off the god-fabricated armor, and donning the hymeneal robe, he became a sacrifice of love in the temple of Apollo. And the Ithacan Ulysses made a virtue of a vice.[829] And indeed his sailing past the Sirens[830] gave evidence that he was destitute of worthy prudence, because he could not depend on his prudence for stopping his ears. Ajax, son of Telamon, who bore the shield of sevenfold ox-hide, went mad when he was defeated in the contest with Ulysses for the armor.

Such things I have no desire to be instructed in. Of such virtue I am not covetous, that I should believe the myths of Homer. For the whole rhapsody, the beginning and end both of the Iliad and the Odyssey is—a woman.

---

[827] Potter would here read *λιπαροῦ*, "elegant;" but the above reading is defended by Sylburg, on the ground that shepherds were so greatly despised, that this is not too hard an epithet to apply to Paris.

[828] Of the many attempts to amend this clause, there seems to be none satisfactory.

[829] Or, won the reputation of the virtue of wisdom by the vice of deceit.

[830] That is, the manner in which he did it, stopping his companions' ears with wax, and having himself bound to the mast of his ship.

Chapter II: *The Greek theogony exposed.*

But since, next to Homer, Hesiod wrote his *Works and Days*, who will believe his driveling theogony? For they say that Chronos, the son of Ouranos,[831] in the beginning slew his father, and possessed himself of his rule; and that, being seized with a panic lest he should himself suffer in the same way, he preferred devouring his children; but that, by the craft of the Curetes, Jupiter was conveyed away and kept in secret, and afterwards bound his father with chains, and divided the empire; Jupiter receiving, as the story goes, the air, and Neptune the deep, and Pluto the portion of Hades.

But Pluto ravished Proserpine; and Ceres sought her child wandering through the deserts. And this myth was celebrated in the Eleusinian fire.[832] Again, Neptune ravished Melanippe when she was drawing water, besides abusing a host of Nereids not a few, whose names, were we to recount them, would cost us a multitude of words. And as for Jupiter, he was a various adulterer, with Antiope as a satyr, with Danaë as gold, and with Europa as a bull; with Leda, moreover, he assumed wings. For the love of Semele proved both his unchastity and the jealousy of Semele. And they say that he carried off the Phrygian Ganymede to be his cup-bearer. These, then, are the exploits of the sons of Saturn.

And your illustrious son of Latona [Apollo], who professed soothsaying, convicted himself of lying. He pursued Daphne, but did not gain possession of her; and to Hyacinthus,[833] who loved him, he did not foretell his death. And I say nothing of the masculine character of Minerva, nor of the feminine nature of Bacchus, nor of the fornicating disposition of Venus.

Read to Jupiter, ye Greeks, the law against parricides, and the penalty of adultery, and the ignominy of pederasty. Teach Minerva and Diana the works of women, and Bacchus the works of men. What seemliness is there in a woman's girding herself with armor, or in a man's

---

[831] Or, Saturn son of Heaven.

[832] In the mysteries of Eleusis, the return of Proserpine from the lower world was celebrated.

[833] Apollo, accidentally killed Hyacinthus by striking him on the head with a quoit. {A quoit is a flattened metal ring or a rope circle used in throwing games; presumably the mythical quoit was of metal.}

decorating himself with cymbals, and garlands, and female attire, and accompanied by a herd of bacchanalian women?

Chapter III: *Follies of the Greek mythology.*

For Hercules, celebrated by his three nights,[834] sung by the poets for his successful labors, the son of Jupiter, who slew the lion and destroyed the many-headed hydra; who put to death the fierce and mighty boar, and was able to kill the fleet man-eating birds, and brought up from Hades the three-headed dog; who effectually cleansed the huge Augean building from its dung, and killed the bulls and the stag whose nostrils breathed fire, and plucked the golden fruit from the tree, and slew the poisonous serpent (and for some reason, which it is not lawful to utter, killed Achelous, and the guest-slaying Busiris), and crossed the mountains that he might get water which gave forth an articulate speech, as the story goes: he who was able to do so many and such like and so great deeds as these, how childishly he was delighted to be stunned by the cymbals of the satyrs, and to be conquered by the love of woman, and to be struck on the buttocks by the laughing Lyda! And at last, not being able to put off the tunic of Nessus, himself kindling his own funeral pile, so he died. Let Vulcan lay aside his envy, and not be jealous if he is hated because he is old and club-footed, and Mars loved, because young and beautiful.

Since, therefore, ye Greeks, your gods are convicted of intemperance, and your heroes are effeminate, as the histories on which your dramas are founded have declared, such as the curse of Atreus, the bed of Thyestes[835] and the taint in the house of Pelops, and Danaus murdering through hatred and making Aegyptus childless in the intoxication of his rage, and the Thyestean banquet spread by the Furies.[836] And Procne is to this day flitting about, lamenting; and her sister of Athens shrills with her tongue cut out. For what need is there of

---

[834] *Τριέσπερον*, so called, as Potter thinks, from his being three nights in the belly of a whale, which swallowed him when shipwrecked, and vomited him safely on shore.

[835] Thyestes seduced the wife of his brother Atreus, whence the tragic career of the family.

[836] There is no apodosis in the Greek. {Apodosis refers to the main clause of a conditional sentence.}

speaking of the goad[837] of Oedipus, and the murder of Laius, and the marrying his mother, and the mutual slaughter of those who were at once his brothers and his sons?

Chapter IV: *Shameless practices of the Greeks.*

And your public assemblies I have come to hate. For there are excessive banquetings, and subtle flutes which provoke to lustful movements, and useless and luxurious anointings, and crowning with garlands. With such a mass of evils do you banish shame; and ye fill your minds with them, and are carried away by intemperance, and indulge as a common practice in wicked and insane fornication.

And this further I would say to you, why are you, being a Greek, indignant at your son when he imitates Jupiter, and rises against you and defrauds you of your own wife? Why do you count him your enemy, and yet worship one that is like him? And why do you blame your wife for living in unchastity, and yet honor Venus with shrines? If indeed these things had been related by others, they would have seemed to be mere slanderous accusations, and not truth. But now your own poets sing these things, and your histories noisily publish them.

Chapter V: *Closing appeal.*

Henceforth, ye Greeks, come and partake of incomparable wisdom, and be instructed by the Divine Word, and acquaint yourselves with the King immortal; and do not recognize those men as heroes who slaughter whole nations. For our own Ruler,[838] the Divine Word, who even now constantly aids us, does not desire strength of body and beauty of feature, nor yet the high spirit of earth's nobility, but a pure soul, fortified by holiness, and the watchwords of our King, holy actions, for through the Word power passes into the soul. O trumpet of peace to the soul that is at war! O weapon that puttest to flight terrible passions! O instruction that quenches the innate fire of the soul! The Word exercises

---

[837] Not, as the editors dispute, either the tongue of the buckle with which he put out his eyes, nor the awl with which his heels were bored through, but the goad with which he killed his father.

[838] *Αὐτὸ; γὰρ ἡμῶν.*

an influence which does not make poets: it does not equip philosophers nor skilled orators, but by its instruction it makes mortals immortal, mortals gods; and from the earth transports them to the realms above Olympus.

Come, be taught; become as I am, for I, too, was as ye are. These have conquered me—the divinity of the instruction, and the power of the Word: for as a skilled serpent-charmer lures the terrible reptile from his den and causes it to flee, so the Word drives the fearful passions of our sensual nature from the very recesses of the soul; first driving forth lust, through which every ill is begotten—hatreds, strife, envy, emulations, anger, and such like. Lust being once banished, the soul becomes calm and serene. And being set free from the ills in which it was sunk up to the neck, it returns to Him who made it. For it is fit that it be restored to that state whence it departed, whence every soul was or is.

Justin's Hortatory Address to the Greeks[839]

Chapter I: *Reasons for addressing the Greeks.*

As I begin this hortatory address to you, ye men of Greece, I pray God that I may know what I ought to say to you, and that you, shaking off your habitual[840] love of disputing, and being delivered from the error of your fathers, may now choose what is profitable; not fancying that you commit any offence against your forefathers, though the things which you formerly considered by no means salutary should now seem useful to you. For accurate investigation of matters, putting truth to the question with a more searching scrutiny, often reveals that things which have passed for excellent are of quite another sort.

Since, then, we propose to discourse of the true religion (than which, I think, there is nothing which is counted more valuable by those who desire to pass through life without danger, on account of the judgment which is to be after the termination of this life, and which is announced not only by our forefathers according to God, to wit the prophets and lawgivers, but also by those among yourselves who have been esteemed wise, not poets alone, but also philosophers, who professed among you that they had attained the true and divine knowledge), I think it well first of all to examine the teachers of religion, both our own and yours, who they were, and how great, and in what times they lived; in order that those who have formerly received from their fathers the false religion, may now, when they perceive this, be extricated from that inveterate error; and that we may clearly and manifestly show that we ourselves follow the religion of our forefathers according to God.

---

[839] {The original editors did not always provide citations to ancient pagan works that Saint Justin relied on for his arguments. This editor has similarly chosen not to provide such citations.}

[840] Literally, "former."

Chapter II: *The poets are unfit to be religious teachers.*

Whom, then, ye men of Greece, do ye call your teachers of religion? The poets? It will do your cause no good to say so to men who know the poets; for they know how very ridiculous a theogony they have composed,—as we can learn from Homer, your most distinguished and prince of poets. For he says, first, that the gods were in the beginning generated from water; for he has written thus:[841]

> Both ocean, the origin of the gods, and their mother Tethys.

And then we must also remind you of what he further says of him whom ye consider the first of the gods, and whom he often calls "the father of gods and men;" for he said:[842]

> Zeus, who is the dispenser of war to men.

Indeed, he says that he was not only the dispenser of war to the army, but also the cause of perjury to the Trojans, by means of his daughter;[843] and Homer introduces him in love, and bitterly complaining, and bewailing himself, and plotted against by the other gods, and at one time exclaiming concerning his own son:[844]

> Alas! he falls, my most beloved of men!
> Sarpedon, vanquished by Patroclus, falls!
> So will the fates.

And at another time concerning Hector:[845]

> Ah! I behold a warrior dear to me
> Around the walls of Ilium driven, and grieve
> For Hector.

---

[841] *Iliad*, xvi. 302.
[842] *Iliad*, xix. 224.
[843] That is, Venus, who, after Paris had sworn that the war should be decided by single combat between himself and Menelaus, carried him off, and induced him, though defeated, to refuse performance of the articles agreed upon.
[844] *Iliad*, xvi. 433. Sarpedon was a son of Zeus.
[845] *Iliad*, xxii.168.

And what he says of the conspiracy of the other gods against Zeus, they know who read these words:[846]

> When the other Olympians—Juno, and Neptune, and Minerva—wished to bind him.

And unless the blessed gods had feared him whom gods call Briareus, Zeus would have been bound by them. And what Homer says of his intemperate loves, we must remind you in the very words he used. For he said that Zeus spake thus to Juno:[847]

> For never goddess pour'd, nor woman yet,
> So full a tide of love into my breast;
> I never loved Ixion's consort thus,
> Nor sweet Acrisian Danaë, from whom
> Sprang Perseus, noblest of the race of man;
> Nor Phoenix' daughter fair, of whom were born
> Minos, unmatch'd but by the powers above,
> And Rhadamanthus; nor yet Semele,
> Nor yet Alcmene, who in Thebes produced
> The valiant Hercules; and though my son
> By Semele were Bacchus, joy of man;
> Nor Ceres golden-hair'd, nor high-enthron'd
> Latona in the skies; no—nor thyself
> As now I love thee, and my soul perceive
> O'erwhelm'd with sweetness of intense desire.

It is fit that we now mention what one can learn from the work of Homer of the other gods, and what they suffered at the hands of men. For he says that Mars and Venus were wounded by Diomed, and of many others of the gods he relates the sufferings. For thus we can gather from the case of Dione consoling her daughter; for she said to her:[848]

> Have patience, dearest child; though much enforc'd
> Restrain thine anger: we, in heav'n who dwell,

---

[846] *Iliad*, i. 299, etc.
[847] *Iliad*, xiv. 315. (The passage is here given in full from Cowper's translation. In Justin's quotation one or two lines are omitted.)
[848] *Iliad*, v. 382 (from Lord Derby's translation).

Have much to bear from mortals; and ourselves
Too oft upon each other suff'rings lay:
Mars had his suff'rings; by Alöeus' sons,
Otus and Ephialtes, strongly bound,
He thirteen months in brazen fetters lay:
Juno, too, suffer'd, when Amphitryon's son
Thro' her right breast a three-barb'd arrow sent:
Dire, and unheard of, were the pangs she bore,
Great Pluto's self the stinging arrow felt,
When that same son of Aegis-bearing Jove
Assail'd him in the very gates of hell,
And wrought him keenest anguish; pierced with pain,
To high Olympus, to the courts of Jove,
Groaning, he came; the bitter shaft remain'd
Deep in his shoulder fix'd, and griev'd his soul.

But if it is right to remind you of the battle of the gods, opposed to one another, your own poet himself will recount it, saying:[849]

Such was the shock when gods in battle met;
For there to royal Neptune stood oppos'd
Phoebus Apollo with his arrows keen;
The blue-eyed Pallas to the god of war;
To Juno, Dian, heav'nly archeress,
Sister of Phoebus, golden-shafted queen.
Stout Hermes, helpful god, Latona fac'd.

These and such like things did Homer teach you; and not Homer only, but also Hesiod. So that if you believe your most distinguished poets, who have given the genealogies of your gods, you must of necessity either suppose that the gods are such beings as these, or believe that there are no gods at all.

Chapter III: *Opinions of the school of Thales.*

And if you decline citing the poets, because you say it is allowable for them to frame myths, and to relate in a mythical way many things about the gods which are far from true, do you suppose you have some

---

[849] *Iliad*, xx. 66 (from Lord Derby's translation).

others for your religious teachers, or how do you say that they themselves[850] have learned this religion of yours? For it is impossible that any should know matters so great and divine, who have not themselves learned them first from the initiated.[851] You will no doubt say, "The sages and philosophers." For to them, as to a fortified wall, you are wont to flee, when anyone quotes the opinions of your poets about the gods.

Therefore, since it is fit that we commence with the ancients and the earliest, beginning thence I will produce the opinion of each, much more ridiculous as it is than the theology of the poets. For Thales of Miletus, who took the lead in the study of natural philosophy, declared that water was the first principle of all things; for from water he says that all things are, and that into water all are resolved. And after him Anaximander, who came from the same Miletus, said that the infinite was the first principle of all things; for that from this indeed all things are produced, and into this do all decay. Thirdly, Anaximenes—and he too was from Miletus—says that air is the first principle of all things; for he says that from this all things are produced, and into this all are resolved. Heraclitus and Hippasus, from Metapontus, say that fire is the first principle of all things; for from fire all things proceed, and in fire do all things terminate. Anaxagoras of Clazomenae said that the homogeneous parts are the first principles of all things. Archelaus, the son of Apollodorus, an Athenian, says that the infinite air and its density and rarity are the first principle of all things. All these, forming a succession from Thales, followed the philosophy called by themselves physical.

Chapter IV: *Opinions of Pythagoras and Epicurus.*

Then, in regular succession from another starting-point, Pythagoras the Samian, son of Mnesarchus, calls numbers, with their proportions and harmonies, and the elements composed of both, the first principles; and he includes also unity and the indefinite binary.[852]

---

[850] I.e., these teachers.

[851] Literally, "those who knew."

[852] *μονάδα χαὶ τὴν ἀόριτον δυάδα.* One, or unity, was considered by Pythagoras as the essence of number, and also as God. Two, or the indefinite binary, was the equivalent of evil. So Plutarch, *De placit. philosoph.* C. 7; from which treatise the above opinions of the various sects are quoted, generally verbatim.

Epicurus, an Athenian, the son of Neocles, says that the first principles of the things that exist are bodies perceptible by reason, admitting no vacuity,[853] unbegotten, indestructible, which can neither be broken, nor admit of any formation of their parts, nor alteration, and are therefore perceptible by reason. Empedocles of Agrigentum, son of Meton, maintained that there were four elements—fire, air, water, earth; and two elementary powers—love and hate,[854] of which the former is a power of union, the latter of separation.

You see, then, the confusion of those who are considered by you to have been wise men, whom you assert to be your teachers of religion: some of them declaring that water is the first principle of all things; others, air; others, fire; and others, some other of these fore-mentioned elements; and all of them employing persuasive arguments for the establishment of their own errors, and attempting to prove their own peculiar dogma to be the most valuable. These things were said by them.

How then, ye men of Greece, can it be safe for those who desire to be saved, to fancy that they can learn the true religion from these philosophers, who were neither able so to convince themselves as to prevent sectarian wrangling with one another, and not to appear definitely opposed to one another's opinions?

Chapter V: *Opinions of Plato and Aristotle.*

But possibly those who are unwilling to give up the ancient and inveterate error, maintain that they have received the doctrine of their religion not from those who have now been mentioned, but from those who are esteemed among them as the most renowned and finished philosophers, Plato and Aristotle.

For these, they say, have learned the perfect and true religion. But I would be glad to ask, first of all, from those who say so, from whom they say that these men have learned this knowledge; for it is impossible that men who have not learned these so great and divine matters from some who knew them, should either themselves know them, or be able correctly to teach others; and, in the second place, I think we ought to

---

[853] *ἀμέτοχα χενοῦ*; the void being that in which bodies move, while they themselves are of a different nature from it.

[854] Or, accord and dissent, attraction and repulsion.

examine the opinions even of these sages. For we shall see whether each of these does not manifestly contradict the other. But if we find that even they do not agree with each other, I think it is easy to see clearly that they too are ignorant.

For Plato, with the air of one that has descended from above, and has accurately ascertained and seen all that is in heaven, says that the most high God exists in a fiery substance.[855] But Aristotle, in a book addressed to Alexander of Macedon, giving a compendious explanation of his own philosophy, clearly and manifestly overthrows the opinion of Plato, saying that God does not exist in a fiery substance: but inventing, as a fifth substance, some kind of ethereal and unchangeable body, says that God exists in it. Thus, at least, he wrote: "Not, as some of those who have erred regarding the Deity say, that God exists in a fiery substance." Then, as if he were not satisfied with this blasphemy against Plato, he further, for the sake of proving what he says about the ethereal body, cites as a witness him whom Plato had banished from his republic as a liar, and as being an imitator of the images of truth at three removes,[856] for so Plato calls Homer; for he wrote: "Thus at least did Homer speak,[857] 'And Zeus obtained the wide heaven in the air and the clouds,'" wishing to make his own opinion appear more worthy of credit by the testimony of Homer; not being aware that if he used Homer as a witness to prove that he spoke truth, many of his tenets would be proved untrue.

For Thales of Miletus, who was the founder of philosophy among them, taking occasion from him,[858] will contradict his first opinions about first principles. For Aristotle himself, having said that God and matter are the first principles of all things, Thales, the eldest of all their sages, says that water is the first principle of the things that exist; for he says that all things are from water, and that all things are resolved into water. And he conjectures this, first, from the fact that the seed of all living creatures, which is their first principle, is moist; and secondly, because all plants

---

[855] Or, "is of a fiery nature."

[856] See the *Republic*, x. 2. By the Platonic doctrine, the ideas of things in the mind of God were the realities; the things themselves, as seen by us, were the images of these realities; and poetry, therefore, describing the images of realities, was only at the third remove from nature. As Plato puts it briefly in this same passage, "the painter, the bed-maker, God—these three are the matters of three species of beds."

[857] *Iliad* xv. 192.

[858] I.e., from Homer; using Homer's words as suggestive and confirmatory of his doctrine.

grow and bear fruit in moisture, but when deprived of moisture, wither. Then, as if not satisfied with his conjectures, he cites Homer as a most trustworthy testimony, who speaks thus:

> Ocean, who is the origin of all.[859]

May not Thales, then, very fairly say to him, "What is the reason, Aristotle, why you give heed to Homer, as if he spoke truth, when you wish to demolish the opinions of Plato; but when you promulgate an opinion contrary to ours, you think Homer untruthful?"

Chapter VI: *Further disagreements between Plato and Aristotle.*

And that these very wonderful sages of yours do not even agree in other respects, can be easily learned from this. For while Plato says that there are three first principles of all things, God, and matter, and form,—God, the maker of all; and matter, which is the subject of the first production of all that is produced, and affords to God opportunity for His workmanship; and form, which is the type of each of the things produced,—Aristotle makes no mention at all of form as a first principle, but says that there are two, God and matter. And again, while Plato says that the highest God and the ideas exist in the first place of the highest heavens, and in fixed sphere, Aristotle says that, next to the most high God, there are, not ideas, but certain gods, who can be perceived by the mind.

Thus, then, do they differ concerning things heavenly. So that one can see that they not only are unable to understand our earthly matters, but also, being at variance among themselves regarding these things, they will appear unworthy of credit when they treat of things heavenly. And that even their doctrine regarding the human soul as it now is does not harmonize, is manifest from what has been said by each of them concerning it. For Plato says that it is of three parts, having the faculty of reason, of affection, and of appetite.[860] But Aristotle says that the soul is not so comprehensive as to include also corruptible parts, but

---

[859] *Iliad*, xiv. 246.

[860] *τὸ λογιχὸν, τὸ θυμιχὸν, τὸ ἐπιθυμτιχὸν*—corresponding to what we roughly speak of as reason, the heart, and the appetites.

only reason. And Plato loudly maintains that "the whole soul is immortal." But Aristotle, naming it "the actuality,"[861] would have it to be mortal, not immortal. And the former says it is always in motion; but Aristotle says that it is immoveable, since it must itself precede all motion.

Chapter VII: *Inconsistencies of Plato's doctrine.*

But in these things they are convicted of thinking in contradiction to each other. And if anyone will accurately criticize their writings, they have chosen to abide in harmony not even with their own opinions. Plato, at any rate, at one time says that there are three first principles of the universe—God, and matter, and form; but at another time four, for he adds the universal soul. And again, when he has already said that matter is eternal,[862] he afterwards says that it is produced; and when he has first given to form its peculiar rank as a first principle, and has asserted for its self-subsistence, he afterwards says that this same thing is among the things perceived by the understanding. Moreover, having first declared that everything that is made is mortal,[863] he afterwards states that some of the things that are made are indestructible and immortal.

What, then, is the cause why those who have been esteemed wise among you disagree not only with one another, but also with themselves? Manifestly, their unwillingness to learn from those who know, and their desire to attain accurate knowledge of things heavenly by their own human excess of wisdom; though they were able to understand not even earthly matters.

Certainly some of your philosophers say that the human soul is in us; others, that it is around us. For not even in this did they choose to agree with one another, but, distributing, as it were, ignorance in various ways among themselves, they thought fit to wrangle and dispute with one another even about the soul. For some of them say that the soul is fire, and some that it is the air; and others, the mind; and others, motion; and others, an exhalation; and certain others say that it is a power

[861] *ἐντελέχεια*,—the completion or actuality to which each thing, by virtue of its peculiar nature (or potentiality, *δύναωις*), can arrive.
[862] Literally, "unbegotten."
[863] Or, "liable to destruction."

flowing from the stars; and others, number capable of motion; and others, a generating water. And a wholly confused and inharmonious opinion has prevailed among them, which only in this one respect appears praise-worthy to those who can form a right judgment, that they have been anxious to convict one another of error and falsehood.

Chapter VIII: *Antiquity, inspiration, and harmony of Christian teachers.*

Since therefore it is impossible to learn anything true concerning religion from your teachers, who by their mutual disagreement have furnished you with sufficient proof of their own ignorance, I consider it reasonable to recur to our progenitors, who both in point of time have by a great way the precedence of your teachers, and who have taught us nothing from their own private fancy, nor differed with one another, nor attempted to overturn one another's positions, but without wrangling and contention received from God the knowledge which also they taught to us. For neither by nature nor by human conception is it possible for men to know things so great and divine, but by the gift which then descended from above upon the holy men, who had no need of rhetorical art,[864] nor of uttering anything in a contentious or quarrelsome manner, but to present themselves pure[865] to the energy of the Divine Spirit, in order that the divine plectrum itself, descending from heaven, and using righteous men as an instrument like a harp or lyre, might reveal to us the knowledge of things divine and heavenly. Wherefore, as if with one mouth and one tongue, they have in succession, and in harmony with one another, taught us both concerning God, and the creation of the world, and the formation of man, and concerning the immortality of the human soul, and the judgment which is to be after this life, and concerning all things which it is needful for us to know, and thus in divers times and places have afforded us the divine instruction.

---

[864] Literally, "the art of words."

[865] Literally, "clean," free from other influences.

Chapter IX: *The antiquity of Moses proved by Greek writers.*

I will begin, then, with our first prophet and lawgiver, Moses; first explaining the times in which he lived, on authorities which among you are worthy of all credit. For I do not propose to prove these things only from our own divine histories, which as yet you are unwilling to credit on account of the inveterate error of your forefathers, but also from your own histories, and such, too, as have no reference to our worship, that you may know that, of all your teachers, whether sages, poets, historians, philosophers, or lawgivers, by far the oldest, as the Greek histories show us, was Moses, who was our first religious teacher.[866] For in the times of Ogyges and Inachus, whom some of your poets suppose to have been earth-born,[867] Moses is mentioned as the leader and ruler of the Jewish nation. For in this way he is mentioned both by Polemon in the first book of his *Hellenics*, and by Appion son of Posidonius in his book against the Jews, and in the fourth book of his history, where he says that during the reign of Inachus over Argos the Jews revolted from Amasis king of the Egyptians, and that Moses led them. And Ptolemaeus the Mendesian, in relating the history of Egypt, concurs in all this. And those who write the Athenian history, Hellanicus and Philochorus (the author of *The Attic History*), Castor and Thallus and Alexander Polyhistor, and also the very well informed writers on Jewish affairs, Philo and Josephus, have mentioned Moses as a very ancient and time-honored prince of the Jews. Josephus, certainly, desiring to signify even by the title of his work the antiquity and age of the history, wrote thus at the commencement of the history: "The Jewish antiquities[868] of Flavius Josephus,"—signifying the oldness of the history by the word "antiquities."

And your most renowned historian Diodorus, who employed thirty whole years in epitomizing the libraries, and who, as he himself wrote, travelled over both Asia and Europe for the sake of great accuracy, and thus became an eye-witness of very many things, wrote forty entire books of his own history. And he in the first book, having said that he had learned from the Egyptian priests that Moses was an ancient lawgiver, and even the first, wrote of him in these very words: "For subsequent to the ancient manner of living in Egypt which gods and heroes are fabled to

---

[866] The incongruity in this sentence is Justin's.

[867] That is, spring from the soil; and hence the oldest inhabitants, the aborigines.

[868] Literally, archaeology.

have regulated, they say that Moses[869] first persuaded the people to use written laws, and to live by them; and he is recorded to have been a man both great of soul and of great faculty in social matters." Then, having proceeded a little further, and wishing to mention the ancient lawgivers, he mentions Moses first. For he spoke in these words:

> Among the Jews they say that Moses ascribed his laws[870] to that God who is called Jehovah, whether because they judged it a marvelous and quite divine conception which promised to benefit a multitude of men, or because they were of opinion that the people would be the more obedient when they contemplated the majesty and power of those who were said to have invented the laws. And they say that Sasunchis was the second Egyptian legislator, a man of excellent understanding. And the third, they say, was Sesonchosis the king, who not only performed the most brilliant military exploits of any in Egypt, but also consolidated that warlike race by legislation. And the fourth lawgiver, they say, was Bocchoris the king, a wise and surpassingly skillful man. And after him it is said that Amasis the king acceded to the government, whom they relate to have regulated all that pertains to the rulers of provinces, and to the general administration of the government of Egypt. And they say that Darius, the father of Xerxes, was the sixth who legislated for the Egyptians."

Chapter X: *Training and inspiration of Moses.*

These things, ye men of Greece, have been recorded in writing concerning the antiquity of Moses by those who were not of our religion; and they said that they learned all these things from the Egyptian priests, among whom Moses was not only born, but also was thought worthy of partaking of all the education of the Egyptians, on account of his being adopted by the king's daughter as her son; and for the same reason was thought worthy of great attention, as the wisest of the historians relate, who have chosen to record his life and actions, and the rank of his descent,—I speak of Philo and Josephus. For these, in their narration of

[869] Unfortunately, Justin here mistook Menes for Moses.
[870] This sentence must be so completed from the context in Diodorus. See the note of Maranus.

the history of the Jews, say that Moses was sprung from the race of the Chaldeans, and that he was born in Egypt when his forefathers had migrated on account of famine from Phoenicia to that country; and him God chose to honor on account of his exceeding virtue, and judged him worthy to become the leader and lawgiver of his own race, when He thought it right that the people of the Hebrews should return out of Egypt into their own land. To him first did God communicate that divine and prophetic gift which in those days descended upon the holy men, and him also did He first furnish that he might be our teacher in religion, and then after him the rest of the prophets, who both obtained the same gift as he, and taught us the same doctrines concerning the same subjects. These we assert to have been our teachers, who taught us nothing from their own human conception, but from the gift vouchsafed to them by God from above.

Chapter XI: *Heathen oracles testify of Moses.*

But as you do not see the necessity of giving up the ancient error of your forefathers in obedience to these teachers [of ours], what teachers of your own do you maintain to have lived worthy of credit in the matter of religion? For, as I have frequently said, it is impossible that those who have not themselves learned these so great and divine things from such persons as are acquainted with them, should either themselves know them, or be able rightly to teach others. Since, therefore, it has been sufficiently proved that the opinions of your philosophers are obviously full of all ignorance and deceit, having now perhaps wholly abandoned the philosophers as formerly you abandoned the poets, you will turn to the deceit of the oracles; for in this style I have heard some speaking. Therefore I think it fit to tell you at this step in our discourse what I formerly heard among you concerning their utterances. For when one inquired at your oracle—it is your own story—what religious men had at any time happened to live, you say that the oracle answered thus: "Only the Chaldeans have obtained wisdom, and the Hebrews, who worship God Himself, the self-begotten King."

Since, therefore, you think that the truth can be learned from your oracles, when you read the histories and what has been written regarding the life of Moses by those who do not belong to our religion, and when you know that Moses and the rest of the prophets were descended from the race of the Chaldeans and Hebrews, do not think that anything incredible has taken place if a man sprung from a godly line, and who lived worthily of the godliness of his fathers, was chosen by God to be honored with this great gift, and to be set forth as the first of all the prophets.

Chapter XII: *Antiquity of Moses proved.*

And I think it necessary also to consider the times in which your philosophers lived, that you may see that the time which produced them for you is very recent, and also short. For thus you will be able easily to recognize also the antiquity of Moses. But lest, by a complete survey of the periods, and by the use of a greater number of proofs, I should seem to be prolix, I think it may be sufficiently demonstrated from the following.

For Socrates was the teacher of Plato, and Plato of Aristotle. Now these men flourished in the time of Philip and Alexander of Macedon, in which time also the Athenian orators flourished, as the Philippics of Demosthenes plainly show us. And those who have narrated the deeds of Alexander sufficiently prove that during his reign Aristotle associated with him. From all manner of proofs, then, it is easy to see that the history of Moses is by far more ancient than all profane[871] histories.

And, besides, it is fit that you recognize this fact also, that nothing has been accurately recorded by Greeks before the era of the Olympiads, and that there is no ancient work which makes known any action of the Greeks or Barbarians. But before that period existed only the history of the prophet Moses, which he wrote in the Hebrew character by the divine inspiration. For the Greek character was not yet in use, as the teachers of language themselves prove, telling us that Cadmus first brought the letters from Phoenicia, and communicated them to the Greeks. And your first of philosophers, Plato, testifies that they were a recent discovery. For in the *Timaeus*[872] he wrote that Solon, the wisest of the wise men, on his return from Egypt, said to Critias that he had heard this from a very aged Egyptian priest, who said to him, "O Solon, Solon, you Greeks are

[871] Literally, "without," not belonging to the true faith.
[872] C. 5.

ever children, and aged Greek there is none." Then again he said, "You are all youths in soul, for you hold no ancient opinion derived through remote tradition, nor any system of instruction hoary with time; but all these things escape your knowledge, because for many generations the posterity of these ancient ages died mute, not having the use of letters."

It is fit, therefore, that you understand that it is the fact that every history has been written in these recently-discovered Greek letters; and if anyone would make mention of old poets, or legislators, or historians, or philosophers, or orators, he will find that they wrote their own works in the Greek character.

Chapter XIII: *History of the Septuagint.*

But if any one says that the writings of Moses and of the rest of the prophets were also written in the Greek character, let him read profane histories, and know that Ptolemy, king of Egypt, when he had built the library in Alexandria, and by gathering books from every quarter had filled it, then learnt that very ancient histories written in Hebrew happened to be carefully preserved; and wishing to know their contents, he sent for seventy wise men from Jerusalem,[873] who were acquainted with both the Greek and Hebrew language, and appointed them to translate the books; and that in freedom from all disturbance they might the more speedily complete the translation, he ordered that there should be constructed, not in the city itself, but seven stadia off (where the Pharos was built), as many little cots as there were translators, so that each by himself might complete his own translation; and enjoined upon those officers who were appointed to this duty, to afford them all attendance, but to prevent communication with one another, in order that the accuracy of the translation might be discernible even by their agreement. And when he ascertained that the seventy men had not only given the same meaning, but had employed the same words, and had failed in agreement with one another not even to the extent of one word; but had written the same things, and concerning the same things, he was struck with amazement, and believed that the translation had been written by divine power, and perceived that the men were worthy of all

[873] {Here, St. Justin begins a history of the origins of what we refer to as the LXX or Septuagint version of the Bible.}

honor, as beloved of God; and with many gifts ordered them to return to their own country. And having, as was natural, marveled at the books, and concluded them to be divine, he consecrated them in that library.

These things, ye men of Greece, are no fable, nor do we narrate fictions; but we ourselves having been in Alexandria, saw the remains of the little cots at the Pharos still preserved, and having heard these things from the inhabitants, who had received them as part of their country's tradition, we now tell to you what you can also learn from others, and specially from those wise and esteemed men who have written of these things, Philo and Josephus, and many others.

But if any of those who are wont to be forward in contradiction should say that these books do not belong to us, but to the Jews, and should assert that we in vain profess to have learnt our religion from them, let him know, as he may from those very things which are written in these books, that not to them, but to us, does the doctrine of them refer. That the books relating to our religion are to this day preserved among the Jews, has been a work of Divine Providence on our behalf; for lest, by producing them out of the Church, we should give occasion to those who wish to slander us to charge us with fraud, we demand that they be produced from the synagogue of the Jews, that from the very books still preserved among them it might clearly and evidently appear, that the laws which were written by holy men for instruction pertain to us.

Chapter XIV: *A warning appeal to the Greeks.*

It is therefore necessary, ye Greeks, that you contemplate the things that are to be, and consider the judgment which is predicted by all, not only by the godly, but also by those who are irreligious, that ye do not without investigation commit yourselves to the error of your fathers, nor suppose that if they themselves have been in error, and have transmitted it to you, that this which they have taught you is true; but looking to the danger of so terrible a mistake, inquire and investigate carefully into those things which are, as you say, spoken of even by your own teachers. For even unwillingly they were on your account forced to say many things by the Divine regard for mankind, especially those of them who were in Egypt, and profited by the godliness of Moses and his ancestry. For I think that some of you, when you read even carelessly the history of Diodorus, and of those others who wrote of these things, cannot fail to see that both Orpheus, and Homer, and Solon, who wrote the laws of the Athenians, and Pythagoras, and Plato, and some others, when they had been in Egypt, and had taken advantage of the history of Moses, afterwards published doctrines concerning the gods quite contrary to those which formerly they had erroneously promulgated.

Chapter XV: *Testimony of Orpheus to monotheism.*

At all events, we must remind you what Orpheus, who was, as one might say, your first teacher of polytheism, latterly addressed to his son Musaeus, and to the other legitimate auditors, concerning the one and only God. And he spoke thus:

> I speak to those who lawfully may hear:
> All others, ye profane, now close the doors,
> And, O Musaeus! hearken thou to me,
> Who offspring art of the light-bringing moon:
> The words I utter now are true indeed;
> And if thou former thoughts of mine hast seen,
> Let them not rob thee of the blessed life,
> But rather turn the depths of thine own heart
> Unto the place where light and knowledge dwell.
> Take thou the word divine to guide thy steps,
> And walking well in the straight certain path,
> Look to the one and universal King—
> One, self-begotten, and the only One,
> Of whom all things and we ourselves are sprung.
> All things are open to His piercing gaze,
> While He Himself is still invisible.
> Present in all His works, though still unseen,
> He gives to mortals evil out of good,
> Sending both chilling wars and tearful griefs;
> And other than the great King there is none.
> The clouds for ever settle round His throne,
> And mortal eyeballs in mere mortal eyes
> Are weak, to see Jove reigning over all.
> He sits established in the brazen heavens
> Upon His golden throne; under His feet

> He treads the earth, and stretches His right hand
> To all the ends of ocean, and around
> Tremble the mountain ranges and the streams,
> The depths, too, of the blue and hoary sea.

And again, in some other place he says:

> There is one Zeus alone, one sun, one hell,
> One Bacchus; and in all things but one God;
> Nor of all these as diverse let me speak.

And when he swears he says:—

> Now I adjure thee by the highest heaven,
> The work of the great God, the only wise;
> And I adjure thee by the Father's voice.
> Which first He uttered when He stablished
> The whole world by His counsel.

What does he mean by "I adjure thee by the Father's voice, which first He uttered?" It is the Word of God which he here names "the voice," by whom heaven and earth and the whole creation were made, as the divine prophecies of the holy men teach us; and these he himself also paid some attention to in Egypt, and understood that all creation was made by the Word of God; and therefore, after he says, "I adjure thee by the Father's voice, which first He uttered," he adds this besides, "when by His counsel He established the whole world." Here he calls the Word "voice," for the sake of the poetical meter. And that this is so, is manifest from the fact, that a little further on, where the meter permits him, he names it "Word." For he said:

> Take thou the *Word* divine to guide thy steps.

Chapter XVI: *Testimony of the Sibyl.*

We must also mention what the ancient and exceedingly remote Sibyl, whom Plato and Aristophanes, and others besides, mention as a prophetess, taught you in her oracular verses concerning one only God. And she speaks thus:

There is one only unbegotten God,
Omnipotent, invisible, most high,
All-seeing, but Himself seen by no flesh.

Then elsewhere thus:

But we have strayed from the Immortal's ways,
And worship with a dull and senseless mind
Idols, the workmanship of our own hands,
And images and figures of dead men.

And again somewhere else:—

Blessed shall be those men upon the earth
Who shall love the great God before all else,
Blessing Him when they eat and when they drink;
Trusting it, this their piety alone.
Who shall abjure all shrines which they may see,
All altars and vain figures of dumb stones,
Worthless and stained with blood of animals,
And sacrifice of the four-fooled tribes,
Beholding the great glory of One God.

These are the Sibyl's words.

Chapter XVII: *Testimony of Homer.*

And the poet Homer, using the license of poetry, and rivaling the original opinion of Orpheus regarding the plurality of the gods, mentions, indeed, several gods in a mythical style, lest he should seem to sing in a different strain from the poem of Orpheus, which he so distinctly proposed to rival, that even in the first line of his poem he indicated the relation he held to him. For as Orpheus in the beginning of his poem had said, "O goddess, sing the wrath of Demeter, who brings the goodly fruit," Homer began thus, "O goddess, sing the wrath of Achilles, son of Peleus," preferring, as it seems to me, even to violate the poetical meter in his first line, than that he should seem not to have remembered before all else the names of the gods. But shortly after he also clearly and explicitly presents his own opinion regarding one God only, somewhere[874] saying to Achilles by the mouth of Phoenix, "Not though God Himself were to promise that He would peel off my old age, and give me the rigor of my youth," where he indicates by the pronoun the real and true God. And somewhere[875] he makes Ulysses address the host of the Greeks thus: "The rule of many is not a good thing; let there be one ruler." And that the rule of many is not a good thing, but on the contrary an evil, he proposed to evince by fact, recounting the wars which took place on account of the multitude of rulers, and the fights and factions, and their mutual counterplots. For monarchy is free from contention. So far the poet Homer.

Chapter XVIII: *Testimony of Sophocles.*

And if it is needful that we add testimonies concerning one God, even from the dramatists, hear even Sophocles speaking thus:

> There is one God, in truth there is but one,
> Who made the heavens and the broad earth beneath,
> The glancing waves of ocean and the winds
> But many of us mortals err in heart,
> And set up for a solace in our woes
> Images of the gods in stone and wood,
> Or figures carved in brass or ivory,
> And, furnishing for these our handiworks,
> Both sacrifice and rite magnificent,
> We think that thus we do a pious work.

Thus, then, Sophocles.

Chapter XIX: *Testimony of Pythagoras.*

And Pythagoras, son of Mnesarchus, who expounded the doctrines of his own philosophy, mystically by means of symbols, as those who have written his life show, himself seems to have entertained

---

[874] *Iliad*, ix. 445.
[875] *Iliad*, ii. 204.

thoughts about the unity of God not unworthy of his foreign residence in Egypt. For when he says that unity is the first principle of all things, and that it is the cause of all good, he teaches by an allegory that God is one, and alone.[876] And that this is so, is evident from his saying that unity and one differ widely from one another. For he says that unity belongs to the class of things perceived by the mind, but that one belongs to numbers. And if you desire to see a clearer proof of the opinion of Pythagoras concerning one God, hear his own opinion, for he spoke as follows:

> God is one; and He Himself does not, as some suppose, exist outside the world, but in it, He being wholly present in the whole circle, and beholding all generations; being the regulating ingredient of all the ages, and the administrator of His own powers and works, the first principle of all things, the light of heaven, and Father of all, the intelligence and animating soul of the universe, the movement of all orbits.

Thus, then, Pythagoras.

Chapter XX: *Testimony of Plato.*

But Plato, though he accepted, as is likely, the doctrine of Moses and the other prophets regarding one only God,[877] which he learned while in Egypt, yet fearing, on account of what had befallen Socrates, lest he also should raise up some Anytus or Meletus against himself, who should accuse him before the Athenians, and say, "Plato is doing harm, and making himself mischievously busy, not acknowledging the gods recognized by the state;" in fear of the hemlock-juice, contrives an elaborate and ambiguous discourse concerning the gods, furnishing by his treatise gods to those who wish them, and none for those who are differently disposed, as may readily be seen from his own statements. For when he has laid down that everything that is made is mortal, he afterwards says that the gods were made.

If, then, he would have God and matter to be the origin of all things, manifestly it is inevitably necessary to say that the gods were

---

[876] Has no fellow.

[877] {Perhaps, more likely, "only one God".}

made of matter; but if of matter, out of which he said that evil also had its origin, he leaves right-thinking persons to consider what kind of beings the gods should be thought who are produced out of matter. For, for this very reason did he say that matter was eternal,[878] that he might not seem to say that God is the creator of evil.

And regarding the gods who were made by God, there is no doubt he said this: "Gods of gods, of whom I am the creator." And he manifestly held the correct opinion concerning the really existing God. For having heard in Egypt that God had said to Moses, when He was about to send him to the Hebrews, "***I am that I am***,"[879] he understood that God had not mentioned to him His own proper name.

Chapter XXI: *The namelessness of God.*

For God cannot be called by any proper name, for names are given to mark out and distinguish their subject matters, because these are many and diverse; but neither did anyone exist before God who could give Him a name, nor did He Himself think it right to name Himself, seeing that He is one and unique, as He Himself also by His own prophets testifies, when He says, "***I God am the first***,"[880] and after this, "***And beside me there is no other God.***"[881] On this account, then, as I before said, God did not, when He sent Moses to the Hebrews, mention any name, but by a participle He mystically teaches them that He is the one and only God. "For," says He; "***I am the Being;***"[882] manifestly contrasting Himself, "the Being," with those who are not,[883] that those who had hitherto been deceived might see that they were attaching themselves, not to beings, but to those who had no being.

Since, therefore, God knew that the first men remembered the old delusion of their forefathers, whereby the misanthropic demon contrived to deceive them when he said to them, "***If ye obey me in transgressing the commandment of God, ye shall be as gods***,"[884] calling

---

[878] Or, "uncreated."

[879] *ὁ ὤν*, "He who is; the Being." {See Exodus 3:14.}

[880] {Isaiah 44:6.}

[881] Isaiah 44:6.

[882] {See Exodus 3:14. OSB: "I AM the Existing One."}

[883] Literally, "with the not-beings."

[884] {Genesis 3:5.}

those gods which had no being, in order that men, supposing that there were other gods in existence, might believe that they themselves could become gods. On this account He said to Moses, "***I am the Being***," that by the participle "being" He might teach the difference between God who is and those who are not.[885]

Men, therefore, having been duped by the deceiving demon, and having dared to disobey God, were cast out of Paradise,[886] remembering the name of gods, but no longer being taught by God that there are no other gods. For it was not just that they who did not keep the first commandment, which it was easy to keep, should any longer be taught, but should rather be driven to just punishment. Being therefore banished from Paradise, and thinking that they were expelled on account of their disobedience only, not knowing that it was also because they had believed in the existence of gods which did not exist, they gave the name of gods even to the men who were afterwards born of themselves. This first false fancy, therefore, concerning gods, had its origin with the father of lies.

God, therefore, knowing that the false opinion about the plurality of gods was burdening the soul of man like some disease, and wishing to remove and eradicate it, appeared first to Moses, and said to him, "***I am He who is.***"[887] For it was necessary, I think, that he who was to be the ruler and leader of the Hebrew people should first of all know the living God. Wherefore, having appeared to him first, as it was possible for God to appear to a man, He said to him, "***I am He who is***;" then, being about to send him to the Hebrews, He further orders him to say, "***He who is hath sent me to you.***"[888]

Chapter XXII: *Studied ambiguity of Plato.*

Plato accordingly having learned this in Egypt, and being greatly taken with what was said about one God, did indeed consider it unsafe to mention the name of Moses, on account of his teaching the doctrine of

---

[885] Literally, "between the God being and the not-beings."

[886] {See Genesis 3:24.}

[887] {Exodus 3:14. Compare above n. 882, and accompanying text.}

[888] {Ibid.}

one only God, for he dreaded the Areopagus;[889] but what is very well expressed by him in his elaborate treatise, the *Timaeus*, he has written in exact correspondence with what Moses said regarding God, though he has done so, not as if he had learned it from him, but as if he were expressing his own opinion. For he said, "In my opinion, then, we must first define what that is which exists eternally, and has no generation,[890] and what that is which is always being generated, but never really is."

Does not this, ye men of Greece, seem to those who are able to understand the matter to be one and the same thing, saving only the difference of the article? For Moses said, "***He* who is**,"[891] and Plato, "That which is." But either of the expressions seems to apply to the ever-existent God. For He is the only one who eternally exists, and has no generation. What, then, that other thing is which is contrasted with the ever-existent, and of which he said, "And what that is which is always being generated, but never really is," we must attentively consider. For we shall find him clearly and evidently saying that He who is unbegotten is eternal, but that those that are begotten and made are generated and perish[892]—as he said of the same class, "gods of gods, of whom I am maker"—for he speaks in the following words:

> In my opinion, then, we must first define what that is which is always existent and has no birth, and what that is which is always being generated but never really is. The former, indeed, which is apprehended by reflection combined with reason, always exists in the same way;[893] while the latter, on the other hand, is conjectured by opinion formed by the perception of the senses unaided by reason, since it never really is, but is coming into being and perishing.

These expressions declare to those who can rightly understand them the death and destruction of the gods that have been brought into being. And I think it necessary to attend to this also, that Plato never names him

[889] {The Areopagus was the highest judicial and legislative body.}
[890] That is, "is not produced or created; has no birth."
[891] {Exodus 3:14.}
[892] Or, "are born and die."
[893] *χατὰ ταύτὰ*, "according to the same things," i.e., in eternal immutability.

the creator, but the fashioner[894] of the gods, although, in the opinion of Plato, there is considerable difference between these two. For the creator creates the creature by his own capability and power, being in need of nothing else; but the fashioner frames his production when he has received from matter the capability for his work.

Chapter XXIII: *Plato's self-contradiction.*

But, perhaps, some who are unwilling to abandon the doctrines of polytheism, will say that to these fashioned gods the maker said, "Since ye have been produced, ye are not immortal, nor at all, imperishable; yet shall ye not perish nor succumb to the fatality of death, because you have obtained my will,[895] which is a still greater and mightier bond." Here Plato, through fear of the adherents of polytheism, introduces his "maker" uttering words which contradict himself. For having formerly stated that he said that everything which is produced is perishable, he now introduces him saying the very opposite; and he does not see that it is thus absolutely impossible for him to escape the charge of falsehood.

For he either at first uttered what is false when he said that everything which is produced is perishable, or now, when he propounds the very opposite to what he had formerly said. For if, according to his former definition, it is absolutely necessary that every created thing be perishable, how can he consistently make that possible which is absolutely impossible? So that Plato seems to grant an empty and impossible prerogative to his "maker," when he propounds that those who were once perishable because made from matter should again, by his intervention, become imperishable and enduring. For it is quite natural that the power of matter, which, according to Plato's opinion, is uncreated, and contemporary and coeval with the maker, should resist his will. For he who has not created has no power, in respect of that which is uncreated, so that it is not possible that it (matter), being free, can be controlled by any external necessity. Wherefore Plato himself, in consideration of this, has written thus: "It is necessary to affirm that God cannot suffer violence."

---

[894] Or, "demiurge or maker."

[895] That is, "my will to the contrary." See Plato, *Tim.* p. 41.

Chapter XXIV: *Agreement of Plato and Homer.*

How, then, does Plato banish Homer from his republic, since, in the embassy to Achilles, he represents Phoenix as saying to Achilles, "Even the gods themselves are not inflexible,"[896] though Homer said this not of the king and Platonic maker of the gods, but of some of the multitude whom the Greeks esteem as gods, as one can gather from Plato's saying, "gods of gods?" For Homer, by that golden chain,[897] refers all power and might to the one highest God. And the rest of the gods, he said, were so far distant from his divinity, that he thought fit to name them even along with men. At least he introduces Ulysses saying of Hector to Achilles, "He is raging terribly, trusting in Zeus, and values neither men nor gods."[898] In this passage Homer seems to me without doubt to have learnt in Egypt, like Plato, concerning the one God, and plainly and openly to declare this, that he who trusts in the really existent God makes no account of those that do not exist. For thus the poet, in another passage, and employing another but equivalent word, to wit, a pronoun, made use of the same participle employed by Plato to designate the really existent God, concerning whom Plato said, "What that is which always exists, and has no birth." For not without a double sense does this expression of Phoenix seem to have been used: "Not even if God Himself were to promise me, that, having burnished off my old age, He should set me forth in the flower of youth." For the pronoun "Himself" signifies the really existing God. For thus, too, the oracle which was given to you concerning the Chaldeans and Hebrews signifies. For when someone inquired what men had ever lived godly, you say the answer was:

> Only the Chaldeans and the Hebrews found wisdom,
> Worshipping God Himself, the unbegotten King.

Chapter XXV: *Plato's knowledge of God's eternity.*

How, then, does Plato blame Homer for saying that the gods are not inflexible, although, as is obvious from the expressions used, Homer said this for a useful purpose? For it is the property of those who expect

---

[896] *Iliad*, ix. 493.
[897] That is, by the challenge of the chain introduced—*Iliad*, viii. 18.
[898] *Iliad*, ix. 238.

to obtain mercy by prayer and sacrifices, to cease from and repent of their sins. For those who think that the Deity is inflexible, are by no means moved to abandon their sins, since they suppose that they will derive no benefit from repentance. How, then, does Plato the philosopher condemn the poet Homer for saying, "Even the gods themselves are not inflexible," and yet himself represent the maker of the gods as so easily turned, that he sometimes declares the gods to be mortal, and at other times declares the same to be immortal? And not only concerning them, but also concerning matter, from which, as he says, it is necessary that the created gods have been produced, he sometimes says that it is uncreated, and at other times that it is created; and yet he does not see that he himself, when he says that the maker of the gods is so easily turned, is convicted of having fallen into the very errors for which he blames Homer, though Homer said the very opposite concerning the maker of the gods. For he said that he spoke thus of himself:

> For ne'er my promise shall deceive, or fail,
> Or be recall'd, if with a nod confirm'd.[899]

But Plato, as it seems, unwillingly entered not these strange dissertations concerning the gods, for he feared those who were attached to polytheism. And whatever he thinks fit to tell of all that he had learned from Moses and the prophets concerning one God, he preferred delivering in a mystical style, so that those who desired to be worshippers of God might have an inkling of his own opinion. For being charmed with that saying of God to Moses, "***I am the really existing***,"[900] and accepting with a great deal of thought the brief participial expression, he understood that God desired to signify to Moses His eternity, and therefore said, "***I am the really existing***;"[901] for this word "existing" expresses not one time only, but the three—the past, the present, and the future. For when Plato says, "and which never really is," he uses the verb "is" of time indefinite. For the word "never" is not spoken, as some

---

[899] *Iliad*, i. 526.
[900] {Exodus 3:14.}
[901] [Ibid.]

suppose, of the past, but of the future time. And this has been accurately understood even by profane writers.

And therefore, when Plato wished, as it were, to interpret to the uninitiated what had been mystically expressed by the participle concerning the eternity of God, he employed the following language: "God indeed, as the old tradition runs, includes the beginning, and end, and middle of all things." In this sentence he plainly and obviously names the law of Moses "the old tradition," fearing, through dread of the hemlock-cup, to mention the name of Moses; for he understood that the teaching of the man was hateful to the Greeks; and he clearly enough indicates Moses by the antiquity of the tradition. And we have sufficiently proved from Diodorus and the rest of the historians, in the foregoing chapters, that the law of Moses is not only old, but even the first. For Diodorus says that he was the first of all lawgivers; the letters which belong to the Greeks, and which they employed in the writing of their histories, having not yet been discovered.

Chapter XXVI: *Plato indebted to the prophets.*

And let no one wonder that Plato should believe Moses regarding the eternity of God. For you will find him mystically referring the true knowledge of realities to the prophets, next in order after the really existent God. For, discoursing in the *Timaeus* about certain first principles, he wrote thus: "This we lay down as the first principle of fire and the other bodies, proceeding according to probability and necessity. But the first principles of these again God above knows, and whosoever among men is beloved of Him."[902] And what men does he think beloved of God, but Moses and the rest of the prophets? For their prophecies he read, and, having learned from them the doctrine of the judgment, he thus proclaims it in the first book of the *Republic*:

> When a man begins to think he is soon to die, fear invades him, and concern about things which had never before entered his head. And those stories about what goes on in Hades, which tell us that the man who has here been unjust must there be punished, though formerly ridiculed, now torment his soul with apprehensions that

[902] Plato, *Tim.* p. 53 D.

> they may be true. And he, either through the feebleness of age, or even because he is now nearer to the things of the other world, views them more attentively. He becomes, therefore, full of apprehension and dread, and begins to call himself to account, and to consider whether he has done anyone an injury. And that man who finds in his life many iniquities, and who continually starts from his sleep as children do, lives in terror, and with a forlorn prospect. But to him who is conscious of no wrong-doing, sweet hope is the constant companion and good nurse of old age, as Pindar says.[903] For this, Socrates, he has elegantly expressed, that "whoever leads a life of holiness and justice, him sweet hope, the nurse of age, accompanies, cheering his heart, for she powerfully sways the changeful mind of mortals."[904]

This Plato wrote in the first book of the *Republic*.

Chapter XXVII: *Plato's knowledge of the judgment.*

And in the tenth book he plainly and manifestly wrote what he had learned from the prophets about the judgment, not as if he had learned it from them, but, on account of his fear of the Greeks, as if he had heard it from a man who has been slain in battle—for this story he thought fit to invent—and who, when he was about to be buried on the twelfth day, and was lying on the funeral pile, came to life again, and described the other world. The following are his very words:[905]

> For he said that he was present when one was asked by another person where the great Ardiaeus was. This Ardiaeus had been prince in a certain city of Pamphylia, and had killed his aged father and his elder brother, and done many other unhallowed deeds, as was reported. He said, then that the person who was asked said: He neither comes nor ever will come hither. For we saw, among other terrible sights, this also. When we were close to the mouth [of the pit], and were about to return to the upper air, and had suffered everything else, we suddenly beheld both him and others likewise, most of whom were tyrants. But there were also some

903 Pind. *Pr.* 233, a fragment preserved in this place.
904 Plato, *Rep.* p. 330 D.
905 Plato, *Rep.* p. 615.

> private sinners who had committed great crimes. And these, when they thought they were to ascend, the mouth would not permit, but bellowed when any of those who were so incurably wicked attempted to ascend, unless they had paid the full penalty. Then fierce men, fiery to look at, stood close by, and hearing the din,[906] took some and led them away; but Ardiaeus and the rest, having bound hand and foot, and striking their heads down, and flaying, they dragged to the road outside, tearing them with thorns, and signifying to those who were present the cause of their suffering these things, and that they were leading them away to cast them into Tartarus. Hence, he said, that amidst all their various fears, this one was the greatest, lest the mouth should bellow when they ascended, since if it were silent each one would most gladly ascend; and that the punishments and torments were such as these, and that, on the other hand, the rewards were the reverse of these.

Here Plato seems to me to have learnt from the prophets not only the doctrine of the judgment, but also of the resurrection, which the Greeks refuse to believe. For his saying that the soul is judged along with the body, proves nothing more clearly than that he believed the doctrine of the resurrection. Since how could Ardiaeus and the rest have undergone such punishment in Hades, had they left on earth the body, with its head, hands, feet, and skin? For certainly they will never say that the soul has a head and hands, and feet and skin. But Plato, having fallen in with the testimonies of the prophets in Egypt, and having accepted what they teach concerning the resurrection of the body, teaches that the soul is judged in company with the body.

Chapter XXVIII: *Homer's obligations to the sacred writers.*

And not only Plato, but Homer also, having received similar enlightenment in Egypt, said that Tityus was in like manner punished. For Ulysses speaks thus to Alcinous when he is recounting his divination by the shades of the dead:[907]

---

[906] The bellowing of the mouth of the pit.

[907] *Odyssey*, xi. 576 (Pope's translation, line 709).

There Tityus, large and long, in fetters bound,
O'erspread nine acres of infernal ground;
Two ravenous vultures, furious for their food,
Scream o'er the fiend, and riot in his blood,
Incessant gore the liver in his breast,
Th' immortal liver grows, and gives th' immortal feast.

For it is plain that it is not the soul, but the body, which has a liver. And in the same manner he has described both Sisyphus and Tantalus as enduring punishment with the body.

And that Homer had been in Egypt, and introduced into his own poem much of what he there learnt, Diodorus, the most esteemed of historians, plainly enough teaches us. For he said that when he was in Egypt he had learnt that Helen, having received from Theon's wife, Polydamna, a drug, "lulling all sorrow and melancholy, and causing forgetfulness of all ills,"[908] brought it to Sparta. And Homer said that by making use of that drug Helen put an end to the lamentation of Menelaus, caused by the presence of Telemachus. And he also called Venus "golden," from what he had seen in Egypt. For he had seen the temple which in Egypt is called "the temple of golden Venus," and the plain which is named "the plain of golden Venus."

And why do I now make mention of this? To show that the poet transferred to his own poem much of what is contained in the divine writings of the prophets. And first he transferred what Moses had related as the beginning of the creation of the world. For Moses wrote thus: "**In the beginning God created the heaven and the earth**,"[909] then the sun, and the moon, and the stars. For having learned this in Egypt, and having been much taken with what Moses had written in the Genesis of the world, he fabled that Vulcan had made in the shield of Achilles a kind of representation of the creation of the world. For he wrote thus:[910]

There he described the earth, the heaven, the sea,
The sun that rests not, and the moon full-orb'd;
There also, all the stars which round about,
As with a radiant frontlet, bind the skies.

---

[908] *Odyssey*, iv. 221.
[909] Genesis 1:1.
[910] *Iliad*, xviii. 483.

And he contrived also that the garden of Alcinous should preserve the likeness of Paradise, and through this likeness he represented it as ever-blooming and full of all fruits. For thus he wrote:[911]

> Tall thriving trees confess'd the fruitful mould;
> The reddening apple ripens here to gold.
> Here the blue fig with luscious juice o'erflows,
> With deeper red the full pomegranate glows;
> The branch here bends beneath the weighty pear,
> And verdant olives flourish round the year.
> The balmy spirit of the western gale
> Eternal breathes on fruits, untaught to fail;
> Each dropping pear a following pear supplies,
> On apples apples, figs on figs arise.
> The same mild season gives the blooms to blow,
> The buds to harden, and the fruits to grow.
> Here order'd vines in equal ranks appear,
> With all th' united labors of the year.
> Some to unload the fertile branches run,
> Some dry the blackening clusters in the sun,
> Others to tread the liquid harvest join.
> The groaning presses foam with floods of wine.
> Here are the vines in early flower descry'd
> Here grapes discolored on the sunny side,
> And there in autumn's richest purple dy'd.

Do not these words present a manifest and clear imitation of what the first prophet Moses said about Paradise? And if any one wish to know something of the building of the tower by which the men of that day fancied they would obtain access to heaven, he will find a sufficiently exact allegorical imitation of this in what the poet has ascribed to Otus and Ephialtes. For of them he wrote thus:[912]

> Proud of their strength, and more than mortal size,
> The gods they challenge, and affect the skies.
> Heav'd on Olympus tottering Ossa stood;
> On Ossa, Pelion nods with all his wood.

---

[911] *Odyssey*, vii. 114 (Pope's translation, line 146).
[912] *Odyssey*, xi. 312 (Pope's translation, line 385).

And the same holds good regarding the enemy of mankind who was cast out of heaven, whom the Sacred Scriptures call the Devil,[913] a name which he obtained from his first devilry against man; and if anyone would attentively consider the matter, he would find that the poet, though he certainly never mentions the name of "the devil," yet gives him a name from his wickedest action. For the poet, calling him Ate,[914] says that he was hurled from heaven by their god, just as if he had a distinct remembrance of the expressions which Isaiah the prophet had uttered regarding him. He wrote thus in his own poem:[915]

> And, seizing by her glossy locks
> The goddess Ate, in his wrath he swore
> That never to the starry skies again,
> And the Olympian heights, he would permit
> The universal mischief to return.
> Then, whirling her around, he cast her down
> To earth. She, mingling with all works of men,
> Caused many a pang to Jove.

Chapter XXIX: *Origin of Plato's doctrine of form.*

And Plato, too, when he says that form is the third original principle next to God and matter, has manifestly received this suggestion from no other source than from Moses, having learned, indeed, from the words of Moses the name of form, but not having at the same time been instructed by the initiated, that without mystic insight it is impossible to have any distinct knowledge of the writings of Moses. For Moses wrote that God had spoken to him regarding the tabernacle in the following words: "***And thou shalt make for me according to all that I show thee in the mount, the pattern of the tabernacle.***"[916] And again: "***And thou shalt erect the tabernacle according to the pattern of all the instruments thereof, even so shalt thou make it.***"[917] And again, a little afterwards:

---

[913] The false accuser; one who does injury by slanderous accusation.

[914] "Ατη, the goddess of mischief, from whom spring all rash, blind deeds and their results.

[915] *Iliad*, xix. 126.

[916] Exodus 25:9.

[917] Ibid.

"Thus then thou shalt make it according to the pattern which was showed to thee in the mount."[918]

Plato, then, reading these passages, and not receiving what was written with the suitable insight, thought that form had some kind of separate existence before that which the senses perceive, and he often calls it the pattern of the things which are made, since the writing of Moses spoke thus of the tabernacle: ***"According to the form showed to thee in the mount, so shalt thou make it."***[919]

Chapter XXX: *Homer's knowledge of man's origin.*

And he was obviously deceived in the same way regarding the earth and heaven and man; for he supposes that there are "ideas" of these. For as Moses wrote thus, "***In the beginning God created the heaven and the earth***,"[920] and then subjoins this sentence, "***And the earth was invisible and unfashioned***,"[921] he thought that it was the pre-existent earth which was spoken of in the words, "***The earth was***," because Moses said, "***And the earth was invisible and unfashioned***;" and he thought that the earth, concerning which he says, "***God created the heaven and the earth***,"[922] was that earth which we perceive by the senses, and which God made according to the pre-existent form. And so also, of the heaven which was created, he thought that the heaven which was created—and which he also called the firmament—was that creation which the senses perceive; and that the heaven which the intellect perceives is that other of which the prophet said, "***The heaven of heavens is the Lord's, but the earth hath He given to the children of men.***"[923] And so also concerning man: Moses first mentions the name of man, and then after many other creations he makes mention of the formation of man, saying, "***And God made man, taking dust from the earth.***"[924]

---

[918] Exodus 25:40.
[919] [Exodus 25:9, 40.]
[920] {Genesis 1:1.}
[921] {Genesis 1:2.}
[922] {Genesis 1:1.}
[923] Psalm 115:15. {Actually Psalm 115:16.}
[924] Genesis 2:7.

He thought, accordingly, that the man first so named existed before the man who was made, and that he who was formed of the earth was afterwards made according to the pre-existent form. And that man was formed of earth, Homer, too, having discovered from the ancient and divine history which says, "***Dust thou art, and unto dust shalt thou return***,"[925] calls the lifeless body of Hector dumb clay. For in condemnation of Achilles dragging the corpse of Hector after death, he says somewhere:[926]

> On the dumb clay he cast indignity,
> Blinded with rage.

And again, somewhere else,[927] he introduces Menelaus, thus addressing those who were not accepting Hector's challenge to single combat with becoming alacrity:

> To earth and water may you all return

resolving them in his violent rage into their original and pristine formation from earth. These things Homer and Plato, having learned in Egypt from the ancient histories, wrote in their own words.

Chapter XXXI: *Further proof of Plato's acquaintance with Scripture.*

For from what other source, if not from his reading the writings of the prophets, could Plato have derived the information he gives us, that Jupiter drives a winged chariot in heaven? For he knew this from the following expressions of the prophet about the cherubim: "***And the glory of the Lord went out from the house and rested on the cherubim; and the cherubim lift up their wings, and the wheels beside them; and the glory of the Lord God of Israel was over them above.***"[928] And borrowing this idea, the magniloquent Plato shouts aloud with vast assurance, "The

---

[925] Genesis 3:19. {Job 34:15; Psalm 104:29; Ecclesiastes 12:7.}
[926] *Iliad*, xxi.
[927] *Iliad*, vii. 99.
[928] Ezekiel 11:22 {-23}.

great Jove, indeed, driving his winged chariot in heaven." For from what other source, if not from Moses and the prophets, did he learn this and so write? And whence did he receive the suggestion of his saying that God exists in a fiery substance? Was it not from the third book of the history of the Kings, where it is written, "***The Lord was not in the wind; and after the wind an earthquake, but the Lord was not in the earthquake; and after the earthquake a fire, but the Lord was not in the fire; and after the fire a still small voice?***"[929] But these things pious men must understand in a higher sense with profound and meditative insight. But Plato, not attending to the words with the suitable insight, said that God exists in a fiery substance.

Chapter XXXII: *Plato's doctrine of the heavenly gift.*

And if anyone will attentively consider the gift that descends from God on the holy men,—which gift the sacred prophets call the Holy Ghost,—he shall find that this was announced under another name by Plato in the dialogue with Meno. For, fearing to name the gift of God "*the Holy Ghost*," lest he should seem, by following the teaching of the prophets, to be an enemy to the Greeks, he acknowledges, indeed, that it comes down from God, yet does not think fit to name it the Holy Ghost, but virtue. For so in the dialogue with Meno, concerning reminiscence, after he had put many questions regarding virtue, whether it could be taught or whether it could not be taught, but must be gained by practice, or whether it could be attained neither by practice nor by learning, but was a natural gift in men, or whether it comes in some other way, he makes this declaration in these very words: "But if now through this whole dialogue we have conducted our inquiry and discussion aright, virtue must be neither a natural gift, nor what one can receive by teaching, but comes to those to whom it does come by divine destiny."

These things, I think, Plato having learned from the prophets regarding the Holy Ghost, he has manifestly transferred to what he calls virtue. For as the sacred prophets say that one and the same spirit is divided into seven spirits, so he also, naming it one and the same virtue, says this is divided into four virtues; wishing by all means to avoid mention of the Holy Spirit, but clearly declaring in a kind of allegory what

---

[929] 1 Kings 19:11, 12.

the prophets said of the Holy Spirit. For to this effect he spoke in the dialogue with Meno towards the close: "From this reasoning, Meno, it appears that virtue comes to those to whom it does come by a divine destiny. But we shall know clearly about this, in what kind of way virtue comes to men, when, as a first step, we shall have set ourselves to investigate, as an independent inquiry, what virtue itself is." You see how he calls only by the name of virtue, the gift that descends from above; and yet he counts it worthy of inquiry, whether it is right that this [gift] be called virtue or some other thing, fearing to name it openly the Holy Spirit, lest he should seem to be following the teaching of the prophets.

Chapter XXXIII: *Plato's idea of the beginning of time drawn from Moses.*

And from what source did Plato draw the information that time was created along with the heavens? For he wrote thus: "Time, accordingly, was created along with the heavens; in order that, coming into being together, they might also be together dissolved, if ever their dissolution should take place." Had he not learned this from the divine history of Moses? For he knew that the creation of time had received its original constitution from days and months and years. Since, then, the first day which was created along with the heavens constituted the beginning of all time (for thus Moses wrote, "***In the beginning God created the heavens and the earth***,"[930] and then immediately subjoins, "***And one day was made***,"[931] as if he would designate the whole of time by one part of it), Plato names the day "time," lest, if he mentioned the "day," he should seem to lay himself open to the accusation of the Athenians, that he was completely adopting the expressions of Moses. And from what source did he derive what he has written regarding the dissolution of the heavens? Had he not learned this, too, from the sacred prophets, and did he not think that this was their doctrine?

[930] {Genesis 1:1.}
[931] {Genesis 1:5.}

Chapter XXXIV: *Whence men attributed to God human form.*

And if any person investigates the subject of images, and inquires on what ground those who first fashioned your gods conceived that they had the forms of men, he will find that this also was derived from the divine history. For seeing that Moses' history, speaking in the person of God, says, "***Let Us make man in our image and likeness,***"[932] these persons, under the impression that this meant that men were like God in form, began thus to fashion their gods, supposing they would make a likeness from a likeness. But why, ye men of Greece, am I now induced to recount these things? That ye may know that it is not possible to learn the true religion from those who were unable, even on those subjects by which they won the admiration of the heathen,[933] to write anything original, but merely propounded by some allegorical device in their own writings what they had learned from Moses and the other prophets.

Chapter XXXV: *Appeal to the Greeks.*

The time, then, ye men of Greece, is now come, that ye, having been persuaded by the secular histories that Moses and the rest of the prophets were far more ancient than any of those who have been esteemed sages among you, abandon the ancient delusion of your forefathers, and read the divine histories of the prophets, and ascertain from them the true religion; for they do not present to you artful discourses, nor speak speciously and plausibly—for this is the property of those who wish to rob you of the truth—but use with simplicity the words and expressions which offer themselves, and declare to you whatever the Holy Ghost, who descended upon them, chose to teach through them to those who are desirous to learn the true religion.

Having then laid aside all false shame, and the inveterate error of mankind, with all its bombastic parade and empty noise, though by means of it you fancy you are possessed of all advantages, do you give yourselves to the things that profit you. For neither will you commit any offence against your fathers, if you now show a desire to betake yourselves to that which is quite opposed to their error, since it is likely

[932] {Genesis 1:26.}

[933] Literally, "those without."

enough that they themselves are now lamenting in Hades, and repenting with a too late repentance; and if it were possible for them to show you thence what had befallen them after the termination of this life, ye would know from what fearful ills they desired to deliver you.

But now, since it is not possible in this present life that ye either learn from them, or from those who here profess to teach that philosophy which is falsely so called, it follows as the one thing that remains for you to do, that, renouncing the error of your fathers, ye read the prophecies of the sacred writers,[934] not requiring from them unexceptionable diction (for the matters of our religion lie in works, not in words), and learn from them what will give you life everlasting. For those who bootlessly disgrace the name of philosophy are convicted of knowing nothing at all, as they are themselves forced, though unwillingly, to confess, since not only do they disagree with each other, but also expressed their own opinions sometimes in one way, sometimes in another.

Chapter XXXVI: *True knowledge not held by the philosophers.*

And if "the discovery of the truth" be given among them as one definition of philosophy, how are they who are not in possession of the true knowledge worthy of the name of philosophy? For if Socrates, the wisest of your wise men, to whom even your oracle, as you yourselves say, bears witness, saying, "Of all men Socrates is the wisest"—if he confesses that he knows nothing, how did those who came after him profess to know even things heavenly? For Socrates said that he was on this account called wise, because, while other men pretended to know what they were ignorant of, he himself did not shrink from confessing that he knew nothing. For he said, "I seem to myself to be wisest by this little particular, that what I do not know, I do not suppose I know." Let no one fancy that Socrates ironically feigned ignorance, because he often used to do so in his dialogues. For the last expression of his apology which he uttered as he was being led away to the prison, proves that in seriousness and truth he was confessing his ignorance: "But now it is time to go away, I indeed to die, but you to live. And which of us goes to the better state, is hidden to all but God." Socrates, indeed, having

[934] Literally, "sacred men."

uttered this last sentence in the Areopagus, departed to the prison, ascribing to God alone the knowledge of those things which are hidden from us; but those who came after him, though they are unable to comprehend even earthly things, profess to understand things heavenly as if they had seen them.

Aristotle at least—as if he had seen things heavenly with greater accuracy than Plato—declared that God did not exist, as Plato said, in the fiery substance (for this was Plato's doctrine) but in the fifth element, air. And while he demanded that concerning these matters he should be believed on account of the excellence of his language, he yet departed this life because he was overwhelmed with the infamy and disgrace of being unable to discover even the nature of the Euripus in Chalcis.[935]

Let not any one, therefore, of sound judgment prefer the elegant diction of these men to his own salvation, but let him, according to that old story, stop his ears with wax, and flee the sweet hurt which these sirens would inflict upon him. For the above-mentioned men, presenting their elegant language as a kind of bait, have sought to seduce many from the right religion, in imitation of him who dared to teach the first men polytheism.

Be not persuaded by these persons, I entreat you, but read the prophecies of the sacred writers.[936] And if any slothfulness or old hereditary superstition prevents you from reading the prophecies of the holy men through which you can be instructed regarding the one only God, which is the first article of the true religion, yet believe him who, though at first he taught you polytheism, yet afterwards preferred to sing a useful and necessary recantation—I mean Orpheus, who said what I quoted a little before; and believe the others who wrote the same things concerning one God. For it was the work of Divine Providence on your behalf, that they, though unwillingly, bore testimony that what the prophets said regarding one God was true, in order that, the doctrine of a plurality of gods being rejected by all, occasion might be afforded you of knowing the truth.

---

[935] This is now supposed to be a fable.

[936] Literally, "sacred men."

Chapter XXXVII: *Of the Sibyl.*

And you may in part easily learn the right religion from the ancient Sibyl, who by some kind of potent inspiration teaches you, through her oracular predictions, truths which seem to be much akin to the teaching of the prophets. She, they say, was of Babylonian extraction, being the daughter of Berosus, who wrote the Chaldean History; and when she had crossed over (how, I know not) into the region of Campania, she there uttered her oracular sayings in a city called Cumae, six miles from Baiae, where the hot springs of Campania are found. And being in that city, we saw also a certain place, in which we were shown a very large basilica cut out of one stone; a vast affair, and worthy of all admiration. And they who had heard it from their fathers as part of their country's tradition, told us that it was here she used to publish her oracles. And in the middle of the basilica they showed us three receptacles cut out of one stone, in which, when filled with water, they said that she washed, and having put on her robe again, retires into the inmost chamber of the basilica, which is still a part of the one stone; and sitting in the middle of the chamber on a high rostrum and throne, thus proclaims her oracles.

And both by many other writers has the Sibyl been mentioned as a prophetess, and also by Plato in his *Phaedrus*. And Plato seems to me to have counted prophets divinely inspired when he read her prophecies. For he saw that what she had long ago predicted was accomplished; and on this account he expresses in the Dialogue with Meno his wonder at and admiration of prophets in the following terms:

> Those whom we now call prophetic persons we should rightly name divine. And not least would we say that they are divine, and are raised to the prophetic ecstasy by the inspiration and possession of God, when they correctly speak of many and important matters, and yet know nothing of what they are saying,

—plainly and manifestly referring to the prophecies of the Sibyl.

For, unlike the poets who, after their poems are penned, have power to correct and polish, specially in the way of increasing the accuracy of their verse, she was filled indeed with prophecy at the time of the inspiration, but as soon as the inspiration ceased, there ceased also the remembrance of all she had said. And this indeed was the cause why some only, and not all, the meters of the verses of the Sibyl were preserved. For we ourselves, when in that city, ascertained from our cicerone, who showed us the places in which she used to prophesy, that there was a certain coffer made of brass in which they said that her remains were preserved. And besides all else which they told us as they had heard it from their fathers, they said also that they who then took down her prophecies, being illiterate persons, often went quite astray from the accuracy of the meters; and this, they said, was the cause of the want of meter in some of the verses, the prophetess having no remembrance of what she had said, after the possession and inspiration ceased, and the reporters having, through their lack of education, failed to record the meters with accuracy. And on this account, it is manifest that Plato had an eye to the prophecies of the Sibyl when he said this about prophets, for he said, "When they correctly speak of many and important matters, and yet know nothing of what they are saying."

Chapter XXXVIII: *Concluding appeal.*

But since, ye men of Greece, the matters of the true religion lie not in the metrical numbers of poetry, nor yet in that culture which is highly esteemed among you, do ye henceforward pay less devotion to accuracy of meters and of language; and giving heed without contentiousness to the words of the Sibyl, recognize how great are the benefits which she will confer upon you by predicting, as she does in a clear and patent manner, the advent of our Savior Jesus Christ; who, being the Word of God, inseparable from Him in power, having assumed man, who had been made in the image and likeness of God, restored to us the knowledge of the religion of our ancient forefathers, which the men who lived after them abandoned through the bewitching counsel of the envious devil, and turned to the worship of those who were no gods.

And if you still hesitate and are hindered from belief regarding the formation of man, believe those whom you have hitherto thought it right to give heed to, and know that your own oracle, when asked by someone to utter a hymn of praise to the Almighty God, in the middle of the hymn spoke thus, "Who formed the first of men, and called him Adam." And this hymn is preserved by many whom we know, for the conviction of those who are unwilling to believe the truth which all bear witness to.

If therefore, ye men of Greece, ye do not esteem the false fancy concerning those that are no gods at a higher rate than your own salvation, believe, as I said, the most ancient and time-honored Sibyl, whose books are preserved in all the world, and who by some kind of potent inspiration both teaches us in her oracular utterances concerning those that are called gods, that have no existence; and also clearly and manifestly prophesies concerning the predicted advent of our Savior Jesus Christ, and concerning all those things which were to be done by Him. For the knowledge of these things will constitute your necessary preparatory training for the study of the prophecies of the sacred writers.

And if any one supposes that he has learned the doctrine concerning God from the most ancient of those whom you name philosophers, let him listen to Ammon and Mercury:[937] to Ammon, who in his discourse concerning God calls Him wholly hidden; and to Mercury,[938] who says plainly and distinctly, "that it is difficult to comprehend God, and that it is impossible even for the man who can comprehend Him to declare Him to others."

From every point of view, therefore, it must be seen that in no other way than only from the prophets who teach us by divine inspiration, is it at all possible to learn anything concerning God and the true religion.

[937]{A later edition reads, "Hermes."}
[938] {Ibid.}

Justin On the Sole Government of God[939]

Chapter I: *Object of the author.*

Although human nature at first received a union of intelligence and safety to discern the truth, and the worship due to the one Lord of all, yet envy, insinuating the excellence of human greatness, turned men away to the making of idols; and this superstitious custom, after continuing for a long period, is handed down to the majority as if it were natural and true. It is the part of a lover of man, or rather of a lover of God, to remind men who have neglected it of that which they ought to know. For the truth is of itself sufficient to show forth, by means of those things which are contained under the pole of heaven, the order [instituted by] Him who has created them.

But forgetfulness having taken possession of the minds of men, through the long-suffering of God, has acted recklessly in transferring to mortals the name which is applicable to the only true God; and from the few the infection of sin spread to the many, who were blinded by popular usage to the knowledge of that which was lasting and unchangeable. For the men of former generations, who instituted private and public rites in honor of such as were more powerful, caused forgetfulness of the catholic[940] faith to take possession of their posterity; but I, as I have just stated, along with a God-loving mind, shall employ the speech of one who loves man, and set it before those who have intelligence, which all ought to have who are privileged to observe the administration of the universe, so that they should worship unchangeably Him who knows all things. This I shall do, not by mere display of words, but by altogether using

[939] *θεοῦ* is omitted in mss., but *μοναρχία* of itself implies it. {The original editors did not always provide specific citations to ancient pagan works that Saint Justin relied on for his arguments. This editor has similarly chosen not to provide such citations.}

[940] I.e., the doctrine that God only is to be worshipped. {This note is by the original editors and it is unclear to what this note refers. The term "catholic" refers generally to the Christ's undivided, universal Church. Of course, when capitalized, the term refers to the Roman Catholic Church, or the Latin Church of the West. The Orthodox believe in the catholicity, or universality, of the Church.}

demonstration drawn from the old poetry in Greek literature,[941] and from writings very common amongst all. For from these the famous men who have handed down as law idol-worship to the multitudes, shall be taught and convicted by their own poets and literature of great ignorance.

Chapter II: *Testimonies to the unity of God.*

First, then, Aeschylus,[942] in expounding the arrangement of his work,[943] expressed himself also as follows respecting the only God:

> Afar from mortals place the holy God,
> Nor ever think that He, like to thyself,
> In fleshly robes is clad; for all unknown
> Is the great God to such a worm as thou.
> Divers similitudes He bears; at times
> He seems as a consuming fire that burns
> Unsated; now like water, then again
> In sable folds of darkness shrouds Himself.
> Nay, even the very beasts of earth reflect
> His sacred image; whilst the wind, clouds, rain,
> The roll of thunder and the lightning flash,
> Reveal to men their great and sovereign Lord.
> Before Him sea and rocks, with every fount,
> And all the water floods, in reverence bend;
> And as they gaze upon His awful face,
> Mountains and earth, with the profoundest depths
> Of ocean, and the highest peaks of hills,
> Tremble: for He is Lord Omnipotent;
> And this the glory is of God Most High.

But he was not the only man initiated in the knowledge of God; for Sophocles also thus describes the nature of the only Creator of all things, the One God:

> There is one God, in truth there is but one,
> Who made the heavens and the broad earth beneath,

[941] Literally, "history."
[942] Grotius supposes this to be Aeschylus the younger in some prologue.
[943] This may also be translated: "expounding the set of opinion prevalent in his day."

The glancing waves of ocean, and the winds;
But many of us mortals err in heart,
And set up, for a solace in our woes,
Images of the gods in stone and brass,
Or figures carved in gold or ivory;
And, furnishing for these, our handiworks,
Both sacrifice and rite magnificent,
We think that thus we do a pious work.

And Philemon also, who published many explanations of ancient customs, shares in the knowledge of the truth; and thus he writes:

Tell me what thoughts of God we should conceive?
One, all things seeing, yet Himself unseen.

Even Orpheus, too, who introduces three hundred and sixty gods, will bear testimony in my favor from the tract called *Diathecae*, in which he appears to repent of his error by writing the following:

I'll speak to those who lawfully may hear;
All others, ye profane, now close the doors!
And, O Musaeus, hearken thou to me,
Who offspring art of the light-bringing moon.
The words I tell thee now are true indeed,
And if thou former thoughts of mine hast seen,
Let them not rob thee of the blessed life;
But rather turn the depths of thine own heart
Unto that place where light and knowledge dwell.
Take thou the word divine to guide thy steps;
And walking well in the straight certain path,
Look to the one and universal King,
One, self-begotten, and the only One
Of whom all things, and we ourselves, are sprung.
All things are open to His piercing gaze,
While He Himself is still invisible;
Present in all His works, though still unseen,
He gives to mortals evil out of good,
Sending both chilling wars and tearful griefs;
And other than the Great King there is none.
The clouds for ever settle round His throne;

And mortal eyeballs in mere mortal eyes
Are weak to see Jove, reigning over all.
He sits established in the brazen heavens
Upon His throne; and underneath His feet
He treads the earth, and stretches His right hand
To all the ends of ocean, and around
Tremble the mountain ranges, and the streams,
The depths, too, of the blue and hoary sea.

He speaks indeed as if he had been an eyewitness of God's greatness. And Pythagoras[944] agrees with him when he writes:

Should one in boldness say, Lo, I am God!
Besides the One— Eternal— Infinite,
Then let him from the throne he has usurped
Put forth his power and form another globe,
Such as we dwell in, saying, This is mine.
Nor only so, but in this new domain
For ever let him dwell. If this he can,
Then verily he is a god proclaimed.

Chapter III: *Testimonies to a future judgment.*

Then further concerning Him, that He alone is powerful, both to institute judgment on the deeds performed in life, and on the ignorance of the Deity [displayed by men], I can adduce witnesses from your own ranks; and first Sophocles, who speaks as follows:—

That time of times shall come, shall surely come,
When from the golden ether down shall fall
Fire's teeming treasure, and in burning flames
All things of earth and heaven shall be consumed;
And then, when all creation is dissolved,
The sea's last wave shall die upon the shore,
The bald earth stript of trees, the burning air
No winged thing upon its breast shall bear.
There are two roads to Hades, well we know;[945]

---

[944] "Pythagorei cujusdam fetus."—*Otto,* after Grotius.

By this the righteous, and by that the bad,
On to their separate fates shall tend; and He,
Who all things had destroyed, shall all things save.

And Philemon[946] again:

Think'st thou, Nicostratus, the dead, who here
Enjoyed whate'er of good life offers man,
Escape the notice of Divinity,
As if they might forgotten be of Him?
Nay, there's an eye of Justice watching all;
For if the good and bad find the same end,
Then go thou, rob, steal, plunder, at thy will,
Do all the evil that to thee seems good.
Yet be not thou deceived; for underneath
There is a throne and place of judgment set,
Which God the Lord of all shall occupy;
Whose name is terrible, nor shall I dare
To breathe it forth in feeble human speech.

And Euripides:[947]

Not grudgingly he gives a lease of life,
That we the holders may be fairly judged;
And if a mortal man doth think to hide
His daily guilt from the keen eye of God,
It is an evil thought; so if perchance
He meets with leisure-taking Justice, she
Demands him as her lawful prisoner:
But many of you hastily commit
A twofold sin, and say there is no God.
But, ah! there is; there is. Then see that he
Who, being wicked, prospers, may redeem
The time so precious, else hereafter waits

---

945 Some propose to insert these three lines in the center of the next quotation from Philemon, after the line "Nay, there's an eye," etc. [I.e., from "There are two roads" to "fates shall tend; and He."}

946 Some say *Diphilus*.

947 Grotius joins these lines to the preceding. Clement of Alexandria assigns them, and the others, which are under the name of Euripides to Diphilus.

For him the due reward of punishment.

Chapter IV: *God desires not sacrifices, but righteousness.*

And that God is not appeased by the libations and incense of evil-doers, but awards vengeance in righteousness to each one, Philemon[948] again shall bear testimony to me:

If anyone should dream, O Pamphilus,
By sacrifice of bulls or goats— nay, then,
By Jupiter— of any such like things;
Or by presenting gold or purple robes,
Or images of ivory and gems;
If thus he thinks he may propitiate God,
He errs, and shows himself a silly one.
But let him rather useful be, and good,
Committing neither theft nor lustful deeds,
Nor murder foul, for earthly riches' sake.
Let him of no man covet wife or child,
His splendid house, his wide-spread property,
His maiden, or his slave born ill his house,
His horses, or his cattle, or his beeves,
Nay, covet not a pin, O Pamphilus,
For God, close by you, sees whate'er you do.
He ever with the wicked man is wroth,
But in the righteous takes a pleasure still,
Permitting him to reap fruit of his toil,
And to enjoy the bread his sweat has won.
But being righteous, see thou pay thy vows,
And unto God the giver offer gifts.
Place thy adorning not in outward shows,
But in an inward purity of heart;
Hearing the thunder then, thou shall not fear,
Nor shall thou flee, O master, at its voice,
For thou art conscious of no evil deed,
And God, close by you, sees whate'er you do.

Again, Plato, in *Timaeus*,[949] says:

---

[948] Some attribute these lines to Menander, others regard them as spurious.

But if anyone on consideration should actually institute a rigid inquiry, he would be ignorant of the distinction between the human and the divine nature; because God mingles many[950] things up into one, [and again is able to dissolve one into many things,] seeing that He is endued with knowledge and power; but no man either is, or ever shall be, able to perform any of these.

Chapter V: *The vain pretensions of false gods.*

But concerning those who think that they shall share the holy and perfect name, which some have received by a vain tradition as if they were gods, Menander in the *Auriga* says:

If there exists a god who walketh out
With an old woman, or who enters in
By stealth to houses through the folding-doors,
He ne'er can please me; nay, but only he
Who stays at home, a just and righteous God,
To give salvation to His worshippers.

The same Menander, in the *Sacerdos*, says:

There is no God, O woman, that can save
One man by another; if indeed a man,
With sound of tinkling cymbals, charm a god
Where'er he listeth, then assuredly
He who doth so is much the greater god.
But these, O Rhode, are but the cunning schemes
Which daring men of intrigue, unabashed,
Invent to earn themselves a livelihood,
And yield a laughing-stock unto the age.

---

[949] P. 68, D. {This is evidently a reference by the prior editors to a source for Plato's works.}

[950] The mss. are corrupt here. They seem to read, and one actually does read, "all" for "many." "Many" is in Plato, and the clause in brackets is taken from Plato to fill up the sense.

Again, the same Menander, stating his opinion about those who are received as gods, proving rather that they are not so, says:

> Yea, if I this beheld, I then should wish
> That back to me again my soul returned.
> For tell me where, O Getas, in the world
> 'Tis possible to find out righteous gods?

And in the *Depositum*:

> There's an unrighteous judgment, as it seems,
> Even with the gods.

And Euripides the tragedian, in *Orestes*, says:

> Apollo having caused by his command
> The murder of the mother, knoweth not
> What honesty and justice signify.
> We serve the gods, whoever they may be;
> But from the central regions of the earth
> You see Apollo plainly gives response
> To mortals, and whate'er he says we do.
> I him obeyed, when she that bore me fell
> Slain by my hand: *he* is the wicked man.
> Then slay him, for 'twas he that sinned, not I.
> What could I do? Think you not that the god
> Should free me from the blame which I do bear?

The same also in *Hippolytus*:

> But on these points the gods do not judge right.

And in *Ion*:

> But in the daughter of Erechtheus
> What interest have I? for that pertains
> Not unto such as me. But when I come
> With golden vessels for libations, I
> The dew shall sprinkle, and yet needs must warn

Apollo of his deeds; for when he weds
Maidens by force, the children secretly
Begotten he betrays, and them neglects
When dying. Thus not you; but while you may
Always pursue the virtues, for the gods
Will surely punish men of wickedness.
How is it right that you, who have prescribed
Laws for men's guidance, live unrighteously?
But ye being absent, I shall freely speak,
And ye to men shall satisfaction give
For marriage forced, thou Neptune, Jupiter,
Who over heaven presides. The temples ye
Have emptied, while injustice ye repay.
And though ye laud the prudent to the skies,
Yet have ye filled your hands with wickedness.
No longer is it right to call men ill
If they do imitate the sins[951] of gods;
Nay, evil let their teachers rather be.

And in *Archelaus*:

Full oft, my son, do gods mankind perplex.

And in *Bellerophon*:[952]

They are no gods, who do not what is right.

And again in the same:

Gods reign in heaven most certainly, says one;
But it is false,—yeah, false: and let not him
Who speaks thus, be so foolish as to use
Ancient tradition, or to pay regard
Unto my words: but with unclouded eye

---

[951] *χαχά* in Euripides, *χαλά* in text.

[952] {The myth of the ancient Greek hero Bellarophon is embedded in Homer's *The Iliad*. Bellerophon is also the subject of a Greek tragedy by that name written by Euripides, a play that is largely lost to history and known only from fragments. From the placement of this passage, it appears to be a quote from the latter.}

Behold the matter in its clearest light.
Power absolute, I say, robs men of life
And property; transgresses plighted faith;
Nor spares even cities, but with cruel hand
Despoils and devastates them ruthlessly.
But they that do these things have more success
Than those who live a gentle pious life;
And cities small, I know, which reverence gods,
Submissive bend before the many spears
Of larger impious ones; yea, and methinks
If any man lounge idly, and abstain
From working with his hands for sustenance,
Yet pray the gods; he very soon will know
If they from him misfortunes will avert.

And Menander in *Diphilus*:[953]

Therefore ascribe we praise and honor great
To Him who Father is, and Lord of all;
Sole maker and preserver of mankind,
And who with all good things our earth has stored.

The same also in the *Piscatores*:

For I deem that which nourishes my life
Is God; but he whose custom 'tis to meet
The wants of men,—He needs not at our hands
Renewed supplies, Himself being all in all.[954]

The same in the *Fratres*:

God ever is intelligence to those
Who righteous are: so wisest men have thought.

And in the *Tibicinae*:

---

[953] These lines are assigned to Diphilus.
[954] The words from "but" to "all" are assigned by Otto to Justin, not to Menander.

Good reason finds a temple in all things
Wherein to worship; for what is the mind,
But just the voice of God within us placed?

And the tragedian in *Phrixus*:

But if the pious and the impious
Share the same lot, how could we think it just,
If Jove, the best, judges not uprightly?

In *Philoctetes*:

You see how honorable gain is deemed
Even to the gods; and how he is admired
Whose shrine is laden most with yellow gold.
What, then, doth hinder thee, since it is good
To be like gods, from thus accepting gain?

In *Hecuba*:

O Jupiter! whoever thou mayest be,
Of whom except in word all knowledge fails;

and,

Jupiter, whether thou art indeed
A great necessity, or the mind of man,
I worship thee!

Chapter VI: *We should acknowledge only one God.*

Here, then, is a proof of virtue, and of a mind loving prudence, to recur to the communion of the unity,[955] and to attach one's self to prudence for salvation, and make choice of the better things according to the free-will placed in man; and not to think that those who are possessed of human passions are lords of all, when they shall not appear

[955] See Chapter I, the opening sentence.

to have even equal power with men. For in Homer,[956] Demodocus says he is self-taught—

> God inspired me with strains

—though he is a mortal. Aesculapius and Apollo are taught to heal by Chiron the Centaur,—a very novel thing indeed, for gods to be taught by a man. What need I speak of Bacchus, who the poet says is mad? or of Hercules, who he says is unhappy? What need to speak of Mars and Venus, the leaders of adultery; and by means of all these to establish the proof which has been undertaken? For if someone, in ignorance, should imitate the deeds which are said to be divine, he would be reckoned among impure men, and a stranger to life and humanity; and if anyone does so knowingly, he will have a plausible excuse for escaping vengeance, by showing that imitation of godlike deeds of audacity is no sin. But if anyone should blame these deeds, he will take away their well-known names, and not cover them up with specious and plausible words.

It is necessary, then, to accept the true and invariable Name, not proclaimed by my words only, but by the words of those who have introduced us to the elements of learning, in order that we may not, by living idly in this present state of existence, not only as those who are ignorant of the heavenly glory, but also as having proved ourselves ungrateful, render our account to the Judge.

---

[956] *Odysseus*, xv. 347.

Extant Fragments of the Lost Work of Justin:

On the Resurrection

Chapter I: *The self-evidencing power of truth.*

The word of truth is free, and carries its own authority, disdaining to fall under any skillful argument, or to endure the logical scrutiny of its hearers. But it would be believed for its own nobility, and for the confidence due to Him who sends it.

Now the word of truth is sent from God; wherefore the freedom claimed by the truth is not arrogant. For being sent with authority, it were not fit that it should be required to produce proof of what is said; since neither is there any proof beyond itself, which is God. For every proof is more powerful and trustworthy than that which it proves; since what is disbelieved, until proof is produced, gets credit when such proof is produced, and is recognized as being what it was stated to be. But nothing is either more powerful or more trustworthy than the truth; so that he who requires proof of this is like one who wishes it demonstrated why the things that appear to the senses do appear.

For the test of those things which are received through the reason, is sense; but of sense itself there is no test beyond itself. As then we bring those things which reason hunts after, to sense, and by it judge what kind of things they are, whether the things spoken be true or false, and then sit in judgment no longer, giving full credit to its decision; so also we refer all that is said regarding men and the world to the truth, and by it judge whether it be worthless or no. But the utterances of truth we judge by no separate test, giving full credit to itself.

And God, the Father of the universe, who is the perfect intelligence, is the truth. And the Word, being His Son, came to us, having put on flesh, revealing both Himself and the Father, giving to us in Himself resurrection from the dead, and eternal life afterwards. And this is Jesus Christ, our Savior and Lord. He, therefore, is Himself both the faith and the proof of Himself and of all things. Wherefore those who follow Him, and know Him, having faith in Him as their proof, shall rest in Him.

But since the adversary[957] does not cease to resist many, and uses many and divers arts to ensnare them, that he may seduce the faithful from their faith, and that he may prevent the faithless from believing, it seems to me necessary that we also, being armed with the invulnerable doctrines of the faith, do battle against him in behalf of the weak.

Chapter II: *Objections to the resurrection of the flesh.*

They who maintain the wrong opinion say that there is no resurrection of the flesh; giving as their reason that it is impossible that what is corrupted and dissolved should be restored to the same as it had been. And besides the impossibility, they say that the salvation of the flesh is disadvantageous; and they abuse the flesh, adducing its infirmities, and declare that it only is the cause of our sins, so that if the flesh, say they, rise again, our infirmities also rise with it.

And such sophistical reasons as the following they elaborate: If the flesh rise again, it must rise either entire and possessed of all its parts, or imperfect. But its rising imperfect argues a want of power on God's part, if some parts could be saved, and others not; but if all the parts are saved, then the body will manifestly have all its members. But is it not absurd to say that these members will exist after the resurrection from the dead, since the Savior said, "***They neither marry, nor are given in marriage, but shall be as the angels in heaven***?"[958] And the angels, say they, have neither flesh, nor do they eat, nor have sexual intercourse; therefore there shall be no resurrection of the flesh.

By these and such like arguments, they attempt to distract men from the faith. And there are some who maintain that even Jesus Himself appeared only as spiritual, and not in flesh, but presented merely the appearance of flesh:[959] these persons seek to rob the flesh of the promise.

First, then, let us solve those things which seem to them to be insoluble; then we will introduce in an orderly manner the demonstration concerning the flesh, proving that it partakes of salvation.

---

957 {A reference to the evil one, or satan.}

958 Mark 12:25. {See also Luke 20:34-36}.

959 {A reference to the Docetists. Docetism was rejected as heresy at the First Council of Nicaea in 325 A.D.}

Chapter III: *If the members rise, must they discharge the same functions as now?*

They say, then, if the body shall rise entire, and in possession of all its members, it necessarily follows that the functions of the members shall also be in existence; that the womb shall become pregnant, and the male also discharge his function of generation, and the rest of the members in like manner. Now let this argument stand or fall by this one assertion. For this being proved false, their whole objection will be removed.

Now it is indeed evident that the members which discharge functions discharge those functions which in the present life we see; but it does not follow that they necessarily discharge the same functions from the beginning. And that this may be more clearly seen, let us consider it thus. The function of the womb is to become pregnant; and of the member of the male to impregnate. But as, though these members are destined to discharge such functions, it is not therefore necessary that they from the beginning discharge them (since we see many women who do not become pregnant, as those that are barren, even though they have wombs), so pregnancy is not the immediate and necessary consequence of having a womb; but those even who are not barren abstain from sexual intercourse, some being virgins from the first, and others from a certain time. And we see men also keeping themselves virgins, some from the first, and some from a certain time; so that by their means, marriage, made lawless through lust, is destroyed.[960] And we find that some even of the lower animals, though possessed of wombs, do not bear, such as the mule; and the male mules do not beget their kind. So that both in the case of men and the irrational animals we can see sexual intercourse abolished; and this, too, before the future world.

And our Lord Jesus Christ was born of a virgin, for no other reason than that He might destroy the begetting by lawless desire, and might show to the ruler[961] that the formation of man was possible to God without human intervention. And when He had been born, and had submitted to the other conditions of the flesh,—I mean food, drink, and

---

[960] That is to say, their lives are a protest against entering into marriage for any other purpose than that of begetting children.
[961] I.e., to the devil.

clothing,—this one condition only of discharging the sexual function He did not submit to; for, regarding the desires of the flesh, He accepted some as necessary, while others, which were unnecessary, He did not submit to. For if the flesh were deprived of food, drink, and clothing, it would be destroyed; but being deprived of lawless desire, it suffers no harm.

And at the same time He foretold that, in the future world, sexual intercourse should be done away with; as He says, "***The children of this world marry, and are given in marriage; but the children of the world to come neither marry nor are given in marriage, but shall be like the angels in heaven.***"[962]

Let not, then, those that are unbelieving marvel, if in the world to come He do away with those acts of our fleshly members which even in this present life are abolished.

Chapter IV: *Must the deformed rise deformed?*

Well, they say, if then the flesh rise, it must rise the same as it falls; so that if it die with one eye, it must rise one-eyed; if lame, lame; if defective in any part of the body, in this part the man must rise deficient. How truly blinded are they in the eyes of their hearts! For they have not seen on the earth blind men seeing again, and the lame walking by His word. All things which the Savior did, He did in the first place in order that what was spoken concerning Him in the prophets might be fulfilled, "***that the blind should receive sight, and the deaf hear***,"[963] and so on; but also to induce the belief that in the resurrection the flesh shall rise entire. For if on earth He healed the sicknesses of the flesh, and made the body whole, much more will He do this in the resurrection, so that the flesh shall rise perfect and entire. In this manner, then, shall those dreaded difficulties of theirs be healed.

---

[962] Luke 20:34, 35 {-36}. {See also Mark 12:25. }

[963] Isaiah 35:5. {See also Isaiah 29:18. For the healing miracles of Christ, see the Gospels of Ss. Matthew, Mark, Luke and John, *passim*.}

Chapter V: *The resurrection of the flesh is not impossible.*

But again, of those who maintain that the flesh has no resurrection, some assert that it is impossible; others that, considering how vile and despicable the flesh is, it is not fit that God should raise it; and others, that it did not at the first receive the promise. First, then, in respect of those who say that it is impossible for God to raise it, it seems to me that I should show that they are ignorant, professing as they do in word that they are believers, yet by their works proving themselves to be unbelieving, even more unbelieving than the unbelievers. For, seeing that all the heathen believe in their idols, and are persuaded that to them all things are possible (as even their poet Homer says,[964] "The gods can do all things, and that easily;" and he added the word "easily" that he might bring out the greatness of the power of the gods), many do seem to be more unbelieving than they. For if the heathen believe in their gods, which are idols (***"which have ears, and they hear not; they have eyes, and they see not"***[965]), that they can do all things, though they be but devils, as saith the Scripture, "***The gods of the nations are devils***,"[966] much more ought we, who hold the right, excellent, and true faith, to believe in our God, since also we have proofs [of His power], first in the creation of the first man, for he was made from the earth by God; and this is sufficient evidence of God's power; and then they who observe things can see how men are generated one by another, and can marvel in a still greater degree that from a little drop of moisture so grand a living creature is formed. And certainly if this were only recorded in a promise, and not seen accomplished, this too would be much more incredible than the other; but it is rendered more credible by accomplishment.[967]

But even in the case of the resurrection the Savior has shown us accomplishments, of which we will in a little speak. But now we are demonstrating that the resurrection of the flesh is possible, asking pardon of the children of the Church if we adduce arguments which seem to be

---

[964] *Odyssey*, ii. 304.

[965] Psalm 115:5.

[966] Psalm 96:5. {Some Bible translations have "idols" instead of "devils." Compare KJV with OSB, for example.}

[967] I.e., by actually happening under our observation.

secular[968] and physical:[969] first, because to God nothing is secular,[970] not even the world itself, for it is His workmanship; and secondly, because we are conducting our argument so as to meet unbelievers. For if we argued with believers, it were enough to say that we believe; but now we must proceed by demonstrations.

The foregoing proofs are indeed quite sufficient to evince the possibility of the resurrection of the flesh; but since these men are exceedingly unbelieving, we will further adduce a more convincing argument still,—an argument drawn not from faith, for they are not within its scope, but from their own mother unbelief,—I mean, of course, from physical reasons. For if by such arguments we prove to them that the resurrection of the flesh is possible, they are certainly worthy of great contempt if they can be persuaded neither by the deliverances of faith nor by the arguments of the world.

Chapter VI: *The resurrection consistent with the opinions of the philosophers.*

Those, then, who are called natural philosophers, say, some of them, as Plato, that the universe is matter and God; others, as Epicurus, that it is atoms and the void;[971] others, like the Stoics, that it is these four—fire, water, air, earth. For it is sufficient to mention the most prevalent opinions. And Plato says that all things are made from matter by God, and according to His design; but Epicurus and his followers say that all things are made from the atom and the void by some kind of self-regulating action of the natural movement of the bodies; and the Stoics, that all are made of the four elements, God pervading them.

But while there is such discrepancy among them, there are some doctrines acknowledged by them all in common, one of which is that neither can anything be produced from what is not in being, nor anything be destroyed or dissolved into what has not any being, and that the elements exist indestructible out of which all things are generated. And

---

968 *ἔξωθεν*, "without" or "outside," to which reference is made to the next clause, which may be translated, "because nothing is outside God," or "because to God nothing is 'without.'"

969 *χοσμιχῶν*, arguments drawn from the laws by which the world is governed.

970 {See above, nn. 965, 966, and accompanying text.}

971 *τὸ χενόν*, the void of space in which the infinity of atoms moved.

this being so, the regeneration of the flesh will, according to all these philosophers, appear to be possible. For if, according to Plato, it is matter and God, both these are indestructible and God; and God indeed occupies the position of an artificer, to wit, a potter; and matter occupies the place of clay or wax, or some such thing. That, then, which is formed of matter, be it an image or a statue, is destructible; but the matter itself is indestructible, such as clay or wax, or any other such kind of matter. Thus the artist designs in the clay or wax, and makes the form of a living animal; and again, if his handiwork be destroyed, it is not impossible for him to make the same form, by working up the same material, and fashioning it anew. So that, according to Plato, neither will it be impossible for God, who is Himself indestructible, and has also indestructible material, even after that which has been first formed of it has been destroyed, to make it anew again, and to make the same form just as it was before.

But according to the Stoics even, the body being produced by the mixture of the four elementary substances, when this body has been dissolved into the four elements, these remaining indestructible, it is possible that they receive a second time the same fusion and composition, from God pervading them, and so re-make the body which they formerly made. Like as if a man shall make a composition of gold and silver, and brass and tin, and then shall wish to dissolve it again, so that each element exist separately, having again mixed them, he may, if he pleases, make the very same composition as he had formerly made.

Again, according to Epicurus, the atoms and the void being indestructible, it is by a definite arrangement and adjustment of the atoms as they come together, that both all other formations are produced, and the body itself; and it being in course of time dissolved, is dissolved again into those atoms from which it was also produced. And as these remain indestructible, it is not at all impossible, that by coming together again, and receiving the same arrangement and position, they should make a body of like nature to what was formerly produced by them; as if a jeweler should make in mosaic the form of an animal, and the stones should be scattered by time or by the man himself who made them, he having still in his possession the scattered stones, may gather them together again, and having gathered, may dispose them in the same way, and make the same form of an animal. And shall not God be able to collect again the decomposed members of the flesh, and make the same body as was formerly produced by Him?

Chapter VII: *The body valuable in God's sight.*

But the proof of the possibility of the resurrection of the flesh I have sufficiently demonstrated, in answer to men of the world. And if the resurrection of the flesh is not found impossible on the principles even of unbelievers, how much more will it be found in accordance with the mind of believers! But following our order, we must now speak with respect to those who think meanly of the flesh, and say that it is not worthy of the resurrection nor of the heavenly economy,[972] because, first, its substance is earth; and besides, because it is full of all wickedness, so that it forces the soul to sin along with it. But these persons seem to be ignorant of the whole work of God, both of the genesis and formation of man at the first, and why the things in the world were made.[973] For does not the word say, "***Let Us make man in our image, and after our likeness***?"[974] What kind of man? Manifestly He means fleshly man. For the word says, "***And God took dust of the earth, and made man.***"[975] It is evident, therefore, that man made in the image of God was of flesh. Is it not, then, absurd to say, that the flesh made by God in His own image is contemptible, and worth nothing? But that the flesh is with God a precious possession is manifest, first from its being formed by Him, if at least the image is valuable to the former and artist; and besides, its value can be gathered from the creation of the rest of the world. For that on account of which the rest is made, is the most precious of all to the maker.

Chapter VIII: *Does the body cause the soul to sin?*

Quite true, say they; yet the flesh is a sinner, so much so, that it forces the soul to sin along with it. And thus they vainly accuse it, and lay to its charge alone the sins of both. But in what instance can the flesh

---

[972] Or, "citizenship."
[973] This might also be rendered, "and the things in the world, on account of which he was made;" but the subsequent argument shows the propriety of the above rendering.
[974] Genesis 1:26.
[975] Genesis 2:7.

possibly sin by itself, if it have not the soul going before it and inciting it? For as in the case of a yoke of oxen, if one or other is loosed from the yoke, neither of them can plough alone; so neither can soul or body alone effect anything, if they be unyoked from their communion. And if it is the flesh that is the sinner, then on its account alone did the Savior come, as He says, "***I am not come to call the righteous, but sinners to repentance.***"[976] Since, then, the flesh has been proved to be valuable in the sight of God, and glorious above all His works, it would very justly be saved by Him.

We must meet, therefore, those who say, that even though it be the special handiwork of God, and beyond all else valued by Him, it would not immediately follow that it has the promise of the resurrection. Yet is it not absurd, that that which has been produced with such circumstance, and which is beyond all else valuable, should be so neglected by its Maker, as to pass to nonentity? Then the sculptor and painter, if they wish the works they have made to endure, that they may win glory by them, renew them when they begin to decay; but God would so neglect His own possession and work, that it becomes annihilated, and no longer exists. Should we not call this labor in vain? As if a man who has built a house should forthwith destroy it, or should neglect it, though he sees it falling into decay, and is able to repair it: we would blame him for laboring in vain; and should we not so blame God? But not such an one is the Incorruptible,—not senseless is the Intelligence of the universe. Let the unbelieving be silent, even though they themselves do not believe.

But, in truth, He has even called the flesh to the resurrection, and promises to it everlasting life. For where He promises to save man, there He gives the promise to the flesh. For what is man but the reasonable animal composed of body and soul? Is the soul by itself man? No; but the soul of man. Would the body be called man? No, but it is called the body of man. If, then, neither of these is by itself man, but that which is made up of the two together is called man, and God has called man to life and resurrection, He has called not a part, but the whole, which is the soul and the body. Since would it not be unquestionably absurd, if, while these two are in the same being and according to the same law, the one were saved and the other not? And if it be not impossible, as has already been proved, that the flesh be regenerated, what is the distinction on the

[976] Mark 2:17.

ground of which the soul is saved and the body not? Do they make God a grudging God? But He is good, and will have all to be saved. And by God and His proclamation, not only has your soul heard and believed on Jesus Christ, and with it the flesh,[977] but both were washed, and both wrought righteousness. They make God, then ungrateful and unjust, if, while both believe on Him, He desires to save one and not the other.

Well, they say, but the soul is incorruptible, being a part of God and inspired by Him, and therefore He desires to save what is peculiarly His own and akin to Himself; but the flesh is corruptible, and not from Him, as the soul is. Then what thanks are due to Him, and what manifestation of His power and goodness is it, if He purposed to save what is by nature saved and exists as a part of Himself? For it had its salvation from itself; so that in saving the soul, God does no great thing. For to be saved is its natural destiny, because it is a part of Himself, being His inspiration. But no thanks are due to one who saves what is his own; for this is to save himself. For he who saves a part himself, saves himself by his own means, lest he become defective in that part; and this is not the act of a good man. For not even when a man does good to his children and offspring, does one call him a good man; for even the most savage of the wild beasts do so, and indeed willingly endure death, if need be, for the sake of their cubs. But if a man were to perform the same acts in behalf of his slaves, that man would justly be called good. Wherefore the Savior also taught us to love our enemies, since, says He, ***what thank have ye?***[978] So that He has shown us that it is a good work not only to love those that are begotten of Him, but also those that are without. And what He enjoins upon us, He Himself first of all does.[979]

Chapter IX: *The resurrection of Christ proves that the body rises.*

If He had no need of the flesh, why did He heal it? And what is most forcible of all, He raised the dead. Why? Was it not to show what

---

[977] Migne proposes to read here *χαὶ οὐν αὐτῇ*, "without the flesh," which gives a more obvious meaning. The above reading is, however, defensible. Justin means that the flesh was not merely partaking of the soul's faith and promise, but had rights of its own.

[978] {See, e.g., Matthew 5:44, 46; Luke 6:27-28, 32, 35.}

[979] It is supposed that a part of the treatise has been here dropped out. {See Luke 23;24, where Jesus prays to the Father while on the Cross for Him to forgive those who crucified Him.}

the resurrection should be? How then did He raise the dead? Their souls or their bodies? Manifestly both. If the resurrection were only spiritual, it was requisite that He, in raising the dead, should show the body lying apart by itself, and the soul living apart by itself. But now He did not do so, but raised the body, confirming in it the promise of life.

Why did He rise in the flesh in which He suffered, unless to show the resurrection of the flesh? And wishing to confirm this, when His disciples did not know whether to believe He had truly risen in the body, and were looking upon Him and doubting, He said to them, "***Ye have not yet faith, see that it is I***;"[980] and He let them handle Him, and showed them the prints of the nails in His hands. And when they were by every kind of proof persuaded that it was Himself, and in the body, they asked Him to eat with them, that they might thus still more accurately ascertain that He had in verity risen bodily; and He did eat honey-comb and fish. And when He had thus shown them that there is truly a resurrection of the flesh, wishing to show them this also, that it is not impossible for flesh to ascend into heaven (as He had said that our dwelling-place is in heaven), "***He was taken up into heaven while they beheld***,"[981] as He was in the flesh. If, therefore, after all that has been said, any one demand demonstration of the resurrection, he is in no respect different from the Sadducees,[982] since the resurrection of the flesh is the power of God, and, being above all reasoning, is established by faith, and seen in works.

Chapter X: *The body saved, and will therefore rise.*

The resurrection is a resurrection of the flesh which died. For the spirit dies not; the soul is in the body, and without a soul it cannot live. The body, when the soul forsakes it, is not. For the body is the house of the soul; and the soul the house of the spirit. These three, in all those who cherish a sincere hope and unquestioning faith in God, will be saved. Considering, therefore, even such arguments as are suited to this world, and finding that, even according to them, it is not impossible that the flesh be regenerated; and seeing that, besides all these proofs, the Savior

[980] Comp. Luke 24:32, etc. {See also John 20:27.}
[981] Acts 1:9. {See also Luke 24:51.}
[982] {See Matthew 22:23, where it is noted that the Sadducees did not believe in resurrection.}

in the whole Gospel shows that there is salvation for the flesh, why do we any longer endure those unbelieving and dangerous arguments, and fail to see that we are retrograding when we listen to such an argument as this: that the soul is immortal, but the body mortal, and incapable of being revived? For this we used to hear from Pythagoras and Plato, even before we learned the truth. If then the Savior said this, and proclaimed salvation to the soul alone, what new thing, beyond what we heard from Pythagoras and Plato and all their band, did He bring us? But now He has come proclaiming the glad tidings of a new and strange hope to men. For indeed it was a strange and new thing for God to promise that He would not keep incorruption in incorruption, but would make corruption incorruption.[983] But because the prince of wickedness could in no other way corrupt the truth, he sent forth his apostles (evil men who introduced pestilent doctrines), choosing them from among those who crucified our Savior; and these men bore the name of the Savior, but did the works of him that sent them, through whom the name itself has been evilly spoken against.

But if the flesh do not rise, why is it also guarded, and why do we not rather suffer it to indulge its desires? Why do we not imitate physicians, who, it is said, when they get a patient that is despaired of and incurable, allow him to indulge his desires? For they know that he is dying; and this indeed those who hate the flesh surely do, casting it out of its inheritance, so far as they can; for on this account they also despise it, because it is shortly to become a corpse. But if our physician Christ, God, having rescued us from our desires, regulates our flesh with His own wise and temperate rule, it is evident that He guards it from sins because it possesses a hope of salvation, as physicians do not suffer men whom they hope to save to indulge in what pleasures they please.

---

[983] {See, e.g., 1 Corinthians 15:50.}

Other Fragments from the Lost Writings of Justin

I

The most admirable Justin rightly declared that the aforesaid demons resembled robbers.

(Tatian's *Address to the Greeks*, chap. xviii.)[984]

II

And Justin well said in his book against Marcion, that he would not have believed the Lord Himself, if He had announced any other God than the Fashioner and Maker [of the world], and our Nourisher. But since, from the one God, who both made this world and formed us, and contains as well as administers all things, there came to us the only-begotten Son, summing up His own workmanship in Himself, my faith in Him is steadfast, and my love towards the Father is immoveable, God bestowing both upon us.

(Irenaeus, *Heresies*, iv. 6.)

III

Justin well said: Before the advent of the Lord, Satan never ventured to blaspheme God, inasmuch as he was not yet sure of his own damnation, since that was announced concerning him by the prophets only in parables and allegories. But after the advent of the Lord learning plainly from the discourses of Christ and His apostles that eternal fire was prepared for him who voluntarily departed from God and for all who, without repentance, persevere in apostasy, then, by means of a man of this sort, he, as if already condemned, blasphemes that God who inflicts judgment upon him, and imputes the sin of his apostasy to his Maker, instead of to his own will and predilection.

(Irenaeus: *Heresies*, v. 26.)

---

[984] [Milton, Pens., line 93.] {The following is supplied in some other versions:

And of those demons that are found
In fire, air, flood, or under ground}

IV

Expounding the reason of the incessant plotting of the devil against us, he declares: Before the advent of the Lord, the devil did not so plainly know the measure of his own punishment, inasmuch as the divine prophets had but enigmatically announced it; as, for instance, Isaiah, who in the person of the Assyrian tragically revealed the course to be followed against the devil. But when the Lord appeared, and the devil clearly understood that eternal fire was laid up and prepared for him and his angels, he then began to plot without ceasing against the faithful, being desirous to have many companions in his apostasy, that he might not by himself endure the shame of condemnation, comforting himself by this cold and malicious consolation.

(From the writings of John of Antioch.)[985]

V

And Justin of Neapolis, a man who was not far separated from the apostles either in age or excellence, says that that which is mortal is inherited, but that which is immortal inherits; and that the flesh indeed dies, but the kingdom of heaven lives.

(From Methodius *On the Resurrection*, in Photius.)[986]

VI

Neither is there straitness with God, nor anything that is not absolutely perfect.

(From ms. of the writings of Justin.)[987]

VII

We shall not injure God by remaining ignorant of Him, but shall deprive ourselves of His friendship.[988]

---

[985] {The original editors did not provide a more specific citation.}

[986] {The original editors did not provide a more specific citation.}

[987] {The original editors did not provide a more specific citation.}

[988] {The lack of citation to the source of the fragment is in the original.}

VIII

The unskillfulness of the teacher proves destructive to his disciples, and the carelessness of the disciples entails danger on the teacher, and especially should they owe their negligence to his want of knowledge.[989]

IX

The soul can with difficulty be recalled to those good things from which it has fallen, and is with difficulty dragged away from those evils to which it has become accustomed. If at any time thou showest a disposition to blame thyself, then perhaps, through the medicine of repentance, I should cherish good hopes regarding thee. But when thou altogether despisest fear, and rejectest with scorn the very faith of Christ, it were better for thee that thou hadst never been born from the womb.

(From the writings of John of Damascus.)[990]

X

By the two birds[991] Christ is denoted, both dead as man, and living as God. He is likened to a bird, because He is understood and declared to be from above, and from heaven. And the living bird, having been dipped in the blood of the dead one, was afterwards let go. For the living and divine Word was in the crucified and dead temple [of the body], as being a partaker of the passion, and yet impassible to God.

By that which took place in the running[992] water, in which the wood and the hyssop and the scarlet were dipped, is set forth the bloody passion of Christ on the Cross for the salvation of those who are sprinkled with the Spirit, and the water, and the blood. Wherefore the material for purification was not provided chiefly with reference to leprosy, but with regard to the forgiveness of sins, that both leprosy might be understood to be an emblem of sin, and the things which were sacrificed an emblem of Him who was to be sacrificed for sins.

---

[989] {The lack of citation to the source of the fragment is in the original.}

[990] {The original editors did not provide a more specific citation.}

[991] See Leviticus 14:49-58.

[992] Literally, "living."

For this reason, consequently, he ordered that the scarlet should be dipped at the same time in the water, thus predicting that the flesh should no longer possess its natural [evil] properties. For this reason, also, were there the two birds, the one being sacrificed in the water, and the other dipped both in the blood and in the water, and then sent away, just as is narrated also respecting the goats.

The goat that was sent away presented a type of Him who taketh away the sins of men. But the two contained a representation of the one economy of God incarnate. For He was wounded for our transgressions, and He bare the sins of many, and He was delivered for our iniquities.

(From ms. of writings of Justin.)[993]

XI

When God formed man at the beginning, He suspended the things of nature on His will, and made an experiment by means of one commandment. For He ordained that, if he kept this, he should partake of immortal existence; but if he transgressed it, the contrary should be his lot.[994] Man having been thus made, and immediately looking towards transgression, naturally became subject to corruption. Corruption then becoming inherent in nature, it was necessary that He who wished to save should be one who destroyed the efficient cause of corruption. And this could not otherwise be done than by the life which is according to nature being united to that which had received the corruption, and so destroying the corruption, while preserving as immortal for the future that which had received it. It was therefore necessary that the Word should become possessed of a body, that He might deliver us from the death of natural corruption. For if, as ye[995] say, He had simply by a nod warded off death from us, death indeed would not have approached us on account of the expression of His will; but none the less would we again have become corruptible, inasmuch as we carried about in ourselves that natural corruption.

(Leontius *against Eutychians*, etc., book ii.)

---

[993] {The original editors did not provide a more specific citation.}

[994] {See Genesis 2:16-17.}

[995] The Gentiles are here referred to, who saw no necessity for the incarnation. {This reference appears to be to pagan Gentiles, not those Gentiles who were illumined and had become Christians.}

XII

As it is inherent in all bodies formed by God to have a shadow, so it is fitting that God, who is just, should render to those who choose what is good, and to those who prefer what is evil, to everyone according to his deserts.

(From the writings of John of Damascus.)[996]

XIII

He speaks not of the Gentiles in foreign lands, but concerning [the people] who agree with the Gentiles, according to that which is spoken by Jeremiah:

> ***It is a bitter thing for thee, that thou hast forsaken Me, saith the Lord thy God, that of old thou hast broken thy yoke, and torn asunder thy bands, and said, I will not serve Thee, but will go to every high hill, and underneath every tree, and there shall I become dissolute in my fornication.***[997]

(From ms. of the writings of Justin.)[998]

XIV

Neither shall light ever be darkness as long as light exists, nor shall the truth of the things pertaining to us be controverted. For truth is that than which nothing is more powerful. Every one who might speak the truth, and speaks it not, shall be judged by God.

(Ms. and works of John of Damascus.)[999]

XV

And the fact that it was not said of the seventh day equally with the other days, "And there was evening, and there was morning," is a distinct indication of the consummation which is to take place in it before it is finished, as the fathers declare, especially St. Clement, and Irenaeus, and Justin the martyr and philosopher, who, commenting with exceeding wisdom on the number six of the sixth day, affirms that the intelligent soul of man and his five susceptible senses were the six works of the sixth

---

[996] {The original editors did not provide a more specific citation.}

[997] Jeremiah 2:19, etc. (LXX).

[998] {The original editors did not provide a more specific citation.}

[999] {The original editors did not provide a more specific citation.}

day. Whence also, having discoursed at length on the number six, he declares that all things which have been framed by God are divided into six classes,—viz., into things intelligent and immortal, such as are the angels; into things reasonable and mortal, such as mankind; into things sensitive and irrational, such as cattle, and birds, and fishes; into things that can advance, and move, and are insensible, such as the winds, and the clouds, and the waters, and the stars; into things which increase and are immoveable, such as the trees; and into things which are insensible and immoveable, such as the mountains, the earth, and such like. For all the creatures of God, in heaven and on earth, fall under one or other of these divisions, and are circumscribed by them.

(From the writings of Anastasius.)[1000]

XVI

Sound doctrine does not enter into the hard and disobedient heart; but, as if beaten back, enters anew into itself.[1001]

XVII

As the good of the body is health, so the good of the soul is knowledge, which is indeed a kind of health of soul, by which a likeness to God is attained.

(From the writings of John of Damascus.)[1002]

XVIII

To yield and give way to our passions is the lowest slavery, even as to rule over them is the only liberty.

The greatest of all good is to be free from sin, the next is to be justified; but he must be reckoned the most unfortunate of men, who, while living unrighteously, remains for a long time unpunished.

Animals in harness cannot but be carried over a precipice by the inexperience and badness of their driver, even as by his skillfulness and excellence they will be saved.

[1000] {The original editors did not provide a more specific citation.}
[1001] {The lack of citation to the source of the fragment is in the original.}
[1002] {The original editors did not provide a more specific citation.}

The end contemplated by a philosopher is likeness to God, so far as that is possible.

(From the writings of Antonius Melissa.)[1003]

XIX

[The words] of St. Justin, philosopher and martyr, from the fifth part of his *Apology*:[1004]—I reckon prosperity, O men, to consist in nothing else than in living according to truth. But we do not live properly, or according to truth, unless we understand the nature of things.

It escapes them apparently, that he who has by a true faith come forth from error to the truth, has truly known himself, not, as they say, as being in a state of frenzy, but as free from the unstable and (as to every variety of error) changeable corruption, by the simple and ever identical truth.

(From the writings of John of Damascus.)[1005]

[1003] {The original editors did not provide a more specific citation.}

[1004] It is doubtful if these words are really Justin's, or, if so, from which, or what part, of his *Apologies* they are derived. {Review of the fifth chapters of both *The First Apology* and *The Second Apology* reveals no discussion similar to that referred to is this fragment. See, above, *The Life and Works of Saint Justin Martyr*, last paragraph, for a discussion of the two *Apologies* and their authenticity, as well as that one may be lost.}

[1005] {The original editors did not provide a more specific citation.}

The Martyrdom of Justin and Others

Rusticus the prefect said, "Unless ye obey, ye shall be mercilessly punished."

Justin said, "Through prayer we can be saved on account of our Lord Jesus Christ, even when we have been punished, because this shall become to us salvation and confidence at the more fearful and universal judgment-seat of our Lord and Savior."

Thus also said the other martyrs: "Do what you will, for we are Christians, and do not sacrifice to idols."

The Martyrdom of Justin and Others

The Martyrdom of the Holy Martyrs Justin, Chariton, Charites, Paeon, and Liberianus, who Suffered at Rome

Introductory Notice.

Though nothing is known as to the date or authorship of the following narrative, it is generally reckoned among the most trustworthy of the Martyria. An absurd addition was in some copies made to it, to the effect that Justin died by means of hemlock. Some have thought it necessary, on account of this story, to conceive of two Justins, one of whom, the celebrated defender of the Christian faith whose writings are given in this volume, died through poison, while the other suffered in the way here described, along with several of his friends.[1006] But the description of Justin given in the following account, is evidently such as compels us to refer it to the famous apologist and martyr of the second century.[1007]

Chapter I: *Examination of Justin by the prefect.*

In the time of the lawless partisans of idolatry, wicked decrees were passed against the godly Christians in town and country, to force them to offer libations to vain idols; and accordingly the holy men, having been apprehended, were brought before the prefect of Rome, Rusticus by name. And when they had been brought before his judgment-seat, Rusticus the prefect said to Justin, "Obey the gods at once, and submit to the kings." [1008]

Justin said, "To obey the commandments of our Savior Jesus Christ is worthy neither of blame nor of condemnation."

Rusticus the prefect said, "What kind of doctrines do you profess?"

[1006] {The friends are, in the order introduced in this martyrdom story: Chariton, Charito, Euelpistus, Hierax, Paeon, and Liberianus.}

[1007] {This editor has formatted the following as a dialogue.}

[1008] I.e., the emperors.

Justin said, "I have endeavored to learn all doctrines; but I have acquiesced at last in the true doctrines, those namely of the Christians, even though they do not please those who hold false opinions."

Rusticus the prefect said, "Are those the doctrines that please you, you utterly wretched man?"

Justin said, "Yes, since I adhere to them with right dogma."[1009]

Rusticus the prefect said, "What is the dogma?"

Justin said, "That according to which we worship the God of the Christians, whom we reckon to be one from the beginning, the maker and fashioner of the whole creation, visible and invisible; and the Lord Jesus Christ, the Son of God, who had also been preached beforehand by the prophets as about to be present with the race of men, the herald of salvation and teacher of good disciples.[1010] And I, being a man, think that

---

[1009] *Μετὰ δόγματος ο'ρθοῦ*, orthodoxy.

[1010] {This statement of faith resembles the Nicene Creed, adopted at the First Ecumenical Council in 325 A.D. This observation is noted with gratitude to this editor's priest, Father Gabriel Bilas. The Nicene Creed as we Orthodox Christians recite it today during our Divine Liturgy and other services states:

> *[I] believe in one God, the Father Almighty, Maker of heaven and earth, and of all things visible and invisible. And in one Lord Jesus Christ, the Son of God, the only-begotten, begotten of the Father before all ages. Light of Light; true God of true God; begotten, not made; of one essence with the Father, by whom all things were made; who for us men and for our salvation came down from heaven, and was incarnate of the Holy Spirit and the Virgin Mary, and became man. And He was crucified for us under Pontius Pilate, and suffered, and was buried. And the third day He rose again, according to the Scriptures; and ascended into heaven, and sits at the right hand of the Father; and He shall come again with glory to judge the living and the dead; whose Kingdom shall have no end."*

The Nicene Creed was supplemented in 381 A.D. at the Second Ecumenical Council, which added:

> *And I believe in the Holy Spirit, the Lord, the Giver of Life, who proceeds from the Father; who with the Father and the Son together is worshipped and glorified; who spoke by the prophets. In one Holy, Catholic, and Apostolic Church. I acknowledge one baptism for the remission of sins. I look for the resurrection of the dead, and the life of the world to come. Amen.*

See https://oca.org/orthodoxy/the-orthodox-faith/doctrine-scripture/ the-symbol-of-faith/nicene-creed. For the text as preserved in various sources, see Nicene and

what I can say is insignificant in comparison with His boundless divinity, acknowledging a certain prophetic power,[1011] since it was prophesied concerning Him of whom now I say that He is the Son of God. For I know that of old the prophets foretold His appearance among men."

Chapter II : *Examination of Justin continued.*

Rusticus the prefect said, "Where do you assemble?"

Justin said, "Where each one chooses and can: for do you fancy that we all meet in the very same place? Not so; because the God of the Christians is not circumscribed by place; but being invisible, fills heaven and earth, and everywhere is worshipped and glorified by the faithful."

Rusticus the prefect said, "Tell me where you assemble, or into what place do you collect your followers?"

Justin said, "I live above one Martinus, at the Timiotinian Bath; and during the whole time (and I am now living in Rome for the second time) I am unaware of any other meeting than his. And if any one wished to come to me, I communicated to him the doctrines of truth."

Rusticus said, "Are you not, then, a Christian?"

Justin said, "Yes, I am a Christian."

Chapter III: *Examination of Chariton and others.*

Then said the prefect Rusticus to Chariton, "Tell me further, Chariton, are you also a Christian?"

Chariton said, "I am a Christian by the command of God."

Rusticus the prefect asked the woman Charito, "What say you, Charito?"

Charito said, "I am a Christian by the grace of God."

Rusticus said to Euelpistus, "And what are you?"

Post-Nicene Fathers, v. 14, Second Series, The Seven Ecumenical Councils of the Undivided Church: Their Canons and Dogmatice Decrees, Together with the Canons of All the Local Synods Which Have Received Ecumenical Acceptance, Henry R. Percival, M.A., D.D., ed., (1900), (reprinted by Hendrickson Publishers, Inc. (Peabody, 1994, 1995)), pp. 3, 163-65.}

[1011] That is, that a prophetic inspiration is required to speak worthily of Christ.

Euelpistus, a servant of Caesar, answered, "I too am a Christian, having been freed by Christ; and by the grace of Christ I partake of the same hope."

Rusticus the prefect said to Hierax, "And you, are you a Christian?"

Hierax said, "Yes, I am a Christian, for I revere and worship the same God."

Rusticus the prefect said, "Did Justin make you Christians?"

Hierax said, "I was a Christian, and will be a Christian."

And Paeon stood up and said, "I too am a Christian."

Rusticus the prefect said, "Who taught you?"

Paeon said, "From our parents we received this good confession."

Euelpistus said, "I willingly heard the words of Justin. But from my parents also I learned to be a Christian."

Rusticus the prefect said, "Where are your parents?"

Euelpistus said, "In Cappadocia."

Rusticus says to Hierax, "Where are your parents?"

And he answered, and said, "Christ is our true father, and faith in Him is our mother; and my earthly parents died; and I, when I was driven from Iconium in Phrygia, came here."

Rusticus the prefect said to Liberianus, "And what say you? Are you a Christian, and unwilling to worship [the gods]?"

Liberianus said, "I too am a Christian, for I worship and reverence the only true God."

Chapter IV: *Rusticus threatens the Christians with death.*

The prefect says to Justin, "Hearken, you who are called learned, and think that you know true doctrines; if you are scourged and beheaded, do you believe you will ascend into heaven?"

Justin said, "I hope that, if I endure these things, I shall have His gifts.[1012] For I know that, to all who have thus lived, there abides the divine favor until the completion of the whole world."

Rusticus the prefect said, "Do you suppose, then, that you will ascend into heaven to receive some recompense?"

[1012] Another reading is *δόγματα*, which may be translated, "I shall have what He teaches [us to expect]."

Justin said, "I do not suppose it, but I know and am fully persuaded of it."

Rusticus the prefect said, "Let us, then, now come to the matter in hand, and which presses. Having come together, offer sacrifice with one accord to the gods."

Justin said, "No right-thinking person falls away from piety to impiety."

Rusticus the prefect said, "Unless ye obey, ye shall be mercilessly punished."

Justin said, "Through prayer we can be saved on account of our Lord Jesus Christ, even when we have been punished,[1013] because this shall become to us salvation and confidence at the more fearful and universal judgment-seat of our Lord and Savior."

Thus also said the other martyrs: "Do what you will, for we are Christians, and do not sacrifice to idols."

Chapter V: *Sentence pronounced and executed.*

Rusticus the prefect pronounced sentence, saying, "Let those who have refused to sacrifice to the gods and to yield to the command of the emperor be scourged, and led away to suffer the punishment of decapitation, according to the laws."

The holy martyrs having glorified God, and having gone forth to the accustomed place, were beheaded, and perfected their testimony in the confession of the Savior. And some of the faithful having secretly removed their bodies, laid them in a suitable place,[1014] the grace of our Lord Jesus Christ having wrought along with them, to whom be glory for ever and ever. Amen.

[1013] This passage admits of another rendering. Lord Hailes, following the common Latin version, thus translates: "It was our chief wish to endure tortures for the sake of our Lord Jesus Christ, and so to be saved."

[1014] {For a discussion of some of the locations of Saint Justin Martyr's relics, see above n. 10.}

Saint Perpetua

Stand fast in the faith, and love one another, all of you, and be not offended at my sufferings.

Saint Perpetua
Last words
as testified to by the eyewitness
The Passion of Saints Perpetua and Felicity

Do not fear, I am here with you, and I am laboring with you.

Saint Perpetua
Account of her last vision
The Passion of Saints Perpetua and Felicity

THE PASSION OF SAINTS PERPETUA AND FELICITY

also known as

The Martyrdom of Perpetua and Felicitas

A Brief Introduction to this Reprint

This edition is taken largely from *Latin Christianity: Its Founder, Tertullian*, Volume III, of *The Ante-Nicene Fathers: Translations of the Writings of the Fathers down to A.D. 325*, edited by the Rev. Alexander Roberts, D.D., and James Donaldson, L.L.D., (American Reprint by Charles Scribner's Sons, arranged with brief notes and prefaces by A. Cleveland Coxe, D.D., of the T. & T. Clark, Edinburgh, edition, 1903). Thus, this is the 1885 translation by the Rev. R. E. Wallis, Ph.D.

A number of printed and digital versions of this work were consulted in the creation of this edition, including: the Kindle edition of Church Fathers (2014-06-12), an eBook version of *The Complete Ante-Nicene & Nicene and Post-Nicene Church Fathers Collection*, originally published by Catholic Way Publishing; *The Passion of Perpetua and Felicity*, by Thomas J. Heffernan (Oxford University Press, 2012), and other versions.

In the present volume, slight modifications have been made to Americanize most British spellings (i.e., *honor* rather than *honour*, for example), and to fix obvious typographical errors, to standardize some paragraph styles, and to add paragraph breaks for dialogue and where there seem to be natural transitions of thought.[1015] The original Introductory Notice of the Translator has been retained.

Original footnotes have been retained, but have been renumbered. Biblical quotations are in ***italicized bold*** font, in block

[1015] {Heffernan breaks out chapters differently than Wallis. Except for this editor's paragraphing alterations, the Chapters set by Wallis are retained.}

quotation form if lengthy (more than fifty words), and their citations are given in a more modern citation form.

Material that has been added or replaced by the editor of this present volume is noted by use of the curly bracket symbols "{" and "}" in place of straight brackets ("[" and "]") which, when used, are of the original editors' use. This includes the extensive footnotes added by this editor, many of which provide citation to relevant Scripture and some limited commentary. To the extent Scripture is quoted, this author has generally cited the King James Version and the Orthodox Study Bible.

Every attempt has been made to ensure accurate rendering of Greek text, usually found in the notes. However, this editor acknowledges that some diacritical marks may be rendered incorrectly because in the editions reviewed some marks were difficult to see.

Any remaining errors or Scriptural misunderstandings are this editor's alone, for which she prays for your indulgence.

* * *

Anyone wanting to make a serious study of this *Passion* should consult Heffernan's scholarly work. His work discusses the one Greek manuscript and the nine Latin manuscripts that exist. His volume offers this *Passion* in its Greek text, his recommended Latin text based on reconciling the nine extant Latin texts, and his new English translation, which is one of the most recent translations available. In addition, his work includes an extensive discussion of the persons mentioned in this *Passion* as well as an extremely detailed commentary, elucidating the textual differences between the various texts and providing historical context as well as his personal observations of the area once known as Carthage, where the events of this *Passion* take place. His evident mastery of ancient Roman and Carthaginian culture, laws and practices, coupled with his understanding of ancient writings, enhance his commentary and serve to give weight to his observations and conclusions.

That having been said, Heffernan's new translation has not been reprinted here for a number of reasons, copyright issues aside, those being in the main difficulties in finding equally scholarly discussions of his observations. For, as much as his work is impressive, this editor is not an antiquities scholar, nor fluent in Greek or Latin, and chooses not to accept his theories and conclusions without reviewing scholarly testing by others.

And, most importantly, although Heffernan's treatment includes numerous references to Scripture, they are incomplete and there is evidence that he approaches the text as someone who may not appreciate the sacredness of the text.[1016] A scholarly approach with review and critique of all the various secular and religious attempts to understand this *Passion*, one that touches on Jungian, Positivist, ancient pagan and Roman religious and cultural beliefs, among many other perspectives of other researchers and authors, as well as the view of this *Passion* as mere literature, is all well and good. So too, is his occasional discussion of "the sacred." Nevertheless, he does not seem to write from a *viewpoint* of sacredness, much less from the perspective of one who understands the spiritual reasons to venerate Saints. These are all important because the narratives themselves claim Divine inspiration.[1017]

In short, Heffernan seems to write from the vantage point of an objective outsider *analyzing*, rather than from a Christian confessor or practitioner *explaining*. One can accomplish the latter while noting all the former. However, this seems lacking in his otherwise impressive work, which he could have titled The Passion of *Saints* Perpetua and Felicity, in accordance with Rev. Wallis's translation. But he did not.

[1016] {See, e.g., Heffernan, p.276, where he talks of the Garden of Eden in rather mythological terms. This is just one example of many.}

[1017] {This is implicit in the writings of Saint Perpetua herself and of Saint Saturus, but explicit in the account by the eyewitness, who claims guidance by the Holy Spirit as well as the command of Saint Perpetua, an acknowledged prophetess, thereby making explicit what is implicit in her narrative. See *Passion* Chapter V.3, below.}

Introductory Notice of the Translator
Rev. R. E. Wallis

Nobody, will blame me for placing here the touching history of these Martyrs. It illustrates the period of history we are now considering, and sheds light on the preceding treatise. I can hardly read it without tears, and it ought to make us love "the noble army of martyrs." I think Tertullian was the *editor* of the story, not its author.[1018] Felicitas is mentioned by name in the *De Anima*: and the closing paragraph of this memoir is quite in his style. To these words I need only add that Dr. Routh, who unfortunately decided not to re-edit it, ascribes the first edition to Lucas Holstenius. He was Librarian of the Vatican and died in 1661.[1019] The rest may be learned from this Introductory Notice of the Translator:

Perpetua and Felicitas suffered martyrdom in the reign of Septimius Severus, about the year 202 A.D. Tertullian mentions Perpetua,[1020] and a further clue to the date is given in the allusion to the birthday of "Geta the Caesar," the son of Septimius Severus. There is, therefore, good reason for rejecting the opinion held by some, that they suffered under Valerian and Gallienus. Some think that they suffered at Tuburbium in Mauritania; but the more general opinion is, that Carthage was the scene of their martyrdom.

The "Acta," detailing the sufferings of Perpetua and Felicitas, has been held by all critics to be a genuine document of antiquity. But much difference exists as to who was the compiler. In the writing itself, Perpetua and Saturus are mentioned as having written certain portions of it; and there is no reason to doubt the statement. Who the writer of the remaining portion was, is not known. Some have assigned the work to Tertullian; some have maintained that, whoever the writer was, he was a Montanist, and some have tried to show that both martyrs and narrator

---

1018 Cap. lv. He calls her *fortissima martyr*, and she is one of only two or three contemporary sufferers he mentions by name.

1019 This first paragraph is attributed to the additional introductory material and notes provided for the American edition by A. Cleveland Coxe.

1020 [In the *De Anima*, cap. lv. as see above.]

were Montanists.[1021] The narrator must have been a contemporary; according to many critics, he was an eye-witness of the sufferings of the martyrs. And he must have written the narrative shortly after the events.

Dean Milman says, "There appear strong indications that the acts of these African martyrs are translated from the Greek; at least it is difficult otherwise to account for the frequent untranslated Greek words and idioms in the text.[1022]

The Passion of Perpetua and Felicitas was edited by Petrus Possinus, Rome, 1663; by Henr. Valesius, Paris, 1664; and the Bollandists. The best and latest edition is by Ruissart, whose text is adopted in Gallandi's and Migne's collections of the Fathers.[1023]

[1021] [Yet see the sermons of St. Augustine (if indeed his) on the Passion of these Saints. *Sermon* 281 and 282, opp. *Tom.* v. pp. 1284-5.]

[1022] *History of Christianity*, vol. i. ch. viii.

[1023] {This final paragraph of the introduction by Wallis is not retained in all editions.}

Preface[1024]

If ancient illustrations of faith which both testify to God's grace and tend to man's edification are collected in writing, so that by the perusal of them, as if by the reproduction of the facts, as well God may be honored, as man may be strengthened; why should not new instances be also collected, that shall be equally suitable for both purposes,—if only on the ground that these modern examples will one day become ancient and available for posterity, although in their present time they are esteemed of less authority, by reason of the presumed veneration for antiquity?

But let men look to it, if they judge the power of the Holy Spirit to be one, according to the times and seasons; since some things of later date must be esteemed of more account as being nearer to the very last times, in accordance with the exuberance of grace manifested to the final periods determined for the world. For

> ***in the last days, saith the Lord, I will pour out of My Spirit upon all flesh; and their sons and their daughters shall prophesy. And upon My servants and My handmaidens will I pour out of My Spirit; and your young men shall see visions, and your old men shall dream dreams.***[1025]

And thus we—who both acknowledge and reverence, even as we do the prophecies, modern visions as equally promised to us, and consider the other powers of the Holy Spirit as an agency of the Church for which also He was sent, administering all gifts in all, even as the Lord distributed to everyone[1026] as well needfully collect them in writing, as commemorate them in reading to God's glory;[1027] that so no weakness or despondency

---

[1024] {Preface by the eyewitness or perhaps by Tertullian.}

[1025] Joel 2:28-29. {See also Acts 2:17-18, a paraphrase of Joel.}

[1026] [Both Perpetua and Felicitas were evidently Montanistic in character and impressions, but, the fact that they have never been reputed other than Catholic, goes far to explain Tertullian's position for years after he had withdrawn from communion with the vacillating Victor.] {The prior editors note Montanistic tendencies in these Saints. This editor would urge caution in associating any Saints of the Church with heresies. The phrase, "as the Lord distributed to everyone," is Scriptural. See 1 Corinthians 7:17; see also Romans 12:3.}

[1027] {It appears these accounts were perhaps meant not only to be read, but to be spoken aloud, perhaps to an assembly of the Church, as they evidently were for some time after

of faith may suppose that the divine grace abode only among the ancients, whether in respect of the condescension that raised up martyrs,[1028] or that gave revelations;[1029] since God always carries into effect what He has promised, for a testimony to unbelievers, to believers for a benefit.

And we therefore, what we have heard and handled,[1030] declare also to you, brethren and little children, that as well you who were concerned in these matters may be reminded of them again to the glory of the Lord, as that you who know them by report may have communion with the blessed martyrs, and through them with the Lord Jesus Christ,[1031] to whom be glory and honor, for ever and ever.[1032] Amen.

---

the martyrdom of these Saints. See the *Preface to This Edition*, above. Orthodox churches today still read aloud the martyrdom stories of Saints at some services. This observation is noted with gratitude to Father Gabriel Bilas, this editor's priest.}

[1028] {Of course the first Christian martyr was Saint Stephen, which by Saint Perpetua's time would have taken place nearly two centuries earlier and thus would seem ancient to them; see Acts 7:55-60.}

[1029] {There are numerous prophecies throughout Scripture, see e.g., the various prophets and the Gospels. Saint Paul acknowledges a number of gifts, including the gift of prophecy at 1 Corinthians 12:8, 10, 28, and indicates that those gifted with prophecy particularly edify the Church. See 1 Corinthians 14:4-5; see also 1 Timothy 4:14. He counsels Christians to covet the best gifts at 1 Corinthians 12:31.}

[1030]{Compare 1 Corinthians 15:1. Again, this seems to indicate the account should be both read and spoken aloud, as Saint Paul wrote in Romans 10:17 that "faith cometh by hearing, and hearing by the word of God." KJV. This passage seems also to refer to those who actually witnessed the martyrdom of Saint Perpetua and her companions, or perhaps those who knew them. See 1 John 1:1, 3.}

[1031] {Perhaps a reference to intercessory prayer to the Saints, and maybe even an oblique reference to veneration of the icons and relics of our Saints.}

[1032] [St. Augustine takes pains to remind us that these *Acta* are not canonical. *De Anima*, cap. 2, opp. *Tom*. x. p. 481.]

Chapter I

Argument: ***When the Saints Were Apprehended, St. Perpetua Successfully Resisted Her Father's Pleading, Was Baptized with the Others, Was Thrust into a Filthy Dungeon. Anxious About Her Infant, by a Vision Granted to Her, She Understood that Her Martyrdom Would Take Place Very Shortly.***

1.[1033] The young catechumens,[1034] Revocatus and his fellow-servant Felicitas, Saturninus and Secundulus, were apprehended. And among them also was Vivia[1035] Perpetua, respectably born, liberally educated, a married matron, having a father and mother and two brothers, one of whom, like herself, was a catechumen,[1036] and a son an infant at the breast. She herself was about twenty-two years of age.

From this point onward she shall herself narrate the whole course of her martyrdom, as she left it described by her own hand and with her own mind.

2.[1037] "While" says she, "we were still with the persecutors, and my father, for the sake of his affection for me, was persisting in seeking to turn me away, and to cast me down from the faith,—'Father,' said I, 'do you see, let us say, this vessel lying here to be a little pitcher, or something else?'

And he said, 'I see it to be so.'

And I replied to him, 'Can it be called by any other name than what it is?'[1038]

[1033] {Author of this introductory section is perhaps the eyewitness or Tertullian, as discussed in the *Preface to This Edition*, above.}

[1034] {The names of all these martyrs are reportedly found in inscriptions from Carthage.}

[1035] {Sometimes translated "Vibia."}

[1036] {A catechumen is someone preparing for his or her baptism into the Orthodox Church. Today, by virtue of *ekonomia*, it may also refer to a convert preparing to enter the Orthodox faith via chrismation alone, with such determinations generally being made by bishops on an individual basis in light of the proposed convert's baptismal history in another Christian denomination.}

[1037] {Commencement of the writing as given by Saint Perpetua herself.}

[1038] {Heffernan throughout his commentaries notes that Saint Perpetua was seemingly very well educated and familiar with the important texts of the day, especially for a woman. See, e.g., Heffernan, p.36, 38. This dialogue is similar to Plato and his theory of

And he said, 'No.'

'Neither can I call myself anything else than what I am, a Christian.'[1039]

Then my father, provoked at this saying, threw himself upon me, as if he would tear my eyes out. But he only distressed me, and went away overcome by the devil's arguments.[1040]

Then, in a few days after I had been without my father, I gave thanks to the Lord; and his absence became a source of consolation[1041] to me. In that same interval of a few days we were baptized, and to me the Spirit prescribed that in the water *of baptism* nothing else was to be sought for bodily endurance.[1042]

After a few days we are taken into the dungeon, and I was very much afraid, because I had never felt such darkness. O terrible day! O

---

forms, i.e., that reality is best described not through its actual physical substance but through ideas of it. See Plato's *Republic* and *Cratylus*.}

[1039] {This is reminiscent of Saint Justin Martyr's *Apologies*, reprinted above, wherein he notes Christians were being persecuted solely on this basis (merely being Christian) and not on the basis of some other long-recognized crime (such as murder, robbery, etc.). See also Tertullian's *Apology*, wherein he discusses the same sort of persecution. Numerous accounts of martyrdom reflect imposition of torture or death sentences upon accusations or testimony that one believed in Christ, or a profession of being "a Christian." See, e.g., *The Prologue from Ochrid: Lives of the Saints and Homilies for Every Day of the Year*, Bishop Nikolai Velimirovic, (1928), Translated by Mother Maria (Birmingham, England: Lazarica Press, 1985); *Let the Little Children Come to Me: Stories of Children Martyrs*, Saint John Chrysostomos Greek Orthodox Monastery (Pleasant Prairie, WI, 2002); *Slain for Their Faith: Orthodox Christian Martyrs Under Moslem Oppression*, Leonidas Papadopoulos, (Ellensburg, WA: Leo Papadopoulos, 2013); *Marriage as a Path to Holiness: Lives of Married Saints*, David and Mary Ford, 2nd ed. (Waymart, PA: St. Tikhon's Monastery Press, 1994, 2013).}

[1040] {Her recognition of the devil's role in persuading her father is a foreshadowing of her visions and her ultimate understanding that in the arena she will be fighting with demonic spiritual forces, not mere men.}

[1041] "Refrigeravit," Græce ἀνέπαυσεν, *scil.* "requiem dedit."

[1042] I.e., the grace of martyrdom. {Thus, this is a foreshadowing of her martyrdom and perhaps as well the coming of her visions. See Chapter I.3, below. Further, it may be recognition of Saint Paul's discussion in Romans 6:3-11 that in baptism into Christ we are also baptized into his death and resurrection into a new life. Heffernan notes in his commentary that this revelatory understanding from the Holy Spirit is evidence of her gift of endurance for the forthcoming physical torture she is about to endure. See Heffernan, p. 160.}

the fierce heat of the shock of the soldiery, because of the crowds![1043] I was very unusually distressed by my anxiety for my infant.

There were present there Tertius and Pomponius, the blessed deacons who ministered to us, and had arranged by means of a gratuity[1044] that we might be refreshed[1045] by being sent out for a few hours into a pleasanter part of the prison. Then going out of the dungeon, all attended to their own wants.[1046]

I suckled my child,[1047] which was now enfeebled with hunger. In my anxiety for it, I addressed my mother and comforted my brother, and commended to their care my son. I was languishing because I had seen them languishing on my account.

Such solicitude I suffered for many days, and I obtained leave[1048] for my infant to remain in the dungeon with me; and forthwith I grew strong and was relieved from distress and anxiety about my infant; and the dungeon became to me as it were a palace,[1049] so that I preferred being there to being elsewhere."

3. "Then my brother said to me, 'My dear sister, you are already in a position of great dignity, and are such that you may ask for a vision,[1050] and that it may be made known to you whether this is to result in a passion or an escape.[1051]

1043 {Heffernan observes that Saint Perpetua's descriptions of her incarceration here and throughout this *Passion* are consistent with what is known of such prisons of the time and lend credence to this *Passion*'s authenticity as historical fact rather than a mere romantic fiction. See Heffernan, e.g., pp. 161-62.}

1044 {I.e., a bribe to or an extortion by the guards.}

1045 {This is arguably not mere physical refreshment, but spiritual refreshment as well, especially since it follows closely on the heels of baptism. See Luke 16:24; Acts 3:19. It may also include emotional or psychological refreshment in terms of being free from her father's persecutions some days earlier, or of a combination of all these types of relief.}

1046 Sibi vacabant.

1047 {Heffernan finds this odd because Roman upper-class women did not nurse their own children but gave them to wet-nurses. See Heffernan, p. 147}

1048 {Saint Perpetua's focus here is on her own power to obtain by her own agency, with the grace of God, relief from the authorities.}

1049 {Again, this may be attributed to the spiritual refreshment following baptism. See above, nn. 1042, 1045.}

1050 {Heffernan speculates that Saint Perpetua may have been known as a prophetess prior to arrest and that this may have led to her arrest. That she agrees to seek such a vision and notes her privilege of speaking with the Lord is some evidence of this. See

And I, who knew that I was privileged to converse with the Lord, whose kindnesses I had found to be so great, boldly promised him, and said, 'Tomorrow I will tell you.' And I asked, and this was what was shown me.[1052]

I saw a golden ladder[1053] of marvelous height, reaching up even to heaven, and very narrow,[1054] so that persons could only ascend it one by one; and on the sides of the ladder was fixed every kind of iron weapon.[1055] There were there swords, lances, hooks, daggers; so that if any one went up carelessly, or not looking upwards, he would be torn to pieces and his flesh would cleave to the iron weapons.

And under the ladder itself was crouching a dragon[1056] of wonderful size, who lay in wait[1057] for those who ascended, and frightened them from the ascent.

And Saturus[1058] went up first, who had subsequently delivered himself up freely on our account, not having been present at the time that we were taken prisoners.

And he attained the top of the ladder, and turned towards me, and said to me, 'Perpetua, I am waiting for[1059] you; but be careful that the dragon do not bite you.'

Heffernan, pp. 167, 170-71. See also Joel 2:28 and Acts 2:17, that dreams are from God, from a pouring out of the Spirit }

[1051] Commeatus. {Heffernan suggests that the question posed to her is one of whether they will be martyred or will be apostates. See Heffernan, p. 171.}

[1052] {See Matthew 7:7, "Ask, and it shall be given you."}

[1053] {This is reminiscent of Jacob's ladder. See Genesis 28:12; see also John 1:51. It also may be a type of the Cross, which we are told by Jesus Christ our Lord to take up. See Matthew 10:38, 16:24; Luke 9:23, 14:27.}

[1054] {Reference to the ladder being "very narrow" is reminiscent of the narrow gate in Matthew 7:13-14. See also Luke 13:24.}

[1055] {Iron and iron weapons are types for the world as the domain of the devil.}

[1056] {Compare Isaiah 27:1, Psalm 74:13, Revelation 12:3-4; 13:1-7. See also Genesis 3:13-15.}

[1057] {This is not unlike the serpent in the Garden of Eden. See Genesis 3:1.}

[1058] {Heffernan's translation identifies Saint Saturus as Saint Perpetua's Christian teacher. See Heffernan, p. 177. One Roman Catholic Church source also identifies him as her instructor in the faith. See https://www.catholic.org/saints/saint.php?saint_id=48. The Orthodox Church in America website identifies Saint Saturus as Saint Perpetua's brother who was arrested with her. See https://oca.org/saints/all-lives/2016/02/01. It is unclear to this editor whether Saint Saturus is a biological brother or a brother in Christ.}

[1059] "Sustineo," Græce ὑπομένω, *scil*. "exspecto."

And I said, 'In the name of the Lord Jesus Christ,[1060] he shall not hurt me.'[1061] And from under the ladder itself, as if in fear of me, he slowly lifted up his head; and as I trod upon the first step, I trod upon his head.[1062]

And I went up, and I saw an immense extent of garden, and in the midst of the garden a white-haired man sitting in the dress of a shepherd,[1063] of a large stature, milking sheep; and standing around were many thousand white-robed ones.[1064]

And he raised his head, and looked upon me, and said to me, 'Thou art welcome, daughter.'

And he called me, and from the cheese as he was milking he gave me as it were a little cake,[1065] and I received it with folded hands; and I ate it, and all who stood around said Amen.

And at the sound of their voices I was awakened, still tasting a sweetness which I cannot describe.

And I immediately related this to my brother, and we understood that it was to be a passion, and we ceased henceforth to have any hope in this world."[1066]

1060 {For references to other invocations of Christ's Name see Mark 9:38-39; Luke 10:17; Acts 2:38, 4:10.}

1061 {See Luke 10:17.}

1062 {Compare Genesis 3:15; Psalm 18:40 ("neck"). See also Saint Augustine's *Sermon* 280.}

1063 This was an ordinary mode of picturing our Lord in the oratories and on the sacred vessels of those days. [This passage will recall the allegory of Hermas, with which the martyr was doubtless familiar.] {For Christ as Shepherd see Psalm 23:1; Isaiah 40:11, 63:11; Matthew 18:12; Luke 15:4; John 10:11; Hebrews 13:20.}

1064 {Perhaps refers to other martyrs; see, e.g. Revelation 6:9-11.}

1065 {Some translations render this as Saint Perpetua taking a mouthful of milk, noting that Tertullian comments on the consumption of milk after baptism in *De Corona* 3.3. It could also relate to the promised land of milk and honey in Exodus 3:8, or meant to show a miracle of changing milk to cheese, such as changing water into wine as in John 2:1-11. See Heffernan, pp. 180-81 (also discussing Eucharist analogy).}

1066 {At this point, Saint Perpetua is distancing from worldly things and turning ever more to the spiritual and her hope and faith in Jesus Christ for an eternal life after being martyred.}

Chapter II

Argument: ***Perpetua, When Besieged by Her Father, Comforts Him. When Led with Others to the Tribunal, She Avows Herself a Christian, and is Condemned with the Rest to the Wild Beasts. She Prays for Her Brother Dinocrates, Who Was Dead.***

1. "After a few days there prevailed a report that we should be heard. And then my father came to me from the city, worn out with anxiety. He came up to me, that he might cast me down, saying,

'Have pity my daughter, on my grey hairs. Have pity on your father, if I am worthy to be called a father by you. If with these hands I have brought you up to this flower of your age, if I have preferred you to all your brothers, do not deliver me up to the scorn of men. Have regard to your brothers, have regard to your mother and your aunt, have regard to your son, who will not be able to live after you. Lay aside your courage, and do not bring us all to destruction; for none of us will speak in freedom if you should suffer anything.'

These things said my father in his affection, kissing my hands, and throwing himself at my feet; and with tears he called me not Daughter, but Lady.

And I grieved over the grey hairs of my father, that he alone of all my family would not rejoice over my passion.[1067]

And I comforted him, saying, 'On that scaffold[1068] whatever God wills shall happen. For know that we are not placed in our own power, but in that of God.'[1069]

[1067] {Presumably by this statement she is testifying that her family is Christian or studying as catachumens to enter the Church, with the exception of her father. And although she is married, she does not refer to her husband at all. It is not clear if "all my family" is meant to include her husband. If so, he too is a Christian or striving to become one. If not, then presumably he is a Roman pagan, or perhaps deceased or divorced. See also discussion above n.23. Heffernan discusses marriage customs of the day , especially as to the custody of the child, and the absence of the husband in the narrative. See Heffernan, pp. 22-28, 147-48. The concern of the father may be that the entire family will be punished if she fails to deny Christ and is sentenced to death.}

[1068] "Catasta," a raised platform on which the martyrs were places either for trial or torture.

[1069] {Saint Perpetua has now more fully placed all her faith in the Lord. Here she also is, in accord with Scripture, giving up all family relationships to follow Christ, come what may

And he departed from me in sorrow."

2. "Another day, while we were at dinner, we were suddenly taken away to be heard, and we arrived at the town-hall. At once the rumor spread through the neighborhood of the public place, and an immense number of people were gathered together. We mount the platform. The rest were interrogated, and confessed.

Then they came to me, and my father immediately appeared with my boy, and withdrew me from the step, and said in a supplicating tone, 'Have pity on your babe.'

And Hilarianus the procurator,[1070] who had just received the power of life and death in the place of the proconsul Minucius Timinianus, who was deceased, said, 'Spare the grey hairs of your father, spare the infancy of your boy, offer sacrifice for the well-being of the emperors.'

And I replied, 'I will not do so.'

Hilarianus said, 'Are you a Christian?'

And I replied, 'I am a Christian.'[1071]

And as my father stood there to cast me down *from the faith*,[1072] he was ordered by Hilarianus to be thrown down, and was beaten with rods.

And my father's misfortune grieved me as if I myself had been beaten,[1073] I so grieved for his wretched old age.[1074]

---

for them, including losing one's own life. See Matthew 8:22; 10:35-39. Thus, she moves one step closer to her martyrdom for Christ.}

[1070] {Hilarianus is a historical figure noted by Tertullian in *Ad Scapulam* iii. 1.}

[1071] {See *The Martyrdom of Justin and Others*, above, Ch.II-III, wherein nearly the exact questions and responses occur, and authorities listed in n. 1039, above.}

[1072] {It would seem that Saint Perpetua views her father's continued efforts to save her physically, and his family from the shame of her death sentence, as the work of the devil. There are also undertones of the beating as a divine rebuke and punishment. See Psalm 2:9 (iron). For reference to rods, see Exodus 4:17, where Moses is told to use a rod as a means to work signs, see also Exodus 7:12. But see Exodus 4:2-4, where the rod is first turned into a serpent and then back into a rod when Moses is told by God to pick up the serpent by the tail. For references to rods in the last days, see Revelation 2:27; 12:5, 19:15 (all referencing a rod of iron).}

[1073] {Compare her sense of pain in sympathy with her father's beating to her lack of perception of her own pain in the arena, below.}

[1074] [St. Augustine opp. iv. 541.]

The procurator then delivers judgment on all of us, and condemns us to the wild beasts, and we went down cheerfully to the dungeon.[1075]

Then, because my child had been used to receive suck from me, and to stay with me in the prison, I send Pomponius the deacon to my father to ask for the infant, but my father would not give it him.

And even as God willed it, the child no long desired the breast, nor did my breast cause me uneasiness, lest I should be tormented by care for my babe and by the pain of my breasts at once."[1076]

3. "After a few days, whilst we were all praying, on a sudden, in the middle of our prayer, there came to me a word, and I named Dinocrates; and I was amazed that that name had never come into my mind until then, and I was grieved as I remembered his misfortune.[1077]

And I felt myself immediately to be worthy, and to be called on to ask on his behalf.[1078] And for him I began earnestly to make supplication, and to cry with groaning to the Lord.[1079]

[1075] {Saint Perpetua is the last to confess faith. All having confessed, she and her companions are now destined to martyrdom without a single one of them succumbing to apostasy, the concern for which her brother requested a vision earlier. Also, see Acts 5:41, where the Apostles rejoiced for having suffered for Christ, except that they rejoiced *after* their beating, unlike Saint Perpetua and her companions who rejoice at merely being sentenced. See also Matthew 5:12.}

[1076] {Her son is the last living family member with whom she must break ties to truly follow Christ. See Matthew 8:22, 10:35-39. She views the child no longer desiring her breast and the lack of breast pain as gifts from God, and which are miraculous. This is also a step toward physical distance from worldly matters. Heffernan discusses the medical effects of terminating breastfeeding and suggests the author's knowledge of such effects is a further indication of the authenticity of Saint Perpetua's account. See Heffernan, pp. 196, 205-207}

[1077] {Note this memory came to her during communal prayer.}

[1078] [The story in 2 Maccabees 12:40-45, is there narrated as a thought suggested to the soldiers under Judas, and not discouraged by him, though it concerned men guilty of idolatry and dying in mortal sin, by vengeance of God. It may have occurred to early Christians that their heathen kindred might, therefore, not be beyond the visitations of Divine compassion. But, obviously, even were it not an Apocryphal text, it can have no bearing whatever on the case of Christians. The doctrine of Purgatory is that nobody dying in mortal sin can have the benefit of its discipline, or any share in the prayers and oblations of the Faithful, whatever.] {Orthodox Christians, and the Eastern Church, do not believe in the Roman Catholic doctrine of Purgatory. They continue to uphold the early and ancient faith that there is an intermediate stage in which the soul, newly freed from

Without delay,[1080] on that very night, this was shown to me in a vision.[1081]

I saw Dinocrates going out from a gloomy place, where also there were several others, and he was parched and very thirsty,[1082] with a filthy countenance and pallid color, and the wound on his face which he had when he died.

This Dinocrates had been my brother after the flesh, seven years of age[1083] who died miserably with disease—his face being so eaten out with cancer, that his death caused repugnance to all men.

For him I had made my prayer, and between him and me there was a large interval,[1084] so that neither of us could approach to the other.

---

the flesh, 'pre-tastes" heaven and hell based on the individual's conduct while in the flesh on earth. As such, there is no possibility of repentance after death. The Orthodox, generally admit, however, that death and the hereafter are a mystery.}

1079 {Saint Perpetua implies the origin of her mind turning to memories of her deceased brother is Divine, rather than of her own accord, that she is called by God to pray for him, and thus necessarily has such power that she may pray for the benefit of non-Christians. See notes following below. See also Heffernan, pp. 207, 211-16.}

1080 {She then records that God responds to her immediately, implying her special favor with God. See also Joel 2:28 and Acts 2:17, that dreams are from God, from a pouring out of the Spirit.}

1081 "Oromate." [This vision, it must be observed, has nothing to do with the prayers for the *Christian* dead, for this brother of Perpetua was a heathen child whom she supposed to be the *Inferi*. It illustrates the anxieties Christians felt for those of their kindred who had not died in the Lord; even for children of seven years of age. Could the gulf be bridged and they received into Abraham's bosom? This dream of Perpetua comforted her with a trust that so it should be. Of course this story has been used fraudulently, to help a system of which these times knew nothing. Cyprian says expressly: "Apud Inferos confessio non est, nec exomologesis *illic fieri* potest." *Epistola lii.* p. 98. Opp Paris, 1574. In the Edinburgh series (translations) this epistle is numbered 51, and elsewhere 54.] {The Latin *di inferi* are the gods below, Roman deities of death and the underworld.}

1082 {Thirst is symbolic of a desire for the living water of Jesus Christ. See John 4:10-15 (conversation between Jesus and the Samaritan woman at the well); see also Jeremiah 2:13, 17:13; Revelation 7:17.}

1083 [There is not the slightest reason to suppose that this child had been baptized: the father a heathen and Perpetua herself a recent catechumen. Elucidation.] {Other translators agree, having noted Dinocrates likely died before baptism. According to Saint Augustine, the boy sinned after baptism. See *De origine animae* 1.12. Heffernan also implies Dinocrates was non-Christian. See Heffernan, p. 207.}

1084 "Diadema," or rather "diastema." [Borrowed from Luke 16:26. But that gulf could not be passed according to the evangelist.] {The story in Luke told by Jesus is that of the beggar Lazarus and the rich man.}

And moreover, in the same place where Dinocrates was, there was a pool full of water, having its brink higher than was the stature of the boy; and Dinocrates raised himself up as if to drink.[1085]

And I was grieved that, although that pool held water, still, on account of the height to its brink, he could not drink.[1086]

And I was aroused, and knew that my brother was in suffering.[1087] But I trusted that my prayer would bring help to his suffering; and I prayed for him every day until we passed over into the prison of the camp, for we were to fight in the camp-show.

Then was the birth-day of Geta Caesar, and I made my prayer for my brother day and night, groaning and weeping that he might be granted to me."[1088]

4. "Then, on the day on which we remained in fetters,[1089] this was shown to me.

I saw that that place which I had formerly observed to be in gloom was now bright; and Dinocrates, with a clean body well clad, was finding refreshment.[1090]

[1085] {This pool of water is reminiscent of the pool at Bethesda where Jesus healed the lame man. See John 5:1-15.}

[1086] {Saint Perpetua's vision is deeply spiritual, reflecting her understanding that her brother has not received Christian salvation, but continues striving for it, water being symbolic not only of baptism but of Jesus Christ as the living water. See John 4:10-15 (conversation between Jesus and the Samaritan woman at the well); see also Jeremiah 2:13, 17:13; Revelation 7:17. Her vision may in some sense also reflect her present conditions of life in an actual hellish prison on earth and her striving toward her martyrdom and union with Christ, although having recently been baptized, see above, she is not in need of baptism as such, but arguably still thirsts for Jesus as living water.}

[1087] {It is not clear here whether she believes Dinocrates is suffering only physically, as she describes that he is in a physical condition of being thirsty, filthy and pale and still bearing his wounds (not a scar), or suffering spiritually as discussed above, or both.}

[1088] {Scripture makes many references to groaning and weeping. See, e.g. Exodus 2:24, 6:5; Psalm 6:8, 30:5, 38:9, 79:11, 102:20; Ezra 10:1; Jeremiah 31:9, 50:4; Acts 7:34. Even when Jesus groaned, God heard Him, see John 11:38-41; the Spirit also groans, see Romans 8:26.}

[1089] "Nervo." {Heffernan discusses at great length the meaning of her being placed in stocks, thereby being rendered helpless, as well as historical facts about such practices. See Heffernan, pp. 227-32.}

[1090] {See discussion of being refreshed, above nn. 1042, 1045, 1049.}

And where there had been a wound, I saw a scar;[1091] and that pool which I had before seen, I saw now with its margin lowered even to the boy's navel. And one drew water from the pool incessantly, and upon its brink was a goblet filled with water; and Dinocrates drew near and began to drink from it, and the goblet did not fail.[1092]

And when he was satisfied, he went away from the water to play joyously, after the manner of children, and I awoke.[1093]

Then I understood that he was translated from the place of punishment."[1094]

[1091] {Here, Saint Perpetua focuses on the physical state and changes in her brother's location. What was all doom and gloom is now bright and his body has been healed, even his wound is now just a scar. There is a sense of light, consistent with Scripture that Jesus is the light of the world and the light of life, see John 8:12, and that we as Christians, hence also Saint Perpetua, are lights in this world, see Philippians 2:15; see also Proverbs 4:18; Matthew 5:14. Her prayers, the content of which she does not reveal, are, to the extent of his physical well-being, answered in full. Also of note is that it seems her understanding of the Christian afterlife includes possession of a physical body cured of its defects. This is certainly in accord with Saint Justin Martyr, see above, *On the Resurrection*. However, she does not go so far as to describe his body in glorious terms, see, e.g., Philippians 3:21.}

[1092] {Again, unfailing water that quenches his thirst seems reminiscent of the Samaritan woman at the well in that she seeks the water which would allow her to never need to walk to the earthly well where she now draws her water, the very living water that Jesus Christ promises. See John 4:10, 14-15. Here, it is quite clear that Saint Perpetua is shown that her prayers for her brother's spiritual condition are also answered, although she never reveals what she prayed for on her brother's behalf. Curiously, Heffernan does not discuss the Scriptural importance of light, nor the obvious connections with the story of the Samaritan woman at the well and Christ being the living water. Note that the supply of water is endless, it did not fail, and is thus perfect.}

[1093] {See Isaiah 12:3, "with joy shall ye draw water out of the wells of salvation."}

[1094] {She trusts now that her brother has been saved through her prayers, again revealing her special relationship with God and the spiritual powers bestowed upon her.}

Chapter III

Argument: ***Perpetua is Again Tempted by Her Father. Her Third[1095] Vision, Wherein She is Led Away to Struggle Against an Egyptian. She Fights, Conquers, and Receives the Reward.***

1. "Again, after a few days, Pudens, a soldier, an assistant overseer[1096] of the prison, who began to regard us in great esteem, perceiving that the great power of God was in us, admitted many brethren to see us, that both we and they might be mutually refreshed.

And when the day of the exhibition drew near, my father, worn with suffering, came in to me, and began to tear out his beard, and to throw himself on the earth, and to cast himself down on his face, and to reproach his years, and to utter such words as might move all creation.[1097]

I grieved for his unhappy old age."[1098]

2. "The day before that on which we were to fight, I saw in a vision that Pomponius the deacon came hither to the gate of the prison, and knocked vehemently.[1099] I went out to him, and opened the gate[1100]

[1095] {This is actually a fourth vision, as she had two separate visions of her brother Dinocrates.}

[1096] Optio.

[1097] {This is the last interaction of Saint Perpetua with her father. While she has depicted herself throughout as a spiritually powerful Christian, her father's entreaties are utterly ineffective; she views them as worldly efforts of a pagan not inspired of God and therefore utterly useless.}

[1098] [St. Aug. opp. *Tom*. v. 1284.] {This perfunctory statement seals her break with her family to follow Christ. See Matthew 8:22, 10:35-39. Her statement of grieving at his old age is in part her grieving for his failure to leave behind his pagan ways, his failure to take on a new Way, that of Christ, and not just her grieving over his conduct or that this is their last meeting, because she is now clearly well on her path away from the worldly and toward the spiritual. To the extent his entreaties are prayers to his gods, they are powerless idols, works of the devil. Although her father's heart remains hardened to her Christianity, Pudens, her jailor, sees the light of Christ in her and her companions. Interestingly, Pudens' order to allow visitors is not fruit of her own requests. Here, she does not focus on her powers to persuade as she does in much of the prior narrative. This is God working through her to call others to Himself while also using them as an instrument of mercy on her behalf.}

[1099] {Of knocking, see Song of Solomon 5:2; Mathew 7:7-8; Luke 11:9-10, 13:25; Revelation 3:20.}

for him; and he was clothed in a richly ornamented white robe, and he had on manifold calliculae.[1101]

And he said to me, 'Perpetua, we are waiting for you; come!'

And he held his hand to me, and we began to go through rough and winding places.

Scarcely at length had we arrived breathless at the amphitheater, when he led me into the middle of the arena, and said to me, 'Do not fear, I am here with you, and I am laboring with you;'[1102] and he departed.

And I gazed upon an immense assembly in astonishment.

And because I knew that I was given to the wild beasts, I marveled that the wild beasts were not let loose upon me.

Then there came forth against me a certain Egyptian,[1103] horrible in appearance, with his backers, to fight with me.

[1100] {Heffernan translates "door" instead of "gate." See Heffernan, p. 129. Both are found hundreds of times throughout the Old Testament and the New Testament, some referring to Jesus as the door, see Luke 13:25; John 10:7, 9. In Acts 5:19, an angel opens prison doors. See also Revelation 3:8, 20, 4:1. These words are also often symbols or types of the Theotokos and Ever-Virgin Mary. However, the context here does not indicate a reference to the Theotokos.}

[1101] It seems uncertain what may be the meaning of the word. It is variously supposed to signify little round ornaments either of cloth or metal attached to the soldier's dress, or the small bells on the priestly robe. Some also read the word *galliculae*, small sandals. {See also Heffernan, p.257-58.}

[1102] {This is one of the most important Christian messages of this *Passion*, that Jesus labors with us so that we should not fear our trials and tribulations. This sentence is quite similar to God's promise of aid in Isaiah 41:10; see also Joshua 1:9, 10:25; 1 Chronicles 28:20; Psalm 3:6, 56:4, 11, and 118:6; cf. Genesis 46:3, Ruth 3:11. Jesus also promises to be always with his Apostles, see Matthew 28:20, the last verse in the Gospel of Matthew. Interestingly, in light of the upcoming contest with the Egyptian, "do not fear" or similar phrases, such as "be not afraid," are repeated in Deuteronomy, often in the context of bringing to mind what efforts God made to bring His people out of Egypt. See e.g., Deuteronomy 1:29-30; 5:5-6, 7:18, 20:1, 3, 31:6, 8. Such phrases are used in the New Testament by angelic messengers, see Luke 1:13;, 30, 2:10; and by Jesus, see Luke 5:10; and as fulfillment of prophecy of the coming of the Messiah in John 12:15. This editor has chosen to use the message of Pomponius, "Do not fear . . . laboring with you," as an epigraph at the beginning of Saint Perpetua's writing in this volume. See above.}

[1103] {Saint Perpetua's vision of an Egyptian is of great spiritual importance as he represents embodiment of the devil. Scriptural references of Egypt and evil abound: Joseph was sold into slavery in Egypt, Genesis 37:28, then later bought all the people and their land in the time of famine, making servants of them, Genesis 47:19-20, 25; and the Pharaoh of Egypt enslaved God's chosen people, Exodus 1:11, 13-14; Pharaoh was also called a great dragon, see Ezekiel 29:3. The evil of Egypt is also referenced in Revelation 11:8.}

And there came to me, as my helpers and encouragers, handsome youths; and I was stripped,[1104] and became a man.[1105]

Then my helpers[1106] began to rub me with oil,[1107] as is the custom for contest; and I beheld that Egyptian on the other hand rolling in the dust.[1108]

And a certain man came forth, of wondrous height, so that he even over-topped the top of the amphitheater;[1109] and he wore a loose tunic and a purple robe between two bands over the middle of the breast; and he had on *calliculae* of varied form, made of gold and silver;

[1104] {Being stripped was perhaps a common occurrence for the arena, however, it is rather at odds with *putting on* the "armor of God," see Ephesians 6:10-17; see also 1 Thessalonians 5:8, so that we can "endure hardness as a good soldier of God." 2 Timothy 2:3. Heffernan discusses this in terms of eroticism. See Heffernan, p.262.}

[1105] [Concerning these visions, see Augustine, *De Anima*, cap. xviii. *el seq.*] {This is an odd reference. It may have import of becoming like Christ, or have a reference to St. Paul's remarks about there being neither "male or females" in Galatians 3:28. There is also the sense of returning to God as originally in the Garden of Eden, where Eve was naked and came to be out of the rib of Adam, who together are "one flesh." See Genesis 2:21-25 ("they were both naked . . . and were not ashamed"). For additional views, see Heffernan's extended discussion, p. 162.}

[1106] {She seems deliberately obscure here. Her helpers could be fellow Christians, martyrs, or, more likely angels sent to help her. See Psalm 91:11, 103:20. Heffernan translates "helpers" as "supporters" and is of the view that Saint Perpetua likely viewed the beings spiritually. See Heffernan, p.162.}

[1107] {This is akin to an anointing, as of priests, alters, sacrifices, kings, and prophets. See, e.g., Exodus 29:21; 1 Samuel 10:1, 15:1, 16:13; Psalm 23:5, 89:20; Isaiah 61:1; see also Daniel 9:24. Anointing oil is also used for healing. See Mark 6:13; John 9:11. And Jesus was anointed, see Mark 14:8, 16:1; Luke 7:38, 46; John 11:2-3. See also Revelation 3:18. See Heffernan, p. 263, for his discussion of this, which notes the customs by athletes and the erotic aspects of the practice.}

[1108] "Afa" is the Greek word ἁφή, *a grip*; hence used of the yellow sand sprinkled over wrestlers, to enable them to grasp one another. {This vision of the Egyptian wallowing in the dust is a further reference to his serpentine or dragon-like nature as the devil. Heffernan, however, notes the practice of rolling in the dust in athletic contests, especially wrestling matches. See Heffernan, p. 264.}

[1109] {There are angelic, Divine and Christ-like implications here. The man is a messenger, perhaps maker of the rules, almighty in appearance and power, and the one who judges and gives awards and punishments for victor and vanquished. Some angels in Revelation are described as "strong" or "mighty" or "powerful." Compare, e.g., different translations of Revelation 5:2. Heffernan's views on this are at pp. 264-65, where he discusses conflation of pagan and Christian concepts.}

and he carried a rod,[1110] as if he were a trainer of gladiators, and a green branch upon which were apples of gold.[1111]

And he called for silence, and said, 'This Egyptian, if he should overcome this woman, shall kill her with the sword; and if she shall conquer him,[1112] she shall receive this branch.'

Then he departed.

And we drew near to one another, and began to deal out blows. He sought to lay hold of my feet, while I struck at his face with my heels;[1113] and I was lifted up in the air,[1114] and began thus to thrust at him as if spurning the earth.

But when I saw that there was some delay I joined my hands so as to twine my fingers with one another; and I took hold upon his head, and he fell on his face, and I trod upon his head.[1115]

And the people began to shout, and my backers[1116] to exalt.[1117]

And I drew near to the trainer and took the branch; and he kissed me,[1118] and said to me, 'Daughter, peace be with you:'[1119] and I began to go gloriously to the Sanavivarian gate.[1120]

[1110] {See discussion in notes, above, regarding Scriptural references to a rod.}

[1111] {This is reminiscent of the Tree of Life in the Garden of Eden, and its fruit, symbolic of eternal life. See Genesis 2-3, especially Genesis 3:22. See also Revelation 22:2, 14. Heffernan also discusses pagan motifs of apples and the use as rewards to victorious athletes, and as symbols of fertility. See Heffernan, p. 267-68.}

[1112] {It does not appear that she must slay him, just conquer or overcome him. It is Christ who ultimately defeats the devil. Saint Perpetua has claimed a great deal of spiritual power for herself, but she does not claim that sort of ultimate power. Given the prophecies of Christ throughout the Gospels, and in Revelation and elsewhere, the devil remains until the last days. She does not seem to perceive her own time as the last days.}

[1113] {See Genesis 3:15, where God puts enmity between the serpent and Eve and their seed so that " it shall bruise thy head, and thou shalt bruise his heel."}

[1114] {Note that she is not thrown by her adversary, but lifted, presumably by Divine intervention. This invokes her prior representation of Pomponius in her vision saying, "I am here with you, and I am laboring with you."}

[1115] [Psalm 45:5, 60:12, 91:13, 108:13.] {See also above n. 1062.}

[1116] {Here the translator uses the word *backers* rather than *helpers*. Heffernan translates "supporters." See Heffernan, p. 130. Again, there is an intimation of angels. See above n. 1106, and Psalm 148:2, and the many references to angels throughout the Book of Revelation.}

[1117] {This exaltation could be for her or for the power of God, or both. See Psalm 18:46, 21:13, 34:3, 57:5, 89:16, 97:9, 99:9, 118:16, 28; see also 1 Peter 5:6.}

[1118] {See Romans 16:16 and 1 Corinthians 16:20 (the holy kiss), 1 Peter 5:14, (kiss of charity).}

Then I awoke, and perceived that I was not to fight with beasts, but against the devil. Still I knew that the victory was awaiting me.[1121]

This, so far, I have completed several days before the exhibition; but what passed at the exhibition itself let who will write."[1122]

[1119] {See the words of Jesus in John 20:26 where He says, "Peace be with you." See also John 14:27; Romans 12:18, 15:13, 33, 16:20 and in closings of many of the Pauline epistles.}

[1120] This was the way by which the victims spared by the popular clemency escaped from the amphitheater. {Or, as another translator has explained, this gate was for gladiatorial victors and for people who were spared to exit the arena. A different gate was used to carry away dead combatants. The gloriousness with which she exits is reminiscent of Philippians 3:21. For discussion of the amphitheater, in general, and its gates, see Heffernan, p. 271 and *passim*.}

[1121] {Now, her understanding is complete that her battle is ultimately spiritual against the forces of the devil. She also has confidence that her martyrdom is assured. Unstated here is her supreme trust in the assistance of her Lord in the arena the next day. Saint Perpetua wakes from her vision confident that her Lord is with her. She is in the Spirit now, awaiting her martyrdom.}

[1122] {Saint Perpetua's account comes to an end, but clearly with a hope that others will report the outcome, and not just anyone, but fellow Christians are expected to tell the remainder of her life and martyrdom. And her prayer is heard and answered in the following sections. See also the *Preface to this Edition* and the very last paragraph of this *Passion*. The many later editions and reprints of her martyrdom, including this present volume, continue to share her testimony, that of the other martyrs with her, and the eyewitness's record of her fate in the arena.}

Chapter IV

Argument: *Saturus, in a Vision, and Perpetua Being Carried by Angels into the Great Light, Behold the Martyrs. Being Brought to the Throne of God, are Received with a Kiss. They Reconcile Optatus the Bishop and Aspasius the Presbyter.*

1. Moreover, also, the blessed Saturus related this his vision, which he himself committed to writing: —[1123]

"We had suffered," says he, "and we were gone forth from the flesh,[1124] and we were beginning to be borne by four angels into the east;[1125] and their hands touched us not.[1126]

And we floated not supine, looking upwards, but as if ascending a gentle slope.[1127] And being set free,[1128] we at length saw the first

---

[1123] {Who wrote this first sentence is unclear, perhaps the eyewitness or Tertullian. What follows is the portion written by Saint Saturus.}

[1124] {Unlike the accounts of Saint Perpetua's visions, wherein she was alive in her body on earth, the account by Saint Saturus of his vision is clear that they have now left their earthly bodies, that they are souls ascending to God and His heavenly Kingdom. His account is only about the spiritual afterlife with God. It is interesting to note that their souls, however, have all the hallmarks of also being in bodies: they walk about, they see others and light, they hear singing, they speak, they wear clothes, they kiss, they prostrate themselves. Moreover, he does not remark on any wounds sustained during their sufferings. See also Saint Justin Martyr, above, *On the Resurrection*. "Gone forth from the flesh" is also reminiscent of Hebrews 5:7 wherein Saint Paul refers to Christ's earthly time as "in the days of His flesh."}

[1125] {Churches generally face East, especially in the Orthodox tradition. It is the direction from which we expect to see the Second Coming of Christ. See Matthew 24:27. In Orthodox churches, the priest also faces East during the liturgy, along with the people, facing icons of Christ and the Saints rather than looking upon each other; whereas Roman Catholic priests and ministers of other denominations generally face the congregation instead. East is also the location for the Garden of Eden. See Genesis 2:8. Heffernan only notes that the reference is to the Garden of Eden. See Heffernan, p. 276.}

[1126] {Note they rise seemingly without aid of the angels, who merely accompany them as guides, not touching them. See John 20:17, where the risen Christ, who has not yet ascended, instructs Mary Magdalene not to touch His body. But see John 20:27, where Jesus encourages the doubting Thomas to inspect his wounds. Heffernan remarks on verse 17, but does not comment on verse 27. See Heffernan, p. 277. Christ was "taken up" or "carried up" at His Ascension. See Acts 1:9 ; Luke 24:51. The beggar Lazarus is also "carried," see Luke 16:22, but Saints Perpetua and Saturus seem to move themselves, float, or move with Divine assistance. Heffernan also does not address these verses.}

boundless light;[1129] and I said, 'Perpetua' (for she was at my side), 'this is what the Lord promised to us; we have received the promise.'

And while we are borne by those same four angels, there appears to us a vast space which was like a pleasure-garden,[1130] having rose-trees and every kind of flower.

And the height of the trees was after the measure of a cypress, and their leaves were falling[1131] incessantly.

Moreover, there in the pleasure-garden four other angels appeared, brighter than the previous ones,[1132] who, when they saw us, gave us honor, and said to the rest of the angels, 'Here they are! Here they are!' with admiration.[1133]

And those four angels who bore us, being greatly afraid, put us down; and we passed over on foot the space of a furlong in a broad path.

1127 {They are not passively on their backs as if laid to rest, but actively rising, looking forward, as if climbing stairs. Whether this movement is of their own accord or volition, or by the Divine is not clear. Heffernan suggests Saint Saturus emphasizes that they are not bodily carried up, as if they had been laid out for a funeral, but are spirits or souls ascending. See Heffernan, p. 277.}

1128 {They are freed of their earthly bodies and their worldly cares. Saint Saturus's vision indicates they pass on to exist in heaven at the time of their death. See Revelation 6:9-11. Heffernan discusses this in terms of the cosmologies of Aristotle and Ptolemy. See Heffernan, p. 279.}

1129 {They are privileged to see the light that "no man can approach." See 1 Timothy 6:16. See also John 8:12, where Jesus explains he is the "light of the world" and that those who follow Him will have the "light of life."}

1130 {This seems a clear allusion to the Garden of Eden.}

1131 "Cadebant;" but "ardebant" — "were burning" — seems a more probable reading. [The imitations of *the Shepherd of Hermas*, in this memoir hardly need pointing out.] {Heffernan urges reliance on Revelation 22:2, where the leaves of the Tree of Life are for the healing of the nations, but notes the divergent views of this passage, dismissing that it is a corruption or that it should be translated as "singing" rather than "falling," as some suggest. See Heffernan, pp. 279-80. But the Scriptural reference in Revelation 22:2 is clearly to the Tree of Life. And the account here does not mention any fruit, of which we are to "eat of the Tree of Life." See Revelation 2:7.}

1132 {Angels are associated with light. See Acts 12:7; Revelation 18:1.}

1133 {See Psalm 116:15; Revelation 14:13.}

There we found Jocundus and Saturninus and Artaxius, who having suffered the same persecution were burnt alive; and Quintus, who also himself a martyr had departed in the prison.[1134]

And we asked of them where the rest were.[1135]

And the angels said to us, 'Come first, enter and greet your Lord.'"[1136]

2. "And we came near to place, the walls of which were such as if they were built of light; and before the gate of that place stood four angels, who clothed those who entered with white robes.[1137]

And being clothed, we entered and saw the boundless light, and heard the united voice of some who said without ceasing, 'Holy! Holy! Holy!'[1138]

And in the midst of that place we saw as it were a hoary man sitting, having snow-white hair, and with a youthful countenance; and his feet we saw not.[1139]

And on his right hand and on his left were four-and-twenty elders, and behind them a great many others were standing.[1140]

[1134] {It would appear that these particular martyrs are named because they would have been known to the likely initial audience—their fellow Christians in Carthage and surrounding areas.}

[1135] {Heffernan wonders who Saint Saturus refers to here, as in which other martyrs. See Heffernan, p. 281-82. Heffernan's speculation that this reference is to those martyred in a prior persecution appears rather tortured. A more natural conclusion is that Saint Saturus is asking about their companions or others who were martyred in the arena with them.}

[1136] {There does not seem to be a clear Scriptural reference for this angelic invitation. But the meaning is clear—tarry not, do not keep your Lord waiting. This is, however, the privilege of any ruler. One would not tarry to meet a President of our country if called to meet with him, likewise for any king or emperor on earth. Heffernan notes liturgical overtones of the response. See Heffernan, p. 283.}

[1137] {See Revelation 6:11, 19:14, for the white robes of martyrs. See also Psalm 51:7; Isaiah 1:18; Daniel 7:9; Matthew 17:2, 28:3; Mark 9:3, Luke 9:29 for garments, hair or features as white as snow or wool or light, including as at the Transfiguration.}

[1138] Agios. {See Revelation 4:8, where four angelic creatures sing night and day, "Holy, holy, holy, Lord God Almighty, Who was and is and is to come." See also Isaiah 6:3, where the seraphim sing, "Holy, Holy, Holy, is the Lord of Hosts; the whole earth is full of His glory!"}

[1139] {See Saint Perpetua's description of the Shepherd, above and accompanying notes, especially nn. 1063 and 1131. See also Daniel 7:9 (ancient of days).}

[1140] {See Revelation 4:4, 10, 5:6, 6:9 (describing, e.g., twenty-four elders on thrones around The Throne).}

We entered with great wonder, and stood before the throne; and the four angels raised us up, and we kissed Him, and He passed His hand over our face.[1141]

And the rest of the elders said to us, 'Let us stand;' and we stood and made peace.

And the elders said to us, 'Go and enjoy.'[1142]

And I said, 'Perpetua, you have what you wish.'

And she said to me, 'Thanks be to God,[1143] that joyous as I was in the flesh,[1144] I am now more joyous here.'"

3. "And we went forth, and saw before the entrance[1145] Optatus the bishop at the right hand, and Aspasius the presbyter, a teacher,[1146] at the left hand, separate and sad; and they cast themselves at our feet, and said to us, 'Restore peace between us, because you have gone forth and have left us thus.'

And we said to them, 'Art not thou our father, and thou our presbyter, that you should cast yourselves at our feet?'[1147]

[1141] {See Saint Perpetua's narration of a kiss and accompanying notes, above n. 1101. See also Saint Justin Martyr's *First Apology*, Ch. 65, above. God touches faces in a number of places in Scripture, always to wipe away tears, see Isaiah 25:8; Revelation 7:17, 21:4. This vision does not include mention of tears, but one can imagine the overwhelmingness of being in the presence of God and that it would be accompanied by tears, of joy and awe, perhaps relief, and numerous other emotions. However, tears are a human response to being overwhelmed, and perhaps not the kind of response our heavenly bodies would have. Revelation 21:4 is significant in that it includes the passage "the former things are passed away."}

[1142] {See Revelation 6:11, that the martyrs were told that they should rest. Compare Saint Perpetua's second vision of her brother Dinocrates, above.}

[1143] {This is a common prayer of thanksgiving. See Psalm 30:12; Daniel 6:10; Acts 27:35; Romans 7:25; 1 Corinthians 15:57; 2 Corinthians 2:14, 8:16, 9:11; 1 Thessalonians 3:9; 2 Thessalonians 2:13; Revelation 11:17.}

[1144] {The reference to the flesh is repetitive of the first sentence in Saturus' account. See above n.1107, and Hebrews 5:7.}

[1145] {Notice Optatus and Aspasius are outside the place where the martyrs now are.}

[1146] A presbyter, that is, whose office was to teach, as distinct from other presbyters. See Cyprian, *Epistles*, vol. i. Ep. xxiii., p. 68, note 113, transl. [One of those brethren referred to by Saint James in James 3:1, and by Saint Paul as elders in 1 Timothy 5:17.]

[1147] {The martyrs protest their bishop and presbyter prostrating before them. This elevates the martyrs over the clergy, which role-reversal the martyrs have difficulty accepting. However, to an Orthodox Christian that often venerates the Saints, this makes eminent sense. The clergy are signifying their recognition that the martyrs are among the

And we prostrated ourselves, and we embraced them; and Perpetua began to speak with them,[1148] and we drew them apart in the pleasure-garden under a rose-tree.

And while we were speaking with them, the angels said unto them, 'Let them alone,[1149] that they may refresh themselves;[1150] and if you have any dissensions between you, forgive one another.'[1151] And they drove them away.

And they said to Optatus, 'Rebuke thy people, because they assemble to you as if returning from the circus, and contending about factious matters.'[1152]

Saints. That they ask something of them, however, is not quite the role of our veneration and prayers. We ask Saints to *intercede* on our behalf, not to directly provide. That is for God alone. On supplication and Saints, see Ephesians 6:18. Heffernan does not discuss veneration of Saints. His discussion of this section revolves around distinctions between charismatic gifts of the martyrs and clerical authority, see Heffernan, p. 291-98, instead arguing that the act of prostration before martyrs is "self-abasement" and an acknowledgment that the martyrs have "power and authority" over the clerics. See Heffernan, p. 291.}

[1148] {Recall, this is Saint Saturus's account. Yet even he accords great power and authority to Saint Perpetua. He is her teacher and yet it is she who speaks to the clergy.}

[1149] {This is, perhaps, an angelic recognition, or the delivering of the message from God, (angels being messengers), that the requests made by the clergy to the martyrs to restore peace are inappropriate. Had they prayed that Saint Perpetua intercede on their behalf with God, that peace be restored to them, perhaps they would not have received the rebuke to leave the martyrs alone. But, then, we would not have had this teaching.}

[1150] More probably, "rest and refresh yourselves." ["Go and enjoy," or, "play," or "take pleasure," in the section preceding.] {See above, nn. 1042, 1045, 1049, and accompanying text.}

[1151] {Regarding Christian forgiveness generally, see Matthew 6:12, 14-15; Mark 11:25-26; Luke 11:4; 2 Corinthians 2:10; Ephesians 4:32. Of course, The Lord's Prayer is clear about our need to forgive others. And, the Pauline Epistles often discuss the need for unity as well as various types of dissension in the Early Church. Heffernan does not discuss Christian forgiveness.}

[1152] {The cause and nature of dissension are unstated. Would the initial readers and listeners of this account have understood its reference? Was it perhaps a matter known to Saint Saturus and these clergy only, and perhaps also to Saint Perpetua? Heffernan speculates there was division in the Carthaginian churches over various doctrines and possible idolatry given the references to the circus. See Heffernan, p. 291-98. There is a hint here of the dissensions and heresies in the Early Church as recorded throughout many of the Pauline Epistles and other Apostolic writings.}

And then it seemed to us as if they would shut the doors. And in that place we began to recognize many brethren, and moreover martyrs. We were all nourished with an indescribable odor, which satisfied us.[1153]

Then, I joyously awoke."[1154]

[1153] {Anyone who has inhaled the scent of chrism or of the relics of Saints would be familiar with this description. It is often a scent similar to that of roses or other flowers, but can be quite intense and fill an entire room or even a large church. The Most Reverend Alexander (Golitzin), Archbishop of Dallas, the South and the Bulgarian Diocese, has described to this editor that the scent of Saints is "the scent of sanctity." Conversation, March 18, 2018, after an agape meal following a Hierarchical Divine Liturgy. Heffernan seems to view the scent as typical poetic descriptions involving appeasement of pagan deities. See Heffernan, p. 298. Heffernan also discusses early Church history tending to be skeptical of using incense and other fragrance. See id. Perhaps Heffernan has never experienced this sacred scent as this editor has had the privilege of experiencing. This editor can witness that these scents arise independently from the relic or weeping icon and are distinct from any incense that may be in use at the same time.}

[1154] {Curiously, Saint Saturus did not describe their own bodies as "glorious," see Philippians 3:21.}

Chapter V[1155]

Argument: *Secundulus Dies in the Prison. Felicitas is Pregnant, But with Many Prayers She Brings Forth in the Eighth Month Without Suffering. The Courage of Perpetua and of Saturus Unbroken.*

1. The above were the more eminent visions[1156] of the blessed martyrs Saturus and Perpetua themselves, which they themselves committed to writing.[1157]

But God called Secundulus, while he has yet in the prison, by an earlier exit from the world, not without favor, so as to give a respite to the beasts. Nevertheless, even if his soul did not acknowledge cause for thankfulness, assuredly his flesh did.[1158]

2. But respecting Felicitas (for to her also the Lord's favor approached in the same way), when she had already gone eight months with child (for she had been pregnant when she was apprehended), as the day of the exhibition was drawing near, she was in great grief lest on account of her pregnancy she should be delayed,—because pregnant women are not allowed to be publicly punished,[1159]—and lest she should

[1155] {The author of the remaining portions is unclear, perhaps Tertullian or the eyewitness.}

[1156] {This implies that the author is aware of other visions not recorded by either Saint Perpetua or Saint Saturus. This is akin to Saint John's comment at the end of his Gospel that Jesus did much that was not written down. See John 21:25.}

[1157] [To be regarded, like *the Shepherd of Hermas*, merely as visions, or allegorical romances.] {Wallis does not see authenticity in these accounts. But Heffernan views much of this *Passion* as containing authentic personal accounts. See, e.g., above nn. 1043, 1076.}

[1158] {This paragraph accounts for the absence of Saint Secundulus from the arena where Saint Perpetua and all her companions are martyred. It assures the reader that he too was martyred and did not escape custody or engage in apostasy. See above n. 1051 and accompanying text noting the concerns about apostasy.}

[1159] {Heffernan, at p. 304, discusses this brief legal explanation as something inserted for the benefit of readers near in time to the event who may have been unaware of the law for various reasons. However, this *Passion* is replete with indications it was intended for far more than edification of other contemporary Christians and was meant for posterity. See this *Passion*'s very last paragraph and *Preface to this Edition*. Indeed, that Saints Perpetua and Saturus memorialized their experiences in writing proves the point. And while Saint Perpetua all but commanded that others write of these events, the eyewitness

shed her sacred and guiltless blood among some who had been wicked subsequently.[1160]

Moreover, also, her fellow-martyrs were painfully saddened lest they should leave so excellent a friend, and as it were companion, alone in the path of the same hope. Therefore, joining together their united cry, they poured forth their prayer to the Lord three days before the exhibition.[1161]

Immediately after their prayer her pains came upon her,[1162] and when, with the difficulty natural to an eight months' delivery, in the labor of bringing forth she was sorrowing, some one of the servants of the *Cataractarii*[1163] said to her, "You who are in such suffering now, what will you do when you are thrown to the beasts, which you despised when you refused to sacrifice?"

And she replied, "Now it is I that suffer what I suffer; but then there will be another in me, who will suffer for me, because I also am about to suffer for Him."[1164]

---

author insists the Holy Spirit wills him to complete the memorialization. Thus, this brief discussion of law is meant to benefit all subsequent readers, including us, today.}

1160 {Saint Felicitas's concern here is not so much that she deliver her child, but that she be martyred with her Christian companions, whose faith is a glory to God and good, rather than be killed with a collection of common criminals whose bad conduct is attributable to the devil.}

1161 {The presumably communal prayer here is reminiscent of Hebrews 10:25; see also Acts 1:14, 2:42; Romans 8:26; Ephesians 6:18.}

1162 {All their prayers are answered in a miraculous way, by her immediately delivering a daughter. That this child is a daughter and Saint Perpetua's child is male may be significant. Saint Perpetua's son, absent a change of heart in the grandfather who is to raise him, will presumably be raised pagan, while this daughter of Felicitas will be raised Christian, and presumably will birth more Christians in time, *ad infinitum*, absent barrenness. See Heffernan, p. 302-05. Nevertheless, undiscussed by Heffernan is the prospect of Saint Perpetua's other relatives who, as discussed earlier, were likely all Christian, having considerable influence on her son. Heffernan's view that Saint Felicitas represents the rise of Christianity and its triumph over pagan Rome is somewhat overwrought. Male seed can be quite fruitful; to wit, the descendants of Abraham.}

1163 "The gaolers," so called from the "cataracta," or prison-gate, which they guarded.

1164 {This statement by Saint Felicitas, which echoes Saint Perpetua's vision, in response to the evil mocking spewed forth from the lips of the jailor, is the summation of the reason for the trials and tribulations of the Saints Perpetua, Felicitas, Saturnus, and their companions: that they will suffer for Christ to His greater glory, but in doing so, He will never leave them to fight the battle alone. See 1 Peter 4:16, 5:10; see also Romans 8:23. Saint Felicitas states succinctly what Saint Perpetua's visions foretell.}

Thus she brought forth a little girl, which a certain sister brought up as her daughter.

3. Since then the Holy Spirit permitted, and by permitting willed, that the proceedings of that exhibition should be committed to writing, although we are unworthy to complete the description of so great a glory; yet we obey as it were the command of the most blessed Perpetua, nay her sacred trust,[1165] and add one more testimony concerning her constancy and her loftiness of mind.[1166]

While they were treated with more severity by the tribune, because, from the intimations of certain deceitful men, he feared lest they should be withdrawn from the prison by some sort of magic incantations,[1167] Perpetua answered to his face,[1168] and said, "Why do you not at least permit us to be refreshed, being as we are objectionable to

---

[1165] {Here is the eyewitness's Divine mandate to complete this account of martyrdom, which also invokes Saint Perpetua's prophetic gifts and blessings from God.}

[1166] {Notice the concern is solely with the culmination of Saint Perpetua's witness and not of the other companions.}

[1167] {This reference to incantations may be to Christian liturgical services. However, Saint Justin's *First Apology* offers another possibility with its appended letter from Marcus Aurelius testifying to the miraculous and withering hail resulting immediately from Christian prayer, and raising concerns about Christians turning such awesome powers against Rome. Romans had good reason to fear the power of Christian prayer, whether liturgical or not. Additionally, Saint Justin Martyr notes the charges against Christians of magic, refuting them. See his *First Apology*, Ch. XIV, and the *Dialogue with Trypho*, Ch. LXIX, both above. Although Heffernan mentions how common such charges of magic were against early Christians, and even cites works by Saint Justin Martyr, see Heffernan, p. 312, 316, he focuses on such charges as ones involving chicanery rather than actual spiritual or supernatural powers granted to Christians as noted by Marcus Aurelius.}

[1168] {Here, we see the eyewitness, rather than just Saint Perpetua herself, documenting the display of and the fruits of Saint Perpetua's spiritual power, especially vis à vis the Roman authorities. This reinforces her own testimony of her power granted by grace.}

the most noble Caesar, and having to fight on his birth-day?[1169] Or, is it not your glory if we are brought forward fatter on that occasion?"[1170]

The tribune shuddered and blushed, and commanded that they should be kept with more humanity,[1171] so that permission was given to their brethren and others to go in and be refreshed with them; even the keeper of the prison trusting them now himself.[1172]

4. Moreover, on the day before, when in that last meal, which they call the free meal, they were partaking as far as they could, not of a free supper, but of an *agape*;[1173] with the same firmness they were uttering such words as these to the people, denouncing *against them* the judgment of the Lord, bearing witness to the felicity of their passion, laughing at the curiosity of the people who came together; while Saturus said, "Tomorrow is not enough for you, for you to behold with pleasure

---

[1169] [A gentle banter, like that of St. Lawrence on the gridiron.] {This editor can see no basis on which the editor could refer to this exchange as gentle banter. Saint Perpetua is directly confronting authority, using her persuasive skills and prominence in the group to assert her spiritual authority on behalf not merely of her companions, but Christ, so that they are a fitting sacrifice and fitting exemplars of Christianity. Moreover, she and her companions are likely near starvation. See Heffernan, p. 318, for a description of Roman prison diets as involving severe deprivation of food.}

[1170] {She is appealing here to the tribune's manifest self-interest in treating well an important prisoner when his ruler's birthday is being celebrated in his presence. See Heffernan, pp. 317-18, for the dates and celebrations.}

[1171] {This may be an allusion to Pontius Pilate, who was caught between the demands of the Jews and fears of rebukes from his superiors should the Jews revolt if he did not accede to their demands to crucify Him. Pilate chose to give in to the demands of the Jews, washing his hands of "the just Person's Blood." See Matthew 27:24; see also Luke 23:4, 14, 22 (repeatedly finding no fault in Him); see also 1 Peter 2:22; Isaiah 53:9. Pilate later converted. See *Encyclopaedia Britannica*, v. 9, p. 440. Pilate was ordered back to Rome for trial on the charge of executing men without providing a proper trial, for which Caligula ordered his death by suicide in 39 A.D. Ibid. His wife is a Saint in the Eastern Orthodox Church. Ibid. She warned her husband to avoid "this innocent Man" on account of her dreams. Matthew 27:19.}

[1172] {Their Christian witness apparently is bearing fruit with at least one of their captors, likely Pudens. This is more explicit in Heffernan's translation. See Heffernan, p. 132, 319.}

[1173] {As we do for those sentenced to capital punishment in the United States, the ancient Romans permitted a last meal. Saint Perpetua and her companions used this opportunity to hold an *agape* meal, or a feast out of Christian-Love. This could be Eucharistic in nature. See Heffernan, p. 320-21. Whatever the nature of the meal, it provides physical and spiritual sustenance, emboldening them for the physical and spiritual battle to come.}

that which you hate. Friends today, enemies tomorrow. Yet note our faces diligently, that you may recognize them on that day of judgment."[1174]

Thus all departed thence astonished, and from these things many believed.[1175]

[1174] {This seems to be an eschatological reference to the last days, not a reference to the upcoming event the next day. Heffernan's translation of this last sentence leaves out any mention of such ultimate judgment. See Heffernan, p. 133. And he opines that these are rhetorical questions, see id., p.321, not a reference to Judgment Day, see id. at p.323 (citing Matthew 7:22). There seems to be no need to tell people to remember their faces for the very next day. But if all people stand before the judgment together, see Matthew 25:32-33, as the wheat is separated from the chaff, the sheep from the goats, this serves as a warning of a reckoning someday for their failure to convert now. The resolve on this point by Saint Saturus perhaps would make it seem very real to those who heard him. This seems especially so because just a few clauses earlier these Christians who are about to be martyred were "denouncing against them the judgment of the Lord."}

[1175] {Here again, the witness of those about to be martyred bears fruit.}

Chapter VI

Argument: ***From the Prison They are Led Forth with Joy into the Amphitheatre, Especially Perpetua and Felicitas. All Refuse to Put on Profane Garments. They are Scourged, They are Thrown to the Wild Beasts. Saturus Twice is Unhurt. Perpetua and Felicitas are Thrown Down; They are Called Back to the Sanavivarian Gate. Saturus Wounded by a Leopard, Exhorts the Soldier. They Kiss One Another, and are Slain with the Sword.***

1. The day of their victory shone forth, and they proceeded from the prison into the amphitheater, as if to an assembly, joyous and of brilliant countenances;[1176] if perchance shrinking, it was with joy, and not with fear.[1177]

Perpetua followed with placid look, and with step and gait as a matron of Christ,[1178] beloved of God; casting down the luster of her eyes from the gaze of all.[1179]

Moreover, Felicitas, rejoicing that she had safely brought forth, so that she might fight with the wild beasts; from the blood and from the midwife to the gladiator, to wash after childbirth with a second baptism.[1180]

[1176] {This is reminiscent of the brightness of the faces of Moses and Jesus. See Exodus 34:29-30, 32-33; Mathew 17:2; Luke 9:29. It is a physical manifestation of the light of Christ within them. Did their faces show as brightly as the face of Jesus at the Transfiguration?}

[1177] {The fortitude of the meal the night before continues and is perhaps strengthened. They are also all in the Spirit and sustained by Christ for whom they fight. Saint Perpetua's visions, shared with her companions, steel all of them for the trials they are about to face, and they all understand they are fighting not just the beasts in the earthly world, but the devil in a spiritual battle. This is a part of God's cosmic struggle, and they are heroic Christian participants, indeed, they represent the Church militant.}

[1178] {She is a bride of Christ, as such she has become a representation of the Church.}

[1179] {This translation renders the meaning somewhat vague. Heffernan's translation indicates that Saint Perpetua has a firm gaze, a stare that is intense, and that it is the spectators gathered in the arena who look away from her. See Heffernan, p. 133, 325. Even so, this description may be the inward, yet focused stare of a person deep in thought, the forward look of determination one might see in an Olympian athlete even in our day, in final preparation for the competition, yet here perhaps focused on concerns not of this world.}

[1180] {Recall that early on they were all baptized. Christians believe in one baptism for the remission of sins. This second baptism is that of martyrdom, see Mark 10:38-39; Luke

And when they were brought to the gate, and were constrained to put on the clothing—the men, that of the priests of Saturn, and the women, that of those who were consecrated to Ceres[1181]—that noble-minded woman resisted even to the end with constancy.[1182]

For she said, "We have come thus far of our own accord, for this reason, that our liberty might not be restrained. For this reason we have yielded our minds, that we might not do any such thing as this: we have agreed on this with you."[1183]

12:50 (both of Christ, already baptized by John the Baptist but who is to receive a second baptism of blood via the Cross). Heffernan notes the increasing believe in a second martyric baptism in Saint Perpetua's era. See Heffernan, p. 329. Saint Gregory of Nazianzus discusses five baptisms in his *Oration on the Holy Lights*:

> Moses baptized but it was in water, and before that in the cloud and in the sea. This was typical as Paul saith; the Sea of the water, and the Cloud of the Spirit; the Manna, of the Bread of Life; the Drink, of the Divine Drink. John also baptized; but this was not like the baptism of the Jews, for it was not only in water, but also "unto repentance." Still it was not wholly spiritual, for he does not add "And in the Spirit." Jesus also baptized, but in the Spirit. This is the perfect Baptism. And how is He not God, if I may digress a little, by whom you too are made God? I know also a Fourth Baptism—that by Martyrdom and blood, which also Christ himself underwent:—and this one is far more august than all the others, inasmuch as it cannot be defiled by after-stains. Yes, and I know of a Fifth also, which is that of tears, and is much more laborious, received by him who washes his bed every night and his couch with tears; whose bruises stink through his wickedness; and who goeth mourning and of a sad countenance; who imitates the repentance of Manasseh and the humiliation of the Ninevites upon which God had mercy; who utters the words of the Publican in the Temple, and is justified rather than the stiff-necked Pharisee; who like the Canaanite woman bends down and asks for mercy and crumbs, the food of a dog that is very hungry.

St. Gregory of Nazianzus, *Oration XXXIX*, Ch. XVII, *Nicene and Post-Nicene Fathers of the Christian Church*, Philip Schaff and Henry Wace, eds. (T & T Clark: Edinburgh), reprinted by Wm B. Eerdmans Publishing Co: Grand Rapids, MI).}

[1181] {The authorities are here requiring them to wear the garb of idols, gods of their own making. See Saint Justin Martyr's discussions, above, of how idols are of the devil in *First Apology*, Ch. IX. This would have been quite offensive to Christians to wear the robes that are for priests and priestesses to idols. Heffernan discusses the attempt to humiliate the martyrs and provides extensive discussion of the pagan gods. See Heffernan, p. 326, 330-31.}

[1182] {There is a hint here of patience, experience and hope from tribulation, as in Romans 5:3-5.}

[1183] {Here, once again, Saint Perpetua asserts herself on behalf of herself and her companions, demonstrating, once again, her spiritual power. And, as the next sentence makes clear, she is again successful.}

Injustice acknowledged the justice; the tribune yielded to their being brought as simply as they were.

Perpetua sang psalms, already treading under foot the head of the Egyptian;[1184] Revocatus, and Saturninus, and Saturus uttered threatenings against the gazing people about this martyrdom.

When they came within sight of Hilarianus, by gesture and nod, they began to say to Hilarianus, "Thou judgest us," say they, "but God will judge thee."[1185]

At this the people, exasperated, demanded that they should be tormented with scourges as they passed along the rank of the *venatores*.[1186]

And they indeed rejoiced that they should have incurred any one of their Lord's passions.

2. But He who had said, "***Ask, and ye shall receive***,"[1187] gave to them when they asked, that death which each one had wished for.

For when at any time they had been discoursing among themselves about their wish in respect of their martyrdom, Saturninus indeed had professed that he wished[1188] that he might be thrown to all the beasts; doubtless that he might wear a more glorious crown. Therefore in the beginning of the exhibition he and Revocatus made trial

---

[1184] {She sings, confident from her visions that she defeats the devil. See Genesis 3:15, Revelation 12:3-4; see also her first vision recounted in Ch. I, 3, above, regarding the serpent or dragon; and her vision in Ch. III, 2, above, regarding the Egyptian; and their accompanying footnotes.}

[1185] {This exhortation is akin to their comments the night before made to people around them at the time of their last meal. Then, it was effective to convert some. Here, it does not convert Hilarianus, at least so far as we are told by the eyewitness.}

[1186] A row of men drawn up to scourge them as they passed along, a punishment probably similar to what is called "running the gauntlet." {They are being scourged as Christ was scourged prior to crucifixion.}

[1187] John 16:24 {Jesus saying, "Ask, and ye shall receive, that your joy may be full." KJV}

[1188] {The translator indicates that Saint Saturninus merely *wishes* to be thrown to all beasts; in Heffernan this is a declaration. See Heffernan, p. 133. Interestingly, neither translates this as "prayed" or "asked" or that he prophesied. Yet it is prophetic because he does meet all the beasts but is unharmed by any except a leopard. It is only in a later section of the narrative that it is acknowledged as prophecy ("foretold"). See prior discussions of prophecy as a gift bestowed by God and the Holy Spirit. See above nn. 1017, 1029, 1030, 1165 (noting that prophecy is a gift which particularly edifies the Church).}

of the leopard, and moreover upon the scaffold they were harassed by the bear.[1189]

Saturus, however, held nothing in greater abomination than a bear; but he imagined[1190] that he would be put an end to with one bite of a leopard. Therefore, when a wild boar was supplied, it was the huntsman rather who had supplied that boar who was gored by that same beast, and died the day after the shows.[1191]

Saturus only was drawn out; and when he had been bound on the floor near to a bear, the bear would not come forth from his den.

And so Saturus for the second time is recalled unhurt.

3. Moreover, for the young women the devil[1192] prepared a very fierce cow,[1193] provided especially for that purpose contrary to custom, rivaling their sex also in that of the beasts.

And so, stripped and clothed with nets, they were led forth.[1194] The populace shuddered as they saw one young woman of delicate frame, and another with breasts still dropping from her recent childbirth. So, being recalled, they are unbound.[1195]

1189 {Heffernan suggests that these two martyrs were not killed by the bear, but that the bear merely *charges* them. See Heffernan, pp. 133, 337. But later text seems to imply they were all sufficiently injured and afterwards simply thrown together, see "cast down with the rest, to be slaughtered in the usual place," below. So it seems they sustained fairly grievous injuries.}

1190 {Here, the translator indicates Saint Saturus. The group's teacher, *imagines* death at the jaws of a leopard. Heffernan translates this as him being *confident* that a leopard would be the means of his martyrdom. Again, it is not portrayed as a prayer or prophecy, here. He does make such a prophetic statement to Pudens, the soldier, later and his prophecy is fulfilled.}

1191 {This ignoble death contrasts with the heroic deaths of all these Saints.}

1192 {Whereas in the previous section various beasts are "supplied," here it is the devil who arranges the beast. This is in keeping with the visions Saint Perpetua shared.}

1193 {See Heffernan's lengthy discussion of why a cow might have been chosen for the women, at pp. 338-39, 344.}

1194 {This is an attempt to humiliate the women. But naked fighters in the arena were evidently common. See Heffernan, p. 345.}

1195 Ita revocatae discinguntur. Dean Milmam prefers reading this, "Thus recalled, they are clad in loose robes." {Saint Perpetua's spiritual power may have moved the crowd to some sympathy. It results in the women being clothed. Again, this reprieve to permit the women some dignity is another gift from God.}

Perpetua is first led in. She was tossed, and fell on her loins; and when she saw her tunic torn from her side, she drew it over her as a veil for her middle, rather mindful of her modesty than her suffering.[1196]

Then she was called for again, and bound up her disheveled hair; for it was not becoming for a martyr to suffer with disheveled hair, lest she should appear to be mourning in her glory.

So she rose up; and when she saw Felicitas crushed, she approached and gave her her hand, and lifted her up.[1197]

And both of them stood together; and the brutality of the populace being appeased,[1198] they were recalled to the Sanavivarian gate.

Then Perpetua was received by a certain one who was still a catechumen, Rusticus by name, who kept close to her; and she, as if aroused from sleep, so deeply had she been in the Spirit[1199] and in an ecstasy,[1200] began to look round her, and to say to the amazement of all, "I cannot tell when we are to be led out to that cow."

[1196] {This passage seems odd, as it seems to reflect an earthly concern for modesty near the end of her spiritual journey. Heffernan sees this largely as an embellishment by the author to emphasize the heroic nature of the scene. See Heffernan, pp. 346-47. The same could be said for the next paragraph, that it is too much of a focus on her earthly body. However, as to the hairpin, Heffernan notes that disarrayed hair signified grief in that culture. See ibid. at 341, 348. In that case, she would be asking to negate any implication that she was in grief over her faith, as the very next clause explains.}

[1197] {This is a demonstration of Christian charity before all of the spectators in the arena. Saint Perpetua is unconcerned about her own fate, dire as it was, and focuses on helping her companion. Heffernan does not discuss this as an act of Christian charity and love.}

[1198] {Heffernan does not comment on this appeasement. This editor would suggest that the crowd being appeased would be shown perhaps by silence or at least fewer calls for more "action." But if there were silence, couldn't that be construed as the crowd being struck dumb by what they were witnessing? Was the crowd so bloodthirsty so as to not be moved by the conduct of these two pious women? They were moved by seeing a noble woman naked and a young mother with breasts dripping milk so much that the women were returned to be clothed. Certainly seeing them act with such poise, modesty and care for one another after facing a beast in the arena would also give them pause. If so, such a show of collective mercy toward these women would be more indicative of the Spirit moving in them to soften their hearts. But all of this is speculation because the text does not elaborate.}

[1199] {See Revelation 4:2, for use of "in the Spirit."}

[1200] {Compare the martyrdom of Saint Stephen, Acts 7:55-60, when he is "full of the Holy Spirit" prior to his martyrdom.}

And when she had heard what had already happened, she did not believe it[1201] until she had perceived certain signs of injury in her body and in her dress, and had recognized the catechumen.

Afterwards causing that catechumen and the brother to approach, she addressed them, saying, "Stand fast in the faith,[1202] and love one another,[1203] all of you, and be not offended at my sufferings."[1204]

4. The same Saturus at the other entrance exhorted the soldier Pudens, saying, "Assuredly here I am, as I have promised and foretold, for up to this moment I have felt no beast. And now believe with your whole heart.[1205] Lo, I am going forth[1206] to that beast, and I shall be destroyed with one bite of the leopard."

And immediately at the conclusion of the exhibition he was thrown to the leopard; and with one bite of his he was bathed with such a quantity of blood, that the people shouted out to him as he was returning, the testimony of his second baptism,[1207] "Saved and washed,

---

[1201] [Routh, *Reliquae,* Vol. I. p. 360.] {Despite the text declaring that Saint Perpetua is "in the Spirit," and Heffernan's similar translation, Heffernan discusses her experience almost exclusively in terms of being in a state of physical shock. See Heffernan, p. 343, 349-51.}

[1202] {See 1 Corinthians 16:13; see also Acts 14:22.}

[1203] {These are Saint Perpetua's last recorded *words*. See the commandment of Jesus in John 13:34 ("A new commandment I give unto you, That ye love one another; as I have loved you, that ye also love one another." KJV), and John 13:35; see also 1 Peter 1:22, 3:8, 1 John 3:23, 4:7, 4:11-12, 2 John 1:5; cf. Romans 12-10, 13:8, Galatians 5:13, Ephesians 4:2, 5:2, 1 Thessalonians 1:3, Hebrews 10:24. However, she has the privilege of making the last mentioned *sound* by later crying out. See below.}

[1204] {This editor has also chosen these last words of Saint Perpetua as an epigraph at the beginning of the writings of Saint Perpetua in this volume. See p. 408.}

[1205] {Remarking on his own prophecy, Saturus exhorts the soldier to convert. Prior discussion of spiritual powers largely belonging to Saint Perpetua now apply equally to Saturus. This section, especially comparing it to the last paragraph of the prior section which mentions her *brother* approaching Saint Perpetua, tends to support a conclusion that Saint Saturus is not her brother because he is at "the other entrance" and the story seems to be told in a chronological fashion. See above, n. 1058, for the disagreement in authorities over whether Saint Saturus is her brother or instructor.}

[1206] {Just as Saint Perpetua often acted boldly and with authority, Saint Saturus does now also. The emphasis is on his decision, of his own accord, to go forth and meet the beast. He is not thrown to the leopard, but willingly meets it.}

[1207] {See discussion above, n. 1180, regarding martyrdom as a second baptism.}

saved and washed."[1208] Manifestly he was assuredly saved who had been glorified in such a spectacle.

Then to the soldier Pudens he said, "Farewell, and be mindful of my faith; and let not these things disturb, but confirm you."[1209]

And at the same time he asked for a little ring from his finger, and returned it to him bathed in his wound, leaving to him an inherited token and the memory of his blood.[1210]

And then lifeless[1211] he is cast down with the rest, to be slaughtered in the usual place.[1212]

And when the populace called for them into the midst, that as the sword penetrated into their body they might make their eyes[1213] partners in the murder,[1214] they rose up of their own accord,[1215] and transferred themselves whither the people wished; but they first kissed one another, that they might consummate their martyrdom with the kiss of peace.[1216]

[1208] A cry in mockery of what was known as the effect of Christian baptism.

[1209] {These are the last words of Saint Saturus who delivers a final Christian witness. It is the group's teacher who delivers it, exhorting the soldier to convert to Christianity, to focus on the faith Saint Saturus demonstrates, and to not let even the physical gore that he has witnessed to disturb him in his own faith.}

[1210] {Heffernan notes that this creates a relic of Saint Saturus that was likely venerated. See Heffernan, p. 353. But he describes this scene as melodramatic. See id. Heffernan also discusses relics and use of blood in pagan, Jewish, and Christian practices, as well as such a gift being a legacy. See id. p. 134-35, 360-61. Yet, the reference to bathing the ring in blood is scripturally based. See Genesis 37:31; Leviticus 9:9; Revelation 19:13 (dipped in blood).}

[1211] {Heffernan's translation indicates he is no longer conscious. See Heffernan, p. 135.}

[1212] {Heffernan describes the customs of the arena at p. 354.}

[1213] {Eyes are the window to our inner being and state of grace. The eyes show when one despises another, see Genesis 16:4-5.}

[1214] {This is a blood-thirsty crowd demanding to view the final slaughtering of these Saints. One can imagine the din and noise of their shouting and jeering. Evidently where their bodies are thrown is not near the center of the arena. See Heffernan, p. 354.}

[1215] {This is seemingly a miraculous outpouring of the Spirit in all of them to have the physical energy to get up on their own, at least as to Saint Saturus who we were just told is lifeless, and Saint Felicitas, who needed assistance from Saint Perpetua after being crushed by the cow.}

[1216] {This too is miraculous, as they are given the physical strength to engage in a final demonstration of Christian love. See Romans 16:16 and 1 Corinthians 16:20 (the holy kiss), 1 Peter 5:14, (kiss of charity).}

The rest indeed, immoveable and in silence,[1217] received the sword-thrust; much more Saturus, who also had first ascended the ladder, and first gave up his spirit, for he also was waiting for Perpetua.[1218]

But Perpetua, that she might taste some pain, being pierced between the ribs,[1219] cried out loudly,[1220] and she herself placed the wavering right hand of the youthful gladiator to her throat.[1221]

Possibly such a woman could not have been slain unless she herself had willed it, because she was feared by the impure spirit.[1222]

O most brave and blessed martyrs! O truly called and chosen[1223] unto the glory of our Lord Jesus Christ! whom whoever magnifies, and honors, and adores, assuredly ought to read[1224] these examples for the

---

1217 {Whatever strength they had to exchange a final kiss of peace, it has now left them.}

1218 {This is a final fulfillment of prophecy as to Saint Saturus. See above, his account of his vision. As Christian teacher, he leads his companions in death.}

1219 {The attempt at killing Saint Perpetua by piercing her ribs is reminiscent of the final thrust of the sword into Jesus Christ after He is crucified, see John 19:34, except that she remains alive until she guides the sword to her own throat.}

1220 {Saint Perpetua utters the last sound made by any of the martyrs.}

1221 [Routh, *Reliquae*, Vol. I. p. 358.] {In a final testament to her spiritual power, *she* guides the sword, not the gladiator who missed the mark. He becomes a passive instrument in her (God's) hand. On a macro level, this symbolizes Roman inability to thwart Christianity. It is also reminiscent of the final sword thrust into the body of Christ. See John 19:34, 37; fulfilling Revelation 1:7; see also Psalm 22:16-17.}

1222 {The final words of the eyewitness's testimony revert back to Saint Perpetua as the focal point of the narrative, concluding with a comment on the extent of her spiritual power, bestowed and aided by God, Christ and the Holy Spirit, and which had been demonstrated throughout by her words, deeds, and ultimately her death. See Revelation 12:11 ("And they overcame him by the blood of the Lamb, and by the word of their testimony, and they loved not their lives unto the death," KJV, "him" being the devil, which here has entered the novice gladiator, as happened with Judas who betrayed Jesus, see Luke 22:3; John 13:2; see also demon possessions in Matthew 4:24, 8:16, 28, 9:32, 12:22; Mark 1:26, 32, 5:15-16, 18; Luke 8:36; Acts 8:7, 16:16. Of note also are the words of Christ recorded in John 12:25: "He that loveth his life shall lose it, and he that hateth his life in this world shall keep it unto life eternal." KJV.}

1223 {See Revelation 17:14. ("they who are with Him are called, and chosen, and faithful")}

1224 {Again, the emphasis is on the preservation of this Christian testimony so that it may be read forever to edify the Church. That this *Passion* continues to be studied and published is further testimony "that one and the same Holy Spirit is always operating even

edification of the Church, not less than the ancient ones, so that new virtues also may testify that one and the same Holy Spirit is always operating even until now, and God the Father Omnipotent, and His Son Jesus Christ our Lord, whose is the glory and infinite power for ever and ever.[1225] Amen.

until now." And this editor feels "called and chosen unto the glory of our Lord Jesus Christ " to play this small part in creating this present volume. May it be blessed to bear fruit.}

[1225] {The final invocation of the Trinity and acknowledgement of its Power and Eternity is used throughout Scripture. See, e.g., Psalm 121:8; Daniel 7:14; Nehemiah 9:5; Matthew 6:13; Galatians 1:5; 1 Timothy 1:17, 6:16; 2 Timothy 4:18, 1 Peter 1:23; Revelation 1:6, 18, 4:9-10, 5:13, 7:12, 10:6, 11:15, 15:7, 19:3, 22:5; see also 1 Chronicles 29:11, 13.}

Elucidation

(Dinocrates, cap. II, p. 701.)[1226]

The avidity with which the Latin controversial writer seize upon this fanciful passage, (which, in fact, is subversive of their whole doctrine about Purgatory, as is the text from the *Maccabees*,) makes emphatic the utter absence from the early Fathers of any reference to such a dogma; which, had it existed, must have appeared in every reference to the State of the Dead, and in every account of the discipline of penitents. Arbp. Usher[1227] ingeniously turns the tables upon these errorists, by quoting the Prayers for the Dead, which were used in the Early Church, but which, such as they were, not only make no mention of a Purgatory, but refute the dogma, by their uniform limitation of such prayers to the blessed dead, and to their consummation of bliss at the Last day and not before. Such a prayer *seems* to occur in {2 Timothy 1:18.} The context (verses 16-18, and 4:19) strongly supports this view; Onesiphorus is spoken of as if deceased, apparently. But as Chrysostom understands it, he was only absent (in Rome) from his household. From {2 Timothy 1:17} we should infer that he had left Rome.[1228]

[1226] {This internal citation is not to the pages in this book. See herein Ch. II. Heffernan does not discuss the Elucidation, perhaps because he seems to have used a different version or printing of the text which may not have contained the Elucidation.}

[1227] Republished, Oxford, 1838. {This may be reviewed at https://www.scribd.com/document/35734680/1835-Archbishop-Ussher-s-Answer-to-a-Jesuit, especially pp. 168-238, the chapter titled "Of Prayer for the Dead" and which sets forth the views of many Early Church Fathers.}

[1228] See *Opp. Tom*. xi. p. 657. Ed. Migne.

Troparia, Kontakia, Akathists, and Hymns
for Saints Perpetua and Justin Martyr

For Saint Perpetua and her Companion Saints

Saint Perpetua, along with her companions, (SS. Felicitas, Saturus, Revocatus, Saturninus, and Secundulus), are commemorated by the Orthodox faithful on February 1st each year. A Troparion for these Saints (Tone 4) may be found at:
https://oca.org/saints/troparia/2019/02/01/100398-martyrs-perpetua-a-woman-of-carthage-and-the-catechumens-saturus

A beautiful Akathist for Saint Perpetua and her companion Saints is available at:
http://grforafrica.blogspot.com/search?q=perpetua

Two Apolytikia, a Kontakion, and a Megalynarion for Saint Perpetua and her companion Saints, that are based on an English translation of Greek hymns set forth in the *Great Synaxarion*, may be found at:
https://2natures.blogspot.com/2018/10/hymns-for-saint-perpetua-martyr-and-her.html

For Saint Justin Martyr and Philosopher

Saint Justin Martyr is commemorated by the Orthodox faithful on June 1st of each year. A Troparion for Saint Justin Martyr (Tone 4) and a Kontakion (Tone 2) may be found at:
https://oca.org/saints/troparia/2019/06/01/101570-martyr-justin-the-philosopher-and-those-with-him-at-rome

Afterword

Dear reader, I hope you have enjoyed and been edified in your faith by reading the writings of Saint Justin Martyr and Saint Perpetua. With these final pages, I wish to provide a few insights into the creation of this work, as well as some acknowledgements.

This project of reprinting, editing, and annotating the works of these Saints began as a special gift to my husband for the blessing of our marriage after we both converted to the Orthodox Faith. I also had prepared it with the thought in mind that I would have it reprinted in a trade binding at a future date, for the volume prepared as a gift was custom designed and bound in leather with a slipcover. Others who saw the finished work urged me to follow through and publish it for the public at large. Thinking I would need to merely correct a few typos and have a few experts read it to make sure I had not inadvertently added doctrinal errors, I could then get it off to the printer quickly. But life intervened. God has a way of doing that.

In short order, both of us lost a parent. My husband lost his remaining parent, his mother, just a few short months after I lost my father. May their memories be eternal. Each of us became the administrators of estates, one of which continues to be difficult. And we welcomed my mother into our home. These added responsibilities and others, as well as additional challenges and life changes, left little time for working on this volume. But, at last, it has been finished and will soon be printed.

Throughout this project I have been filled with grace in many ways. Indeed, I can feel God's Providential hand at work in my life, often quite powerfully. And I have been the beneficiary of what I can only describe as miracles. Some pertain to this work. I would like to share a few of them with you because from the start I felt I was drawn to engage in this project through the call of the Holy Spirit and these events only confirm that this project was blessed from the start. I share with you not to boast, but so you may see that God often actually works powerfully in one's life, even in seemingly little things, for it is always to His greater glory. This is why we should share such stories with each other. For if we choose to retain secretly what He has given us, it does not work for His greater glory, but for our own destruction.

* * *

The first instances of the miraculous occurred when this work was initially prepared primarily as a gift for my husband. The speed with which I was able to find the necessary sources and the speed with which I revised and added to the work were almost super-human. But it was with the design of the binding and its structure that revealed the powerful workings of the Lord and how much this effort was blessed.

I was planning on a special binding for a single-volume custom leather edition. My publishing company has worked with a specialty bindery a number of times and I chose to use it again for this work. Originally, the bookbinder, I will call him Michael, and I had settled on certain endpapers, leather for the cover, and a complementary slipcase color. They would be blue. The paper would be off-white. When the leather came in, it was gorgeous, but much to our surprise the goat skin was not a true blue but tending slightly toward aqua and was of a slightly lighter hue than I had anticipated. Each goat skin is different and takes dye differently. After all, each is from an individual animal and every goat is unique. So one must always be prepared for a color which may not quite match the sample.

Michael warned me prior to my visit to the bindery to view the goat skin that we would likely need to select other fabric for the slipcover. It was his opinion that the blues did not work together. He was right. Instead of being complementary, the leather and fabric clashed—horribly. By now, I was getting close to a deadline. For, if I was to present this work to my husband for our marriage blessing ceremony, the binding and slipcover had to be completed. I recall looking at Michael with some dismay and wondering how new cloth could be ordered and received and then used in time to create the slipcover, or whether there was still time to order a different goat skin.

Well, Michael disappeared into the back room for a few minutes. When he returned he was carrying a bolt of beautiful red silk fabric with a slight texture to it. All I could think was, *Wow!* We then discussed a few other changes to how the pages would be bound.

One of these changes was the endpaper. I wanted it to be very special. It so happened that I had in stock some gold metallic paper I thought might be nice to use. (I have designed and published greeting cards for over a decade. My company stocks scores of different paper types and weights.) This was the same paper from which I had made custom invitations to invite people to our marriage blessing and the reception to follow. Incorporating this paper into the binding would eternally tie this physical book to our sacred ceremony. But I was not certain it was suitable for bookbinding. So I had sent some samples of different paper weights for the bookbinder to evaluate. By the time of that visit, Michael had determined one of the gold papers was suitable to use for an endpaper.

Another change was to alter the color of the font for chapter titles and certain other headings to a bright red. I had seen this practice in a number of better quality Orthodox books. Moreover, that design component seemed quite in keeping with the overall design of the book I was creating, especially now with that red silk fabric for the slipcover. It also matched the font color of our invitations, further tying together all aspects of our marriage blessing with this gift commemorating it and our Name Saints and their works written so very long ago.

In the meantime, I had been looking for some particular paper I had once bought. Laid paper is expensive. But years ago I had run across a single ream at a paper dealer on deep discount that seemed then to have my name on it and so I bought it. Yet, I could never seem to find a proper use for that high quality paper. Over the years it occasionally would come to mind and I would find it again and look at it again and wonder how I could use it. But it always seemed too nice to use for greeting card inserts and, because I had only a single ream, it just would not do for printing mass quantities of a card design. At some point, I stopped re-evaluating it for using with greeting cards or stationery products and had decided it had been a wasted investment, unlikely ever to be used.

However, that ream of paper was suddenly calling me to finally use it for the pages of this work. I literally looked everywhere and could not find it. I looked for that ream of laid paper on and off for days and days. I just could not let go of the idea that perhaps this book had been its purpose all along.

Then, I was nearing the point that I had to print the pages of the book to have them finished in time to take to the bindery. And, on the very last day I could print, I looked up at a spot where a lone ream of paper sat on a top shelf and I could not recall if I had looked at that particular ream. It was one of those times when you talk to yourself back and forth, *"ah, don't bother, just use the plain paper, it can't be that laid paper,"* then, *"oh, go ahead and look at it; you've got time,"* and *"just use the paper you already put in the printer, you have to take it to the bindery first thing tomorrow morning, you don't have time for this anymore,"* and *"besides, you already looked at it, just press print!"* And literally just as I was about to print, I decided I must look at that ream. Lo and behold, there it was—the laid paper! It felt like my Guardian Angel had given me an assist. And so, I printed a few test pages to ensure it worked well, for laid paper has a texture that could have made it unsuitable given the font I had selected. It looked absolutely gorgeous! Then, I printed the pages on that beautiful, creamy laid paper and carefully placed it in a covered manuscript box.

The next morning, I hurried to the bindery and left those beautiful pages in Michael's capable hands.

Later, I thought about all that had happened just pertaining to the book's physical design, the colors and their spiritual meanings, the structure of the book binding, how much it honored God, how much it honored our Saints who wrote so long ago, how the gold paper made it almost like a work of iconography, how miraculous some of these events really were. And, I later wrote the following in an email to Michael summarizing many of these thoughts:

> Dear Michael,
>
> I wanted to let you know that my husband adores the book. He is awed by all the symbolism in the design—the blue for human, the red for the Divine. He even took it to the church to show everyone who came to our marriage blessing and who stayed for the reception afterward. And, best of all, he took to reading it from the moment he received it. So, indeed, prayers are answered.
>
> Since the inception of this project, I have known that it is inspired by the Holy Spirit—from the initial spark of the idea, to finding the texts, to further annotating them, to writing the portions I contributed, and to the textual design. Even finally finding the laid paper at the very last moment had to be from the spark of the Divine. And, frankly, most importantly, your assistance in the design and physical structure of the book was also inspired

by the Spirit. For the presentation of any book is a large part of how it is viewed and welcomed by the reader, or not. For ugly or poorly designed books are often passed over and never read.

I haven't been certain whether you are a Christian. But I wanted to let you know that the Holy Spirit certainly used you as a means in creating this work of art and inspiration for my husband (and others, everyone wants a copy once I prepare it for a trade version). The red silk was known only to you. Without you being inspired to bring that fabric out, I would not have known that this humanly created book (in blue leather) could be wrapped in the Divine (red silk slipcase).

It was my knowledge of the color of the slipcase—and its deeply spiritual symbolism—that prompted me to change the font color for all the titles and chapter headings throughout the book at the last minute. Without you being Divinely inspired, I could not have been so inspired to alter the format of the interior, so that the Divine permeates the text as well.

And, the interior red leather hinges you offered, another feature I could not have known to consider and which actually function to physically support and bind the book, is also of the Divine—the Divine is truly holding it all together. Moreover, this is all very Trinitarian. The piece of red leather for the title on the spine, with the support of the two interior hinges in matching red leather makes the three: Father, Son and Holy Spirit.

Our fellow church members are awed by the working of the Spirit through you on our behalf. You have certainly played an important role in the blessing of our marriage. So, words really cannot express my gratitude for your assistance in helping design this book. I can only add:

May the Lord continue to bless you and keep you always, Michael. May your knowledge of how the Holy Spirit used you to create this special volume bring you to faith or deepen your faith, as the case may be. And, may you wonder in awe, as we have, at the amazing beauty of God working in our lives.

In honor of the custom edition, the cover for this paperback edition mimics the colors of the original custom binding.

* * *

But God did not stop His efforts with that first custom edition of this work. He also was quite helpful with this trade edition. And how He arranged everything has opened such new and amazing spiritual richness in my life.

During Lent, just a few short months after my father passed, our priest invited me to go on a pilgrimage to some Orthodox monasteries in Pennsylvania. After arranging with my sister to host our mother for a few days, I was able to go. I had already visited and attended services at Dormition of the Mother of God Orthodox Monastery in Rives Junction, Michigan, a monastery for women that happens to have icons of both Saint Justin Martyr and Saint Perpetua, and St. Sabbas the Sanctified Orthodox Monastery, in Harper Woods, Michigan, a monastery for men. But those visits were for Vespers or Liturgical services or other special events and so lasted but a few hours. This pilgrimage would include staying overnight at one of the monasteries. Seven other pilgrims from our church accompanied us, but my husband could not go. So, I was on my own.

We visited the Orthodox Monastery of the Transfiguration, in Ellwood, Pennsylvania, a monastery for women, and the Monastery of St. Tikhon of Zadonsk, in Waymart, Pennsylvania, a monastery for men and where St. Tikhon's Orthodox Theological Seminary is also located. A number of little miracles occurred over the course of this trip, but I will share two.

The one miracle pertained directly to the preparation of this work for publication in this trade edition. At the recommendation of my priest, I had mailed the manuscript to one of the librarians at St. Tikhon's, Michael Skors, for his review and to check for doctrinal errors. I had added information and commentary in footnotes and introductory material. So, I wanted to be sure everything I had said was in keeping with our Orthodox faith. Happily, Father was able to set an appointment for me to sit down with Michael while we were visiting the monastery and seminary. I thought I would just have a chance to meet him briefly and discuss my project and the manuscript.

When I arrived, much to my surprise, he handed me the manuscript and told me that he had completed the review. So we spent a little time going over his notations. I had been very careful in the additions I made to the footnotes, and in the various prefatory commentaries. But it turned out that there was only one small error that was incorrect as a matter of doctrine, by the grace of God blessing my effort. He had also taken the time to comment on a variety of issues, and to note various typos needing correction. He was so generous with his time, both in reviewing the manuscript and in talking with me. That he had been able to review this rather large manuscript in so short a time and for us to be able to meet in person were truly miraculous events, and such a blessing of this project.

The other miracle had nothing to do with this work. About halfway through our trip, we visited St. George's Orthodox Church in Taylor, Pennsylvania, where our small group was able to privately pray and venerate a very special icon of the Theotokos. This icon, the Theotokos Kardiotissa (Icon of the Tender Heart) is a myrrh-weeping icon, sometimes referred to as myrrh-seeping or myrrh-streaming. If you have never seen such an icon, never experienced the unique flowery fragrance of its scent, a powerful and overwhelming scent that is nearly intoxicating, or never experienced the sight of the myrrh dripping or collecting on its surface, you might not believe these phenomena are genuine. But we each received an anointing of our foreheads with the streaming myrrh, and drops of myrrh that fell as the icon was tipped over our cupped hands. And one young lady received the privilege of a tiny piece of cotton streaming a copious amount of myrrh into her hands.

In case you doubt such phenomena, I can witness to you that this is very real. There were no tricks. As the time spent with the icon unfolded, there was no possibility that it was faked. I watched as the priest of the church took a small piece of cotton that was wet with the myrrh and squeezed it into this young woman's cupped hands. However, that little piece of cotton, even highly saturated, could not have physically contained the amount of oil I saw descending into her hands. There was so much of it that she shared it with all of us, eight other people. It was *awe*-some, in the true sense of the word, astonishing, breathtaking. All you wanted to do was fall on your knees—and we all did as we each venerated the Mother of God and her Son, the Christ Jesus.

In truth, when I heard we would be seeing this icon, I was not certain what to expect. And, I had my doubts about such phenomena. At one time in my life I was going to be a scientist, a polymer chemist or pharmaceutical researcher, until I veered off into another path. But this type of experience defies the principles of our natural world, our understanding of the ways things work here. I can understand such events not as some sort of odd, unexplainable exceptions to the regular and natural order of things, but only in terms of miracles from God. This experience was not one that could be understood stemming from belief alone, in my humble opinion. This was at an elemental, fundamental level a grant of knowledge, a window into the Divine and its revelatory powers. And I felt so unworthy to have experienced it. I still do.

That pilgrimage started with a visit to the monastery in Ellwood. That visit to Transfiguration Monastery was brief. But it was truly transformative. I was able to go back two additional times to the Transfiguration Monastery in 2018—a Trinity of visits in just one year to that monastery alone! Each time I have been to a monastery I have found such calm, such serenity, such restorative peace for my complicated and challenging life—and so much holiness that I often do not know what to make of it all. This is especially true of my visits to Transfiguration Monastery.

I pray that each of you, dear readers, will be able to make a monastery pilgrimage someday and to find such peace. I pray also that someday you may witness and experience, up close and personal, a weeping icon.

* * *

Finally, I would like to comment briefly on the *Preface to This Edition*, and some history since it was written.

Terrorism was much in the news just before and during the preparation of this work originally. This was documented in footnotes in the *Preface*. With the inauguration of a new President in our country, and more recently the mid-term elections, the media has focused more on politics than the war on terror. However, horrific and despicable persecution of Christians continues to occur the world over, still largely by Islamic state and non-state actors. It is just more difficult to find reports about it. But even as I write this *Afterword*, in just the past few days, ISIS has claimed responsibility for more bloodshed, more success for its jihad.

And there have been reports that Boko Haram has destroyed over one thousand Christian churches in Nigeria.

This is a battle that has gone on for many centuries and it will continue. But it is not limited to adherents of Islam. Though largely not bloody, Christians are persecuted in other ways in our country, mostly through regulations and attacks on freedoms related to our religious expression and faith-informed speech. I have in mind here the Christian bakers of wedding cakes, for example, who are fined or sued for failing to create same-sex wedding cakes or transsexual or other themed cakes. So far, those of faith are usually vindicated, but they must defend against such legal suits, sometimes all the way up to our United States Supreme Court. Such legal battles are costly, psychologically, emotionally, and financially, driving some people out of business. And, we are seeing unprecedented coordinated efforts by some who bully, threaten to assault or even threaten to kill, and who defame Christians and others who support them, most especially through various social media platforms and some members of the press. The most recent online mob of this sort involved Catholic high school students.

We still need to be bold in our faith, come what may. And those of us who are not directly caught up in any persecution for our Christian faith must pray for those who suffer such onslaughts. But even more importantly, we must pray for those who persecute us or our fellow Christians. It is what Jesus Christ calls us to do. And, as Saint Perpetua reported hearing during her last vision, "Do not be afraid, I am here with you, and I am laboring with you."

Acknowledgments

First and most importantly, I am grateful to the Father, Son and Holy Spirit, who guided me to Orthodoxy in the first place, and then inspired me to prepare and edit this work, and who sustained me throughout the preparation of this edition during some of the most challenging trials and tribulations. I could not have done it—any of it—without their Divine help and blessings. I also thank Saints Justin Martyr and Perpetua for writing what they wrote so long ago, as well as their inspiration and prayers. And, I thank the Guardian Angels of me and my husband for watching over us during this time.

Thank you Father Gabriel Bilas for being a manuscript reader and for recommending someone who could review this work for doctrinal errors. Specific helpful comments that Father shared are acknowledged in the relevant footnotes. I also appreciate very much Michael Skors for his doctrinal review and his other helpful comments. I also thank Archbishop Alexander for his remarks after an agape meal about holy icons that eventually were added to this edition, which were also acknowledged in the relevant footnotes.

Thank you also to everyone who read portions, helped edit, or who were involved in designing the cover. This includes Michael, whose masterful design work for the custom edition was used as the inspiration for the cover of this trade edition.

I also want to express gratitude to all my family and friends who urged me to complete this project and who supported me through it in one way or another, most especially Tatiana and her husband John; Kathy, a dear friend; Alisha and all the other waitresses at our local Big Boy who served countless cups of decaf coffee to me as I edited this edition; Leticia, my aunt, who so often sustains me; and my mom, Carol.

And to my husband, with whom together we are one flesh, words cannot express my love and gratitude for your patience with me and my work—on this book, other works that are in some stage of writing, and so much more.

As Divinely inspired as I view this work, and as much effort as has gone into it, there are bound to be errors. Of course, any such remaining errors are my own. Again, I pray none are significant, and that our Lord and you forgive me for any errors or oversights.

About the Author

Donna Perpetua is an Orthodox Christian living in southeast Michigan with her husband, and her mother, who they welcomed into their home after the death of her father. She edited and wrote the introductions and supplementary materials for the first volume of the series *Ancient Examples: Writings of the Early Christians for Today*. It includes the works by Saint Justin Martyr and Saint Perpetua.

She has a number of other Orthodox Christian works planned.

Donna Perpetua enjoys making pilgrimages to Orthodox monasteries in America. She was pleased to discover an icon of her and her husband's name Saints at the Holy Dormition of the Mother of God Orthodox Monastery in Rives Junction, Michigan. She is considering learning how to write icons.

A Note from the Publisher

We hope you enjoyed this first volume of what we plan to be a series of similar titles, *Ancient Examples: Writings of the Early Christians for Today*. As conceived, this series will focus on Early Christians who wrote commentaries on Scripture or who delivered sermons about our ancient Christian Faith, and martyrdom stories of Saints. We believe strongly that such works are necessary for the edification of the Church today, just as much as they were necessary when they were initially written so very long ago.

This first volume contains works by Saint Justin Martyr and Saint Perpetua, including their martyrdom stories. In honor of these two Saints we developed, just for Orthodox works, the imprint *Saints Justin and Perpetua Orthodox Christian Books*. We pray that you look forward to the release of other titles in the series.

DMS Onge Publishing, LLC,
publishes fiction and nonfiction works
under a number of imprints, including this imprint,
Saints Justin and Perpetua Orthodox Christian Books,
as well as greeting cards and other printed products.